AF773652

THE EUROPEAN UNION APPROACH TOWARDS WESTERN SAHARA

P.I.E. Peter Lang
Bruxelles · Bern · Berlin · Frankfurt am Main · New York · Oxford · Wien

EUROCLIO is a scientific and editorial project, a network of research institutions and researchers, and an ideas forum. EUROCLIO as an editorial project consists of two aspects: the first concerns studies and documents, the second concerns tools. Both are aimed at making the results of research more accessible, and also at opening up paths through the history of European construction/integration/unification.

The EUROCLIO series meets a dual objective:
- to provide reference tools for research,
- to provide a platform for this research in terms of the publication of results.

The series thus consists of two sub-series that satisfy these requirements: the Studies and Documents series and the References series. These two series are aimed at general libraries and/or university history departments, teachers and researchers, and in certain cases, specific professional circles.

The Studies and Documents series consists of monographs, collections of articles, conference proceedings, and collections of texts with notes for teaching purposes.

The References series consists of bibliographies, guides and other tools. It thus contributes to the creation of a database making up a "Permanent catalogue of sources and bibliographies on European construction".

Edited by
Éric Bussière, Université de Paris-Sorbonne (France),
Michel Dumoulin, Louvain-la-Neuve (Belgique),
& Antonio Varsori, Universitá degli Studi di Padova (Italia)

THE EUROPEAN UNION APPROACH TOWARDS WESTERN SAHARA

Marco Balboni and Giuliana Laschi (eds.)

Euroclio
Vol. 98

Volume pubblicato nell'ambito dei progetti di cooperazione internazionale decentrata con il contributo della Regione Emilia Romagna, promossi da:

Rete Tifariti

Sostenuta da Comune di Ravenna, Comune di Forlì, Comune di Nonantola (MO), CISP-ER, Nexus (Bologna), Peace Games (Bologna), Comune di Ponte San Nicolò (PD), AUSER ER (Bologna), CGIL (Ravenna); Associazioni: Kabara Lagdaf (Modena), El Ouali (Bologna), 1514 Oltre il muro (Ponte San Nicolò – PD), TreCaSma (Trento).

The book was subject to a double blind refereeing process.

No part of this book may be reproduced in any form, by print, photocopy, microfilm or any other means, without prior written permission from the publisher. All rights reserved.

© P.I.E. PETER LANG S.A.
Éditions scientifiques internationales
Brussels, 2017
1 avenue Maurice, B-1050 Brussels, Belgique
www.peterlang.com; brussels@peterlang.com

Printed in Germany

ISSN 0944-2294
ISBN 978-2-8076-0103-1
ePDF 978-2-8076-0104-8
ePub 978-2-8076-0105-5
Mobi 978-2-8076-0106-2
DOI 10.3726/b10720
D/2017/5678/12

Library of Congress Cataloging-in-Publication Data: Names: Balboni, Marco, editor. | Laschi, Giuliana, 1962- editor. Title: The European Union approach towards Western Sahara / Marco Balboni and Giuliana Laschi (eds.). Description: Brussels : P.I.E. Peter Lang, 2016. | Series: Euroclio, ISSN 0944-2294 ; Vol. 97 | Includes bibliographical references. | English; one contribution in French. Identifiers: LCCN 2016039419 (print) | LCCN 2016052135 (ebook) | ISBN 9782807601031 | ISBN 9782807600768 | ISBN 9782807600775 (ePDF) | ISBN 9782807600782 (ePub) | ISBN 9782807600799 (Mobi) | ISBN 9782807601048 () | ISBN 9782807601055 () | ISBN 9782807601062 ( ) Subjects: LCSH: European Union countries--Foreign relations--Morocco. | Morocco--Foreign relations--European Union countries. | European Union countries--Foreign economic relations--Morocco. | Morocco--Foreign economic relations--European Union countries. | Western Sahara--International status. Classification: LCC D2025.5.M67 E87 2016 (print) | LCC D2025.5.M67 (ebook) | DDC 341.242/209648--dc23 LC record available at https://lccn.loc.gov/2016039419

Bibliographic information published by "Die Deutsche Nationalbibliothek"

"Die Deutsche Nationalbibliothek" lists this publication in the "Deutsche Nationalbibliografie"; detailed bibliographic data is available on the Internet at http://dnb.d-nb.de.

Table of Contents

Introduction

Marco BALBONI & Giuliana LASCHI

University of Bologna[1]

Colonialism left an indelible mark on Africa and the Sahrawi people are one of the many groups who are still reckoning with the inheritance left them by Europeans. The Western Sahara was subjected to more than a century of illegal occupation firstly with Spanish colonisation and subsequently under Moroccan occupation. After winning their independence from Spain the Sahrawi people fought a resistance war against Moroccan occupation until the United Nations negotiated a ceasefire in exchange for a self-determination referendum. Morocco has never allowed this referendum to take place, however, and has consistently blocked UN mediation efforts[2].

The Sahrawi people are the victims of rushed decolonisation and after the Spanish departed they were obliged to abandon the land they had lived on for centuries. Immediately after the withdrawal of the Spanish colonial occupiers in 1976 Moroccan troops from the north and Mauritanian soldiers from the south invaded the Western Sahara and the Sahrawi people were forced into refugee camps on Algerian territory. Morocco has continued to illegally occupy the territory and the Sahrawi have been a divided people ever since. Approximately 70% of them live in occupied areas and 30% in refugee camps. They have been a people in exile for forty years and have never succeeded in exercising their right to self-determination. The crisis in the Western Sahara is emblematic of the frequent ineffectiveness of the international community and its principal bodies.

For more than forty years, then, the Western Sahara has been the site of acute international crisis weighed down by the interests of the great

1 Giuliana Laschi wrote the first part until the paragraph "The international crisis" included; Marco Balboni wrote the paragraph "Questioning the legality of agreements concluded between Morocco and the EU under international and European law".

2 K. Arts and P. Pinto Leite (eds.), *International Law and the Question of Western Sahara*, Oporto, IRJET, 2007.

Western powers who, for economic, strategic, security and immigration containment reasons, have consistently put a firm partnership with Morocco before self-determination for the Sahrawi people[3]. On the other hand, whilst capable of powerful resistance to occupation, the Sahrawi have shown themselves to be peaceful, preferring non-violent, international mediation to armed struggle. Their pacifism, respect for UN resolutions and efforts not only to survive in and from the Algerian desert but also to create a functional and evolved society are not such as to prompt fears of destabilisation and thus neither governments nor the international media have taken any interest in this serious unresolved international crisis.

The European Union and the UN feed these refugees in their Saharan camps but at the same time they have signed treaties with Morocco and, above all, a fishing convention which encompasses the Western Sahara's territorial waters thereby indirectly and illegally recognising Moroccan sovereignty over the occupied territories. Member states continue to exploit profitable business opportunities with Morocco and the press keep quiet, evidently considering information on a crisis which has been quite literally kept in deafening silence as of no public interest.

The Western Sahara crisis, then, is one of the international community's key failures. A solution has been postponed for decades in a resounding media silence paralleled by scholarly disinterest. The volume we are introducing here is intended to supply an academic basis to an analysis of the crisis in chapters which deal with various aspects of the matter written by scholars, experts and also the main players in the international action designed to manage the crisis. The book attempts to fill the void in academic work and is thus designed as a reference tool on the Western Sahara question. It is made up of an analytical section together with an appendix which lists the main documents relating to this international dispute.

Africa's last colony

Francesco Correale's chapter analyses the history of the crisis in depth and is our reference for thorough information. In this introduction our objective is to present an overview of the various stages in the international

3 J.M. Murphy, "The Functioning of Realpolitik in Protracted Conflict and the Transformative Capacity of Self-Determination. A case study of Western Sahara, Africa's Last Colony", doctoral thesis, Universitat Jaume I, Castellon (Spain), 2010; S. Zunes and J. Mundy, *Western Sahara: War, Nationalism, and Conflict Irresolution*, Siracuse-New York, Syracuse University Press, 2010; Y.H. Zoubir and D. Volman (eds.), *International Dimensions of the Western Sahara Conflict*, Westport, Praeger Publisher, 1993.

crisis analysed here and to put it in context in the international academic sphere[4].

In the pre-colonial era the geographical area of modern day Western Sahara, which lies directly along the Atlantic Ocean on one side and the vast Sahara desert on the other, fell within the orbit of Islamic civilisation and culture and was a trading crossroads. As a result of migratory fluidity of the people who inhabited the area it had no well-defined borders or social immobility which was a colonial imposition and constitutes one of the gravest attempts to cancel out African history. In the 7th century Sahrawi society underwent a first migration of Muslim peoples from the Arabic peninsula and then a second Arab migration in the 12th century. These events gradually Islamicised the Maghreb, a process which was then consolidated by the purely trading activities of the first Islamicised Berbers. Its crossroads position on the trading routes made the Western Sahara attractive to the first Europeans to arrive on its coast in the 15th century where the first Spanish settlement was set up in 1478 though it was only from 1881 that Spanish occupation took root. With a royal decree of 1884 the Spanish government set up a protectorate in the area between Cap Blanc and Cape Bojador on the basis of pacts with the chiefs of the independent tribes living on this part of the coast. The Spanish colonisation of the Western Sahara was officially recognised by the European powers at the Berlin Africa Conference (1884-85) and thus in 1885 Spain declared its protectorate over the region. True exploration and then occupation of the area began only at the end of the 1940s under the Franco dictatorship whilst previously the mother country's main interest had been in the Atlantic coast's prolific fishing. In fact Spain limited its initial settlements to the coastal areas. It was the discovery of phosphates in Bou-Craa (1949-50) which prompted further Spanish intervention in the Sahara and gave the region its exceptional economic value.

When, in 1956, the French government brought its protectorate in Morocco to an end the latter laid claim to the Sahara and Mauritania territories on the basis of the so-called "Greater Morocco" line of thought. In the same years the Sahrawi people began mobilising against colonial occupation and in November 1957 launched an attack on Spanish troops in Tarfaya province allying themselves for the occasion with the Moroccan Liberation Army and penetrating southwards to attack the 'colonial yoke' in Mauritania. Spain thus decided to join forces with France to bring the insurrection to an end. In February 1958, therefore, operation *Ecouvillon* was launched and the two colonial powers defeated the Sahrawi rebels

[4] For a more in-depth account of this international crisis see also my *L'Europa e gli altri. Le relazioni esterne della Comunità dalle origini al dialogo Nord-Sud*, Bologna, Il Mulino, 2015.

with help of the Royal Armed Forces of Sultan Mohammed V who subsequently personally claimed the Sahara as Moroccan for the first time without, however, making any precise territorial references.

At the beginning of the 1970s, following on from pressing demands by the United Nations, Spain began to consider decolonising the area[5], reinforcing the independence ambitions of the Sahrawi people who formed full blown independence movements in this period, including the Saguia El Hamra and Rio de Oro Liberation Movement (MSL) set up in early 1967 under the leadership of Mohamed Sid Brahim Bassiri. The birth of the Western Sahara independence movement involved fighting Spanish occupation and Morocco's territorial demands at the same time. The first manifestations of Sahrawi ability to mobilise against Spain was a peaceful demonstration organised in Zemla on 17th June 1970 which met with bloody repression in which Bassiri was killed. This violent reaction to their peaceful demands for independence persuaded the Sahrawi people that the time had come for a different form of resistance and to this end the Polisario Front (Popular Front for the Liberation of Saguia el Hamra and Rio de Oro) was set up on 10th May 1973 and just ten days later armed struggle was set in motion[6].

On 24th May 1975 the Spanish governor of the Western Sahara, General Gomez de Salazar, announced plans to evacuate the area in Operation *Hirondelle* and negotiations with the Polisario Front began. Determined to occupy the territories liberated by Spain, however, Hassan II prompted a peaceful march of Moroccan 'volunteers' to take control of what he called "the Moroccan provinces of the Sahara". The so-called Green March, re-christened the Black March by the Sahrawi people, began on 6th November 1975. 350,000 Moroccans moved into the area from the North-West and met with no opposition from Spain. A curfew was imposed on the whole of the Western Sahara.

The international crisis

The principle of self-determination for the Western Sahara was recognised by the UN for the first time in the 1960s in response to demands that Spain decolonise the area[7]. Article 73 of the UN Charter

[5] J. de Piniés, *La Descolonización Española en la Naciones Unidas*, Madrid, Centro de Estudios Políticos y Costitucionales, 2001.

[6] T. Hodges, *Western Sahara: The Roots of a Desert War*, Westport, Lawrence Hill, 1983.

[7] This principle was established by the UN in 1960 in Assembly Resolution 1514: "All peoples have the right to self-determination; by virtue of that right they freely determine their political status and freely pursue their economic, social and cultural development". UN, Declaration on the Granting of Independence to Colonial Countries and Peoples Adopted by General Assembly resolution 1514 (XV) of 14th December 1960.

sets out that the "Governing state's obligations include notifying the Secretary General on any independence granted to the peoples governed. In the 1950s annual reports on the Western Sahara were the competence of Spain although the latter was initially reluctant to do so as it considered the area a province across the seas, a metropolitan area with a Spanish population not a people with the right to self-determination, and thus its government as legitimate. However, in the context of the Cold War, fears that the issue might trigger off disputes in other metropolitan territories in which Spain had significant interests, such as the Canary Islands, prompted Spain to fulfil its duties. The Western Sahara was thus included in the territories covered by Resolution 1514 of 1960 which sanctioned the right to self-determination and thus the right of the Sahrawi people to this same self-determination.

In 1965-66, moreover, two specific resolutions were approved – A/Res/20/2072 and A/Res/21/2229 – which reiterated this right to self-determination and established the principle that it was the Sahrawi people who should decide whether to set up their own state or join an existing state in a referendum. Still fearful of possible repercussions for the Canary Islands, Spain did not oppose the resolution and decided to call a referendum in 1974 after completing a census. Morocco expressed its opposition to Spain's decision and set in motion action designed to disrupt the General Assembly prompting Spain to proclaim the existence of a judicial dispute over the Sahara and pass the task of sorting it out onto the International Court of Justice. In reiterating that the Western Sahara had always been under its control, however, Spain was responding to Moroccan ambitions and denying the existence of a dispute. The appropriateness of referring the matter to the International Court of Justice, however, split the General Assembly. On the 13th of December 1974 Resolution 3292 requesting an opinion on two key issues was adopted with a great many abstentions. The first of these was the issue of whether the Western Sahara had been a *terra nullius* at the moment of its occupation by Spain and, in the event that this had not been the case, what legal bonds existed between the Sahara, Morocco and Mauritania. As there was no dispute underway over the Western Sahara as the two resolutions confirming its right to self-determination had both been approved by Spain, the Court could have abstained from expressing an opinion.

But the Court expressed an advisory opinion on 16th October 1975 stating that the Western Sahara was not a *terra nullius* – a land occupied by people with no social or political organisation – in the 19th century, though one which had nothing in common with the concept of state sovereignty as conceived of in Western political culture. The area was inhabited by a people who were predominantly nomadic but divided politically and socially into tribes led by chiefs who were recognised as legitimate representatives. It was these same tribal chiefs who had signed the protectorate treaty in 1884 with Spain which had rapidly degenerated into full blown colonial domination. The Court noted the existence of certain bonds of servitude between the Sultan of Morocco and a number of tribes living in the area but ruled out any form of territorial sovereignty over the Western Sahara by Morocco and Mauritania. In conclusion, the opinion thus denied the existence of elements capable of casting doubt on the applicability of 1960 Resolution 1514 on the decolonisation of the Western Sahara and, in particular, the applicability of the principle of self-determination as the free and authentic expression of the will of the area's people.

The Court's opinions were never put into practice, however. In fact, having lost its legal battle the Rabat government moved onto the politics of the *de facto* and, on the 16th of October, the day the Court's advisory opinion was published, King Hassan II launched his Green March to bring the 're-integration' of the Western Sahara into the Moroccan kingdom to fruition. Although this march was presented as peaceful it was a full blown violation of the border and thus of the principle of territorial integrity. As the General Assembly had no jurisdiction over the dispute Spain turned to the Security Council, appealing to Chapter VI and specifically to Article 35 and demanding that a meeting be called to condemn the Moroccan government's plans which it saw as an invasion threatening international peace and security. The Council opted to call for direct negotiations between those involved, in the first place, with great moderation. It condemned the Green March but made no reference to violations of international borders.

Aware of its inability to protect the Western Sahara, Spain entered negotiations with Morocco and Mauritania which led to the Madrid Tripartite Accord known as the Declaration of Principles on Western Sahara on 14th November 1975. The solution adopted was that Spain would give up its mandatory powers and a joint government would be set up which was to lead to total decolonisation together with Djemaa, the Sahrawi people's representative body. Despite the doubts which were raised on several sides on the validity of the agreement the General Assembly limited itself to approving two resolutions which confirmed the rights of the Sahrawi people to self-determination. The first of these referred to Spain's organisation of a self-determination consultation together with the United Nations. The latter, on the other hand, reiterated the final objective of total decolonisation but constituted a *de facto* acceptance of the Madrid Accords, as formalised by the Rabat Pact of 1976 in which Morocco and Mauritania divided up the area between them, for the temporary government of the area. Further significant developments in the General Assembly's stance followed with resolutions 34/37 in

November 1979 which called for partnership with the Organisation of African Unity (OUA) to begin.

The General Assembly also acknowledged the peace treaty signed in Algiers on 10th August 1979 between Mauritania, which thus exited the dispute and abandoned the occupied area, and the Polisario Front which was recognised, for the first time, as the official "representative of the Sahrawi people". This resolution was the model for subsequent, yearly, virtually carbon copy declarations by the General Assembly while the OUA was entrusted with the decolonisation of the area.

In 1976 the Sahrawi people founded the RASD, the Sahrawi Arab Democratic Republic, which attempted to demonstrate the legitimacy of its declaration of independence right from the start in a memorandum in which it maintained that "the Sahrawi people have natural and original sovereignty [...], possess inalienable rights to self-determination and the most natural situation is independence". The proclamation was entirely legal because it accorded fully with the opinions expressed by the International Court of Justice and the UN resolutions, in particular that dating to 1960 relating to the Granting of Independence to Countries and Peoples Subject to Colonialism. Despite the legal foundations for their actions, however, the Sahrawi people struggled to gain political recognition as a state for the RASD. Membership of the Organisation of African Unity (OUA) in 1982 contributed to the official legitimation of its political status which was accompanied by recognition by 76 mainly non-aligned states, former colonies and countries in the southern hemisphere which had fought such battles themselves and made similar claims in the past. This was not, however, accompanied by recognition from world powers and the northern hemisphere and today RASD has access only to certain international forums and solely in an observer capacity with consequent reduced weight and credibility.

Morocco even went to the lengths of leaving the OUA when RASD was granted membership and has carried out an active diplomatic offensive against its recognition over the years inviting states which had already recognised it to withdraw their diplomatic support, on occasions successfully. Mauritania has taken a different path and in 1979 formally distinguished its own diplomatic position from Morocco's by withdrawing its troops from the Western Sahara and joining Algeria in supporting the Sahrawi people.

A solution to the crisis seemed imminent in 1988 when the UN Security Council authorised the Secretary General to appoint a special representative assisted by a "support group" in Resolution 621 with "sole and exclusive responsibility for all matters relating to the organisation and implementation of the referendum". The responsibilities of the special representative encompassed potentially legislating in the Western Sahara, action to free prisoners on both sides and all measures designed to facilitate refuge return to the area. Lastly an immediate ceasefire was called for to enable the referendum to be implemented, a condition which was achieved on 6th September 1991[8].

The decisive document for the creation of the United Nations Mission for the self-determination referendum (MINURSO) was the project drawn up, a couple of years later, by the then Secretary General Javier Perez de Cuellar and approved by the Security Council on 27th June 1990. The foundation stones of the project were the Sahrawi people's right to choose between independence and incorporation into Morocco; the use of the census compiled by the Spanish authorities in 1974 and supplemented by a 'demographic update' (this expression has been the subject of various interpretation disputes over the years) as the basis for the electoral lists; a reduction in numbers of Moroccan and Sahrawi troops in the region; the deployment of UN peacekeeping troops and the appointment of a special representative reporting to the Secretary General responsible for all referendum related issues assisted by MINURSO. As far as MINURSO's functions were concerned, the Secretary General classified these into three groups under the responsibility of various units: a) a civil unit made up principally of UN functionaries entrusted with responsibility for administrative tasks and refugees; b) security units responsible for maintaining order and legality in voter registration and monitoring the action of the local police forces to ensure that no intimidation or bullying took place during the referendum; c) a military unit in charge of monitoring the ceasefire. The implementation of the UN mission was unanimously approved by the Security Council on 29th April 1991 in Resolution 690. In accordance with the explicit mandate provided by this resolution the mission was categorised as a peacekeeping mission, in particular because it required the prior consent of the parties to the dispute.

Despite respect for the ceasefire and MINURSO deployment in the area, after 1991 no significant progress was made in the direction of a referendum.

A 'compromise proposal' was put forward in 1993 by the new UN Secretary General Boutros Ghali which was accepted unreservedly by Morocco and conditionally by the Polisario Front given that it would have swollen the electoral lists with around 60,000 Moroccan citizens living in the area at the time of the census but not Sahrawi. The Polisario Front's refusal to accept these conditions paralysed the peace process which made no further progress until Boutros Ghali's mandate expired. The first official date for the referendum was 1992 but it was then postponed every year.

8 T. Schelley, *Endgame in the Western Sahara*, London, Zed Books, 2004.

Kofi Annan nominated a special representative for the Western Sahara, James Baker, in 1997 whose mission consisted of re-examining the situation together with two sides to assess the applicability of the regulation plan; studying potential amendments acceptable to both sides and capable of increasing the chances of a more rapid implementation of the process; and lastly, in the event of failure, coming up with other possible options. After lengthy negotiations in Houston from 14th to 16th September 1997 Morocco and the Polisario Front reached agreement on voting conditions and an 'honest' code of conduct under the attentive and constant supervision of the United Nations. This agreement settled the electoral register, the return of the refugees, a code of conduct for the election campaign, an exchange of war prisoners, the freeing of political prisoners, the positioning of the Morocco and Sahrawi armed forces and the partial withdrawal of Moroccan armed forces. Special identification commissions were then set up in the territories occupied by Morocco, in the liberated territories and in the refugee camps. However, Moroccan objections to the criteria used to identify the electorate led to time consuming and unproductive work by the commissions. In December 1999 the disputed groups were definitively identified and only very few entered onto the electoral roll – 2,000 out of 51,000 identified; new appeals were made to MINURSO, around 55,000, almost all of them by Morocco.

Given the impasse in the work of the commissions after the year 2000, Baker and Annan began to make plans for an alternative to the referendum to side-step the issue, a solution which met with Moroccan support. This 'third way' proposed the 'concession' of wide ranging autonomy in the Western Sahara which would become an official part of Morocco. This solution by the Secretary General was taken up by the Security Council in Resolution 1349 on 3rd April 2001. In May Baker presented this autonomy plan in the form of a framework agreement to the Polisario Front and Algeria. The plan proposed the integration of the Western Sahara into the Moroccan state with an autonomy statute for a transitory period of 5 years at the end of which the definitive status of the Western Sahara would be sanctioned by a referendum in which those resident there for at least one year, whatever their origins, would be entitled to the vote.

The agreement in this form has been the subject of intense criticism by the Sahrawi people. While Morocco argued that the proposal was based on the legitimacy of its presence in the area, a thesis which was given partial credence by the Secretary General who defined Morocco as a 'governing power', the Polisario Front noted that the powers which the Moroccan government was to grant to the Western Sahara were in actual fact illegally exercised over an occupied territory. However, despite dissent on its contents, the Sahrawi people subsequently accepted this plan prompting an immediate withdrawal from the negotiating table by Morocco. In February

2002 Kofi Annan relaunched this agreement placing four options before the Security Council: a) implementing the peace plan even without the consent of the two sides; b) applying a revised framework agreement and presenting it to the two sides as non-negotiable; c) dividing up the Western Sahara; d) pulling MINURSO out. Debate within the Security Council shifted with Baker arguing that agreement between the two sides was now unattainable. With Resolution 1429 in July 2002 the Security Council came down in favour of none of these solutions, declared its belief in the validity of the peace plan and asked Baker to come up with a solution which guaranteed the right to self-determination without expressly calling for a referendum as the means for enforcing this right. With the same resolution the Council argued for yet another extension of MINURSO on 31st January 2003. Since the failure of the second Baker plan and the resignation of the special representative, no agreement between the two sides has been reached.

In addition to the UN the European Union has also played a very important role supporting the Sahrawi people, pushing for a definitive solution to the problem and applying pressure to ensure that the plight of this people is not ignored as well as offering practical help for Sahrawi refugees in the form of huge financial aid. Unfortunately its organisational structure – involving the interaction of EC and inter-governmental dynamics – has meant that the EU's attitude to this people has frequently been ambiguous and contradictory[9]. Alongside action in support of the Sahrawi people, promoted mainly by the most fully community based EC bodies such as its Parliament and Commission, the Council's internal dynamics have led to greater support for Morocco being given by member states such as the Association Agreement with Morocco in 1996 and the more recent 2006 fishing agreement.

Any discussion of the relationship between the Western Sahara and the EU necessarily also touches on the bonds which exist between the European Union and Morocco which are deep rooted. The first important document here was the 1996 Association Agreement between the European Union and Morocco followed by fruitful trading links and financial bonds and the more recent fishing agreement. The agreement was encompassed by the Euro-Mediterranean partnership action plan whose ambitious ultimate objective was the creation, in 2010, of a free trade area. This project was launched with the Barcelona summit of 1995 at which the European Union and ten Mediterranean partners took part in an attempt to set up a free trade area via a network of bilateral agreements between Brussels and the region's individual states. The treaty drawn up with Morocco fell under this plan. The kingdom of Morocco has also been

---

9 J. Vaquer i Fanés, "The European Union and Western Sahara", in *European Foreign Affairs Review*, 9, 2004, pp. 93-113.

one of the main beneficiaries of the MEDA programme. In accordance with the new generation of association agreements the preface to this agreement highlighted the importance of the United Nations Charter and specifically respect for human rights, democratic principles and economic freedom and the text makes clear that one of the aspects which favoured its creation was precisely the importance accorded by the two sides to the United Nations Charter and specifically respect for human rights and economic and political freedom.

However, the illegal occupation of the Western Sahara by Morocco, its ambiguous and uncooperative attitude to the various solutions to the crisis put forward over the years by the UN and its violation of the human rights of the Sahrawi people, and of Moroccans themselves, clearly contravene the agreement.

Furthermore, although the importance of the UN Charter was recognised in prior agreements, in 2006 Morocco and the European Union signed an agreement relating to the potential exploitation of Morocco's coastal fishing waters by European fishing boats in which the coastal surface area calculations used included the Western Sahara. This clearly contravenes United Nations provisions on the exploitation of the resources of illegally occupied countries.

These few elements suffice to highlight a certain ambiguity in the European Union's attitude to the Western Sahara.

Despite the attention paid to the crisis by the two main international organisations the Western Sahara is still today occupied by Morocco and the Sahrawi people have still not been given the chance to put their rights to self-determination into practice.

Questioning the legality of agreements concluded between Morocco and the EU under international and European law

A major question is the legality either under international law or European Union law of the conclusion between Morocco and third parties of Agreements which may affect the Western Sahara's territory. This is especially true for the European Union, an actor deeply involved in a cooperative process with Morocco.

As E. Hagen underlines, the European Union has reached several Agreements with Morocco and Morocco is now the first partner of the Union in the region. All these Agreements are bilateral and have been concluded within the framework of the Barcelona process[10]. They aim

10 The Barcelona Declaration of 1995 is the founding document of the Euro-Mediterranean Partnership (EMP).

at implementing economic cooperation between the countries party and at exploiting the natural resources of the same parties, in exchange of financial compensations.

The first Agreement adopted between the parties is the EU-Morocco Association Agreement which entered into force in 2000. It is the current legal basis of the relations between the EU and its North African neighbour, setting out in detail the specific areas in which the Barcelona Process' objectives can be developed bilaterally. Among the other aims, the development of a Euro-Mediterranean free trade area is envisaged.

In July 2005, within the framework of the European Neighbourhood Policy, Morocco has signed with the European Union an Action Plan which includes priorities and objectives for cooperating in the political, economic and commercial spheres. The Action Plan facilitates the implementation of the instruments provided for in the Association Agreement between the EU and Morocco and fosters the economic integration with Morocco.

Since 2008, Morocco benefits also of an Advanced Status with the European Union, being the first country in the Southern Mediterranean region to have granted such a status. This development paves the way to a gradual integration of Morocco into EU policies, to deepen free trade Agreements by the establishment of a common economic area based on the rules of the European Economic Area and to extend them to new areas such as intellectual property rights, capital movements and sustainable development[11].

Following the grant of the Advanced Status, a new Action Plan has been adopted in 2013, strengthening and deepening several of the above mentioned advanced status' objectives.

Thanks to this framework, a number of specific Agreements have been concluded between the Parties, related mainly to the trade of agriculture products and fishing[12]. The most important Agreements in force are the Agreement on reciprocal liberalisation measures on agricultural products, processed agricultural products, fish and fishery products, entered into force in 2012[13], and the Fisheries Partnership Agreement (FPA), entered into force

---

11 Commission européenne, Déclaration de l'Union européenne, Septième Session du Conseil d'Association UE-Maroc, Luxembourg, 13 October 2008, DG E V, No.13653/08.

12 European Commission, 3 April 2008, COM (2008) 164, *Implementation of the European neighbourhood policy in 2007*; European Neighbourhood and Partnership Instrument – Morocco Strategy Paper 2007-2013.

13 Council Decision of 8 March 2012 on the conclusion of an Agreement in the form of an Exchange of Letters between the European Union and the Kingdom of Morocco concerning reciprocal liberalisation measures on agricultural products, processed agricultural products, fish and fishery products, the replacement of Protocols 1, 2 and 3

in 2007 and implicitly renewed since then[14]. As recalled by R. Passos, the FPA needs to be implemented by specific Protocols in order to be executed. The adoption of such Protocols has been a major issue of debate within the European Union, especially within the European Parliament. The last Protocol has been adopted in 2013 and entered into force in 2014[15].

At present, the conclusion of a Deep and Comprehensive Free Trade Agreement (DCFTA) is under discussion with the aim of replacing and extending significantly the scope of the Association Agreement in force[16].

The legality of the conclusion of such agreements is subject to two preliminary issues, deeply discussed in all the contributions of this book: the status of the Territory of Western Sahara and their territorial scope of application, i.e. whether they will apply or not to the Territory of Western Sahara.

R. Passos suggests in his contribution that there are two different possible approaches concerning the qualification of the status of Western Sahara. A first approach is supported by those who claim that Western Sahara's people has a right to self-determination which has been violated by the invasion of Morocco. A second approach qualifies Western Sahara as a Non-Self-Governing Territory and is grounded on the famous opinion given by H. Corell, the Under-Secretary-General for Legal Affairs at that time[17]. Accordingly, Morocco would be the Power assuming *de facto* the responsibilities for the administration of the Territory as provided by Article 73 of the Charter of the United Nations regarding precisely Non-Self-Governing Territories. While the adoption of the first approach leads to affirm the illegality as such of the exploitation of Western Sahara's natural resources, according to the supporters of the second approach the conclusion of Agreements in the same field would be possible, although certain conditions would need to be met.

---

and their Annexes and amendments to the Euro-Mediterranean Agreement establishing an association between the European Communities and their Member States, of the one part, and the Kingdom of Morocco, of the other part, in *Official Journal of the European Union*, L 241, 2012, p. 2 ff.

14 Fisheries Partnership Agreement between the European Community and the Kingdom of Morocco, Council Regulation (EC) No.764/2006, 22 May 2006, in *Official Journal of the European Union*, L 141, 2006, p. 1 ff.

15 Council Decision on the conclusion, on behalf of the European Union, of the Protocol between the European Union and the Kingdom of Morocco setting out the fishing opportunities and financial contribution provided for in the Fisheries Partnership Agreement in force between the two parties, in *Official Journal of the European Union*, L 349, 2013, p. 1 ff.

16 In http://ec.europa.eu/trade/policy/countries-and-regions/countries/morocco/.

17 UN Security Council, Letter dated 29 January 2002 from the Under-Secretary-General for Legal Affairs, the Legal Counsel, addressed to the President of the Security Council, S/2002/161, 12 February 2002.

The above distinction is reflected also in the current debate. While some qualify Morocco as an occupying power[18], others – especially within the European Union – refer to it as an administrative power, *de facto* administering power or administering power *tout-court*[19].

A similar distinction is not only doubtful, but mixes different things. As a consequence, it could be very misleading, as other contributors here underline, starting from H. Corell himself.

In international law's terms, as well as those of the United Nations, the qualification of administrative power recalls the position of any country which has an effective control over a territory, irrespective of the legality of illegality of such control. As such, also an occupying power is an administrative power. In fact, this qualification is mainly intended to recall to States which control territories which do not belong to them under international law that, nevertheless, they have certain obligations vis-à-vis the people under administration, especially concerning their protection. Put in this way, Morocco is certainly, at present, the administrative power of Western Sahara, being therefore obliged by the international rules applicable thereof, starting with human rights rules[20]. As specified by the High Commissioner for Human Rights (OHCHR) after a visit to Western Sahara, this obligation is without prejudice of the status of the territory concerned[21].

On the contrary, the qualification of administering power or of *de facto* administering power is meant to identify States which administer a Non-

---

18 For instance, J. Soroeta Liceras, *El conflicto del Sahara Occidental, reflejo de las contradicciones y carencias del Derecho internacional*, Bilbao, 2001.

19 The qualification as *de facto* administering or administrative power mainly comes from the Opinion of the Legal Service of the European Parliament, Doc. sj-0085/06, 20 February 2006, and from the EU Commissioners, while the qualification as administering power *tout-court* comes from national politicians, especially from Spain. On the matter, C. Ruiz Miguel, *El acuerdo de pesca UE-Marruecos o el intento español de considerar a Marruecos como "potencia administradora" del Sahara Occidental*, http://www.umdraiga.com; P. San Martin, *EU-Morocco Fisheries Agreement: The Unforeseen Consequences of a Very Dangerous Turn*, in *Grupo de Estudios Estratégicos GEES*, 2006, http://eng.gees.org.

20 International Court of Justice (ICJ), 9 July 2004, Advisory Opinion, *Legal Consequences of the Construction of a Wall in the Occupied Palestinian Territory*, para. 102 ff.; European Court of Human Rights (ECHR), 18 December 1996, *Loizidou v. Turkey*.

21 See OHCHR, *Report of the OHCHR Mission to Western Sahara and the Refugee Camps in Tindouf – 15/23 May and 19 June 2006*, Geneva, 8 September 2006, para. 11: the assessment of violations on the basis of international law on human rights binding an occupying State should not be "interpreted as constituting a position vis-à-vis the status of the territory according to international law or attributing any legitimacy to claims of sovereignty, but rather constitutes an evaluation of the *de facto* enjoyment of human rights by the people" of the territory concerned .

Self-Governing Territory in accordance with Article 73 of the Charter, thus acquiring the status and the responsibilities provided by this provision.[22]

Western Sahara is certainly a Non-Self-Governing Territory, but this does not mean that Morocco is the administering power or a *de facto* administering power according to Article 73 of the Charter. The qualifications of Non-Self-Governing Territory and of administering power or of *de facto* administering power are not reciprocally interdependent but depend instead on different historical processes. As C. Ruiz Miguel here explains in his reconstruction of the principle of self-determination and the people of Western Sahara, it is hardly to say that the historical process which has characterized the presence of Morocco in Western Sahara could be framed in the context of Article 73 of the Charter.[23]

The letter of the Under-Secretary-General for Legal Affairs clearly confirms this interpretation: while Morocco is certainly an administrative power of the Western Sahara in the first sense and has the obligations resulting from that status, it is not certainly an administering power or a *de facto* administering power under art. 73 of the Charter. Consequently, it does not have the international status connected to it[24].

---

[22] Art. 73 of the Charter says that "Members of the United Nations which have or assume responsibilities for the administration of territories whose peoples have not yet attained a full measure of self-government recognize the principle that the interests of the inhabitants of these territories are paramount, and accept as a sacred trust the obligation to promote to the utmost, within the system of international peace and security established by the present Charter, the well-being of the inhabitants of these territories, and, to this end: a. to ensure, with due respect for the culture of the peoples concerned, their political, economic, social, and educational advancement, their just treatment, and their protection against abuses; b. to develop self-government, to take due account of the political aspirations of the peoples, and to assist them in the progressive development of their free political institutions, according to the particular circumstances of each territory and its peoples and their varying stages of advancement; c. to further international peace and security; d. to promote constructive measures of development, to encourage research, and to co-operate with one another and, when and where appropriate, with specialized international bodies with a view to the practical achievement of the social, economic, and scientific purposes set forth in this Article; and e. to transmit regularly to the Secretary-General for information purposes, subject to such limitation as security and constitutional considerations may require, statistical and other information of a technical nature relating to economic, social, and educational conditions in the territories for which they are respectively responsible other than those territories to which Chapters XII and XIII apply".

[23] This is why Morocco doesn't appear as the administering power of Western Sahara in the UN list of Non-Self-Governing Territories (cf., https://www.un.org/en/decolonization/nonselfgovterritories.shtml), nor it could be said a de facto administering power because it has never assumed de facto the responsibilities implied by art. 73 (spontaneously or recognized by any other international subject, starting from the United Nations itself).

[24] See the Letter quoted above, para. 7: "On 26 February 1976, Spain informed the Secretary-General that as of that date it had terminated its presence in Western Sahara

A different issue arises when we take into account the obligations incumbent on Morocco because of its presence in Western Sahara, in particular as far as the conclusion of Agreements with third parties is concerned. As administrative power of a Non-Self-Governing Territory, there is no doubts that Morocco has at least the obligations which are due to a Non-Self-Governing Territory. This is the reason why the Under-Secretary-General for Legal Affairs in his Letter to the President of Security Council decided to dwell on the obligations of an administering power in the matter at issue[25]. However, again, this does not mean that Morocco is or could be qualified as an administering power (or a *de facto* administering power) under Article 73 of the Charter. As stated above, the international obligations of an administrative power are to be defined according to the reasons for the presence in the interested territory. Hence, these obligations or responsibilities may be different, or going further, of those related to an administering power within the meaning of Article 73 of the Charter.

Secondly, the legality under international law of the Agreements concluded by Morocco and the European Union depends on their territorial scope of application, i.e. on the inclusion or not of the territory of Western Sahara in such Agreements. In this regard, none of the aforementioned Agreements expressly specifies whether the territory of Western Sahara falls or not within their scope of application. This differs from the attitude adopted by other international actors. For instance, the Free Trade Agreement between United States and Morocco explicitly excludes Western Sahara[26].

Therefore, the only way in order to understand if these agreements are intended to be or not applicable to the Territory of Western Sahara is to refer to the interpretative criteria established by international law[27]. In

---

and relinquished its responsibilities over the Territory, thus leaving it in fact under the administration of both Morocco and Mauritania in their respective controlled areas. Following the withdrawal of Mauritania from the Territory in 1979, upon the conclusion of the Mauritano-Sahraoui agreement of 19 August 1979 (S/13503, annex I), Morocco has administered the Territory of Western Sahara alone. Morocco, however, is not listed as the administering Power of the Territory in the United Nations list of Non-Self-Governing Territories, and has, therefore, not transmitted information on the Territory in accordance with Article 73[e] of the Charter of the United Nations".

25 See the Letter quoted above, para. 8: "*Notwithstanding the foregoing, and given the status of Western Sahara as a Non-Self-Governing Territory,* it would be appropriate for the purposes of the present analysis to have regard to the principles applicable to the powers and responsibilities of an administering Power in matters of mineral resource activities in such a Territory".

26 See the appendix in this book.

27 See Vienna Convention on the Law of Treaties between States and International Organizations or between International Organizations of 1986. The Convention has not been ratified so far neither by Morocco nor by the EU. However, it seems largely

this sense, the FPA is the typical example discussed in the legal as well as political debate.

The FPA text establishes that the Agreement is applicable to the Territories under the sovereignty or jurisdiction of Morocco. While the term *sovereignty* is clear, the term *jurisdiction* is not. It may refer to the exclusive economic zone or any other territory on which Morocco does not have full sovereignty, but over which it exercises some forms of control, e.g. Western Sahara.

According to an opinion of the European Parliament's legal service, the FPA does neither include nor exclude the waters of Western Sahara and therefore it is up to the Moroccan authorities to apply the Agreement in compliance with its obligations under international law[28].

While practice is probably the most useful criterion in order to overcome the ambiguity of the Agreement, the position of the legal service is not acceptable since the European Union cannot discharge its responsibilities by simply leaving Morocco free to solve the issue. Instead, practice of both parties must be taken into account as well as the knowledge which a Party could have, in good faith, of the practice adopted by the other Party[29]. As different contributors point out, the EU plays a central role in the execution of the Agreement and the practice of both Parties clearly demonstrates that the Agreement is intended to include the Territory of Western Sahara[30]. However, it should be noticed that this practice seems inconsistent with the interpretation adopted by the Court of Justice of the European Union in other similar situations which has recognized that the Association agreement concluded with Israel is not applicable to the import of goods from the Occupied Palestinian Territories (OPT) while the Association agreement with Cyprus is not applicable to Northern Cyprus[31].

In light of the above, several concerns are raised in relation to the compliance of these agreements not only with International law, but also with European Union law.

---

reproductive of the international customary law on the matter, as confirmed by the Vienna Convention on the Law of Treaties of 1969, which provides for the same provisions.

28 Legal Opinion of the Legal Service of the Parliament, Doc. SJ-0085/06, cit. For large passages of the Opinion, see E. Milano, *The new Fisheries Partnership Agreement between the European Community and the Kingdom of Morocco: Fishing Too Far South?*, in *Anuario Español de Derecho Internacional*, 2006 and in http://eng.gees.org.

29 See art. 31.3.b) of the Vienna Convention.

30 In fact, it does not seem that the present practice differs significantly from the previous one adopted as a result of the implementation of the earlier fisheries agreements.

31 ECJ, case C-386/08, *Brita* (2010) ECR I-1289; case C-432/92, *Anastasiou I* (1994) ECR I-3087. Doubts on the exact meaning of this practice are expressed by E. Milano, *The New Fisheries Partnership*, cit., para. 6.

As far as international law is concerned, a first issue to analyse is related to the legal capacity of Morocco under international law to conclude an Agreement on behalf of Western Sahara.

According to a standard which seems generally accepted under international law, it should be recalled that even an administering power does not have the right to conclude an Agreement on behalf of the territory under administration once the process of decolonisation has begun or, at least, has acquired an international relevance. This has been stated by the International Arbitration Tribunal in the case *Guinea-Bissau v. Senegal* and seems to reflect largely international customary law[32].

Second, in a clear consistent way with the principle above mentioned, constraints derive also from the principle of sovereignty over natural resources. As recognized by the Under-Secretary-General for Legal Affairs in the above mentioned Letter and recalled in his contribution in this book[33], international customary law allows even an administering power to conclude an international agreement on behalf of the people concerned only if two conditions are met: the Agreement must be concluded in accordance with the interests *and* with the will of the people concerned. Both elements (interests and will) must be satisfied at the same time, being just one of them insufficient. The need for both elements is confirmed by many United Nations General Assembly's resolutions as well as by international practice[34].

This implies that the FPA and other Agreements must be concluded not only taking care of the interests or the benefits of the people, but also in accordance with their will. Moreover, it could be said that it is impossible to respect the people's interests without taking into account its

---

32 Arbitration Tribunal for the Determination of the Maritime Boundary, Decision of 31 July 1989, *Guinea-Bissau v. Senegal*, RIAA (vol. XX), para. 40 ff. The Tribunal specified also that the above mentioned principle cannot be inferred from the right to self-determination, but from the principle of effectiveness and the rules governing the formation of States in the international sphere, has not character of a rule of *jus cogens* and is applicable only when the activity of the national liberation movement has "acquired an international impact".

33 UN Security Council, Letter dated 29 January 2002, quoted above. The request was not related to the stipulation of agreements between subjects of international law but to the stipulation of contracts between the Moroccan authorities and foreign companies. However, the Opinion is based largely on the practice between States. Hence, there is no reason for not applying its conclusions also to agreements between States.

34 Since 1995, the General Assembly has affirmed "the value of foreign economic investment undertaken in collaboration with the peoples of Non-Self-Governing Territories and in accordance with their wishes in order to make a valid contribution to the socio-economic development of the Territories": Res. 50/33 of 6 December 1995, para. 2, on Economic and other activities which affect the interests of the peoples of the Non-Self-Governing Territories, annually reiterated.

will, being it the only subject who can legitimacy identify what exactly corresponds to its own interest.

However, as E. Milano notices, the European Union's political institutions seem to suggest that the principle of sovereignty over natural resources is satisfied whenever it could be said that a benefit is engendered for the interested people according to the view of the Parties to the Agreement, especially according to the view of the European Union itself. As a consequence, it can be said that not only the will of the people concerned seems to be neglected, but also the interests or the benefits of this people seem to be determined in a unilateral way.

From both the principles just mentioned, it comes that an Agreement concerning Western Sahara cannot be concluded without consulting the Saharawi people. As far as the latter is internationally represented by a subject legally entitled at representing it under international law, i.e. the *Frente Polisario*, it seems that any Agreement cannot be concluded without consulting this subject or, in other words, a similar agreement can be concluded only when its participation is granted.

Third, all the members of the international community have the obligation not to recognise international situations created in breach of international law, at least when this breach is serious and involves international rules of a peremptory character[35]. As clarified by the Special Rapporteur *Crawford*, the "*attempted* acquisition of sovereignty over territory through the denial of the right of self-determination of peoples" is such a breach[36].

The obligation not to recognise international illegal situations encompasses also the so-called implicit recognition. As the International Court of Justice has stated, the conclusion of bilateral agreements may give rise to such an implicit recognition[37].

As E. Milano points out, the conclusion of the Agreements between Morocco and the European Union without any tentative to differentiate

---

35 In the words of Art. 41 para. 2 of the *Draft Articles on Responsibility of States for Internationally Wrongful Acts*, 2001, "no State shall recognize as lawful a situation created by a serious breach within the meaning of article 40", i.e. a serious breach of "an obligation arising under a peremptory norm of general international law".

36 *Report of the International Law Commission*, 53rd session, 2001, pp. 287 ff., italic of the author. According to E. Milano, *The doctrine(s) of non-recognition: theoretical underpinnings and policy implications in dealing with de facto regimes*, 2007, in http://www.esil-sedi.eu/fichiers/en/Agora_Milano_060.pdf, the obligation of not recognition should arise also in the absence of the peremptory character of the breached norm.

37 International Court of Justice (ICJ), *Legal Consequences For States of the Continued Presence of South-Africa in Namibia not-withstanding Security Council Resolution 276* (1970), Advisory Opinion, ICJ Reports, p. 56. See also, ICJ, *Legal Consequences of the Construction of a Wall in the Occupied Palestinian Territory*, Advisory Opinion, 9 July 2004, para. 154 ff.

the regime of the Western Sahara or taking into account its special status sounds strongly as an implicit recognition by the European Union of a Moroccan authority over Western Sahara.

As far as European Union Law is concerned, it should be remembered that the respect for human rights and the rule of law binds the European Union also in its external action. While it doesn't seem that the EU has taken in duly account these principles before the conclusion of the Agreements, the Agreements in force are generally based on the so-called democratic or essential clause. This clause implies that the respect of human rights should be appreciated as an essential part of these Agreements. Therefore, if a serious breach of human rights occurs, this is to be considered as a substantial violation of the Agreements with the consequence that the other Party is authorised to suspend or extinguish the treaty[38].

Now, the human rights situation in the Territory is particularly worrying[39]. Going beyond the right of self-determination, which from a rigorous point of view is an human right in itself as provided by the International Covenant on Civil and Political Rights and the International Covenant on Economic, Social and Cultural Rights[40], the protection of human rights in the Territory seems far from satisfactory.

However, the European Union seems quite reluctant to draw up the necessary conclusions from the above analysis. The situation concerning the respect of human rights in the Territory of Western Sahara has never acquired relevance either before the conclusion of the Agreements or afterwards[41].

As R. Passos explains, the 2014 Fisheries Protocol reinforces the clause creating a system of monitoring especially aimed to assess if its application engenders benefits for the people concerned. The system would be set up with a special attention for people of Western Sahara, even if not expressly nominated, in order to verify whether or not the Agreement corresponds indeed to their interests or is beneficial for it.

---

38 See art. 60 Vienna Convention on the Law of Treaties.

39 Strictly speaking, the obligation to take into account the respect of human rights at the moment of the conclusion of the Agreements or the application of the clause is not limited to the Territory of Western Sahara, but concerns all the territories under control of Morocco. In other words, for applying the principle or the clause, it doesn't matter if the Agreements include or not the Territory of Western Sahara and, therefore, it is not necessary to demonstrate that the Agreements are applicable to this Territory.

40 OHCHR, *Report of the OHCHR Mission to Western Sahara*, *op. cit.*, paras. 9 and 52, according to which almost all the violations recorded stem from the non-realization of the right of self-determination.

41 A. Karmous, *Les enjeux des ressources halieutiques du Sahara Occidental*, Fondation France Libertés, 23 October 2002, in http://membres.lycos.fr/tomdsm/analyses.html, p. 8 ff., wondering whether the essential clause is just a style clause.

A negative assessment would bring to the suspension of the Agreement. However, the clause is not in position to remedy to the different problems that the conclusion of the Agreement raises under international law. With the consequence, as R. Passos himself observes, that the application of the clause, at least at the moment, seems hardly to fulfil the scope for which it has been elaborated.

As pointed out by H. Corell, after so many years of unsatisfactory situation in the field, the political (as well as legal) world seems to remain quite unaware of the real implications of the principle of the rule of law to the case of Western Sahara and of the possible sensitive risks of this attitude in the field.

However, these implications seem quite full of consequences if properly considered as demonstrated by the recent judgement of the General Court of the Court of Justice of the European Union, which has led to the annulment of the Council of the European Union's decision on the conclusion of the Agreement concerning reciprocal liberalisation measures on agricultural products, processed agricultural products, fish and fishery products[42].

[42] Although some critics remain in relation to specific aspects. See General Court of the Court of Justice of the European Union, *Front Polisario v. Council*, T-512/12.

Les origines de la "question du Sahara Occidental"

Enjeux historiques, défis politiques

Francesco CORREALE

CNRS UMR 7324 CITERES (CNRS/Univ. F. Rabelais), Tours

Un beso,
solamente un beso,
separa
la boca de África
de los labios de Europa

(Limam Boisha, 2004)

Une question ouverte et actuelle

En 1975, les dernières régions du continent africain sous domination coloniale secouent le joug que les métropoles européennes font encore peser sur elles. Toutes n'accèdent pas rapidement à une véritable liberté. Alors que le Mozambique, l'Angola et le Cap Vert, après avoir forcé les Portugais à évacuer leurs pays, s'engagent sur le chemin des indépendances[1] qui s'avéra long et douloureux, le Sahara Occidental[2] est abandonné par l'Espagne au Maroc et à la Mauritanie (Accords de Madrid du 14 novembre 1975). L'Organisation des Nations Unies (ONU), qui demande depuis 1965 que la population puisse s'exprimer à travers un référendum d'autodétermination, est ignorée. Une grande partie de la population, les Sahraouis, pour éviter de succomber aux armées mauritaniennes et marocaines – ces dernières n'hésitant pas à bombarder de napalm les campements nomades et à empoisonner les puits – doit se réfugier en Algérie. Progressivement, les civils rescapés aménagent des camps à proximité de Tindouf pour

1 Sur la décolonisation de l'Afrique portugaise, voir S. Lloyd-Jones & A. Costa Pinto, *The Last Empire: Thirty years of Portuguese decolonisation,* Bristol & Portland, Oregon, Intellect Books, 2003.

2 Le terme "Sahara Occidental", avec un "O" majuscule désigne le territoire anciennement dénommé "Sahara espagnol" tandis qu'avec un "o" minuscule définit l'espace géographique.

échapper à la guerre. Puis de véritables "camps de réfugiés" (reconnus comme tels par la communauté internationale et en particulier par le Haut-Commissariat des Réfugiés de l'ONU, HCNUR) sont aménagés pour les familles tandis tous les hommes valides rejoignent les forces de l'Armée populaire sahraouie, émanation du Front Polisario créé en 1973 pour lutter contre la domination espagnole. Pendant plus de quinze ans le Front tente de s'opposer par les armes à l'invasion maroco-mauritanienne du territoire. Après l'armistice signé avec le Maroc en 1991 – la Mauritanie s'étant retirée du conflit en 1978 –, les tentatives de l'ONU pour organiser le référendum échouent systématiquement, et cela, malgré la mise en place d'une Mission des Nations Unies pour l'Organisation d'un Référendum au Sahara Occidental – la MINURSO[3]. Quarante ans plus tard, la "question du Sahara Occidental" demeure ouverte, ignorée par les médias internationaux, voire assez méconnue même par les "experts" – à différents niveaux – de l'histoire et de la géopolitique de l'Afrique du Nord. Pourtant, les raisons qui devraient pousser à l'élever au rang de "question prioritaire" dans la recherche d'une résolution favorisant la stabilité du Maghreb et du Sahara-Sahel, sont bien évidentes et peuvent être ainsi énoncées :

– Une décolonisation inaccomplie : le Sahara Occidental est actuellement le dernier pays d'Afrique, avec l'île de St-Hélène, à être inscrit dans les listes de la 4e Commission de l'Assemblée Générale de l'ONU concernant les territoires non autonomes, où l'on reconnait l'exercice inaliénable du droit à l'autodétermination[4] aux populations. De fait, c'est le plus vaste territoire non autonome au monde.
– Dans une perspective historique, la "question du Sahara Occidental" peut être considérée comme paradigmatique des contradictions nées de l'implantation sur certains espaces africains d'États *ex nihilo* par la colonisation européenne ; une création arbitraire, génératrice de conflits liés soit au refus des frontières coloniales – ou à la notions même de frontière –, soit à des difficultés des sociétés ainsi sommées de construire un système étatique postcolonial, ou encore à la mauvaise gestion de la phase de décolonisation par l'ancienne métropole, en l'occurrence, l'Espagne.
– D'un point de vue géopolitique, elle est l'une des causes des blocages de l'Union du Maghreb Arabe (UMA), fondé à Marrakech en février 1989 sur le modèle de la Communauté économique

[3] Pour plus d'informations sur le rôle de la MINURSO, voir son site internet http://www.un.org/en/peacekeeping/missions/minurso/ (consulté le 7 avril 2015).

[4] Pour le rôle de la Quatrième Commission de l'Assemblée Générale des Nations Unies, voir son site internet http://www.un.org/fr/ga/fourth/index.shtml (consulté le 7 avril 2015).

européenne et réunissant cinq pays nord-africains : le Maroc, la Mauritanie, la Tunisie, l'Algérie et la Libye[5]. L'appui offert par le gouvernement algérien au Front Polisario ne fait qu'aiguiser le différend algéro-marocain sur les frontières des deux pays, différend qui avait déjà provoqué une guerre en 1963 (qu'on a appelé la "Guerre des sables")[6]. Ainsi, le Sahara Occidental est potentiellement un terrain d'affrontement armé.

Les enjeux politiques et économiques en sont également multiples. On remarque :

- L'existence de ressources naturelles importantes telles les mines de phosphates, le sable (exporté vers les Canaries), les ressources halieutiques et vraisemblablement du pétrole, ce qui constitue un enjeu économique d'envergure[7].
- La présence d'un ancien mouvement nationaliste très fort, incarné par le Front Polisario, qui a proclamé en 1976 la "République Arabe Sahraouie Démocratique" (RASD). Les origines du Front se trouvent sans doute dans l'Organisation Avancée pour la Libération du Sahara (OALS)[8], cellule nationaliste fondée en 1969 par Mohammed Sidi Basiri ; voire dans le combat mené par une bonne partie des populations du territoire entre 1956 et 1958 contre les colonialismes espagnol et français, mené à l'instigation et en partie sous la direction de l'Armée de Libération Nationale Marocaine. Ceci a rapidement posé des problèmes entre résistants marocains et résistants sahraouis, les premiers voulant contrôler les seconds qui n'acceptaient pas d'être dirigés par des étrangers, fussent-ils leurs alliés.
- Une population partagée entre les zones occupées actuellement par le Maroc et celles administrées par la RASD, à la fois dans la partie

5 Pour les enjeux de l'UMA, voir R. Weexsteen, "Une construction supranationale postcoloniale : l'Union du Maghreb Arabe (UMA), Enjeux, réalités et perspectives", in Sophie Caratini (dir.), *La question du pouvoir en Afrique du Nord et de l'Ouest. Vol. 2 : Affirmation identitaires et enjeux de pouvoir*, L'Ouest Saharien, Hors-Série n° 9-2, p. 131-138.

6 Pour une analyse détaillée de la "Guerre des sables", voir A. Torres García, *La guerra de las arenas. Conflicto entre Marruecos y Argelia durante la guerra fría (1963)*, Barcelone, Edicions Bellaterra, S.L., 2012.

7 Pour une documentation assez complète sur les ressources du Sahara occidental, voir le site de l'ONG Western Sahara Resource Watch (WSRW : http://www.wsrw.org/) (consulté le 7 avril 2015).

8 Sur les origines de l'OALS, voir C. Barona Castañeda, *Hijos de la nube. El Sahara Español desde 1958 hasta la debacle*, Madrid/San Lorenzo del Escorial, Libros C. De Langre, 2004, p. 169-174 et T. Bárbulo, *La historia prohibida del Sáhara Español*, Barcelona, Ediciones Destino S.A., 2002, p. 66-95.

du territoire du Sahara Occidental qu'elle contrôle et dans les camps de réfugiés proches de Tindouf. La population des camps estimée à 150.000/200.000 individus vit depuis quarante ans dans des conditions de dépendance économique quasi absolue à la coopération internationale. La région est en effet impropre à toute production agricole, du fait de la nature de ses sols et de l'extrême aridité de son climat. Au cours de la dernière décennie, les remises de l'étranger envoyées à leur famille par la diaspora sahraouie – en particulier les jeunes – vivant pour la plupart en Espagne, ainsi que le développement du commerce, activité traditionnelle aux confins sahariens, ont contribués à améliorer les conditions d'une partie de la population ; la majorité, sans autres ressources économiques que les dons, ne cesse de s'appauvrir. Quarante ans d'exil ont transformé les camps de réfugiés, initialement des tentes, en véritables petites villes, avec des structures quasi-urbaines.

– Dans le même temps, dans les territoires sahraouis occupés, la situation des populations n'est pas non plus très brillante. Si un certain nombre de Sahraouis a plus ou moins accepté le régime d'occupation, la plupart d'entre eux subissent le joug de l'administration marocaine. De fait, les Sahraouis sont aujourd'hui minoritaires dans leur propre territoire, devant l'arrivée de nombreux citoyens/colons marocains venant des milieux pauvres du nord.

Cette liste d'enjeux et d'éléments qui devraient susciter une plus grande attention de la communauté internationale pour la question sahraouie n'est pas exhaustive. Pour réellement les comprendre, il est nécessaire de remonter dans le passé des populations qui habitent et/ou habitaient ce territoire et recourir à l'histoire. Ainsi, se basant sur le dépouillement d'une importante bibliographie et de fonds d'archives tant français qu'espagnols, cet article vise-t-il à proposer une esquisse des origines de la "question du Sahara Occidental". Il se focalise sur les dynamiques internes au territoire et aux populations qui le parcourent, et donne ainsi à comprendre leur impact sur la situation actuelle.

Une ébauche de géographie et histoire précoloniale

Le Sahara occidental en tant que région géographique est bien plus vaste que le territoire strictement circoncis par les frontières établies sur le papier par les Français et les Espagnols entre la fin du 19e et le début du 20e siècle. Ainsi délimité, l'espace alors désigné comme le "Sahara Occidental" s'étend entre les parallèles 27°40' au Nord et 21°20' au Sud. Il possède à l'ouest plus de 1000 km de littoral atlantique, est séparé du Maroc au nord au niveau de la région de Tarfaya, de l'Algérie au nord-est par une frontière d'environ 150 km et de l'actuelle Mauritanie à l'est et au sud suivant une ligne qui bifurque au niveau de mines de fer de Zouerate. Il est composé de deux régions : la Sagyat al-Hamra dans la partie nord, et le Wādī ad-Dhahab, ou Rio de Oro dans la partie sud.

Jusqu'au 13e siècle, l'espace du Sahara occidental était habité par deux grandes confédérations berbères : les Zanata, plutôt sédentaires, et les Sanhaga, éleveurs nomades. Au 11e siècle, ces dernières se déplacent du centre de l'actuelle Mauritanie vers le Nord et au-delà du détroit de Gibraltar, atteignant l'Andalousie et fondent l'Empire Almoravide (1060-1147). Au 13e siècle toute la région est submergée par des populations arabes nomades en provenance du Yémen, les Arabes Maqīl. Une fraction des Maqīl, les Banī Hasān, émigre jusqu'au Sahara occidental, se mélangeant au cours des années, avec les Sanhaga. C'est à ce moment qu'on peut faire remonter la naissance d'un mélange ethnique autochtone, les bidān, parlant une langue assez proche de l'arabe classique, le Hassanya, et habitant la région qui s'étend du Wadi Drā'a (sud de l'actuel Maroc) au Sénégal et au Niger et de l'Atlantique à l'actuelle Mauritanie. Ce *melting pot* arabo-berbère n'est pas toujours paisible. En particulier, à la moitié du 17e siècle, une rébellion des populations berbères déclenche la "guerre de Shūr Būbā" dont l'issue marque le début d'un processus de hiérarchisation de la société ouest-saharienne, avec un premier hiatus entre les populations du Sahara Occidental et celles de la Mauritanie[9]. Ces dernières en effet s'organisent politiquement en Émirats, avec un chef au sommet tandis que les nomades sahariens demeurent politiquement acéphales[10]. Ces populations maures arabophones, appelées communément "Maures" sont donc constituées par le mélange de trois éléments culturels dominants : les Berbères Zanata et Sanhaja, les Arabes arrivés par vagues dans la région depuis le 13e siècle, et des Noirs de l'Afrique sub-saharienne réduits en esclavage et/ou objets d'un très ancien commerce transsaharien.

À la fin du 19e siècle, trois grandes confédérations de tribus parcourent non exclusivement le territoire qui va devenir le "Sahara Occidental" ou "Sahara espagnol". Elles peuvent être déclinées géographiquement du nord au sud de la manière suivante :

– les Takna, installés en bordure du désert sont essentiellement des commerçants. Ils sont divisés en divers groupes économiquement

9 Pour approfondir cette période de l'histoire du Sahara occidental, voir J. R. Diego Aguirre, *El oscuro pasado del desierto. Aproximación a la Historia del Sáhara*, Madrid, Sial Ediciones/Casa de África, 2004.

10 M. al Muhtar W. As-Sa'Ad, "Émirats et espace émiral maure. Le cas du Trârza aux XVIIIe-XXe siècles", in *Revue du Monde Musulman et de la Méditerranée*, n° 54, 1989, pp. 53-82.

complémentaires et partagés en deux *leff* ou factions rivales. La plus septentrionale, à dominante sédentaire, tient les marchés de la région du wādī Nūn (dont Gūlimīn est le centre). L'autre faction, composée de pasteurs itinérants, guerriers et chameliers, nomadise plus au sud dans la région côtière selon un mouvement nord/sud en fonction des saisons. Il faut bien comprendre que le wādī Nūn qui coule au pied de l'Anti-Atlas sud, marque la limite entre le monde berbérophone marocain et le monde arabophone maure de l'Ouest-saharien. Les factions Takna sédentaires, souvent bilingues, sont donc à la lisière. Ils alimentent les marchés de l'Anti-Atlas au nord, et envoient vers le sud leurs caravanes de marchandises le long des pistes transsahariennes qui traversent la Mauritanie. Dans les oasis des villes d'étape de ce commerce, les Takna, comme d'autres confédérations commerçantes, ont installé des relais, en particulier dans l'Adrār[11] ;

- les Rgaybāt, éleveurs et guerriers, nomadisent des confins septentrionaux du désert à l'Adrar mauritanien et de l'océan atlantique aux frontières actuelles du Nord-malien. Ils sont divisés en deux groupes alliés : les Rgaybāt Charg ou Rgaybāt al-Gwāsim au nord et les Rgaybāt Sahel (*al-Sāhil*) au sud[12] ;
- les Awlād Dalīm, guerriers également réputés, dont les terrains de parcours, les plus méridionaux, s'étendent de la côte aux territoires mauritaniens qui jouxtent la frontière avec le Sahara Occidental, et qui sont composés de cinq fractions apparentées : Ludaikat, Serhana, Awlād Baamar, Awlād Khaliga, Awlād Taggaddi)[13].

D'autres groupes de pasteurs, soit d'importance numérique mineure, soit protégés par l'un ou l'autre des trois grands groupes de guerriers dominants, nomadisent également de manière permanente, régulière ou exceptionnelle sur les pâturages du Sahara Occidental. Lorsque les Espagnols ont débarqué dans la péninsule de Dakhla, en novembre 1884, leur première préoccupation a été de chercher un interlocuteur qui ait sur l'ensemble des habitants de la région une légitimité politique suffisante pour traiter avec eux. Mais qui ? Dans une société acéphale où, contrairement à l'espace de la Mauritanie actuelle, aucun groupe ne s'est jamais doté d'un quelconque "émir", le problème était de taille. À partir

---

11 Sur les Takna, voir M. Naimi, *Le Sahara à travers le pays Takna : histoire des relations commerciales et politiques*, Rabat, Matba 'at 'Ukaz, 1988.

12 Sur les Rgaybāt, voir S. Caratini, *Les Rgaybāt (1610-1934)*, Paris, L'Harmattan, 1989, 2 vol.

13 Sur les Awlād Dalīm, voir A. López Bargados, *Arenas coloniales. Los Awlād Dalīm ante la colonización franco-española del Sáhara*, Barcelone, Edicions Bellaterra, S.L., 2003.

de cette première question, qui va devenir cruciale pour le gouvernement espagnol, nous nous interrogerons sur les caractéristiques principales de l'emprise coloniale espagnole. Nous chercherons à comprendre comment ce colonisateur "autre" va-t-il contribuer à différencier les populations nomades qui n'avaient de cesse de franchir une frontière n'existant pas pour eux de leurs voisins des espaces marocains et mauritaniens "sujets de la France".

L'Espagne et les populations du Sahara occidental : quelle colonisation ?

En 1884 Emilio Bonelli y Hernando[14] guide une expédition au Sahara pour le compte de la Société Espagnole des Africanistes et Colonialistes et fonde une première factorerie commerciale dans la péninsule de Dakhla (la future Villa Cisneros). Il noue une sorte d'alliance avec les Awlād Bū Sba'a un groupe guerrier récemment venue du Maroc bouleverser l'échiquier des forces sahariennes, et disputant au moment de son arrivée leur territoire aux Awlād Dalīm. Bonelli y Hernando méconnait évidemment la réalité sociale et politique du Sahara occidental et croit avoir traité avec le groupe dominant. Quelques mois plus tard les Awlād Dalīm prennent leur revanche, et lorsqu'ils attaquent les Awlād Bū Sba'a, ils s'en prennent en toute logique à leurs amis étrangers et assaillent le maigre contingent espagnol qui défend la factorerie[15]. Les escarmouches se poursuivent jusqu'en 1895, jusqu'à ce que les Espagnols, comprenant qui est le véritable maître des lieux mais surtout du moment, signent un traité commercial avec les Awlād Dalīm. Les attaques à la factorerie cessent, mais les Espagnols restent isolés sur la côte, malgré quelques tentatives de pénétration à l'intérieur du territoire[16]. Faiblement armés, très peu nombreux, ils sont considérés par les Awlād Dalīm – et par l'ensemble des populations de la région – comme des vassaux, voire de simples intermédiaires d'un petit commerce qui s'effectue alors avec les îles Canaries.

---

14 Emilio Bonelli y Hernando est auteur d'un ouvrage dans lequel il décrit les premiers "exploits" des Espagnols sur la côte saharienne : *El Sahara. Descripción geográfica, comercial y agrícola desde Cabo Bojador a Cabo Blanco, viajes al interior, habitantes del desierto y consideraciones generales*, Madrid, Tipolitografía de L. Péant é Hijos, 1887.

15 Sur les conflits de la fin du 19e siècle entre les populations de la région, dans lesquels s'inscrit le conflit entre les Awlād Dalīm et les Awlād Bū Sba'a, A. López Bargados, *op. cit.*, p. 272-278 ; S. Caratini, *op. cit.*, vol. 1, p. 90-102.

16 Parmi les expéditions à l'intérieur du territoire il faut mentionner celle "scientifique" dénommée Cervera-Quiroga-Rizzo de 1886 qui avait pour objectif d'atteindre les salines d'Idjil, voir J. A. Rodríguez Esteban (dir.), *Conmemoración de la expedición científica de Cervera-Quiroga-Rizzo al Sáhara Occidental en 1886*, Madrid, Consejo Superior de Investigaciones Científicas, 2008.

Il faut attendre décembre 1903 pour que l'Espagne nomme un véritable gouverneur militaire du Río de Oro[17]. Francisco Bens d'Argandoña est né à Cuba en 1867. Il prend son poste en 1904, avec très peu de moyens militaires et économiques[18]. Il prône donc la "pénétration pacifique", et inaugure la politique dite "du pain de sucre". Il s'agit d'amadouer les populations par des dons de denrées alimentaires, d'argent, de marchandises diverses et parfois d'armes. Par cette stratégie, il paye en quelque sorte, aux tribus dominantes la permission de rester stationné sur la côte. Il se comporte donc comme ses prédécesseurs, mais pour marquer sa position, il institutionnalise la "dîme" qu'il verse aux différents notables, et la fait figurer dans le budget de la colonie[19].

Au cours de ces premières années de la "colonisation espagnole", qui n'en est pas encore une, deux événements importants – et dans un certain sens, involontairement spéculaires – ont lieu parallèlement à la politique de lente pénétration entamée par Bens. Entre 1904 et 1912 les gouvernements de Paris et de Madrid signent une série d'accords pour définir précisément les contours de leurs possessions territoriales respectives tant au Maroc que dans l'Ouest-saharien. En ce qui concerne le Sahara, la région de Tarfaya est baptisée "zone méridionale du protectorat marocain" et reste donc, nominalement, sous l'autorité du Sultan 'alawite. La Sagyat al-Hamra est définie comme la "zone où

---

17 Avant la nomination de Bens, l'administration de la colonie avait été assurée par Emilio Bonelli y Hernando, Sous-Gouverneur, puis Commissaire Royal, du 3 novembre 1884 à 1902 ; et par Angel Villalobos, Sous-Gouverneur de 1902 au 1er décembre 1903. Bonelli y Hernando et Villalobos faisaient partie du Corps d'Infanterie de la Marine.

18 Sur les premières années de la présence espagnole au Sahara Occidental, voir J. M. Martínez Milán, *España en Sáhara Occidental y en la zona sur del Protectorado en Marruecos, 1885-1945*, Madrid, UNED Ediciones, 2003, p. 73-92.

19 "Je commençais la captation du Maure par cette politique que certains définissent du 'pain de sucre', puisque par ces cadeaux et d'autres j'attirais l'indigène vers moi [...]. En échange de ces cadeaux (bracelets en argent Hassani ou de douros Alphonse, verroterie en argent pour ornements de coiffure, amulettes, mouchoirs de coloris divers, des babioles des Canaries, vêtements aux couleurs qui déteignaient, donnant une couleur bleue à leur peaux), les femmes maures me tenaient au courant de tout ce dont les nomades discutaient pendant la nuit dans leurs tentes, des conversations autour des puits du Sahara [...], des différends qui existaient parmi les tribus, de l'esprit des chefs des clans, de la propagande et de l'enseignement des marabouts, des combats entre les tribus et du caractère des Maures les plus importants et les plus turbulents", F. Bens Argandoña, *Mis memorias (ventidos años en el desierto)*, Madrid, Selecciones Gráficas, 1947 p. 42-45. Pour les cadeaux qu'il donne aux différents populations, Bens fait figurer dans le budget du Gouvernement de 1904 1.074 Ptas et 1.250 Ptas en 1905 et 1906, lettre n° 62, le Sous-Secrétaire au Ministère d'État au Gouverneur Politico-Militaire du Rio de Oro, Madrid, 27/12/1907, Archivo General de la Administración (AGA), Alcalá de Henares, Sección n°15 : Africa – Fondo No.24 – Gobierno General del Sahara : Caja S 3743.

l'Espagne a un droit exclusif d'occupation" alors que le Río de Oro est "colonie espagnole"[20]. Tous ces accords sont évidemment conclus à l'insu des populations de ces espaces dont certaines sont déjà engagées dans la résistance à la pénétration coloniale.

En effet, dans les mêmes années, le *shaykh* Mā' al-'Aynayn, érudit soufi de grande réputation originaire du Sud-est mauritanien, encourage la résistance à la pénétration française au nord comme au sud, et réunit autour de lui une coalition de guerriers qui s'oppose par les armes à l'avancée des conquérants dans les territoires mauritaniens. Le Sultan du Maroc[21], auquel il a fait appel, soutient cette coalition par l'envoi d'armes et d'argent jusqu'en 1907, quand la mission qu'il a envoyée auprès du *shaykh* rentre au Maroc à la suite de différends avec les guerriers maures. Cependant, Mā' al-'Aynayn ne cessera son combat qu'il poursuivra jusqu'à sa mort, en octobre 1910, sous les murs de Tiznit. Son fils, Ahmad al-Hayba, lui succède alors et sera proclamé Sultan à Marrakech en août 1912[22].

Mais le *shaykh* ne s'occupe pas seulement de coordonner et guider la résistance. Entre 1898 et 1902, Mā' al-'Aynayn fonde un carrefour caravanier au milieu de la Sagyat al-Hamra, Smara[23]. Avec ses disciples, il s'efforce de drainer le trafic caravanier vers cette région qui paraît "sûre" car aucun infidèle n'y est jamais venu. À tort, car Smara est évacuée en 1909 à cause de la pénétration coloniale française dans les espaces mauritaniens. Il faut remarquer qu'au contraire de la présence française, les populations de ces régions considèrent l'établissement des Espagnols sur la côte comme une ressource. C'est donc à Bens que le fils de Mā' al-'Aynayn, Ahmad al-Hayba, se faisant leur porte-parole, propose d'occuper Tarfaya et d'aménager un port à l'abri de l'administration coloniale française. L'installation espagnole sur ce point de la côte et l'établissement d'une nouvelle factorerie commerciale après celle de

[20] L'étude plus complète sur la délimitation des frontières du Sahara occidental est F. E. Trout, *Morocco's Saharan Frontiers*, Genève, Droz, 1969.

[21] Sur la résistance à la pénétration française guidée par Mā' al-'Aynayn, F. Correale, "Mā' al-'Aynayn, il Marocco e la resistenza alla penetrazione coloniale (1905-1910)", in *Oriente Moderno*, Nuova Serie, anno XVIII (LXXVIII), indice vol. 2, 1998, p. 227-278.

[22] Sur l'épopée d'Ahmad al-Hayba en 1912, voir D. Rivet, *Lyautey et l'institution du Protectorat français au Maroc 1912-1925*, Paris, L'Harmattan, 1996, 3 vol., 1 vol., p. 136-137. Rivet analyse dans les pages successives les composantes du mouvement hibiste, les raisons qui en déterminent le succès et, ensuite, la chute. D'autres détails sur la résistance d'Ahmad al-Hayba pendant cette période se trouvent dans T. Garcia Figueras, *Africa en la acción española*, Madrid, Inst. de estudios africanos, 1949, p. 208-210.

[23] Sur la fondation de Smara, voir J. Caro Baroja, *Estudios Saharianos*, Madrid, Consejo Superior de Investigaciones Científicas, 1955, p. 306-318.

Villa Cisneros se feront en juin 1916[24]. Le débarquement à Tarfaya a été en effet retardé par l'éclatement de la Première Guerre mondiale et les affrontements navals qui ont opposés Alliés et troupes allemandes au large des côtes sahariennes[25]. Dans le même but déclaré, en 1920, Bens fonde une factorerie à La Güera, à l'extrême sud de la colonie du Río de Oro. L'objectif de ce troisième emplacement au Sahara est double. D'un côté il s'agit de permettre aux caravanes qui ne veulent plus écouler leurs marchandises par Port-Etienne – contrôlé par la colonisation française – de le faire en territoire "espagnol"[26] ; de l'autre de répondre aux exigences des lobbies de la pêche canariennes qui réclament une plus forte présence militaire de l'Espagne dans la péninsule de Cap Blanc, afin de développer un commerce qui puisse rivaliser avec celui de Port-Etienne. Il faut souligner que malgré l'appui du Gouvernement espagnol, Bens n'est guère enthousiaste de l'occupation de La Güera car d'un côté il ne veut pas entrer en conflit avec les Français, et de l'autre il aurait préféré voir l'installation d'une troisième factorerie commerciale aux environs de Villa Cisneros, afin de ne pas "éparpiller" les maigres forces espagnoles présentes au Sahara[27].

Tandis que la résistance à l'occupation française de l'espace maure se concentre du côté espagnol de la frontière où les guerriers nomades ont compris qu'ils pouvaient jouir d'une sécurité relative, les Espagnols mettent timidement en place un instrument de contrôle de leur zone en même temps qu'un embryon d'administration des populations en créant en 1928 une Police du Sahara (*Tropas de Policía del Sahara*)[28]. En réalité, ils stationnent presque uniquement sur la côte jusqu'en 1934, date de "bouclage" des régions septentrionale de la Mauritanie et méridionales du Maroc et de l'Algérie qui marquent la fin des "pacifications" françaises de ces régions sahariennes. Les Espagnols, à l'instar de leurs voisins, construisent alors des postes dans différents points de leur portion de désert où ils installent des garnisons sans pour autant réellement contrôler leur territoire et les populations qui y nomadisent, et occupent Smara inhabitée depuis 1909. Toujours en 1934, le Gouvernement républicain confie la

24 Sur l'occupation de Tarfaya, F. Bens Argandoña, *Memoria relativa a la ocupación de Cabo Juby por España efectuada en 29 junio 1916*, Cabo Juby, 1917, document dactylographié conservé à la Bibliothèque Nationale de Madrid (côte *Afr Ga F. Ca 390-15*).

25 *Ibidem.*

26 Sur l'occupation de La Guëra M. Fernández-Aceytuno, *Ifni y Sáhara. Una encrucijada en la historia de España*, Palencia, Simancas Ediciones, S.A., 2001, p. 314-316.

27 Sur ces aspects, voir J. M. Martínez Milán, *op. cit.*, p. 90-92.

28 *Tropas de Policía del Sahara* in J. Tejero Molina, *El Sahara Español de la 'A' a la 'Z'*, 2 vol., Madrid, Torres de Papel, 2013-2014, 1 vol., p. 662-663.

charge de Gouverneur Général des Territoires d'"*Ifni, Sahara Español et Río de Oro*" au Haut-Commissaire espagnol au Maroc[29], à Tétouan.

Malgré quelques épisodes secondaires, la guerre civile espagnole (1936-1939) n'a pas de véritable impact sur la gestion des territoires sahariens dont l'administration passe rapidement aux mains des phalangistes[30]. Très peu de troupes sont levées pour la guerre en Espagne parmi les populations sahariennes, alors que le recrutement des Marocains dans le Protectorat est assez important. Notons également que la région sert de lieu d'internement pour les Républicains pendant le conflit et après la victoire de Franco[31].

En 1946, pour contrecarrer le nationalisme marocain naissant, le Gouvernement de Madrid décide d'unifier ses possessions africaines, créant l'Afrique Occidentale Espagnole (A.O.E.), une entité administrative qui regroupe les territoires du Maroc déjà sous protectorat espagnol, le Sahara Occidental et l'enclave d'Ifni. La réalité montre qu'il s'agit d'un véritable imbroglio institutionnel, car le Gouverneur de l'A.O.E., qui dépend directement de la Présidence du Gouvernement par la Direction Générale du Maroc et des Colonies, siège à Ifni, alors que le véritable centre décisionnel continue d'être Tétouan, la capitale du Protectorat. Cette création de l'A.O.E. a-t-elle des conséquences sur les imaginaires que les populations, réunies pour la première fois sous une même administration, s'en font ? Pour esquisser une réponse à cette question, il convient de prendre en considération deux données : Tétouan est le véritable centre politique du Gouvernement espagnol en Afrique, et le personnel de l'administration coloniale au Sahara depuis 1934 provient de plus en plus du Protectorat espagnol au Maroc. La nouvelle configuration a donc pour conséquence intérieure que les décisions adoptées à Tétouan doivent être appliquées à Ifni, Tarfaya et El Ayoun, ce qui ne se fait pas sans heurts : les sources témoignent de conflits fréquents, notamment entre les administrateurs coloniaux périphériques[32]. Plus

---

29 À la suite de cette décision, le Gouverneur du Sahara devint Délégué Gouvernemental du Sahara.

30 Sur les effets de l'éclatement de la guerre civile espagnole au Sahara, voir M. Fernández-Aceytuno, *op. cit.*, p. 349-353.

31 Voir à ce propos J. Sahareño, *Villa Cisneros. Deportación y fuga de un grupo de antifascistas*, La Laguna, Tierra de fuego, 2007 ; et, plus en général, sur les déportations politiques au Sahara entre 1932 et 1936, J. R. Diego Aguirre, *Historia del Sahara Español. La verdad de una traición*, Madrid, Kayeda, 1988, p. 245-266.

32 Sur les conséquences politiques de ces changements, voir C. Ruíz Miguel, *El Sahara Occidental y España : Historia, Política y Derecho. Análisis crítico de la política exterior española*, Madrid, Editorial Dykinson, 1955, p. 69-71 (consulté le 8 avril 2015 sur le site http://saharalibre.es/modules/Libros/libros/ESOYEHPYDACDLPEE%28cruizmiguel%29.pdf).

tard, ce rattachement administratif du Sahara Occidental à Tétouan sera utilisé par les nationalistes marocains qui s'y référeront pour affirmer la "marocanité" des territoires sahariens[33].

Le deuxième point est que l'unité administrative de cet ensemble colonial espagnol (bien que dans la région de Tarfaya, protectorat méridional du Maroc, le Gouverneur de l'A.O.E. exerce les fonctions de Délégué du Haut-Commissaire à Tétouan), produit un ensemble assez homogène. Cette continuité casse de fait le principe des divisions territoriales dues à différentes administrations coloniales et, faisant abstraction complète des frontières décidées par les Gouvernements de Paris et de Madrid, crée une continuité politique et sociale qui se correspond en partie aux parcours des populations nomades et semi-nomades de l'Ouest Saharien. Si les statuts coloniaux tous artificiels des territoires visaient à morceler les espaces pour mieux les contrôler, l'unification – certes courte, car elle n'a duré que douze ans – de ces zones est théoriquement susceptible de provoquer la genèse d'un sentiment différent dans les populations "soumises" désormais à une même autorité supra-tribale – l'Etat colonial – du wādī Dra'a, qui constitue la limite septentrionale de la région de Tarfaya, à la Mauritanie. De quelque manière, les frontières coloniales constituent ainsi l'humus dans lequel se foisonne une identité sahraouie dont les fondements reposent sur le territoire et non plus sur la traditionnelle structure politique et sociale propre au monde bidān, dont le nomadisme constitue le trait essentiel.

Après l'indépendance du Maroc (1956), le Sahara espagnol est inclus dans l'idée du "Grand Maroc", développée par Allāl al Fāsi, leader du parti *Istiqlāl* en juillet 1956, au Caire[34]. En même temps il est infiltré par des membres de l'Armée de Libération Nationale (ALN) provenant du Sud du Maroc et qui mènent une importante propagande au nom du *jihad* auprès des populations. Les Sahraouis répondent nombreux à cet appel, mais la nouvelle Armée de Libération – qui est parfois dans les documents espagnols et français appelée "Armée de Libération du Sahara" – n'a que

33 *Ibidem.*

34 Allāl al-Fāsi, *Livre rouge et documentaires*, Tanger, M. Peretti, 1961 ; M. Barbier, *Le conflit du Sahara Occidental*, Paris, L'Harmattan, 1982, p. 78. A. Gaudio in *"Sahara Espagnol", fin d'un mythe colonial*, Rabat, Éditions Arrissala, 1975, p. 179, soutient que la carte du "Grand Maroc" avait été présentée au Caire en 1955, et avait été diffusée par l'Ambassade du Maroc à Londres ; J. Serjac in "Mauritanie et Maroc", *L'Afrique et l'Asie*, n° 45, 1959, p. 11-21, p. 11, affirme qu'au moment de la création de l'Armée de Libération Nationale du Maroc, en juillet 1955, Allāl al-Fāsi incitait les combattants à lutter pour "la réalisation du Grand Maroc, de Colomb-Béchard à Saint-Louis du Sénégal", et non seulement pour la libération des territoires soumis au Protectorat français. Le "Grand Maroc" fixait la frontière du Royaume au fleuve Sénégal et comprenait tout le Sahara Occidental et la Mauritanie, le sud-ouest de l'Algérie et le nord-ouest du Mali.

des cadres marocains. Quelques contingents de l'AL tentent une percée dans le nord de la Mauritanie, mais ils sont battus par les troupes coloniales françaises (janvier – février 1957). Quelque mois plus tard (automne 1957), ils attaquent également les forces espagnoles, les obligeant à abandonner tous les postes de l'intérieur et à se replier sur la côte. Le gouvernement de Madrid réagit. Dans un premier temps, en janvier 1958, il dissout l'AOE et transforme ses colonies en Provinces métropolitaines. Puis, les Gouvernements espagnols et français s'accordent pour mener une opération militaire conjointe d'envergure, dite "opération Ecouvillon/Ouragan", qui prend en tenaille les différents bataillons de l'ALN. Ceux d'entre eux qui échappent aux bombardements se replient alors majoritairement vers le nord, les armées espagnoles et françaises bloquant le sud et l'est. Deux mois plus tard, l'Espagne cède définitivement la région de Tarfaya au Royaume du Maroc (traité d'Angra de Cintra, 2 avril 1958).

Le passage de l'Armée de Libération sur le territoire saharien et le combat anticolonial qu'elle mène enrôlant massivement les populations du Sahara auront ainsi produit des effets qu'on peut résumer en deux points :

- une méfiance accrue des pasteurs nomades sahariens vis-à-vis de l'Espagne à la suite de bombardements aveugles, ciblant à la fois le bétail, les puits et les caravanes ; et en raison de la cession de la région de Tarfaya au Royaume du Maroc, ce qui marque une rupture dans la représentation que les Sahraouis se faisaient de "leur territoire" allant jusqu'aux limites du wādī Drā'a[35] ;
- une frustration vis-à-vis des pays limitrophes qui ont obtenu leur indépendance, tel que le Maroc, ou sont sur le point de l'obtenir comme la Mauritanie et surtout l'Algérie, dont les échos de la guerre de libération du FLN atteignent tant les centres urbains du Sahara espagnol que les campagnes. Par ailleurs, le Maroc et la Mauritanie indépendantes tentent d'attraire dans leurs pays les Sahraouis en leur promettant des subsides pour les troupeaux.

D'une manière générale, on constate que les actions conjointes menées contre la France et l'Espagne ont ravivé l'esprit de résistance des populations du Sahara Occidental contre les Européens et ont donné vie à des alliances politiques momentanées entre les Sahraouis se retrouvant ensemble dans les bataillons formés par l'ALN, sans aucune référence

[35] Il est intéressant de remarquer que l'une des phrases les plus recourant que les Sahraouis emploient pour manifester leur désarroi vis-à-vis de la cession de la région de Tarfaya au Maroc dit : "on s'endormit espagnols et on se réveilla marocains", soulignant ainsi le fait que Tarfaya et ses alentours avaient été l'objet d'un échange sans aucune implication des populations qui y habitaient.

aux dynamiques ou aux intérêts de telle ou telle autre tribu.[36] Pourtant, un certain nombre d'effectifs sahraouis enrôlés dans l'ALN prennent leur distance par rapport aux officiers marocains déjà quelques mois après les opérations militaires franco-espagnoles[37]. En décembre 1958, dans le sud du Maroc, les contingents sahraouis de l'ALN se battent contre les cadres de l'Armée de Libération et les FAR, et revendiquent leur autonomie par rapport au Royaume du Maroc. Ils rentrent, après quelques hésitations, dans la zone espagnole. Cet épisode, appelé par les Sahraouis l'"opération du *ksar makhzin*" car il débute par l'assaut à un dépôt d'armes à Tan Tan verrouillé par les cadres de l'ALN, marque un point de non-retour dans les relations entre le Maroc et les Sahraouis. Ces derniers vont jusqu'à accuser les Marocains de l'Armée de Libération de les avoir trompés avec leur propagande au nom du *jihad* contre les chrétiens, pour la libération de tous les territoires encore colonisés, alors que le véritable objectif de l'AL aurait été l'annexion du Sahara et de la Mauritanie par le Royaume du Maroc[38]. Face à ces événements quelle est la réaction de l'administration coloniale espagnole ?

Renouant avec la tradition inaugurée par Bens, l'administration espagnole remet en place une véritable stratégie de cooptation des populations moyennant le versement d'indemnités pour les pertes humaines et de bétail provoquées par les bombardements de 1957-1958. Puis, à partir de décembre 1958, le Gouvernement espagnol s'engage dans une campagne d'aides sociales (*Ayuda Social*), à savoir une allocation, tant aux notables qu'aux nomades, en denrées alimentaires et parfois en argent. Cet instrument vise à attirer les populations vers l'administration, à s'assurer la fidélité des notables qui sont les premiers bénéficiaires des aides, et cela jusqu'en 1975[39]. Il faut souligner que la sècheresse de ces années facilite la tâche des du gouvernement espagnol.

---

36 Ainsi qu'il ressort du discours tenu par les Sahraouis interviewés au cours des séjours dans les camps de réfugiés en 2007-2008 et en 2014.

37 Sur ces derniers point, voir F. Correale, "Le Sahara espagnol : histoire et mémoire du rapport colonial. Un essai d'interprétation", in S. Caratini (dir.), *La question du pouvoir en Afrique du Nord et de l'Ouest.* Vol. 1 : *Du rapport colonial au rapport de développement, L'Ouest Saharien*, Hors-Série n° 9-1, p. 103-152, p. 132-133.

38 Ce discours est tenu presque à l'unanimité par les ex-guérilleros interviewés, qui soulignent ainsi leurs différences par rapport au Marocains. Il n'en reste pas moins que les Sahraouis s'enrôlèrent massivement dans l'AL et qu'aujourd'hui, dans les camps de réfugiés, le récit de cette "alliance" avec les Marocains ne se fait pas sans provoquer quelque embarras.

39 Ces points ont été développés plus en détail dans l'article cité à la note précédente, p. 133-143. Sur les *Ayudas Social*, voir aussi J. E. Alonso del Barrio, *Sáhara-Ifni. ¿Encrucijada o abandono ? 1956-1963*, Saragosse, Mira Editores, 2010, 2 vol., vol. 2 : p. 341-350.

Pour contrer les visées expansionnistes du Maroc, l'Espagne envoie des troupes dans sa province saharienne. Le dispositif de contrôle territorial est ensuite renforcé par la mise en place de six (puis quatre) *harka* (contingents) d'irréguliers sahraouis – non intégrés officiellement dans l'armée espagnole – à la frontière nord du territoire saharien. Ces *harka*, organisées sur une base tribale à la différence des bataillons qui étaient structurés au sein de l'ALN, ont pour tâche de mener des incursions et des contre-incursions en territoire marocain, contre telle ou telle autre tribu, afin d'alimenter un climat d'insécurité. Comme le relatent les nombreux documents consultés à ce sujet à l'*Archivo General de la Administración* d'Alcalá de Henares[40], au Centre des Archives Diplomatiques de Nantes[41] et aux Archives Nationales d'Outre-Mer[42], il s'agit en effet de manière délibérée d'aiguiser les rivalités intertribales latentes dans le Sud-marocain[43]. Les forces espagnoles sont aidées dans cette tâche par les forces françaises de Mauritanie, le gouvernement français étant opposé aux revendications territoriales du Maroc sur le territoire mauritanien. À l'instar des Espagnols, les Français créent dans l'Adrar des "milices" dénommés "*partisans*", qui jouent exactement le même rôle que les *harka*[44].

Les stratégies d'attraction des Sahraouis mises en place par l'administration espagnole s'accompagnent d'une véritable politique de modernisation et d'urbanisation de la nouvelle "province saharienne", avec notamment le développement des centres urbains – essentiellement de El Ayoun, Villa Cisneros et Smara –, les tentatives de sédentarisation de la population, et la mise en œuvre de l'exploitation des ressources du territoire, notamment celle les phosphates[45]. En effet, non loin d'El

---

40 Fonds du Gouvernement Général du Sahara.

41 Fonds des Ambassades de France à Nouakchott et à Rabat.

42 Fonds du Gouvernement Général de l'Algérie et du Ministère des Colonies, puis de la France d'Outre-Mer.

43 Notamment entre les Takna – Ayt Lahsan et les Rgaybāt.

44 La question des troupes irrégulières aux frontières n'a été développée que marginalement (voir M. Fernández-Aceytuno, *op. cit.*, p. 624-627). On en trouve des traces assez importantes dans les fonds de l'AGA à Alcalá de Henares, dans la correspondance provenant de l'Ambassade et des Consulats de France au Maroc et en Mauritanie, conservée au Centre des Archives Diplomatiques de Nantes (CADN) ; dans les fonds des "Territoires du Sud" du Gouvernement Général de l'Algérie, conservés au Archives Nationales d'Outre-Mer (ANOM) d'Aix-en-Provence et chez les Sahraouis des camps de réfugiés eux-mêmes, qui ont un souvenir souvent assez précis du fonctionnement des *harka* et des *partisans* – interviews menées en 2007-2008 et en 2014.

45 Sur les développements des centres urbains au Sahara Espagnol, voir J. A. Rodríguez Esteban et D. A. Barrado Timón, "Los procesos de urbanización en el Sahara español (1884-1975) : un componente esencial del proyecto colonial", in *Les Cahiers d'EMAM*

Ayoun, à Bū Crāa, d'importants gisements de ce minerai avaient été découverts en 1947. Leur extraction systématique ne commença qu'au cours des années 1960[46].

Ces investissements du gouvernement espagnol au Sahara sont tardifs (74 ans après le débarquement de Bonelli y Hernando). Ils rencontrent la faveur d'une partie de la population, très appauvrie par les années de sècheresse, et en situation de marginalité dans l'ensemble des pays de la zone. La construction d'infrastructures se fait en effet même grâce au recrutement massif de main d'œuvre sahraouie qui, malgré les maigres salaires par rapport à ceux des Espagnols employés dans les mêmes secteurs, trouvent là une source économique pour vivre et maintenir leurs familles dans les villes. Les notables – chefs de tribus et/ou chefs de fractions – profitent aussi de cette politique. De fait, les Espagnols font de plus en plus appel à eux pour assurer le rôle d'intermédiaires entre l'administration[47] et les habitants de la Province. La réussite partielle de cette stratégie de cooptation est évidente. Elle s'accompagne de l'octroi du droit de vote aux hommes chefs de familles résidant dans les centres urbains pour les élections des conseils municipaux. Cependant, seulement la moitié de ces conseillers est élus, l'autre moitié est nommée parmi les représentants du commerce, de l'industrie, de la culture et des professions libérales où les Espagnols sont majoritaires. La Province du Sahara a également trois représentants aux Cortès, le Parlement espagnol, choisis par le Gouvernement parmi les membres les plus influents. En 1963, les trois représentants sont le maire d'El Ayoun, celui de Villa Cisneros et le président du Conseil provincial (*Cabildo provincial*). En 1967, le nombre des représentants aux Cortès est porté à six, deux d'entre eux étant élus parmi les chefs des familles et les autres nommés par le Gouvernement[48]. Les premières élections ont lieu en 1963. L'étape successive de cette politique destinée à montrer la volonté de l'Espagne d'associer les Sahraouis au gouvernement est créée au niveau provincial : la Djemaa, ou Assemblée Générale, qui continuait à exister pour chaque tribu, avec des fonctions purement symboliques. Ses membres sont élus

[en ligne], 24-25 2015, numéro thématique *Sahara occidental : mémoires, culture, histoires* (dir. F. Correale et J. C. Gimeno Martín), consulté le 9 avril 2015 [DOI : 10.4000/emam.796] ; et P. Rabasco Pozuelo, *Laayoune, Sidi Ifni and Dakhla: Ramón Estalella's modernist projects in Spanish West Africa, 1961–1969*, in "Planning Perspectives", 2015 [DOI : 10.1080/02665433.2014.989452].

46 Sur la découverte et l'exploitation par les Espagnols des gisements de Bū Crāa, voir J. R. Diego Aguirre, *Historia del Sahara Español*..., *op. cit.*, p. 437-445.

47 Sur l'ambiguïté des notables, voir F. Correale, *Le Sahara espagnol*..., *op. cit.*, p. 139-140.

48 Pour plus de détails sur la création d'institutions "représentatives" dans la Province du Sahara, voir T. Hodges, *Sahara occidental. Origines et enjeux d'une guerre du désert*, Paris, L'Harmattan, 1987, p. 179-188.

pour la première fois en 1967, puis de nouveau en 1971 : 37 députés par suffrage direct, 46 choisis parmi les chefs des tribus. En 1973, le nombre des membres de la Djemaa passe de 82 à 102, une tentative presque désespérée des Espagnols pour élargir leur assise politique et sociale[49].

En effet, alors que l'Espagne développe sa politique de colonisation, les appels des Nations Unies sont de plus en plus forts pour que le territoire soit décolonisé. Sur le plan strictement politique, les revendications territoriales du Maroc et de la Mauritanie ainsi que celles du premier mouvement nationaliste sahraoui organisé, l'Organisation Avancée pour la Libération du Sahara de Mohammed Sidi Basiri qui apparait entre 1968 et 1969 et est durement réprimée par les Espagnols en juin 1970[50], sont sans doute plus importantes que les pressions de l'ONU.

En 1973, les rescapés de la répression espagnole de 1970 fondent le Front Polisario, dont l'action est aux antipodes de celle entreprise par l'administration de la Province. Entre 1973 et 1975, le Front mène des actions contre les troupes espagnoles, en essayant aussi de recruter ses effectifs parmi les Sahraouis qui servent dans l'armée[51]. À la veille du retrait de l'Espagne, le mouvement est bien structuré, avec une proposition politique forte qui vise l'indépendance. Néanmoins, pour comprendre comment la décolonisation du Sahara Occidental n'a pas été possible, il faut faire un pas en arrière et revenir au moment de la transformation administrative de 1958.

La décolonisation inaccomplie

La transformation en Province de la colonie espagnole du Sahara Occidental[52] répond à une volonté précise du Gouvernement franquiste de se maintenir en Afrique, malgré la vague des décolonisations qui s'annoncent. Cinq ans plus tard, en 1963, l'ONU inscrit les populations du Sahara Occidental dans les listes des populations auxquelles doit être appliqué le principe d'autodétermination des peuples colonisés prévu par la résolution n° 1514 du 14 décembre 1960. La résolution n° 2072 du 16 décembre 1965 de l'Assemblée Générale des NU demande ensuite

---

49 "Administración Local y provincial", in J. Tejero Molina, *El Sahara Español de la 'A' a la 'Z'*, 2 vol., Madrid, Torres de Papel, 2013-2014, 1 vol., p. 158-161.

50 Sur la répression du mouvement nationaliste de 1970, voir T. Bárbulo, *op. cit.*, p. 78-88.

51 Sur cette phase de la lutte armée contre les Espagnols, comparer les deux versions idéologiquement aux antipodes de M. Fernández-Aceytuno, *op. cit.*, p. 686-691, et J. R. Diego Aguirre, *Historia del Sahara Español...*, *op. cit.*, p. 658-683. Les deux hommes étaient pourtant deux militaires engagés, dans des services différents, au Sahara Espagnol.

52 C. Barona Castañeda, *op. cit.*, p. 19-27.

officiellement à l'Espagne de se retirer du territoire[53]. Notons que les résolutions sur l'autodétermination des Sahraouis sont adoptées par l'ONU au moment où les revendications territoriales du Maroc et de la Mauritanie sur le Sahara Occidental se durcissent.

La France octroie l'indépendance à la République Islamique de Mauritanie (RIM) en 1960, après deux ans d'autonomie. La première revendication de la Mauritanie sur le Sahara espagnol remonte à 1957 lorsque Mokhtar Ould Daddah, vice-président du premier Conseil du Gouvernement de Mauritanie, lance un appel aux populations du Sahara espagnol afin qu'elles s'unissent à la future "Grande Mauritanie Indépendante" en vertu de leurs affinités avec les populations mauritaniennes. L'objectif est d'éloigner les Sahraouis de l'Armée de Libération Nationale et donc de l'influence marocaine. En 1963, Ould Daddah, devenu premier Président de la nouvelle République de la Mauritanie, tout en souhaitant officieusement le maintien du statu quo colonial pour le Sahara Occidental, déclare à l'Assemblée Générale des Nations Unies que les Sahraouis ont droit à l'autodétermination, ce qui aurait dû également rendre possible leur intégration à la Mauritanie. En 1969, la reconnaissance de la RIM par le Roi du Maroc amène à l'établissement de relations diplomatiques entre les deux pays, et un quasi-attendu retours aux positions de 1957[54], mais il faut remarquer que la Mauritanie maintient au cours des années 1960 trois positions différentes au sujet du Sahara : la revendication du territoire, l'acceptation implicite du statu quo et l'autodétermination des Sahraouis. Si on l'analyse les motivations poussant Ould Daddah à soutenir des postures aussi contradictoires entre elles, on peut supposer qu'elles répondent d'un côté à des exigences de politique intérieure, faisant face aux partis pro-marocains qui, malgré le fait d'avoir été mis à l'écart de la vie politique mauritanienne, gardent leurs sympathisants[55]. Déplacer l'attention à l'extérieur est une manière classique d'écarter un danger intérieur. D'un autre côté, l'exigence de maintenir aussi loin que possible le Maroc du Sahara Occidental signifie en même temps ne pas partager avec un voisin plus puissant une large frontière commune, mise en doute par la revendication du "Grand Maroc".

---

53 C. Ruiz Miguel, *op. cit.*, analyse de manière systématique les résolutions de l'ONU et leur impact dans le développement des événements qui amènent aux accords de Madrid de 1975.

54 Sur les revendications mauritaniennes, voir T. Hodges, *op. cit.*, p. 131-134.

55 Sur le rôle joué par les partis mauritaniens pro-marocains à l'intérieur de la RIM et, une fois en exil, au Maroc, voir F. De la Serre, "Les revendications marocaines sur la Mauritanie", in *Revue Française de Science Politique*, vol. 16, n° 2, avril 1966, p. 320-331 ; et J. Serjac, *op. cit.*

La revendication marocaine du Sahara espagnol est bien plus constante dans le temps. Ses origines se trouvent dans la carte du "Grand Maroc". Malgré l'action politique des nationalistes marocains pour la décolonisation espagnole du territoire auprès de l'ONU, la revendication reste discrète au cours des années 1960. En effet, le Gouvernement de Rabat met tout d'abord en avant ses plaintes contre l'indépendance de la Mauritanie et doit faire face à une importante crise avec l'Algérie à propos de leurs frontières communes. Cette crise débouche sur la "guerre des sables" d'octobre-novembre 1963 et sanctionne une victoire politique de l'Algérie indépendante qui garde le tracé des limites fixées par les Français pendant la domination coloniale[56].

La revendication du Sahara espagnol est remise au centre de l'agenda politique marocain par Hassan II au début des années 1970, et notamment après les deux tentatives de coup d'état militaire de 1971 et 1972[57]. À part l'annexion du territoire, l'objectif du Roi à l'égard du Sahara est double : d'un côté, distraire l'attention de l'opinion publique nationale de la crise politique et sociale que traverse le Maroc depuis 1965[58], en évoquant un objectif fédérateur pour favoriser un climat d'unité nationale ; de l'autre, il s'agit de trouver le moyen pour éloigner du territoire marocain une bonne partie de l'armée et la détourner des tentatives de renversement de la monarchie[59]. Il se peut qu'à ces deux raisons s'en ajoute une troisième, à savoir : "pacifier" la région de Tarfaya, qui rattachée au Maroc depuis 1958, continue d'être un espace de troubles causés à la fois par la présence d'une forte communauté sahraouie marginalisée par l'administration marocaine et soumise à un régime militaire en tant que région frontalière du Sahara revendiqué. Enfin, la conjoncture politique internationale – la Guerre Froide – semble favorable au Maroc, considéré par les États-Unis comme le paladin de l'Occident contrairement à l'Algérie dont le gouvernement est notoirement prosoviétique. Il reste que les revendications marocaines sur le Sahara provoquent des réactions assez contradictoires en Espagne.

Sur suggestion de l'administration espagnole, en février 1973 la *Djemaa* demande au Gouvernement espagnol de définir son avenir par référendum. Elle prône une amélioration des institutions représentatives sahraouies

---

56 Cependant c'est seulement en 1972, par le traité de Rabat, que le Gouvernement marocain reconnait officiellement la frontière algérienne. Le traité est ratifié par l'Algérie en 1973 mais seulement en 1992 par le Maroc.

57 Sur les deux tentatives de coup d'état, voir G. Perrault, *Notre ami le roi*, Paris, Gallimard, 1990, p. 117-187 ; et I. Dalle, *Les trois rois. La monarchie marocaine de l'indépendance à nos jours*, Paris, Fayard, 2004, p. 363-383.

58 Quand Hassan II suspend la Constitution et proclame l'état de siège dans tout le pays, jusqu'en 1970.

59 G. Perrault, *op. cit.*, p. 246-249.

déjà mises en place par Madrid, afin d'assurer une participation de plus en plus large de la population à l'administration du territoire. Quelque mois plus tard, le Gouvernement franquiste envisage un Sahara autonome lié à l'Espagne qui assurerait les relations extérieures du territoire. Toutefois, ces intentions ne se réalisent pas à cause de l'assassinat, en décembre 1973, de l'Amiral Carrero Blanco, bras droit de Francisco Franco pour le Sahara et destiné à lui succéder au sommet de l'État. La position du Gouvernement central évolue vers un désengagement progressif du territoire. Mais à El Ayoun les administrateurs de la Province[60] essayent d'amener le Sahara à une indépendance "téléguidée" par l'octroi d'un Statut d'autonomie interne (juillet 1974) qui transférerait la responsabilité des affaires intérieures du Sahara à un gouvernement saharien dont l'entrée en vigueur est envisagée après quelques mois. Quelque semaine plus tard, le Gouvernement adopte des mesures pour que la population puisse s'exprimer, et prévoit notamment la tenue d'un référendum sous les auspices de l'ONU au cours du premier semestre 1975. Dans ce contexte, l'administration espagnole procède au recensement (assez grossier) de la population, comptant 73.497 Sahraouis ayant droit de vote dans le référendum d'autodétermination[61]. Le pouvoir marocain réagit en décembre 1974 – après avoir obtenu l'accord de la Mauritanie[62] – en incitant l'Assemblée Générale de l'ONU à demander un avis consultatif sur le statut du territoire à la Cour de Justice de la Haye. La demande de l'Assemblée Générale bloque le processus politique engagé par les Espagnols. La Cour doit statuer sur deux questions :

1) "*Le Sahara occidental (Río de Oro et Sagyat al-Hamra) était-il, au moment de la colonisation par l'Espagne, un territoire sans maître (terra nullius) ?*",

et en cas de réponse négative :

2) "*Quels étaient les liens juridiques de ce territoire avec le Royaume du Maroc et l'ensemble mauritanien ?*"[63]

L'avis consultatif, rendu le 16 octobre 1975[64], stipule que le territoire de l'ancienne "province saharienne de l'Espagne" n'était pas *terra nullius* avant la colonisation, que certaines populations au cours de l'histoire

---

60 Sur la schizophrénie politique des autorités espagnoles à propos du Sahara Occidental, voir T. Barbúlo, *op. cit.*, p. 212-234.

61 Notamment C. Barona Casteñeda, *op. cit.*, p. 169-190.

62 Après de longs pourparlers entre Hassan II et M. Ould Daddah, voir à ce propos M. Ould Daddah, *La Mauritanie contre vents et marées*, Paris, Khartala, 2003, p. 451-480 ; et Tony Hodges, *op. cit.*, p. 232-236.

63 T. Hodges, *op. cit.*, p. 234.

64 Pour une documentation détaillée sur l'avis de la Cour internationale de justice de La Haye, voir le site de la Cour (consulté le 9/04/2015) : http://www.icj-cij.org/docket/index.php?p1=3&p2=4&k=69&case=61&code=sa&p3=0.

avaient maintenu un lien avec le Sultan 'alawite tandis que d'autres étaient liés avec l'"ensemble mauritanien"[65]. Selon les juges de la Haye, ceci ne remet pas en question le principe du référendum d'autodétermination[66], mais Hassan II décide de ne pas prendre en compte la seconde partie de l'avis de la Cour et ordonne la mobilisation de l'armée et de l'ensemble des populations de son Royaume. Entre le 24 et le 30 octobre, les Forces Armées Royales (FAR) pénètrent dans le Sahara Occidental pour empêcher le Front Polisario d'occuper les postes déjà évacués par l'armée espagnole[67]. Le 6 novembre 1975, 350 000 Marocains arrivés depuis quelque jour dans la région de Tarfaya, rentrent sur le territoire sahraoui en brandissant le drapeau marocain, le portrait d'Hassan II et le Coran. C'est la "Marche verte" (verte, de la couleur de la couverture du livre sacré), un événement médiatique essentiellement symbolique dont la fonction est de renforcer une légitimité politique – celle de la monarchie – tout en créant un mythe unificateur – celui d'une marche libératrice et pacifique. Même si elle est condamnée par le Conseil de Sécurité de l'ONU le jour même (résolution n° 380 du 6 novembre 1975), elle est en fait la dernière étape d'une série de pressions exercées sur l'Espagne franquiste pour la forcer à accepter de céder le territoire du Sahara Occidental au Maroc[68], en la mettant devant le fait accompli[69].

Pour sa part, le Front Polisario réunit autour de lui la grande partie de la société/population sahraouie. Le prestige du Front grandit au lendemain de la reconnaissance comme seul représentant du peuple sahraoui par l'ONU, dont une mission guidée par le Secrétaire Générale Kurt Waldheim s'était rendu à El Ayoun en mai 1975[70]. Cela avait permis au Polisario aussi de couper court à toute ambition du PUNS – Parti d'Union Nationale Sahraouie –, une formation politique voulue par les Espagnols et qui avait fini par se dissoudre[71]. Le 12 octobre 1975, les

---

65 Voir à ce sujet M. Flory, "L'ensemble mauritanien en tant que notion juridique", in CRESM-CEAN (eds.), *Introduction à la Mauritanie*, Paris, Éditions du CNRS, 1979, p. 403-412.

66 T. Hodges, *op. cit.*, p. 263-264.

67 *Ibidem*, p. 730-731.

68 Sur la démythification de la "Marche Verte", voir le beau dossier de D. Bennani, M. Sekkouri Alaoui et N. Benkacem, "La vérité sur la Marche Verte", in *Tel Quel*, n° 198, 2002, http://w.telquel-online.com/archives/198/sujet1.shtml (consulté le 9 avril 2015).

69 Et à ce propos, de nombreux attentats avaient été commis au cours de l'année 1975 contre des cibles espagnols par des infiltrés marocains, en faisant retomber, dans un premier temps, la responsabilité sur le Front Polisario : J. R. Diego Aguirre, *Historia del Sahara Español...*, *op. cit.*, p. 704-711.

70 Sur la mission de l'ONU, voir T. Hodges, *op. cit.*, p. 248-253.

71 Sur le PUNS et les autres formations politiques au Sahara, dont certaines téléguidées par le Gouvernement marocain, voir J. R. Diego Aguirre, *Historia del Sahara Español...*, *op. cit.*, 684-692 et 709-711 et M. Barbier, *op. cit.*, p. 98-103.

porte-parole de différentes tribus se réunissent pour proclamer l'Unité nationale, annoncer la fin du système tribal et la naissance du "Peuple"[72], ce qui représente une véritable révolution sociale sur laquelle va se fonder l'essence de l'autorité du Front. Or, si le Polisario ne peut pas s'opposer à la signature des Accords de Madrid, du 14 novembre 1975, qui sanctionnent le partage du Sahara entre le Maroc et la Mauritanie[73], il n'en reste pas moins que sa réaction est politiquement importante. Le dernier soldat espagnol quitte le territoire le 26 février 1976. Le lendemain, pour remplir le vide institutionnel et juridique provoqué par le départ de l'armée espagnole, les cadres du mouvement nationaliste sahraoui proclament la "République Arabe Sahraouie Démocratique" (RASD)[74]. La première Constitution, adoptée par la RASD à la fin août 1976[75], reflète complétement la révolution sociale impulsée par le Front Polisario : elle ne comporte plus de traces des appartenances tribales et de la traditionnelle organisation lignagère de la société[76], tout le "peuple sahraoui" devant se reconnaitre désormais dans la "nation sahraouie".

La guerre du Sahara

Ainsi structuré, soutenu militairement par la Libye, puis par l'Algérie[77], le Polisario peut contenir l'invasion marocaine et battre militairement la Mauritanie. La guerre du Sahara connait deux phases [78] :

---

72 S. Caratini, "De la tribu au peuple : le rôle paradoxal de l'oubli dans les constructions identitaires sahraouies", in M. Lahlou (dir.), *Histoires familiales, identité, citoyenneté*, Lyon-Limonest, L'interdisciplinaire, coll. Psychologie(s)", 2002, p. 124-136 ; et S. Caratini, *La république des sables. Anthropologie d'une révolution*, Paris, L'Harmattan, 2003, p. 65-75. Encore aujourd'hui, le 12 octobre est célébré comme la journée de l'"Unité nationale".

73 Pour une analyse intéressante des Accords de Madrid, voir C. Barona Castañeda, *op. cit.*, p. 290-295.

74 On peut trouver la vidéo de la proclamation de la RASD sur le site https://www.youtube.com/watch?v=GnRmuhF4-0Y (consulté le 10 avril 2015).

75 Pour le texte (en espagnol) de la 1re Constitution de la RASD, voir le site http://es.scribd.com/doc/44798553/CONSTITUCION-DE-LA-RASD#scribd (consulté le 10 avril 2015).

76 Sur les contradictions historiques de la construction identitaire sahraouie réalisée par le Front Polisario, F. Correale, "La narration de l'histoire en situation de crise. Revendications et contradictions dans la construction mémorielle sahraouie", in *Les Cahiers d'EMAM* [en ligne], 24-25, 2015, numéro thématique *Sahara occidental : mémoires, culture, histoires* (dir. F. Correale et J. C. Gimeno Martín), consulté le 10 avril 2015 [DOI : 10.4000/emam.838].

77 Sur les soutiens internationaux dont jouit le Front Polisario, T. Barbúlo, *op. cit.*, p. 123-134.

78 Le conflit étant décrit dans beaucoup des ouvrages déjà cités, je me limiterai à ajouter deux travaux qui me semblent essentiels : J. R. Diego Aguirre, *Guerra en el Sáhara*, Madrid, Ediciones Istmo, 1991 ; et S. Zunes and J. Mundy, *Western Sahara. War,*

- de 1976 à 1979 : le Front attaque la Mauritanie sur son propre sol, notamment le train des mines de fer de Zouerate qui débarque le minerai au port de Nouadhibou, provoquant le collapse de l'économie de la RIM. Nouakchott est bombardé. Malgré l'aide du Maroc et de la France – qui en 1977 s'engage directement dans le conflit avec l'opération "Lamantin" – la Mauritanie se retire du conflit en 1979. L'année précédente, un coup d'État militaire avait déposé Mokhtar Ould Daddah. Le nouveau président, Moustapha Ould Salek signe un accord de paix avec le Front Polisario le 5 août 1979. La RIM reconnait la RASD le 27 février 1984 [79] ;
- de 1979 à 1991 : la guerre du Sahara devient une guerre sahraouie-marocaine. Entre 1975 et 1979 le Maroc occupe une partie du territoire sans jamais parvenir à le contrôler pleinement. En 1979, pour montrer que le Maroc ne contrôle même pas son sol national, le Front occupe temporairement Tan Tan, puis Assa, Zaq, Leiborat. Il s'agit d'incursions rapides qui ne visent pas à maintenir le contrôle des postes attaqués et qui rappellent plutôt les *gazzi* ou les raids des *harka* et des *partisans*. Tout en continuant la guerre, au cours des années 1980, l'armée marocaine se replie sur des points stratégiques comme les villes et les centres miniers pour les phosphates. Inspirés par le mur qu'Israël a élevé dans le Sinaï au lendemain de sa conquête en 1967 à la suite de la "guerre des six jours" – la Ligne Bar-Lev –, les FAR décident d'isoler les régions qu'elles occupent par la construction d'une succession de six murs qui aujourd'hui encore coupent longitudinalement le territoire en deux, sur environ 2720 km[80]. L'armistice du 6 septembre 1991 sanctionne cette situation de fait : d'un côté le Maroc qui occupe le 80% de l'ex-Sahara espagnol, de l'autre la RASD qui essaye d'administrer les 20% restant ainsi que les camps de réfugiés.

Parallèlement à la guerre, le Front Polisario et le Maroc s'affrontent sur le terrain diplomatique. Le premier obtient à la fois la reconnaissance de la RASD par de nombreux pays africains, asiatiques, et latino-américains (parmi ceux-ci la Libye, l'Algérie, l'Iran, le Mexique, le

---

Nationalism, and Conflict Irresolution, Syracuse-New York, Syracuse University Press, 2010.

79 La meilleure analyse de la guerre avec la Mauritanie et de ses conséquences politiques et économiques est faite par T. Hodges, *op. cit.*, p. 299-344.

80 Sur les murs marocains, voir H. Braica, "El muro del Sáhara Occidental : acecho de la muerte", in *Grupo de Estudios Estratégicos*, juillet 2006 [en ligne] http://www.gees.org/articulos/el_muro_del_sahara_occidental_acecho_de_la_muerte_2706 (consulté le 10 avril 2015) ; et J. R. Diego Aguirre, *Guerra...*, *op. cit.*, 229-236. Sur la guerre maroco-sahraouie, voir le même ouvrage de D. Aguirre ainsi que (jusqu'en 1985) T. Hodges, *op. cit.*, p. 345-416, et S. Zunes and J. Mundy, *op. cit.*, p. 3-29.

Venezuela, le Nigeria et, dernièrement, l'Afrique du Sud) et l'admission officielle de la RASD au sein de l'Organisation de l'Unité Africaine (1982-1984). Cela provoque le retrait du Maroc de l'OUA bien qu'il en avait été l'un des membres fondateurs[81]. Pour sa part, le Royaume du Maroc continue à jouir du soutien des Etats-Unis et surtout de la France[82], ainsi que de la plupart des pays de la Ligue Arabe. Néanmoins, au début des années 1980, Hassan II fait face à une crise économique et sociale dont les causes sont imputables, en grande partie, aux coûts de la guerre du Sahara. Des émeutes “pour le pain” éclatent dans plusieurs villes du pays (Casablanca, Nador) entre 1981 et 1984. En même temps, la barrière constituée par les murs devient l'objet d'incursions de plus en plus fréquentes du Polisario, ce qui fait craindre que la supériorité marocaine sur le plan militaire ne soit que temporaire. C'est vraisemblablement pour ces raisons qu'en 1988 Hassan II accepte le principe du référendum d'autodétermination qui conduit à l'armistice trois ans plus tard.

Une mission des Nations Unies, la MINURSO, est chargée d'identifier les votants pour le référendum et de son déroulement. Un nouveau terrain d'affrontement s'ouvre alors : celui de la reconnaissance du corps électoral, le Front Polisario considérant comme valide le recensement espagnol de 1974 et le Maroc soutenant que le recensement ne comprend pas beaucoup d'ayants droits sahraouis résidant au Maroc et non inclus dans les listes électorales établies par l'administration espagnole[83]. Écrire l'histoire des vingt-cinq dernières années serait l'objet d'un autre article et je me limiterai donc à quelques données principales.

La question du corps électoral devient centrale. En la soulevant toutes les fois que la date du referendum approche, le Maroc boycotte de fait la tenue du référendum même ainsi que cela est le cas en 1992 et en 1997. Cette stratégie qui vise à gagner du temps pour créer une situation de non-retour permet au Royaume de réaliser une véritable politique coloniale dans les territoires qu'il contrôle : construction d'infrastructures, exploitation des ressources naturelles, cooptation des Sahraouis qui acceptent d'entrer dans les rouages de l'administration marocaine, peuplement par vagues successives de colons originaires surtout des régions les moins favorisées

---

81 Sur la bataille diplomatique à l'OUA, T. Hodges, *op. cit.*, 369-393 et J. R. Diego Aguirre, *Guerra...*, *op. cit.*, p. 237-260.

82 Voir à ce sujet T. Barbulo, *op. cit.*, p. 231-234 ; T. Hodges, *op. cit.*, p. 473-487 ; J. R. Diego Aguirre, *Guerra...*, *op. cit.*, p. 209-219 ; et surtout S. Zunes et J. Mundy, *op. cit.*, p. 59-88.

83 Voir à ce sujet E. Jensen, *Western Sahara: Anatomy of a Stalemate?*, Boulder, Colorado, Lynne Rienner Publishers, 2011 ; et J. Besenyő, *op. cit.*, p. 131-164. Les deux ouvrages ont une valeur remarquable car les deux auteurs ont été respectivement chef de la MINURSO et officier ayant servi dans la même mission.

du territoire marocain telles celles du Nord[84]. En même temps, cela se passe sans la participation de la majeure partie de la population sahraouie, marginalisée dans son propre territoire, ce qui provoque de nombreuses manifestations qu'on n'hésite pas à définir, du côté pro-sahraoui, d'intifadāt : 2005, 2008, 2010[85].

Dans les campements de réfugiés trois générations grandissent enfermées dans une condition de non-paix et de dépendance des aides humanitaires[86]. Si la société sahraouie reste malgré tout dynamique, avec une explosion d'associations auto-organisées qui à l'intérieur des camps se mobilisent pour améliorer la situation des autres réfugiés et à l'étranger répandent le "verbe" de l'indépendance, la situation politique stagne : le non-renouvellement des cadres du Front Polisario semble aujourd'hui être un piège politique qui favorise le désenchantement des jeunes générations vis-à-vis de son projet politique. Cela n'empêche qu'après quarante années les camps se sont transformées en véritables villes, avec une économie propre qui facilite la stratification sociale et accentue les divergences entre ceux qui ont accès à certains types de ressources à partir de l'"extérieur", aux aides humanitaires – telles les remises de l'étranger ou les revenus provenant de trafics parfois douteux – et ceux qui ne l'ont pas[87].

La question du Sahara représente donc aujourd'hui une sorte de "bombe" prête à exploser. Les décisions qui seront prises par les institutions internationales chargées de l'affaire détermineront pour

---

[84] Voir à ce sujet les travaux de Victoria Veguilla del Moral et notamment : "Transformaciones demográficas y competición política. Obstáculos al autogobierno saharaui en clave electoral", in *Revista de Estudios Internacionales Mediterráneos* n° 14 janvier-juin 2013 [en ligne] : https://sites.google.com/site/teimrevista/numeros/numero-14-enero-2013-junio-2013/transformaciones-demograficas-y-competicion-politica-obstaculos-al-autogobierno-saharaui-en-clave-electoral ; "La política marroquí de viviendas en Dajla (Sáhara Occidental). Ajustes a un contexto demográfico en mutación", in *RIPS ; Revista de investigaciones políticas y sociológicas*, vol. 12, nº 2, 2013 [en ligne] : [DOI : 10.15304/rips.12.2.1580] (consultés le 10 avril 2015).

[85] Sur les révoltes à l'intérieur des territoires occupés, voir S. Zunes & J. Mundy, *op. cit.*, p. 140-166 ; C. Barona Castañeda, "Memorias de una resistencia. La otra historia del Sahara Occidental", in *Les Cahiers d'EMAM* [en ligne], 24-25, 2015, numéro thématique *Sahara occidental : mémoires, culture, histoires* (dir. F. Correale et J. C. Gimeno Martín), consulté le 10 avril 2015 [DOI : 10.4000/emam.859].

[86] Sur la transformation des camps, voir S. Caratini, "*La prisión del tiempo : los cambios sociales en los campamentos de refugiados saharauis*", in *Cuadernos Bakeaz 77* (octobre 2006), p. 1-15 ; et le travail inédit d'A. Courbet, "Nés dans les camps. Changements identitaires de la nouvelle génération de réfugiés sahraouis et transformation des camps", thèse soutenue en 2008, Paris, École de Hautes Études en Sciences Sociales.

[87] Ce qui a pu être observé par l'auteur au cours de ses séjours dans les camps en décembre 2007-janvier 2008 et avril-mai 2014.

combien de temps encore les Sahraouis devront attendre une solution non-armée du conflit, ou plutôt donneront une idée de l'état de santé du projet nationaliste sahraoui dont l'actualisation pourrait encore une fois provoquer un affrontement par les armes.

Mise en perspective

Pour conclure cet excursus (incomplet) sur les origines de la "question du Sahara Occidental", je voudrais mettre en perspective trois éléments : la construction/définition de l'identité sahraouie ; le rôle/rappel de l'histoire dans la question du Sahara Occidental ; les traces/héritages de l'histoire comme support à une éventuelle résolution du conflit.

En ce qui concerne l'identité sahraouie, on peut aisément récapituler qu'elle se structure autour de trois périodes :

- entre les 13e et le 17e siècle par le mélange des populations arabes provenant du Yémen avec les populations berbères qui habitent la région ;
- entre 1884 et 1976, par la présence d'un colonialisme "autre" que le français qui forge, à l'intérieur de frontières bien définies, un ensemble hispanophone et crée les conditions pour un processus d'"assemblage" social et politique des populations du territoire, traditionnellement organisées selon un schéma segmentaire et hiérarchique ;
- entre 1976 et la période que l'on pourrait définir de postcoloniale (ou coloniale marocaine), correspondant à la phase de consolidation du sentiment nationaliste dont les germes remontent à la fin des années 1950. Le Front Polisario incarne ce sentiment et propose à la population sahraouie un dessein politique qui vise à dépasser les structures sociales traditionnelles pour affermir la "nation sahraouie" et lui permettre de survivre dans des conditions assez particulières et difficiles telles que la guerre et l'exil. Il faut souligner qu'après quarante ans, le projet nationaliste sahraoui, bien que pleinement assumé par les réfugiés des camps, peine à se renouveler et à offrir d'autres dispositifs de cohésion politique et sociale que ceux pensés par le (désormais) vieux leadership du Front[88].

Sur un autre plan, face aux projets expansionnistes du Maroc et de la Mauritanie, le Polisario propose un contre-nationalisme qui, au début des années 1970, finit pour permettre aux Sahraouis éparpillés

[88] Pour une réflexion critique sur les atouts politiques actuels du Front Polisario, voir A. Wilson, "Democratising elections without parties : reflections on the case of the Sahrawi Arab Democratic Republic", in *The Journal of North African Studies*, n° 15-4, 2010, p. 423-438.

en dehors du Sahara espagnol de retrouver une patrie (et une identité supra-tribale). Or, les rappels continuels des partisans du "Grand Maroc" ou de la "Grande Mauritanie" à une histoire qui aurait figé à jamais les tenants sociaux et politiques des populations sahraouies, les liant inévitablement aux destins de l'un et l'autre des pays, constituent un oxymore historique. Pour paradoxal que cela puisse paraître, on pourrait suggérer l'hypothèse que la question du Sahara Occidental ne trouve pas sa résolution à cause d'un...refus d'histoire. En effet, les thèses nationalistes des deux pays (et notamment la revendication marocaine) ne prennent pas en considération que :

- Les équilibres précoloniaux ont été rompus par l'irruption des Européens en Afrique du Nord qui, à leur tour, en ont engendré des nouveaux ;
- La Mauritanie et le Maroc d'aujourd'hui sont le fruit d'une pacification coloniale qui a changé en profondeur les paramètres traditionnels de la souveraineté dans la région : *de jus sanguinis/ jus religionis a jus loci*[89].
- Le Maroc d'aujourd'hui (et de 1956) n'est plus le Sultanat 'alawite des 17-20e siècles, dont les territoires étaient floues et dépendaient de la force d'attraction/coercition du pouvoir politico-religieux du Sultan, mais un Royaume dont la structure étatique, ainsi que ses frontières, ont été définies par le colonialisme français.

La présence de ces césures ne peut pas occulter que même au cours de l'histoire récente, des *moments confédératifs* ont vu le jour et ont pu faire penser à des "recompositions historiques". Sans donc remonter aux Empires Almoravide et Almohade, fruits de mouvements politico-religieux provenant du Sahara des 11e-13e siècles, on peut rappeler :

- les alliances entre les populations saharo-mauritaniennes et marocaines dans la lutte contre les invasions coloniales françaises, au cours des deux premières décennies du 20e siècle ;
- la collaboration participative des populations sahraouies avec l'Armée de Libération Nationales (ALN), née au Maroc, pour la décolonisation des territoires sahariens entre 1956 et 1958 (événements qui, au contraire, aujourd'hui se prêtent à une lecture partisane tant de la part des Sahraouis que de la part des Marocains) ;
- la complicité/convergence idéologique entre certains mouvements politiques de gauche du Maroc et les noyaux nationalistes sahraouis au cours des années 1960, qui cessèrent à cause de la Marche Verte.

---

89 Voir à ce sujet le bel article de M. Flory, "La notion de territoire arabe et son application au problème du Sahara", in *Annuaire français de droit international*, vol. 3, 1957, pp. 73-91 [DOI : 10.3406/afdi.1957.1308].

Ainsi, l'humus historique d'une éventuelle rencontre entre les parties en conflit est encore loin de donner tous ses fruits et, au contraire, constitue une source symbolique prioritaire dans la construction de nouveaux équilibres. Si la résolution du conflit du Sahara Occidental ne peut que passer par l'application du principe d'autodétermination et, donc, le libre choix des populations sahraouies, il n'en reste pas moins que dans un cadre supra-étatique (telle l'UMA par exemple), la rencontre et la collaboration des Sahraouis avec les autres parties autrefois en conflit ne serait pas une nouveauté en soi mais s'inscrirait dans une continuité historique avérée des relations entre les différentes populations de la région.

The Principle, the Right of Self-determination and the People of Western Sahara

Carlos Ruiz MIGUEL

University of Santiago de Compostela

Historical development of the idea of the "self-determination of people" in international law until 1945

James Brown Scott showed how the Spanish scholars who reflected on the colonisation of America set the foundations of modern International Law[1]. They reflected about the lawfulness and the conditions of colonisation. In such a debate we could find the first antecedent of self-determination when, in 1540, the professor of the University of Valladolid *Bartolomé de Carranza* said that a colonisation is lawful but only if it is provisory, so that in a short period of time the colonized people may recover their independence:

> "Should them (the barbarians) be instructed by honest men so that they don't return to their barbary; and when this task was accomplished after 16 or 18 years and the land be plain, because there is no risk that they return to their primitive way of life, they should be left in their original and own freedom because they don't need more trusteeship"[2].

Some scholars argue that the processes that lead to the independence of the American States, subjected to English or Spanish rule are based upon the idea of "self-determination of peoples". They see under this frame the (North-) American Revolution that proclaimed the right of peoples to govern themselves in the Declaration of Independence (July 4th 1776).

1 J. Brown Scott, *The Spanish Origin of International Law*, Oxford, The Clarendon Press, 1934.

2 B. de Carranza, *Ratione fidei potest Caesar debellare et tenere indos novi Orbis?*, 1540 (in J. de la Peña, *De bello contra insulanos: intervención de España en América: Escuela Española de la Paz, segunda generación, 1560-1585: testigos y fuentes*, Madrid, CSIC, Vol. 1, p. 1982, p. 552 ss.): "Et debet eos docer per homines probos, ne illi redeant ad vomitum (...) quia non timetur periculum redeundi ad suam sectam, sunt reliquendi in sua prima et propria libertate, quia iam non indigent tutore" (p. 554).

They also consider under the same idea the Declaration of Independence of the Argentinian Provinces (July 9th 1816)[3]. However, both cases are different and they don't invoke expressly "self-determination". In the case of the North-American Declaration it is clear that the Law of Nations is not invoked to justify the independence[4]; if we consider the case of Argentina, it is true that the peoples of the provinces make their proclamation "in face of all the nations and men of the globe"[5], but there is no explicit reference to an international right to "self-determination". The case of the American territories could then be considered as a "secession" of some territories from their State because it is difficult to argue that these peoples who proclaimed at that time the independence did existed before.

The practice of the "plebiscite" began after the French Revolution[6], and suggested the substitution of an objective basis for the establishment of a political community by a subjective one. However, in the 19th century we don't find a development of the idea of "self-determination" of "peoples". However, we find another idea that is related to it: the "principle of nationality", formulated by the Italian Mancini. According to Mancini the "nation" and not the "State" is the primary element *of International Law* (Mancini speaks of "Foreign Public Law"). Mancini argues that there is a "right to free and harmonic development of nationality" (diritto al libero e armonico sviluppo della Nazionalità). The content of this principle was summarized in this way: every *nation* has the *right* to establish its own *State* or to federate to another, and every State should constitute a single nation[7]. But this principle, which grants this right to "nations" and not to "peoples", was neglected by the literature in international law. What is clear is that it did not get a positive recognition in any legal instrument.

3 See for example, I. Brownlie, "An Essay in the History of the Principle of Self-Determination", in C.H. Alexandrowicz (ed.), *Grotian Society Papers 1968: Studies in the History of the Law of Nations*, Vol. 2, 90 ff.; A. Truyol y Serra, *La sociedad internacional*, Madrid, Alianza, 1985, p. 44 ss.

4 "That whenever any Form of Government becomes destructive of these ends, it is the Right of the People to alter or to abolish it, and to institute new Government".

5 "Por la autoridad de los pueblos que representamos, protestando al cielo, a las naciones y hombres todos del globo la justicia, que regla nuestros votos, declaramos solemnemente a la faz de la tierra que, es voluntad unánime e indudable de estas provincias romper los violentos vínculos que las ligaban a los reyes de España, recuperar los derechos de que fueron despojadas, e investirse del alto carácter de una nación libre e independiente".

6 Wambaugh has exhaustedly documented the practice of plebiscite in three periods: during the French Revolution (1791-1798), between 1848-1870 and between 1871-1914. Cf. S. Wambaugh, *A Monograph on Plebiscites. With a Collection of Official Documents*, New York, Oxford University Press, 1920.

7 P. Stanislao Mancini, *Della nazionalità come fondamento del diritto delle genti: prelezione al corso di diritto internazionale e marittimo pronunziata nella R. Università di Torino*, Torino, Tipografia Eredi Botta, 1851.

The "principle of nationality" is both a category of Domestic and Foreign Public Law in the Mancini's contribution.

It is worth to mention that Friedrich Engels, who wrote in 1864 that "the whole thing is an absurdity" and that it seemed "a Russian invention concocted to destroy Poland", did not warmly welcome the "principle of nationality"[8].

The explicit reference to the "self-determination" of "peoples" appear on two different levels in Europe at the beginning of the 20th century.

On the one hand, already in 1913, Josif Vissariónovich "Stalin", one of the leading Marxist Russian leaders, despite the opinion of Engels on this question, published a paper upholding the right to self-determination, according to which nations have the right not only of autonomy but also of secession[9]. In the same sense, in 1914, Vladimir Ilich Ulianov "Lenin" published a paper with the title "The right of nations to self-determination"[10]. In this paper, Lenin considers that "the self-determination of nations means the political separation of these nations from alien national bodies and the formation of an independent national State". Hence, the subject of this right is the "nation", not the "people". We may say, then, that this "right of nations to self-determination" is not far from the "principle of nationality", but it may be considered as a similar idea formulated with a different expression. Lenin proclaims this right but does not pay any importance to International Law. It could be considered (as it later was the case) more a right to be introduced in Domestic Public Law.

On the other hand, four years later, in 1918, US President Woodrow Wilson will support the same idea as Lenin when he presented his "Fourteen Points" in his Speech delivered on the 8th January 1918. Although Wilson does not explicitly use the expression "right to self-determination", it is implicit in his Speech. The Wilson's idea of the right to self-determination seems very close to the Mancini's "principle of nationality". First, it takes into account the "nationality" as a primary basis to establish legal institutions as it can be clearly seen precisely in his points number XI (Balkan States) and IX (Italy: "A readjustment of

8 F. Engels, "What have the working classes to do with Poland?", in *The Commonwealth*, No.150, 24 March 1866. Reproduced in Karl Marx/Friedrich Engels, *Gesamtausgabe*, Berlin, Akademie Verlag, -1 Abteilung, Vol.20, 193 ff.

9 J. V. Stalin, "Marxism and the national and the national question", in *Prosveshcheniye*, No.3-5, March-May 1913. English version in J. V. Stalin, *Works*, Moscow, Foreign Languages Publishing House, 1953, Vol.2, p. 300-381.

10 V. I. U. Lenin, "The right of nations to self-determination", in *Prosveshcheniye*, No.4-6, April-June 1914. English version in Lenin, *Collected Works*, Moscow, Progress Publishers, 1972, Vol.20, pp. 393-454. Translated: Bernard Isaacs and The Late Joe Fineberg.

the frontiers of Italy should be effected along clearly recognizable lines of nationality"). Second, as in Mancini, self-determination has both a domestic and a foreign meaning: in the Preamble of his Speech, Wilson reminds that what he demands in the international level is what the USA recognizes in the domestic one ("What we demand in this war, therefore, is nothing peculiar to ourselves. It is that the world be made fit and safe to live in; and particularly that it be made safe for every peace-loving nation which, like our own, wishes to live its own life, determine its own institutions"). This kind of self-determination is what Wilson advocates for Russia (point VI) and Belgium (point VII). However, in the Wilson's points the right to self-determination loses weight when it comes to deal with colonial territories (point V). Not to mention that Wilson does not make any reference to a right to self-determination for the Southern States of the USA.

There was a wide use of the "plebiscite" after the I World War to settle territorial questions in Europe on the basis of the principle of self-determination. But despite the Wilson's points, the right to self-determination did not receive international legal recognition after the First World War[11]. This became crystal clear with the "Aaland case". Although populated by Swedish speaking population, the Aaland Islands were part of the Great Duchy of Finland that was part of the Russian Empire. When Finland got its independence in 1917, they became part of Finland. Then, Sweden and the Aaland population claimed that the latter had a "right to self-determination" which allowed it to decide on integration into Sweden. The parties submitted the case to the Counsel of the League of Nations, which dismissed the claims of self-determination favouring the solution proposed by Finland, that is a territorial autonomy with international guarantees[12].

During the Second World War the two main western Allies, USA & UK, issued a Statement of major relevance regarding self-determination, the "Atlantic Charter" (14th August 1941). Two of the eight points of this Charter related to self-determination, which was clearly implied even if not explicitly mentioned as such:

> "Second, they desire to see no territorial changes that do not accord with the freely expressed wishes of the peoples concerned;

---

[11] J. Mattern, *The Employment of the Plebiscite in the Determination of Sovereignty*, The Johns Hopkins Press, 1920, p. 194.

[12] *(1920) L.N.O.J. Spec. Supp. No. 3*. On Aaland see, L. Hannikainen, "Autonomy in Finland: The Territorial Autonomy of the Aland Islands and the Cultural Autonomy of the Indigenous Saami People", in *Baltic Yearbook of International Law*, Vol.2 (2002), p. 175-197.

Third, they respect the right of all peoples to choose the form of government under which they will live; and they wish to see sovereign rights and self-government restored to those who have been forcibly deprived of them".

In this mention we could find "*in nuce*" the further developments of self-determination.

Once the Second World War finished in Europe on 26 June 1945, 50 of the United Nations 51 original members signed in San Francisco the Charter of the United Nations. For the first time in History, the Charter granted an international legal status to "self-determination". It was explicitly considered in Articles 1.2 and 55. Article 73 does not use the expression "self-determination" but refers to "self-government".

Article 1.2 of the Charter grants a paramount importance to the "principle of equal rights and self-determination of peoples" as it is considered one of the "Purposes of the United Nations". Article 55 reiterates the reference to "the principle of equal rights and self-determination of peoples".

Self-determination in the Charter presents two interesting features considering the above-mentioned historical background: first, it is predicated not to "nationalities" or nations but to "peoples"; second, it is not considered as a "right" but as a "principle". However, some scholars considered that the way "self-determination" was embodied in the UN Charter admitted different interpretations, especially related to the deadline to for its implementation[13]. Those ambiguities disappeared with the Resolution 1514 of 1960.

The legal nature of self-determination: from principles to right

"Self-determination" was firstly considered in the UN Charter as a "principle" embodied in a "purpose" of the United Nations.

In the first stage, just after the approval of the UN Charter, no specific obligations for its member States were established regarding non-autonomous territories. Certainly, the Charter was a step beyond the former treaties on Colonial Law. But initially this change affected only the United Nations as such and not their member States. No reference is made in Article 2 of the UN Charter to an obligation for member States regarding the colonies, if not already involved in the colonization process. But Article 1.2 imposes on the United Nations as a whole the obligation "to develop friendly relations among nations based on *respect for* the *principle* of equal rights and *self-determination of peoples*".

[13] Truyol y Serra, *La sociedad internacional*, *op. cit*, p. 85.

The legal nature of self-determination was that of a "principle" and not of a "right". This is why the "Draft Declaration on Rights and Duties of States"[14] of 1949 has no reference neither to the "right" to self-determination or to the "obligation" of the States to respect it. Actually, the Permanent Representative of the Union of Socialist Soviet Republics, Vladimir M. Koretsky, voted against the draft of this declaration arguing that "it deviated from such fundamental principles of the United Nations as the sovereign equality of all the Members thereof and the right of self-determination of peoples".

Actually there was some ambiguity on the notion of "peoples". This may explain what could be considered as a certain "passivity" of the United Nations in the period 1945-1960 regarding the process of decolonization where the UN policy was "reactive" rather than "proactive". The position of the UN may be understandable considering that it seemed that there was not unanimity about the idea of "peoples" and, hence, we may find an explanation to this "reactive" policy of the UN in the decolonization conflicts that blew up after 1945.

In 1960 the idea of "self-determination" experienced a deep transformation when the General Assembly's Resolution 1514 was passed. This transformation was three-folded. First, it was considered not only as a UN-"principle" but also as a "right". Second, the content of "self-determination" was further developed. And, third, the colonial peoples were identified as "peoples" entitled to this "right" to self-determination. The General Assembly's Resolution 1514, which refers to "colonial countries and peoples", declared that: "All peoples have the right to self-determination. By virtue of that right they freely determine their political status and freely pursue their economic, social and cultural development"[15] (emphasis added).

This consideration of self-determination as a "right" was also enshrined in the common Article 1.1 of the two Covenants of 1966[16], which reiterated the text of the second paragraph of the General Assembly's Resolution 1514.

The International Court of Justice (ICJ) has confirmed this evolution, firstly, concerning the trusteeships. In the Namibia case it said that:

---

14 A/RES/375, 6 December 1949.

15 A/RES/1514 (XV), 14th December 1960, para. 2.

16 International Covenant on Civil and Political Rights, Adopted and opened for signature, ratification and accession by General Assembly resolution 2200A (XXI) of 16 December 1966 (entry into force 23 March 1976, in accordance with Article 49); International Covenant on Economic, Social and Cultural Rights, Adopted and opened for signature, ratification and accession by General Assembly resolution 2200A (XXI) of 16 December 1966 (entry into force 3 January 1976, in accordance with article 27).

> "In the domain to which the present proceedings relate, the last fifty years, as indicated above, have brought important developments. These developments leave little doubt that the ultimate objective of the sacred trust was the self-determination and independence of the peoples concerned"[17].

Then, concerning the non-self-governing territories, in the Western Sahara case the Court said that

> "in the exercise of its functions it is necessarily called upon to take into account **existing rules of international law** which are directly connected with the terms of the request and indispensable for the proper interpretation and understanding of its Opinion"[18] (emphasis added).

And actually, the Court considered that Resolution 1514 and other General Assembly's Resolutions directly related (1541 and 2625) were the Law to be applied[19].

Finally, this legal evolution has been confirmed in the Timor case where the ICJ has stated that:

> "In the Court's view, Portugal's assertion that the right of peoples to self-determination, as it evolved from the Charter and from United Nations practice, has an erga omnes character, is irreproachable. The principle of self-determination of peoples has been recognized by the United Nations Charter and in the jurisprudence of the Court (see Legal Consequences for States of the Continued Presence of South Africa in Namibia (South West Africa) notwithstanding Security Council Resolution 276 (1970), Advisory Opinion, I.C.J. Reports 1971, pp. 31-32, paras. 52-53; Western Sahara, Advisory Opinion, I.C.J. Reports 1975, pp. 31-33, paras. 54-59); it is one of the essential principles of contemporary international law"[20].

The legal nature of self-determination as a "*right*" meant that new *obligations* arose also for UN member States. The obligations imposed on third States to implement the respect of this right are of two kinds: political and economic.

Politically, third States are obliged to observe, respect and promote the right to self-determination. The development of the principle of self-determination by the resolutions of the General Assembly and the case-law of the International Court of Justice has led to impose obligations not only to the UN as such but also to all the member States, even if not

---

17 Legal Consequences for States of the Continued Presence of South Africa in Namibia (South West Africa) notwithstanding Security Council Resolution 276 (1970), Advisory Opinion, I.C.J. Reports 1971, p. 16. (para. 53).

18 Western Sahara, Advisory Opinion, I.C.J. Reports 1975, p. 12. (para. 52).

19 Western Sahara, Advisory Opinion, I.C.J. Reports 1975 (para. 55-59).

20 *East Timor (Portugal v. Australia),* Judgment, I.C.J, Reports 1995, p. 90 (para. 29).

involved in a colonization. As a result, it has been declared that "self-determination" is not only a general *principle* of the Law of the UN but also a *right* of the peoples that from now on have a separate, own *international* status. This transformation of self-determination from being a principle to being a principle and a right has an important consequence, i.e. that, as a right, has an *erga omnes* character that necessarily implies a correspondent obligation for all UN member States to respect it.

The "Declaration on the granting of independence to colonial countries and peoples" states that "*All States* shall observe faithfully and strictly the provisions of the ... present resolution"[21].

The "Declaration on Principles of International Law Concerning Friendly Relations and Co-operation Among States in Accordance with the Charter of the United Nations"[22] affirms:

> "Every State has the duty to promote, through joint and separate action, realization of the principle of equal rights and self-determination of peoples, in accordance with the provisions of the Charter, and to render assistance to the United Nations in carrying out the responsibilities entrusted to it by the Charter regarding the implementation of the principle".

> "the territory of a colony (...) has, under the Charter, a status separate and distinct from the territory from the State administering it; and such separate and distinct status shall exist until the people of the colony (...) have exercised their right of self-determination in accordance with the Charter".

Economically, the fight against colonialism developed a new obligation previously ignored. The "Programme of Action for the full implementation of the Declaration on the granting of independence to colonial countries and peoples"[23] established the obligation to avoid any economic practice in non-autonomous territories on behalf of the colonial power, as it is a major obstacle to achieve decolonization:

> "Member States shall wage a vigorous and sustained campaign against activities and practices of foreign economic, financial and other interests operating in colonial Territories and on behalf of colonial Powers and their allies, as these constitute a major obstacle to the achievement of the goals embodied in resolution 1514 (XV). Member States shall consider the adoption of necessary steps to have their nationals and companies under their jurisdiction discontinue such activities and practices; these steps should also aim at preventing the systematic influx of foreign immigrants into colonial Territories, which disrupts the integrity and social, political and cultural unity of the peoples under colonial domination".

---

21 A/RES/1514 (XV), para. 7.

22 A/RES/2625 (XXV), 24 October 1970.

23 A/RES/2621 (XXV), 12 October 1970, para. 4.

We may then conclude that third States have *not only* an obligation to respect politically the separated, different and specific status of "non-autonomous territories", *but also* an obligation to prevent any economic action blurring it or supporting the continuation of the colonial rule. This obligation exists also regarding those third States that claim to have some legal ties with the "non-autonomous territory" before it was colonized by the administering power. This is self-evident if we consider that even the administering power, which was entitled with a legitimate and valid title to occupy the territory, has its title affected by the principle of self-determination.

The holders of self-determination

When the UN Charter was elaborated it was clear that the "States" considered themselves as "peoples" whose "self-determination" was proclaimed in the Charter. It became clear, in any case, that the Charter of the United "Nations" did not refer explicitly to "nations" when self-determination was at stake. The absence of a reference to "nations" in this regard seems to be a subtle way to discard the "principle of nationality" whose effects, after the First World War, were highly destabilizing in Europe. But the question remained open: certainly "self-determination" of "peoples" referred to "States", but… did it refer also to other kinds of "peoples" who were not "States"?

The first resolutions of the General Assembly avoided the references concerning "self-determination" to "peoples" other than "States". It is quite interesting to see how a 1946 General Assembly's resolution concerning the non-self-governing territories has no reference to the "self-determination" of the "peoples" who have yet not attained a full measure of self-government"[24]. And as we have already noticed, the 1949 "Draft Declaration on Rights and Duties of States" did not included neither a "right" to enjoy nor a "duty" to respect the self-determination of the peoples.

The issue did evolved when, in 1960, the General Assembly approved its "Declaration on the granting of independence to colonial countries and peoples" (A/RES/1514). This declaration, explicitly aimed to "colonial peoples", made it clear that "all peoples" had the "right to self-determination".

The determination of the "peoples" who are also "States" is relatively easy despite some cases of States that, although recognized by a big or small number of other States or international organizations, are not members of the United Nations (as in the case of the Saharawi Arab Democratic Republic).

---

[24] A/RES/9 (I), 9 February 1946.

But it was necessary to identify the "colonial peoples" entitled with a "right" to "self-determination". In order to grant legal security to the international system, the United Nations established a system to identify clearly who the "colonial peoples" are. Although Article 73 e) of the United Nations' Charter imposed on the administering power the obligation to transmit information concerning the non-autonomous territories under their administration, some States were reluctant to do it considering that those territories were not "non-autonomous" but an integral part of the national territory. This is why a day after the General Assembly approved its "Declaration on the granting of independence to colonial countries and peoples", it passed a resolution concerning the "Principles which should guide Members in determining whether or not an obligation exists to transmit the information called for under Article 73 e) of the Charter"[25]. Two principles were especially relevant:

> "Principle IV
>
> Prima facie there is an obligation to transmit information in respect of a territory which is geographically separate and is distinct ethnically and/or culturally from the country administering it.
>
> Principle V
>
> Once it has been established that such a prima facie case of geographical and ethnical or cultural distinctness of a territory exists, other elements may then be brought into consideration. These additional elements may be, inter alia, of an administrative, political, juridical, economic or historical nature. If they affect the relationship between the metropolitan State and the territory concerned in a manner which arbitrarily places the latter in a position or status of subordination, they support the presumption that there is an obligation to transmit information under Article 73 e) of the Charter".

The General Assembly established in 1961 a "Special Committee" to examine the application of the "Declaration on the granting of independence to colonial countries and peoples" composed by 17 Members[26] that were enlarged to 24 Members in 1962[27]. Member States may submit information regarding the non-autonomous territories under their administration, thus qualifying those territories as "peoples", with some exceptions explicitly admitted by the International Court of Justice, as mentioned *infra*. However, the General Assembly may also decide to enlist a certain Territory as "non-autonomous" and to qualify it as a "people" with a "right" to "self-determination". And also the Security Council may qualify a certain territory as a "people" entitled

---

25 A/RES/1541 (XV), 15 December 1960.

26 A/RES/1654 (XVI), 27 November 1961; A/RES/1700 (XVI), 19 December 1961.

27 A/RES/1810 (XVII), 17 December 1962.

to "self-determination". Hence, when the General Assembly or the Security Council refer *nominatim* to a certain people there is no doubt about the international recognition of such a "people".

The International Court of Justice has declared that:

> "State practice during this period points clearly to the conclusion that international law contained no prohibition of declarations of independence. During the second half of the twentieth century, the international law of self-determination developed in such a way as to create a right to independence for the peoples of non-self-governing territories and peoples subject to alien subjugation, domination and exploitation"[28].

In 2007, the United Nations' General Assembly passed a resolution containing the "United Nations Declaration on the rights of the indigenous peoples"[29], that introduces some nuances related to this question. This Declaration considers that "indigenous peoples" are "peoples" and, as such, are entitled to a "right to self-determination". That's what the Preamble says in several sentences,[30] while the dispositive section of the resolution specifies it further:

> "Article 3
>
> Indigenous peoples have the right to self-determination. By virtue of that right they freely determine their political status and freely pursue their economic, social and cultural development".
>
> However, as we will see further on, the content of the right to self-determination of those peoples is NOT the same as the content of the right of other "peoples" and, particularly, the "States" and the "colonial peoples".

Outside the frame of the "State", the "colonial peoples" and the "indigenous peoples", International Law does not seem to accept, at least until this moment, a "people" with a "right of self-determination"[31].

---

28 *Accordance with International Law of the Unilateral Declaration of Independence in Respect of Kosovo*, Advisory Opinion, I.C.J. Reports 2010, p. 403 (para. 79).

29 A/RES/61/295, 10th December 2007.

30 "Acknowledging that the Charter of the United Nations, the International Covenant on Economic, Social and Cultural Rights and the International Covenant on Civil and Political Rights, as well as the Vienna Declaration and Programme of Action, affirm the fundamental importance of the right to self-determination of all peoples, by virtue of which they freely determine their political status and freely pursue their economic, social and cultural development, bearing in mind that nothing in this Declaration may be used to deny any peoples their right to self-determination, exercised in conformity with international law".

31 Olivier Corten, "A propos d'un désormais 'classique': *Le droit à l'autodétermination en dehors des situations de décolonisation* de Théodore Christakis", *Revue Belge de Droit International*, XXXII [1999], 1, pp. 329-349; Cesáreo Gutiérez Espada y Romualdo Bermejo García, "El derecho de libre determinación de los pueblos no coloniales a

Certainly, there have been several authors who have suggested the possibility "*in abstracto*" of another holder of this right to self-determination in addition to "States" and "colonial peoples", when this right was still not recognized to "indigenous peoples". Maybe Cassese is the first to say that UN General Assembly's Resolution 2625 contains a "saving clause" related to *internal* self-determination, so that the respect due to it should be guaranteed with *external* self-determination[32]. To this aim, in my view, this author offers a very strained interpretation of the UN General Assembly's Resolution 2625 (XXV) that establishes (emphasis added):

> "Nothing in the foregoing paragraphs shall be construed as authorizing or encouraging any action which should dismember or impair, totally or in part, the territorial integrity or political unity of sovereign and independent States conducting themselves in compliance with the principle of equal rights and self-determination of peoples as described above and thus possessed of a government representing the whole people belonging to the territory without distinction as to race, creed or colour".

This being considered, the interpretation offered by Cassese to this provision clearly does not seem to respect the literal, historical, systematic and teleological methods for the interpretation of norms. First of all, Cassese "forgets" the basic assumption that the paragraph of the UN General Assembly's resolution 2625 on which he construes his thesis refers to only ONE people and hence it is difficult to see how this one people could self-determine and separate from itself. Additionally, there is not a single historic argument supporting his interpretation. Moreover, it seems evident that this paragraph is located inside a set of provisions that regulate international, not domestic, relations. Finally, and because of all the above said, the aim of this norm is to impede external interferences in a State. There is even another author who does not appeal to the UN General Assembly's Resolution 2625 to recognize a "people" entitled to a (international) "right to self-determination" in other cases which is (in my view) different from the abovementioned, such as the South-Sudan[33].

There have been some failed attempts to grant the recognition at the international justice level of the "right to self-determination" of "peoples" who are neither "States", nor "colonial peoples" or even "indigenous

---

la luz del Derecho Internacional", en Juan José Solozábal Echevarría (coord.), *La autodeterminación a debate*, Fundación Pablo Iglesias, Madrid, 2014, p. 93-118.

32 Antonio Cassese, *Self-determination of peoples. A legal reappraisal*, Cambridge University Press, Cambridge (UK), 1995, p. 109 ss.

33 J. Day, "The remedial right of secession in International Law", in *Potentia*, No.4 (2012), p. 19 ss.

peoples". This is showed by the analysis of the cases related to the "Turkish-Republic of Northern Cyprus" (TRNC) and Kosovo.

In relation to the first of those territories, in the Loizidou case, the government of Turkey alleged that the TRNC's legislation was valid because it came from a State created by the exercise of the right to self-determination of the Cyprus-Turkish people[34]. However, the European Court of Human Rights did not pay attention to this argument.

As far as the Kosovo case is concerned, the ICJ said that:

> "Whether, outside the context of non-self-governing territories and peoples subject to alien subjugation, domination and exploitation, the international law of self-determination confers upon part of the population of an existing State a right to separate from that State is, however, a subject on which radically different views were expressed by those taking part in the proceedings and expressing a position on the question. Similar differences existed regarding whether international law provides for a right of "remedial secession" and, if so, in what circumstances. There was also a sharp difference of views as to whether the circumstances which some participants maintained would give rise to a right of "remedial secession" were actually present in Kosovo"[35].

The Advisory Opinion in the Kosovo case is especially important because in the proceedings some parties argued that the UN General Assembly's Resolution 2625 (XXV) contained a "saving clause" following the idea suggested by Cassese. However, the Court did not assume this position.

The Content of Self-determination

The problem of the content of self-determination has known an important development after the adoption of the "United Nations Declaration on rights of the indigenous peoples". This resolution is relevant because it modulates the content of self-determination depending on the type of "people" entitled with such right. Put in this way, the plurality of holders of this right implies a plurality of contents.

The content of the right to self-determination of "colonial peoples" has been clearly specified in UN General Assembly's Resolution 1514 which distinguishes between a "political" and an "economic" content.

According to the General Assembly's Resolution 1514, the political content of the right to self-determination bears a domestic and an external content. When the Resolution 1514 says that *by virtue of that right (the*

---

[34] ECtHR, Loizidou v. Turkey, 18th December 1996. The claim of the Turkish Government is in para. 35 of the ruling.

[35] ICJ, Kosovo, 2010, para. 82.

peoples) freely determine their political status", this provision may be interpreted at the domestic level as the faculty of all peoples to determine without any constraint their political system. This provision may also be understood at the external level as the faculty of all peoples to determine if they want to be independent, associated or integrated into another State as the Resolution 1541 exposed[36]. However, the ICJ has made clear that the application of the right to self-determination requires a free and genuine expression of the will of the peoples concerned[37]. No association or integration is admissible under constraints, against or without the free and genuine expression of the will of the peoples. This is why the Resolution 1514 states that "the subjection of peoples to alien subjugation, domination and exploitation constitutes a denial of fundamental human rights" and "is contrary to the Charter of the United Nations".

The external level of the right to self-determination is closely related to the "right to independence". The Resolution 1514 affirms that:

> "Immediate steps shall be taken, in Trust and Non-Self-Governing Territories or all other territories which have not yet attained independence, to transfer all powers to the peoples of those territories, without any conditions or reservations, in accordance with their freely expressed will and desire, without any distinction as to race, creed or colour, in order to enable them to enjoy complete independence and freedom"[38].

What is the relation between self-determination and independence? In my opinion the Resolution 1514 and the doctrine developed by the ICJ lead to the notion that there is a presumption "*iuris tantum*" that a people wants to be independent. Only if it is proved otherwise, a people may not be independent. And the proof comes from a "free and genuine expression of the will" of the people concerned.

Certainly, the Court has established that:

> "The validity of the principle of self-determination, defined as the need to pay regard to the freely expressed will of peoples, is not affected by the fact that in certain cases the General Assembly has dispensed with the requirement of consulting the inhabitants of a given territory. Those instances were based either on the consideration that a certain population did not constitute a "people" entitled to self-determination or on the conviction that a consultation was totally unnecessary, in view of special circumstances"[39].

---

36 A/RES/1541 (XV), 15 December 1960 (Principle VI).

37 ICJ, Western Sahara, 1975, para. 55.

38 A/RES/1514 (XV), para. 5.

39 ICJ, Western Sahara, 1975, para. 59.

This doctrine provides for two cases. The first is the case where there are "inhabitants of a given territory" who don't constitute a "people", such as the case of Hong-Kong or Gibraltar where the decolonization is not to be implemented through a "referendum". The second is the case where there is a "conviction that a consultation was totally unnecessary, in view of special circumstances" as it was for many colonies where the will for independence is so clear that the colonial power just granted the independence without consulting the population.

The economic content of self-determination is set in para. 2 of the Resolution 1514, according to which by virtue of the right to self-determination peoples "*freely pursue their economic, social and cultural development*". The Preamble of this resolution provides for a more detailed explanation of the economic content:

> "Convinced that the continued existence of colonialism prevents the development of international economic co-operation, impedes the social, cultural and economic development of dependent peoples and militates against the United Nations ideal of universal peace,

Affirming that peoples may, for their own ends, freely dispose of their natural wealth and resources without prejudice to any obligations arising out of international economic co-operation, based upon the principle of mutual benefit, and international law".

The economic content of this right has been further explicated in para. 2 of the common Article 1 of the International Covenants of 1966:

> "All peoples may, for their own ends, freely dispose of their natural wealth and resources without prejudice to any obligations arising out of international economic co-operation, based upon the principle of mutual benefit, and international law. In no case may a people be deprived of its own means of subsistence".

The UN General Assembly's Resolution 61/295, that approves the "United Nations Declaration on rights of the indigenous peoples", is extraordinary relevant to the question here examined. After granting the "indigenous peoples" the right to self-determination, this Declaration establishes for them a DIFFERENT content than the one established for "colonial peoples". In fact, just after granting to "indigenous peoples" the right to self-determination (Article 3), the Declaration specifies what is the content of such a right:

> "Article 4
>
> Indigenous peoples, in exercising their right to self-determination, have the right to autonomy or self-government in matters relating to their internal and local affairs, as well as ways and means for financing their autonomous functions".

This means that the content of the self-determination of "indigenous peoples" has ONLY an internal, but not external, political content. And this marks an essential difference with "colonial peoples". For this reason, in my view, it is difficult to share the opinion of Klabbers stating that "now [...] self-determination can no longer simply be construed as a right of colonies to Independence, it has evolved into a right of peoples to take part in decisions affecting their future [...]. Self-determination is best understood as a procedural right; that is, entities have a right to see their position taken into account whenever their futures are being decided. That may not amount to a right to secede or even a right to autonomy or self-government, but it does amount to a right to be taken seriously"[40]. The position of Klabbers, who completely ignores the difference between "colonial peoples" and "indigenous peoples", voids the International Law in force and substitutes it with his personal view or preference.

Limits and legal remedies to self-determination

The right to self-determination allows a people to establish and shape its own State in the concert of nations. However, the will of a people to establish and shape its own State may be the expression of a nationalist will or ideology that may affect other peoples. In this sense, the principle/right to "self-determination" may be opposed, paradoxically, to the "principle of nationality". In order to avoid any destabilization arisen from the exercise of the right to self-determination, the Resolution 1514 established certain limits.

As well as the "Declaration on the granting of Independence to Colonial Countries and Peoples" imposes to the peoples-States the obligation to respect the "integrity" of the "national territory" of colonial peoples[41], the latter also have the obligation to respect the "national unity and the territorial integrity" of the peoples-States[42]. It is clear, however, that the "territorial integrity" of a certain State can never include the territory of any other international recognized "people". If this were the case, such a claim should be considered illegitimate and contrary to International Law.

It is well known that the International legal system is an imperfect one, because there is no Executive branch (or the Executive branch has a limited capacity to implement International Law).

40 J. Klabbers, "The Right to Be Taken Seriously: Self-Determination in International Law", in *Human Rights Quarterly*, Vol.28, No.1 (2006), p. 186-206 (p. 189).

41 A/RES/1514 (XV), para. 4 ("The integrity of their national territory shall be respected").

42 A/RES/1514 (XV), para. 6 ("Any attempt aimed at the partial or total disruption of the national unity and the territorial integrity of a country is incompatible with the purposes and principles of the Charter of the United Nations").

Instead of asking what should be the guarantee of the right to self-determination internationally recognized, international legal scholars have posed the question related to the "right to self-determination (and specifically, the secession) as guarantee or "remedy" for the respect of other human rights. This has been the theory of "remedial secession". This theory, which has been raised as hypothetical at the national level in Canada[43], has been evoked at international level in a separate opinion to the decision of the European Court of Human Rights in the Loizidou case[44]. Later, it aroused again in another separate opinion[45] in the Kosovo case, although the ICJ considered that it shouldn't take a position on it[46].

There have been voices opposed[47] and others in favour[48] of this formula. However, what seems clear is that Kosovo was not the best case to invoke this idea. Some scholars argue that those who invoked that "right to secede" did it when the human rights situation of Kosovars were not anymore facing a risk of violation by Serbian authorities[49]. But there is still another reason to consider particularly inadequate the case of Kosovo to invoke a "remedial secession". Those who tried to get profit from this theory hid that the secession from Serbia was used, at the same time, to guarantee the impunity of those authorities or Kosovar agents responsible of serious human rights violations against Serbians (particularly in the case of the body organ extractions from Serbian prisoners)[50]. In the case of Kosovo we found the paradox that the "remedial secession" would have

---

43 Re Secession of Quebec, [1998] 2 S.C.R. 217 (p. 285-286).

44 ECtHR, Loizidou v. Turkey, 18th December 1996, Concurrent Opinion of Judges Wildhaber and Ryssdal.

45 *Accordance with International Law of the Unilateral Declaration of Independence in Respect of Kosovo*, Advisory Opinion, I.C.J. Reports 2010, Separate Opinion of the Judge Cançado Trindade, p. 593, para. 175.

46 *Accordance with International Law of the Unilateral Declaration of Independence in Respect of Kosovo*, Advisory Opinion, I.C.J. Reports 2010, p. 403, para. 79.

47 S. F. Van den Driest, *Remedial Secession: A Right to External Self-Determination as A Remedy to Serious Injustices?*, Cambridge, Intersentia, 2013.

48 O. Corten, *A propos d'un désormais 'classique': Le droit à l'autodétermination en dehors des situations de décolonisation, de Théodore Christakis*, *op. cit.*, pp. 340-44.

49 S. R. Bermejo García and C. Gutiérrez Espada, *La declaración unilateral de independencia de Kosovo a la luz de la Opinión Consultiva de la Corte Internacional de Justicia, de 22 de julio de 2010 y de las declaraciones, opiniones individuales y disidentes a la misma*, in "*Anuario español de derecho internacional*", No.26 (2010), p. 7-59 (p. 41); C. B. Jiménez Piernas, *Los principios de soberanía e integridad territorial y de autodeterminación de los pueblos en la opinión consultiva sobre Kosovo: una oportunidad perdida*, in "*Revista Española de Derecho Internacional*", Vol. 63, No.1 (2011), p. 29 ss. (p. 44-47).

50 Report of the Council of Europe "Inhuman treatment of people and illicit trafficking in human organs in Kosovo", AS/Jur (2010) 46, in http://assembly.coe.int/nw/xml/News/FeaturesManager-View-EN.asp?ID=964.

operated as impunity guarantee concerning the human rights violations committed by the separatists.

If we focus on the question of the guarantee of the right to self-determination, it is worth to recall that International Law is, with a high degree, dependent of its duty-bearers: mainly, the States themselves. States have a duty to fulfil their international obligations in good faith. Regarding the International Law of self-determination, there is another duty-bearer in addition to them: the colonial peoples. The fulfilment of the International legal provisions regarding the right to self-determination relies also on the holders themselves of this right.

The "Declaration on the granting of Independence to Colonial Countries and Peoples" shows how the duty-bearer must fulfil its international legal obligations:

> "All armed action or repressive measures of all kinds directed against dependent peoples shall cease in order to enable them to exercise peacefully and freely their right to complete Independence"[51].

This is again stressed in the "Declaration on Principles of International Law Concerning Friendly Relations and Co-operation among States in accordance with the Charter of the United Nations"[52] which says:

> "The establishment of a sovereign and independent State, the free association or integration with an independent State or the emergence into any other political status freely determined by a people constitute modes of implementing the right of self-determination by that people.
>
> Every State has the duty to refrain from any forcible action which deprives peoples referred to above in the elaboration of the present principle of their right to self-determination and freedom and Independence".

But the question is how to proceed when the duty-bearer does not fulfil its obligations. The "Declaration on Principles of International Law Concerning Friendly Relations and Co-operation among States in accordance with the Charter of the United Nations" has provided for a remedy, even if not always satisfactory:

> "In their actions against, and resistance to, such forcible action in pursuit of the exercise of their right to self-determination, such peoples are entitled to seek and to receive support in accordance with the purposes and principles of the Charter".

This remedy is inspired by the resolutions adopted by the first Conference of independent African heads of State and Government held

---

51 A/RES/1514 (XV), para. 4.

52 A/RES/2625 (XXV).

in Addis Ababa, Ethiopia, from 22 to 25 may 1963, by the Organization of African Unity (OAU) since the very first moment of its existence:

> "Reaffirming that it is the duty of all African Independent States to support dependent peoples in Africa in their struggle for freedom and Independence"[53].

The United Nations took their inspiration from this source to adopt a resolution on Namibia where the General Assembly:

> "Appeals to All States to give the indigenous people of South West Africa all necessary moral and material support in their legitimate struggle for freedom and independence"[54].

The colonial peoples have the right to struggle for their right to self-determination, their freedom and independence. In legal terms, the continuation of the colonial rule is to be considered as presumption *iuris et de iure* of an aggression of the colonial State against the colonial people, which legitimates the latter's self-defence.

In the case of certain African colonies the United Nations went further to adopt a resolution condemning the economic practices, carried by States or by individuals that hindered the right to self-determination[55]. In the specific case of Namibia the General Assembly established a "United Nations Council for South West Africa"[56]. This Council at its 209th meeting on 27 September 1974 approved the Decree on the natural resources of Namibia[57]. The Decree even allowed the Council to seize every product or resource originated in Namibia and intended to be exported.

The right to self-determination of the Saharawi people

It is clear that the "people of Western Sahara" (WS), whose existence is continuously affirmed by the United Nations' Resolutions on Western Sahara from 1966 until now, has an "inalienable right to self-determination" and "independence".

The "right to self-determination" of the "people of Western Sahara" was firstly recognized in 1966[58] under the Spanish rule. Since 1965, the General Assembly considered the question of Western Sahara under the "Declaration on the granting of Independence to Colonial Countries

---

53 CIAS/Plen.2/Rev.2.

54 A/RES/2074 (XX), 17 December 1965.

55 A/RES/2288, 7 December 1967.

56 A/RES/2248 (S-V), 19 May 1967.

57 A/Ac.131/33.

58 A/RES/2229 (1966).

and Peoples"[59]. However, in order to avoid any confusion which could led to the conclusion that the "independence" should be reached by the integration of the WS in another country, the bodies of the United Nations expressly recognized that the people of Western Sahara has a "right to self-determination and independence". In order to cast any doubts about the right to independence of the people of Western Sahara the General Assembly asked the International Court of Justice about "what were the legal ties between this territory and the Kingdom of Morocco and the Mauritanian entity"[60]. The answer of the International Court of Justice in its Advisory Opinion dated 16 October 1975 was crystal clear:

> "The Court's conclusion is that the materials and information presented to it do not establish any tie of territorial sovereignty between the territory of Western Sahara and the Kingdom of Morocco or the Mauritanian entity. Thus the Court has not found legal ties of such a nature as might affect the application of resolution 1514 (XV) in the decolonization of Western Sahara and, in particular, of the principle of self-determination through the free and genuine expression of the will of the peoples of the Territory"[61].

This right to self-determination and independence has been reaffirmed when Spain decided to abandon the Territory[62] and later when the major part of the Territory was occupied by Morocco[63]. This recognition has been made continuously by the General Assembly until now[64], as well as by the Security Council[65].

The political and economic content of this right of self-determination has been developed in different degrees by the United Nations.

The law of the United Nations is very clear on how this right to self-determination should be exercised: holding a "*referendum*". The referendum as the way to complete the self-determination of the people of Western Sahara is a clear and continuous requirement of the Law of the United Nations, when the Territory was under Spanish rule but also when Spain decided to abandon the Territory[66] and, later, when the major part

---

59 A/RES/1514 (1960).

60 A/RES/3292 (1974).

61 ICJ Western Sahara, 1975, para. 162.

62 A/RES/3458-A (1975) & A/RES/3458-B (1975).

63 A/RES/33/31 (1978), A/RES/34/37 (1979), A/RES/35/19 (1980).

64 A/RES/64/101 (2010), A/RES/65/112 (2011), A/RES/66/86 (2012), A/RES/67/129 (2013), A/RES/68/91 (2013), A/RES/69/101 (2014).

65 S/RES/1871 (2009), S/RES/1920 (2010), S/RES/1979 (2011), S/RES/2044 (2012), 2152 (2014), 2218 (2015).

66 A/RES/3458-A (1975) & A/RES/3458-B (1975).

of Western Sahara was occupied by Morocco[67]. Still now, the Security Council[68] maintains a Mission in the Territory, established in 1991, that is the "United Nations Mission for the *Referendum* in Western Sahara" (MINURSO, in its Spanish acronym).

This could not be in any other way, because according to the "Declaration of Principles of International Law concerning Friendly relations and cooperation among States in accordance with the Charter of the United Nations":

> "The establishment of a sovereign and independent State, the free association or integration with an independent State or the emergence of any other political status freely determined by a people constitute modes of implementing the right of self-determination by that people"[69].

Since the very first moment when the United Nations established that the "referendum" was the correct instrument for the exercise of the "right to self-determination" and the decolonization of the territory of Western Sahara, the UN established the requirements of this referendum. The legality of the United Nations requires that the "referendum" should be "conducted on an entirely free, democratic and impartial basis"[70]. In order to guarantee the fairness of the decolonization process, the referendum should be conducted "without any administrative or military constraints"[71].

VI.2.B. The economic obligations imposed to all UN member States regarding all non-autonomous territories were *explicitly referred also to the Western Sahara* in General Assembly's Resolution 3292 (XXIV):

> "(the General Assembly) Reiterates its invitation to all States to observe the resolutions of the General Assembly regarding the activities of foreign economic and financial interests in the Territory and to abstain to contribute by their investments or immigration policy to the maintenance of a colonial situation in the Territory"[72].

The Legal Opinion of the Under-Secretary-General for Legal Affairs, the Legal Counsel of the United Nations from 2002, has reiterated these obligations. In its Advisory opinion, the UN Legal Counsel said:

---

67 A/RES/33-31 (1978), A/RES/34-37 (1979), A/RES/35-19 (1980).

68 S/RES/1871 (2009), S/RES/1920 (2010), S/RES/1979 (2011), S/RES/2044 (2012).

69 A/RES/2625 (1970).

70 A/RES/2229 (1966).

71 A/RES/38/40 (1981).

72 A/RES/3292 (1974).

> "If further exploration and exploitation activities were to proceed in disregard of the interests and wishes of the people of Western Sahara, they would be in violation of the principles of international law applicable to mineral resource activities in Non-Self-Governing Territories"[73].

Although the first General Assembly's Resolution on Western Sahara[74] just referred to the "territory" of Western Sahara, the next General Assembly's Resolutions made clear who is the holder of this right being recognized as a "people" not only under Spanish rule[75], but also when Spain decided to abandon the Territory[76] and later when major part of Western Sahara was occupied by Morocco[77]. The General Assembly[78] and the Security Council[79] of the UN have affirmed in a consistent and continuous way the existence of the "*people of Western Sahara*". It is worth to mention that Morocco itself has accepted the existence of the "people of Western Sahara" when it has voted in favour of the Security Council's Resolutions 2044 (2012) and 2099 (2013) when it was a non-permanent member of this body.

Certainly the resolutions of the United Nations speak about the "people of Western Sahara". But, how should be determined who constitute this people? The United Nations made it clear that only the "indigenous people of the Territory" compose the "people of Western Sahara". This has been clearly stated by the General Assembly under Spanish rule[80], but also when Spain decided to abandon the Territory[81].

But, then, one may ask who those indigenous people are. The answer with detailed names lies in the census of the "people of Western Sahara" that has been completed by the United Nations. The report of the Secretary-General dated 17 February 2000 reveals that, contrary to some opinions, the MINURSO has already completed the list of the voters allowed to participate to the referendum for self-determination. This list was communicated to the two parties of the conflict on 17 January 2000[82].

---

73 Letter dated 29 January 2002 from the Under-Secretary-General for Legal Affairs, the Legal Counsel, addressed to the President of the Security Council, S/2002/161 (para. 25).

74 A/RES/2072 (1965).

75 A/RES/2229 (1966).

76 A/RES/3458-A (1975) & A/RES/3458-B (1975).

77 A/RES/33/31 (1978), A/RES/34/37 (1979), A/RES/35/19 (1980).

78 A/RES/64/101 (2010), A/RES/65/112 (2011), A/RES/66/86 (2012), A/RES/67/129 (2013), A/RES/68/91 (2013), A/RES/69/101 (2014).

79 S/RES/1920 (2010), S/RES/1979 (2011), S/RES/2044 (2012), S/RES/2099 (2013), 2152 (2014), 2218 (2015).

80 A/RES/2229 (1966).

81 A/RES/3458-A (1975) & A/RES/3458-B (1975).

82 S/2000/131, para. 6.

The legal remedy to this right has been also explicated by the United Nations. In this moment, the Security Council still relies on the duty-bearer to fulfil on good faith its obligations. This is why the Security Council since 2007 asks both parties to negotiate the solution of this conflict. However, it is difficult to set aside the fact that Morocco does not want to negotiate in good faith the fulfilment of its legal obligations since it is ready to negotiate only a "solution" that denies the right of the People of Western Sahara to freely choose their political status.

It is time to remember that in a similar context (the war of Western Sahara, 1975-1991), where Morocco was not ready to fulfil its legal obligations, while the United Nations deplored the military occupation of the Territory by one of the "two parties to the conflict" (i.e., Morocco) and urged this country to terminate its occupation, the General Assembly has recognized "the legitimacy of the struggle" of the people of Western Sahara "to secure the enjoyment of that right"[83].

This recognition is perfectly consistent with the "Declaration of Principles of International Law concerning Friendly relations and cooperation among States in accordance with the Charter of the United Nations":

> "Every State has the duty to refrain from any forcible action which deprives peoples referred to above in the elaboration of the present principle of their right to self-determination and freedom and independence.
>
> In their actions against, and resistance to, such forcible action in pursuit of the exercise of their right to self-determination, such peoples are entitled to seek and to receive support in accordance with the purposes and principles of the Charter"[84].

The latest developments of the case show that the economic issues lie in the core of the conflict and that a formula similar to the one adopted in the Namibia case is the most likely to bring the solution to the conflict.

In the case of the Western Sahara no scholar has suggested to apply the "remedial secession" doctrine. Certainly there is a difficulty in principle: insofar the Western Sahara is NOT part of the territorial integrity of Morocco, a "secession" is conceptually impossible. Notwithstanding, it could be possible to suggest a certain modulation of this theory to the context of a Non-Autonomous Territory under the shape of a "remedial independence" arguing that, in the current situation, not only there are massive human rights violations, but also that these occur with a nearly absolute impunity.

---

83 A/RES/34/37 (1979), A/RES/35/19 (1980).

84 A/RES/2625 (1970).

The former South-African President, Thabo Mbeki, already advanced the idea of a "remedial independence", even if not formulated in this way, in his letter to the King of Morocco dated 1st August 2004. In this letter, President Mbeki said that, in light of the blockage by Morocco of the process of the Referendum for self-determination with independence as an option, South Africa considered that the Moroccan position was a denial of the right to self-determination. This is why, in such a situation, South-Africa considered that the recognition of the SADR (Saharawi Arab Democratic Republic) as an independent State was a way to support the right to self-determination[85]. Although the South-African letter does not use the Word "remedy", its meaning is obvious.

However, South Africa did not refer to the human rights situation (outside the human right to self-determination) in Western Sahara in its position. The human rights situation in Western Sahara has been officially verified as regrettable by the United Nations, by some States (even one State, USA, allied to the Kingdom of Morocco itself)[86] and by international human rights organisations[87]. In this regard, it is necessary to recall that the Report of the United Nations High Commissioner for Human Rights dated 8th September 2006 stated that "the human rights situation is of serious concern, particularly in the Moroccan-administered territory of the Western Sahara". In the same sense, we may add the reports from many other bodies of the United Nations system (Human Rights Committee, Commission on Human Rights, Committee against Torture, Special Rapporteur on Torture, Special Rapporteur in the field of Cultural Rights, Special Rapporteur on the situation of human rights defenders, in addition to the Reports of the Secretary-General to the General Assembly and the Security Council), all of them noting the regrettable situation of human rights in the part of the Western Sahara occupied by Morocco[88]. Nevertheless, the most worrying fact is the nearly absolute impunity. In all these years, only two policemen have been sentenced because of a human rights violation (the death provoked to a peaceful demonstrator), but they just remained two years in prison[89].

---

85 The text of this document of paramount relevance may be found in http://arso.org/MBK.htm.

86 Cf., Annual Reports on Human Rights of the US Department, in http://www.state.gov/j/drl/rls/hrrpt.

87 Not to mention that the Kingdom of Morocco, itself, officially has recognized part of the human rights violations produced before the access of Mohamed VI to the power in July 1999. Cf. C. Ruiz Miguel, "La responsabilité internationale et les droits de l'homme: le cas du Sahara Occidental", in *Cahiers de la Recherche des Droits Fondamentaux*, No.11 (2013), p. 105-130 (p. 107-111).

88 See *ibidem*, p. 120-129.

89 See *ibidem*, p. 111.

Very few cases may show, as clearly as the Western Sahara case does, how the independence is not just a right but may also be a remedy to terminate a situation characterised by systematic and unpunished human rights violations.

Fish before Peace

The EU's Controversial Fisheries in Occupied Western Sahara

Erik Hagen

Western Sahara Resource Watch

"The financial aspect is not necessarily the most important aspect of this agreement. The political aspect is just as important"[1].

In one short statement, Morocco's fisheries minister summarized the entire problem of the EU's former fish agreement with Morocco. The year was 2006, and the debates had been running high in European institutions on the upcoming EU-Moroccan fisheries agreement. A new pact, in which the EU would pay money to the Moroccan government to fish in Western Sahara waters, was just about to be concluded after months of dispute.

The statement underlined the problem with the entire deal: Morocco was about to reel in a large and controversial political catch. As a leading beneficiary of the EU's Neighbourhood Policy, Morocco has been advantaged with a number of trade deals with the EU; some of these deals directly affect the territory of Western Sahara. Morocco naturally has an agenda in these kinds of agreements. By attracting foreign companies and governments to sign accords for the management of the natural resources of the territory, Morocco normalizes its long-standing illegal occupation of Western Sahara, and creates an impression of international support for its presence in the Saharawi territory.

"International agreements which do not exclude 'the Moroccan Sahara' from their application, prove that the area is Moroccan", the Moroccan Minister of Communication asserted in an interview years later.

However, on one occasion, this project of including Western Sahara as part of the Kingdom through EU agreements crumbled. In a historical decision 14 December 2011, the European Parliament rejected the

1 Aujourd'hui le Maroc, 24.05.2006, Accord de pêche: naufrage polisarien http://www.fishelsewhere.eu/files/dated/2009-10-25/laenser_2006_in_alm.pdf.

fisheries in the territory. It was one of the very unique occasions in the history of the EU that a trade deal has been blocked by the lawmakers, and the only time it has happened to a fisheries agreement. From a political victory in 2006, the Moroccans five years later had suffered a bitter loss on the same deal.

This article outlines the saga behind the blocking of the EU-Morocco fisheries agreement in 2011, and looks at the arguments used by its supporters. For several years did the defenders of the EU fisheries in Western Sahara argue that the fisheries accord was not a political act, but one of mere fishing. They blamed the opponents for taking advantage of a simple trade agreement for political agenda.

But as the agreement was up for continuation in 2011, all arguments to support the continued fisheries had been undermined by the EU's own investigations. The same supporters that had stressed the apolitical nature of fisheries, only had political arguments left to defend continued fisheries. In the end, it seemed all to be about politics, as the Moroccan government had admitted itself. Even the documented environmental destruction and multi-million Euro losses for the union turned unimportant, as long as its Spanish fleet were kept busy.

The EU fisheries had to continue since it was politically important for Morocco, they said.

EU interest with Morocco

Due to its occupation of Western Sahara, Morocco is the only African country that is not part of the African Union. Yet, it is the African state with the closest ties to the EU. Strategic reasons why the EU needs to maintain the goodwill of the Moroccan government are numerous: Migration and drug control across the Gibraltar Strait, intelligence exchange on terrorism, overlapping maritime and land claims with its member state Spain, just to name a few.

According to figures from the European Commission, the EU is Morocco's biggest trading partner, by far, accounting for around 50% of the country's total trade. The trade in goods between the EU and Morocco is ever increasing, and was in 2012 at more than 26 billion Euros[2]. Through the trade cooperation, the European Community has entered into several agreements with its neighbouring country in the south west, that in practice cover natural resources in Western Sahara.

It appears that two EU states in general have the definition power over the EU policy on the Western Sahara conflict: Morocco's neighbor

---

2 European Commission, 22.04.2013, EU and Morocco start negotiations for closer trade ties, http://trade.ec.europa.eu/doclib/press/index.cfm?id=888.

country Spain and the Kingdom's long term ally, France. The remaining 26 states in the Union appear not to invest much political capital, if any, in the dispute, in order not to upset Madrid and Paris.

"We know what international law guides us to do, but in this matter we follow Spain", stated a representative of one of the country delegations to Brussels regarding the EU fisheries in Western Sahara[3]. There are some noble exceptions, where governments stress the legitimate rights of the Saharawi people, most of all governments in Northern Europe. But they seldom go in direct confrontation with the Spanish-French duo. Also the European Parliament, consisting of the democratically elected representatives from the 28 EU states, repeatedly issue statements about the human rights in Western Sahara. The Parliament for instance "expresses its concern at the continued violation of human rights in Western Sahara; calls for the protection of the fundamental rights of the people of Western Sahara, including freedom of association, freedom of expression and the right to demonstrate; demands the release of all Sahrawi political prisoners"[4].

The position of the European Parliament is also supported by key documents by the UN Secretariat and leading human rights organisations. The US organization Freedom House, for instance, rates Western Sahara at the bottom of ratings on political freedom – together with states such as North Korea. However, on the other end of the scale, one would find players within the EU system with a completely different view.

At key moments in Western Sahara conflict, the EU ambassador to Morocco has actively pursued the Moroccan position on diverting human rights abuses in Western Sahara, to focus on spreading Moroccan versions of the turn of events[5]. The ambassador is even quoted stating that "Morocco and the EU share the same values of democracy and freedom", at a seminar of media freedom in Rabat[6].

---

3 Conversation with the author, November 2010.

4 European Parliament, 7.02.2013, http://www.europarl.europa.eu/sides/getDoc.do?type=TA&language=EN&reference=P7-TA-2013-55. See also: 13.12.2012 – Annual report on human rights and democracy in the world 2011 and the European Union's policy on the matter http://www.europarl.europa.eu/sides/getDoc.do?type=REPORT&language=EN&reference=A7-0377/2012.

5 La Razón, 12.11.2010, http://www.larazon.es/detalle_hemeroteca/noticias/LA_RAZON_341773/historico/769-la-ue-prefiere-evitar-el-conflicto-con-marruecos#.UXjX7Mp7N7k.

6 MAP, 27.09.2013, Eneko Landaburu: "Le Maroc et l'UE partagent les mêmes valeurs de démocratie et de liberté", http://www.aufaitmaroc.com/actualites/maroc/2010/9/27/eneko-landaburu-le-maroc-et-lue-partagent-les-memes-valeurs-de-democratie-et-de-liberte#.UXjarcp7N7l.

This illustrates a key part of the dynamics of the EU processes and what happened during the battle of the fisheries agreement. Sometimes the European Parliament and the Commission could take highly differing views. Sometimes, they could even be in direct conflict with one another.

Integrating into the European Market

It is in the overall framework of political cooperation between Morocco and the EU that the fisheries agreement must be viewed.

At the very same day in December 2011 as the European Parliament wrote history by rejecting the fisheries agreement, ironically, the Council of Ministers mandated the Commission to negotiate a so-called Deep and Comprehensive Free Trade Agreement (DCFTA)[7]. The DCFTA negotiations formally started 16 months later[8]. The main objective of this agreement is to facilitate Morocco's gradual alignment with the EU single market.

"These negotiations show the EU's strong commitment to further developing its trade and investment ties with Southern Mediterranean partners who are committed to political and economic reforms", stated the EU Trade Commissioner[9].

But there was a hatch. As always, as the EU is reluctant to properly exclude the occupied parts of Western Sahara from its trade deals with Morocco. Through the DCFTA talks, which will probably not be concluded for a few years, Morocco will negotiate the agreement with the EU as if the Moroccan-controlled parts of Western Sahara were part of the Kingdom.

31 Saharawi civil society organisations from occupied Western Sahara and the Saharawi refugee camps in Algeria have appealed to the European Commission to exclude their country from the DCFTA-talks. The European Commission has not taken their wish into account, and has not consulted them so far in the process[10].

The DCFTA talks illustrate how Western Sahara is the elephant in the room during EU-Moroccan negotiations. It is the topic seldom raised, but all institutions know should be. Overall, the EU tends to follow a say-as-little-as-possible approach.

---

7 European Council, Deep and Comprehensive Free Trade Area, EU-Morocco, Questionnaire, 2013, http://trade.ec.europa.eu/doclib/docs/2013/february/tradoc_150521.pdf.

8 European Commission, 22.04.2013, EU and Morocco start negotiations for closer trade ties, http://trade.ec.europa.eu/doclib/press/index.cfm?id=888.

9 European Commission, 22.04.2013, EU and Morocco start negotiations for closer trade ties, http://trade.ec.europa.eu/doclib/press/index.cfm?id=888.

10 WSRW, 26.06.2012, 31 Saharawi NGOs call for change in EU's trade policy, http://www.wsrw.org/a214x2338.

"The EU confirms its support to the UN Secretary General and his Personal Envoy in their efforts to reach a just, lasting and mutually acceptable political solution", stated the EU's spokesperson on human rights as the situation in Western Sahara was at its most intense since the ceasefire in 2010[11]. The quote is not untypical to the EU's approach to the conflict. To comparison, a general UN Security Council resolution would normally state exactly the same, but then ending with the formulation "… which will provide for the self-determination of the people of Western Sahara"[12]. The omission is often made by the EU, cutting through the entire EU approach to the conflict and its trade relations with Morocco. It illustrates how Saharawi people is not taken into account by the EU. When dealing with Saharawi natural resources, the EU negotiates with Rabat, and lends a deaf ear to the Saharawi protests.

Overgrown fishing Fleet

The EU struggles with a massive overcapacity in its fishing fleet. In short, there are far too many fishermen and fishing vessels for the always decreasing fish stocks available in European waters. 88% of the EU's own waters are overfished. The main problem is Spain: 80% of the EU fishing vessels, and 65% of the EU fishermen are Spanish. To cope with the problem of sleeping fleet and unemployed fishermen, the EU enters into so-called Fisheries Partnership Agreements, or "FPAs", through which the Union pays African and Pacific governments to issue fishing licences for the EU vessels in their waters. The model is not without controversy. The fleet often overuses the fish stocks where it operates, and enters in conflict with the traditional small-scale, often poor, fishing communities operating from the coast. Some of the governments that sign fisheries deals with the EU are known to be un-democratic or corrupt, and with limited resources to monitor the visiting European fleet. In Western Sahara the problem is that the EU even inked the agreement with the wrong government: its occupying power.

Spanish fishermen have been fishing in the waters offshore Western Sahara for centuries. As the territory was to be decolonized from Spain in the autumn of 1975, the weak and collapsing Franco regime signed the Madrid Accords with Morocco and Mauritania, allowing the two neighbour countries to invade the territory. The deal was in direct conflict with the obligation Spain had to decolonize the territory. In return, Spain

11 10.11.2010, Statement by the Spokesperson of EU HR Ashton on Western Sahara, http://www.eu-un.europa.eu/articles/en/article_10352_en.htm.

12 UNSC resolution 2044 (2012), Security Council Extends Mandate of United Nations Mission in Western Sahara, http://www.un.org/News/Press/docs/2012/sc10621.doc.htm

would be allowed to keep its fishing rights and partly its ownership in the phosphate industry in Western Sahara. In that way, the massively overgrown fishing fleet that the Franco regime had built could maintain its unsustainable fisheries even after it unilaterally, and thus illegally, renounced from its colonial obligations.

While the Saharawi people was left on its own to escape to refugee camps in Algeria or to confront the occupiers at home, the fish stocks and phosphate deposits of the territory became part of the package that Spain gained from ignoring its obligation to decolonize Western Sahara properly. The Spanish tradition of fishing in Western Sahara after 1975 is thus part of the explanation as to why Western Sahara is not decolonized in the first place. It is a profit that Spain gained from allowing Morocco to occupy the territory in violation of the rights of the people that inhabited in the former Spanish province.

In 1986, Spain joined the Union. From then on it would be the EU that negotiated foreign fisheries agreements with Morocco on Spain's behalf. From 1988, the EU for the first time signed such an agreement with Morocco, allowing for 800 licences annually for Spanish and Portuguese fishermen. No ceiling on catches was introduced, and Morocco was paid 282 million Euros for the deal. A new agreement was signed in 1992, the same year that the referendum in Western Sahara was supposed to have taken place. The agreement was even more lucrative for Morocco: the Moroccan government was paid 310 million Euros, for an activity almost exclusively taking place in Western Sahara waters. In 1995, the latter agreement was redefined and prolonged, for a payment of 500 million Euros, and in turn terminated by Morocco in 1999. By then, the fish stocks in Western Sahara were about to collapse[13].

The halt of fisheries offshore Western Sahara at the turn of the century struck hard on the Spanish fishing communities. "In Andalusia, more than 200 vessels have been affected and a total of 151 vessels remain tied up pending an improvement in fishing relations between Morocco and the EU. As a result of this crisis, business has dropped by half in the markets of the ports of Almería, Barbate, Huelva, Malaga and Algeciras", stated a Spanish Member of European Parliament (MEP) in the autumn of 2004.

"Would the Commission be prepared to make a fresh attempt at rapprochement with Morocco with the aim of facilitating cooperation on fishing-related matters?", she asked[14].

---

13 T. Shelley, *Endgame in the Western Sahara: What Future for Africa's Last Colony?*, London-New York, Zed books, 2004, p. 75.

14 MEP María Salinas García, Written question to European Commission, 29.10.2004, http://www.europarl.europa.eu/sides/getDoc.do?type=WQ&reference=E-2004-2679&format=XML&language=EN.

In 2005, the Commission responded to the pressure from Spain, and commenced talks for yet another agreement, which, as we shall see, entered into force in 2007[15]. This was the first time the EU entered into such an agreement after the UN legal office had issued its 2002 legal opinion on oil exploration in Western Sahara. The principles outlined in the UN opinion were clear, even for natural resources other than oil: if the people of Western Sahara did not benefit from it, and if they did not consent, such operation would be in violation of international law. So did the Saharawi people consent? Were they to benefit from an agreement that the EU signed with the government that oppress them?

Selective reading

We will perhaps never know how the legal staff of the European Commission and Council actually argued in the defense for the EU fisheries agreement that the Spanish fisheries industry had pushed for. The opinions that the two legal offices made have to this date been kept confidential. Yet, the statements given by the Commission when confronted in public, reveals a clear misrepresentation of UN documents and international law that in more spotlighted conflict situations would have created headlines in themselves. But not in the matter of the little known issue of Western Sahara.

In the year up until the adoption of the agreement, the Commission and key governments went to great lengths to obfuscate the whereabouts of the future fisheries, to lay the responsibility on Morocco and to misrepresent the legal opinion of the UN.

The EU-Moroccan fisheries agreement of 2007-2011 did not make any efforts to specify that Western Sahara is excluded from the agreement with Morocco. Actually, it did not mention Western Sahara at all. Instead, the agreement allowed for EU fisheries under Morocco's "sovereignty and jurisdiction". It was clear for everyone that the fisheries would happen in Western Sahara, but the defenders went to great lengths to avoid saying it.

The only legal reference that the European Commission used to defend its agreement was the mentioned UN opinion from 2002, as well as its own, internal, confidential analysis.

The UN legal opinion was written by the then UN secretary-general for legal affairs, Ambassador Hans Corell, to the Security Council in 2002. The analysis concluded that natural resource activity in Western Sahara is illegal if it was "to proceed in disregard of the interests and wishes of the people of Western Sahara".

---

15 EU-Morocco Fisheries Partnership Agreement, http://www.vest-sahara.no/files/dated/2008-05-15/fisheries_partnership_agreement_eu-morocco.pdf.

However, the EU consistently misrepresented the report. Never did the Commission refer to the final conclusion of the legal opinion, only segments inside which do not reflect the conclusion. Never did the Commission consult the Saharawi people over the agreement, and never did the Commission even refer to the wishes of the Saharawis regarding the agreement.

More than 100 UN resolutions have established that the people of Western Sahara have the right to self-determination. This right applies also to the resources of the territory. No states in the world recognise the Moroccan sovereignty over Western Sahara.

Still, the Saharawi's wishes were simply ignored every time the Commission was confronted with the legality of the agreement. Each time, the UN legal opinion was misrepresented:

> "Regarding the compliance of the current Agreement with international law, and the legal opinion of the European Parliament [...], we would like to reiterate that in his letter of 2002, Mr. Corell, concluded that (economic) activities in a Non-Self-Governing Territory by an administering Power are illegal 'only if conducted in disregard of the needs and interests of the people of that Territory'"[16].

In this way, by referring to other parts of the text than the final conclusion, the Commission never needed to take into account the "wishes" or aspects of self-determination for the Saharawis. By doing this, the EU gave the image that it can decide, on their behalf, what it is that the Saharawis are wishing. It also stresses something that the EU mentions repeatedly: that Morocco is the de facto administering power over the territory. "Morocco is the de facto administrator of Western Sahara", stated Commissioner Borg in 2006. "So, the Commission proposal is in conformity with the legal opinion of the United Nations issued in January 2002," he argued[17]. This is in fact *the contrary* to what is stated in the UN legal opinion. The UN legal opinion clearly states Western Sahara has no such administering Power[18]. The opinion was made by analogy, *as if* Western Sahara had had one.

---

16 Letter from European Commission to WSRW, 27.06.2010, http://www.fishelsewhere.eu/index.php?parse_news=single&cat=140&art=1151.

17 EU Observer, 09.03.2006, Commission under fire over Morocco fisheries agreement, http://euobserver.com/news/21092.

18 This is also mentioned in European Parliament Legal Service, Legal Opinion Re: Proposal for a Council Regulation on the conclusion of the Fisheries Partnership Agreement between the European Community and the Kingdom of Morocco – Compatibility with the principles of international law, 20.06.2006, http://www.wsrw.org/files/dated/2013-04-26/parliament_legal_opinion_fpa_20.02.2006.pdf.

Another way of diluting Corell's conclusion was by inversing the meaning into a double negation:

> "[…] 'according to the legal adviser to the Secretary-General of the United Nations (12 February 2002) […], activities related to natural resources undertaken by an administering power in a non-self-governing territory are not illegal so long as they are not undertaken in disregard of the needs, interests and benefits of the people of that territory', stated the European Commissioner for Fisheries and Maritime Affairs"[19].

The Commission had spent two entire years in preparing the agreement, and defended the text fiercely in the debates. The statements were consistently vague. Never did they want to state that the fishing would take place in Western Sahara.

"According to the provisions of the agreement, it is up to the Moroccan authorities as the contracting party concerned to define the fishing zones on the basis of which fishing licences will be issued", Commissioner Borg stated just before the vote in the European Parliament plenary session, 15 May 2006[20].

The opinion of the European Council was not discussed as much as the one from the Commission. Seven years after it was written, in July 2013, the Council stated it could not disclose it. The argument? Due to its "great political sensitivity"[21].

Also the European Parliament undertook a legal analysis. But unlike the legal opinions of the European Commission and Council, the one from the Parliament was published. The report warned of the illegality of the agreement. However, it was hard for the Parliament's legal staff to draw a conclusion, since the proposed agreement did not actually specify that fishing would take place in Western Sahara. If that were to happen, however, and if Morocco did not respect the rights of the Saharawis, it would be illegal, the Parliament legal service stated:

> "[…] The text of the Agreement is not sufficiently clear as to its territorial area of application", the legal opinion from 2006 noted.
>
> This does not mean that the agreement is, as such, contrary to the principles of international law. At this stage, it cannot be prejudged that Morocco will not comply with its obligations under international law vis-à-vis the people of

19 Fishelsewhere.eu, 14.10.2009, EU ignores the Sahrawis' wishes – again, http://www.fishelsewhere.eu/a169x1005.

20 Commissioner Joe Borg in European Parliament, 15.052006, http://www.europarl.europa.eu/sides/getDoc.do?type=CRE&reference=20060515&secondRef=ITEM-018&format=XML&language=EN.

21 WSRW.org, 04.07.2013, EU Council refuses to disclose 2006 legal opinion on Morocco fish deal, http://www.wsrw.org/a105x2617.

Western Sahara. It depends on how the agreement will be implemented. [...] In case the Moroccan authorities disregard manifestly their obligations under international law vis-à-vis the people of Western Sahara, the Community could eventually enter into bilateral consultations with a view to suspending the agreement"[22].

The debates ran high in the Parliament. While parliamentarians objected to the Commission's fact blurring and likely inclusion of Western Sahara, underlining that the agreement would violate international law, the Commission itself worked intensively to calm down the opposition.

"[T]he Commission thoroughly evaluated the political, legal and economic implications of an eventual agreement. In this case, as in others, the Commission is taking care to avoid a situation where the conclusion of new agreements in the field of fisheries could become a factor in international disputes or conflicts", the Commissioner stated[23].

The sector that had pushed for the agreement, mostly the Spanish parliamentarians, praised the Commissioner for the negotiating of the agreement.

"I would like to express my gratitude to a section of the population who I represent", stated a Spanish parliamentarian on the Commission's work. "I am talking about the population of the Canary Islands, which also neighbours these waters, which has always fished in these waters and not, despite what some people have said, in a colonialist fashion. My great-grandfather signed an agreement with the population of the coast in order to fish there, on the basis of the principle of mutual interest. We had been fishing in those waters, we shall go back to fishing there, and I would like to thank the Commission for the effort it has made. I hope that this Parliament will approve this Agreement by a large majority, since it is very fair and very correct from the point of view of international law"[24].

Other defenders said that the debate over the Saharawis people had nothing to do in such a forum.

---

22 European Parliament Legal Service, Legal Opinion Re: Proposal for a Council Regulation on the conclusion of the Fisheries Partnership Agreement between the European Community and the Kingdom of Morocco – Compatibility with the principles of international law, 20.06.2006, http://www.wsrw.org/files/dated/2013-04-26/parliament_legal_opinion_fpa_20.02.2006.pdf.

23 Debates, European Parliament, 04.04.2006, http://www.europarl.europa.eu/sides/getDoc.do?type=CRE&reference=20060404&secondRef=ITEM-014&format=XML&language=EN.

24 MEP Manuel Medina Ortega in European Parliament, 15.06.2006, http://www.europarl.europa.eu/sides/getDoc.do?type=CRE&reference=20060515&secondRef=ITEM-018&format=XML&language=EN.

"We believe that the Committee on Fisheries is not the place to resolve extremely important and complex international political problems", Spanish MEP Carmen Fraga said 15 May 2006.[25]

She thanked her Spanish countryman that had prepared the dossier for the Plenary session, and the "balance he has achieved in relation to the political issues that have arisen".

The debate up until the vote in the Plenary session of the European Parliament was also used by pro-Moroccan parliamentarians to score political points, promoting rather absurd political statements in support of the Moroccan claims to the territory, in which legal references were even more twisted: "I welcome this agreement, which is reasonable on two grounds", stated a French MEP who in the past had served as fiscal advisor of the Moroccan monarch[26].

> "Firstly, it is reasonable as far as the fishery resources in the Moroccan provinces of Western Sahara are concerned. It is not the opinion of Parliament's legal service that counts, but that of the International Court of Justice. For centuries, Morocco has exercised a certain form of sovereignty over that territory. If Algeria wants an outlet into the Atlantic, that is its problem, but that is not a good enough reason to invent laws. It is also reasonable because it is good to retain the benefits derived from these agreements and to transfer them to the Saharan provinces of Morocco and to the people. […] we must take delight in the fact that we have concluded this reasonable and balanced agreement with Morocco. Let us not pick a quarrel with the Moroccans"[27].

Wrapping up

The deal was eventually approved in 2006, and entered into force from 28 February 2007. The EU fleet would be given 114 licences, in return of a 36 million Euros annual payment to the Moroccan government. It meant a total package of 144 million Euros to fish – mostly in a territory that Morocco has never laid a maritime claim over.

The vagueness of the territorial scope led Sweden to vote against the agreement in the European Council, stating that "Western Sahara is not part of the territory of Morocco under international law". "How can

[25] MEP Carmen Fraga, in European Parliament, 15.05.2006, http://www.europarl.europa.eu/sides/getDoc.do?type=CRE&reference=20060515&secondRef=ITEM-018&format=XML&language=EN.

[26] MEP Jean-Claude Martinez in European Parliament, 15.05.2006, http://www.europarl.europa.eu/sides/getDoc.do?type=CRE&reference=20060515&secondRef=ITEM-018&format=XML&language=EN.

[27] MEP Jean-Claude Martinez in European Parliament, 15.05.2006, http://www.europarl.europa.eu/sides/getDoc.do?type=CRE&reference=20060515&secondRef=ITEM-018&format=XML&language=EN.

the EU on the one hand support the United Nations resolution and not recognise the annexation of the Western Sahara and on the other hand have a fisheries agreement with Morocco that covers the occupied areas? We want to be a neutral part in solving this conflict", a Swedish official stated as the deal was up for vote[28]. Finland, Ireland and the Netherlands agreed with the Swedish position, but did not vote against the deal, opting instead to abstain, issuing their own statements. The remaining states endorsed the agreement in the Council. Several representatives of EU governments stated that in either case, if fisheries were in fact to take place in Western Sahara, Morocco would have to make sure that the benefits would go to the "local population" and could not prejudge how Morocco would comply or not.

But no specific reference whatsoever was made in the protocol to whom that local population was. Were they Moroccan or Saharawi?

In the end, Morocco had four years to deliver proof that the "local population" would benefit. As we should see later, what they coughed up was, mildly speaking, not really what the states had asked for.

"Please, friends of the Sahrawi people, tell the EU that they first help solve the Western Sahara conflict, then they can exploit our fish. The way they do it now will only make problems for us and for the UN peace process", stated Saharawi human rights activists from the occupied territories in a letter to the Parliamentarians they day before the vote[29].

A third of the parliamentarians voted against the Council's decision in a parliament vote on 15 May 2006. It was not enough for majority. And since the Parliament did not have decision making power, it would still have had no importance if the parliament had disagreed. The Council's decision would in either case have gone through.

The Commission still claimed they had everything covered. "I repeat that concerning Western Sahara the wording used in the agreement was formulated very carefully. I repeat that it neither defines nor prejudges the legal status of the waters concerned. Again, with regard to […] the question as to whether Morocco can conclude agreements that concern the exploitation of the natural resources of Western Sahara, the United Nations legal adviser gives a clear answer," were Commissioner Borg's last words in European Parliament, before the Plenary vote[30].

---

28 Financial Times, 14.06.2006, EU fishing deal set to proceed despite Sahara dispute, http://www.ft.com/cms/s/0/7d092668-e380-11da-a015-0000779e2340.html.

29 WSRW.org, Letter, 16.05.2006, http://www.wsrw.org/a193x1999.

30 Commissioner Joe Borg in European Parliament, 15.06.2006, http://www.europarl.europa.eu/sides/getDoc.do?type=CRE&reference=20060515&secondRef=ITEM-018&format=XML&language=EN.

As the deal was sealed, and the fishing activity started, the critique would come from, probably, the highest authority possible.

Corell concerned

"I am afraid that Commissioner Borg has been ill advised", ambassador Hans Corell, then retired from his UN position, stated during a conference on international law in 2008[31].

The EU Commission's continuous misuse of the UN text had not passed unnoticed by the author. He saw it peculiar that the Commission was reading his text as if Morocco is a de facto administering power, and that the agreement "therefore" would be in conformity with the legal opinion. What Corell thought about the EU's use of his UN document deserves a generous quote:

> "I must confess that I was quite taken aback when I learnt about this agreement. Without doubt, good relations between Europe and Morocco are of greatest importance. [...] But I am sure that it would have been possible to find a formulation that would have satisfied both parties while at the same time respecting the legal regime applicable in the waters off Western Sahara. Any jurisdiction over those waters is subject to the limitations that flow from the rules on self-determination.
>
> It has been suggested that the legal opinion I delivered in 2002 has been involved by the European Commission in support of the Fisheries Partnership Agreement. I do not know if this is true. But if it is, I find it incomprehensible that the Commission could find any such support in the legal opinion, unless, of course, it has established that the people of Western Sahara had been consulted, had accepted the agreement, and the manner in which the profits from the activity were to benefit from them. However, an examination of the agreement leads to a different conclusion. [...] It is very difficult to identify the Saharawi in this enumeration. [...] In all the pages of the Agreement, there is not one word about the fact that Morocco's "jurisdiction" is limited by the international rules of self-determination.
>
> As a European, I feel embarrassed. Surely, one would expect Europe and the European Commission – most of all – to set an example by applying the highest possible international legal standards in matters of this nature. Under all circumstances, I would have thought that it was obvious that an agreement of this kind that does not make a distinction between the waters adjacent to Western Sahara, and the waters adjacent to the territory of Morocco, would violate international law."

---

31 Amb Hans Corell, 05.12.2008, The legality of exploring and exploiting natural resources in Western Sahara, http://www.havc.se/res/SelectedMaterial/20081205pretoriawesternsahara1.pdf.

Also other legal scholars concluded on the illegality of the agreement[32], as did the government of Sweden.

The Legal Service of the European Parliament fell on the same conclusion as the former UN legal chief. In a new legal opinion from 2009, made public in 2010, the office did not find any proof that the Sahrawi have ever been consulted in relation to the fisheries agreement in Western Sahara, which had by then been in effect for more than two years.

> "It is not demonstrated that the [...] financial contribution [to Morocco] is used for the benefit of the people of Western Sahara. Yet, compliance with international law requires that economic activities related to the natural resources of a Non-Self-Governing Territory are carried out for the benefits of the people of such Territory, and in accordance with their wishes"[33].

It concludes:

> "In the event that it could not be demonstrated that the FPA was implemented in conformity with the principles of international law concerning the rights of the Saharawi people over their natural resource, principles which the Community is bound to respect, the Community should refrain from allowing vessels to fish in the waters off Western Sahara by requesting fishing licences only for fishing zones that are situated in the waters off Morocco."

For the period that this legal opinion from the parliament was still confidential, the leader of the Fisheries Committee told Western Sahara Resource Watch that the Parliament's legal opinion "supported the legality" of continued fisheries in Western Sahara. When the document was made public, it was clear that it was not really the case.

Benefiting whom?

"I think each refugee should have one slice of bread with fish every day", researcher Ingrid Barikmo told her colleagues in the refugee camps in Algeria, at a time when the four year fisheries agreement was half way through its application. The chronic malnutrition level in the refugee

32 The same conclusion of illegality of the EU fisheries agreement was given by the French lawyers NGO Sherpa (2006, http://www.wsrw.org/index.php?cat=193&art=1479), by the Association of the Bar of the City of New York (2011, http://www.wsrw.org/index.php?parse_news=single&cat=105&art=1894), by a group of Swedish jurists from 4 universities (2011, http://www.wsrw.org/files/dated/2011-02-17/swedish_legal-opinion_16.02.2011.pdf) and by the European Association of Lawyers for Democracy & World Human Rights, ELDH (2011, http://www.eldh.eu/publications/publication/press-release-fishery-agreement-between-european-union-and-morocco-illegal-61/).

33 Fishelsewhere.eu, 23.02.2010, Here is the secret legal opinion from the EU Parliament, http://www.fishelsewhere.eu/a140x1077.

camps is worrisome. Studies have shown that in periods, one in every five Sahrawi children is acutely malnourished[34].

Ms Barikmo has studied the nutrition levels in the Saharawi refugee camps in Algeria for the last 14 years. Her colleagues during a meeting and her team often gather to discuss how to respond to the malnutrition among a population completely depending on aid. Their research has uncovered a worrisome situation for the Sahrawi people that fled their homeland in mid 1970s, as Morocco ignored the opinion of the International Court of Justice and invaded Western Sahara to the UN's condemnation.

The refugees struggle with donor fatigue and malnutrition. 93% of the refugee children have an unacceptable diet, according to the team's research[35]. Ms Barikmo's suggestion of more fish in the diet was well-placed, but there are too few funds.

"My colleagues simply laughed at me. They thought I was joking", Barikmo said later.

The European Union's humanitarian organization, ECHO, donates in average 10 million Euros annually in humanitarian aid to these camps[36]. However, to compare, the EU paid 3.6 times as much to Morocco annually under the Fisheries Partnership Agreement for access to the fish stocks that are owned by the same refugees. The EU buys the Saharawis' fish from Western Sahara's occupation power, while the children in the refugee camps suffer from lack of protein.

The other half of the Saharawis still living in the occupied territory, also find the EU's plans to be unfortunate. They say they do not benefit from it. When 799 international organisations in 2010 protested the EU's plunder in a letter to the European Commission, all Saharawi groups were among the signatories[37].

Meanwhile, expressing opposition to the Moroccan management of the territory it occupies can lead to harsh punishments.

Any person being critical to the illegal Moroccan presence, will risk being subjected to human rights violations. This has been documented, year after year, by leading international human rights organisations. Morocco

---

34 World Food Programme, Medicos Del Mundo, Norwegian Church Aid, Akershus University College, Nutritional and Food Security Survey among the Saharawi refugees in Camps in Tindouf, Algeria (October 2008), http://vest-sahara.no/files/dated/2013-05-02/nutritional_survey_2008.pdf.

35 Interview, 2013, researcher Ingrid Barikmo, Oslo and Akershus University College.

36 European Commission, ECHO Factsheet, Saharawi refugees, April 2013, http://reliefweb.int/sites/reliefweb.int/files/resources/sahrawi_en_0.pdf.

37 WSRW.org, 29.09.2010, 799 organisations, and a refugee in Brussels, protest EU fisheries, http://www.wsrw.org/a159x1614.

has recently rejected a recommendation in the UN Human Rights Council to apply international minimum standards for registering organisations, including for Saharawi groups advocating for the Saharawi right to self-determination[38].

Leading Saharawi activists that took part in the organizing of the October-November 2010 protest camp outside of El Aaiún, in which socio-economic rights were called for, were convicted to severe punishments in a Moroccan military court. One of them, the secretary-general of Committee for Protection of Natural Resources, got sentenced to lifetime in jail. He has been an outspoken critic of the EU's fisheries activities of Western Sahara – and was one of nine to get such sentence.

The European Parliament has repeatedly expressed its concern over the abuses[39]. So have the reports from UN Secretary-General Ban Ki-Moon, who in 2013 requested from the Security Council a mandate to the MINURSO that would allow for human rights monitoring. The same two countries that lobby for EU trade deals covering Western Sahara – Spain and France – prevented such an inclusion in April 2013, even after pressure from the US to do otherwise.

As the fisheries operations of the EU continued, Saharawis would carry homemade banners or tag on the walls of buildings in El Aaiún; "Where is our right in fishing treaty?"

> "We never had a voice in this undertaking, and the only outcome of the fisheries agreement that our people have noticed, is that our voices are suppressed even more, as Morocco feels itself supported by the European Union in its illegal and unfounded claim over our homeland. Since the Saharawi people have not agreed to nor benefits from the agreement, as required under international law, we respectfully ask that all European fisheries in Saharawi waters be halted immediately",

Stated a group of Saharawi political prisoners in a letter to the president of the European Parliament[40].

Most importantly, however, the Western Sahara liberation movement Frente Polisario repeatedly objected to the agreement. On numerous

---

38 UN General Assembly, Human Rights Council, 06.07.2012, Report of the Working Group on the Universal Periodic Review, http://www.upr-info.org/IMG/pdf/a_hrc_21_3_morocco_e.pdf#page=3&zoom=auto,0,539.

39 7.02.2013, http://www.europarl.europa.eu/sides/getDoc.do?type=TA&language=EN&reference=P7-TA-2013-55; 13.12.2012, http://www.europarl.europa.eu/sides/getDoc.do?type=REPORT&language=EN&reference=A7-0377/2012; 12.09.2012, http://www.europarl.europa.eu/sides/getDoc.do?type=TA&reference=P7-TA-2012-0334&language=EN.

40 WSRW.org, 14.09.2010, Saharawi political prisoners demand halt to EU fisheries, http://www.wsrw.org/a159x1591.

occasions did representatives of Polisario contact the EU institutions protesting the agreement. They have also called on the UN to intervene[41].

Before the agreement was adopted in the first place, in April 2006, the Fisheries Committee in fact took the initiative to have the two parties to the conflict, Morocco and Polisario, to participate in the Parliament for a joint consultation. However, as Morocco did not want to present its case at the same table as Polisario, the entire joint consultation was cancelled, to the joy of the Spanish socialists on the committee that had tried to prevent the initiative. The organisers stated that there would not be any such consultation if both parties were not present at the same time[42]. The consequence was the Polisario's view was never heard in meetings with the Fisheries Committee. In all future consultations, it would be Morocco that was to be invited instead by the EU institutions, alone, to discuss the management of the Western Sahara fish stocks.

At the time when the fisheries agreement was adopted in 2006, states, parliamentarians and the EU legal service stated that one cannot prejudge how or whether Morocco would comply with its obligations. When the four years came to an end, Morocco had never presented one shred of evidence on whether the people of Western Sahara benefited from the fisheries. One has every reason to wonder what was actually discussed at the annual meetings between the Commission and Morocco. They had had four years to find out.

In the end, the parliamentarians needed to take the issue into their own hands. A delegation from the European Parliament's Fisheries Committee was supposed to visit Western Sahara in 2010 to assess how the people were consulted and benefiting. After months went by without any official reply, Morocco officially rejected the Fisheries Committee's proposal of visiting the territory, claiming the timing for such a visit was "not opportune"[43].

Five other known European delegations of journalists, civil society groups and students that travelled to the territory under-cover to investigate the matter application of the former agreement in 2010-2011, were expelled from Morocco or Western Sahara[44].

---

41 E.g. Fishelsewhere.eu, 28.11.2012, Polisario expresses concern to Security Council over EU fisheries, http://www.fishelsewhere.eu/a140x1388.

42 ABC, 04.04.2006, Marruecos sopesa no acudir a la UE para opinar sobre el acuerdo pesquero, http://www.abc.es/hemeroteca/historico-02-04-2006/abc/Economia/marruecos-sopesa-no-acudir-a-la-ue-para-opinar-sobre-el-acuerdo-pesquero_142988229026.html.

43 Fishelsewhere.eu, 04.06.2010, Morocco rejects visit from European Parliament, http://www.fishelsewhere.eu/a140x1143.

44 WSRW.org, 29.11.2010, Danish journalist deported from Morocco after covering EU fisheries, http://www.wsrw.org/a159x1705; WSRW.org, 11.01.2011, Member of WSRW expelled from Western Sahara, http://www.wsrw.org/a204x1813; WSRW.org,

Morocco never presented any evidence to prove that the fisheries activities in Western Sahara under the agreement benefited the Saharawi people, nor that they have been consulted.

The silence from Morocco was frustrating for those European interests that lobbied for the agreement. “Morocco will not give it to us”, the leader of the Fisheries Committee stated[45].

Many also raised the question what purpose it had to ask Morocco give such a report to begin with. They do not represent the Saharawis, do they?

Corell, the former UN legal chief that the EU had lent all its argument on, came back on the stage.

“The fisheries agreement is now (October 2010) up for a renewal. It has been suggested to me that the European Commission is of the opinion that it is for Morocco to see to it that the agreement is implemented in a manner that the interests of the Saharawi are taken into consideration. In view of the circumstances, in particular the political dispute over many years between Morocco and the Frente Polisario, this position is simply not acceptable. An honourable actor in the international arena must demonstrate a higher standard. This applies in particular to Europe where actions by States should be based on the Charter of the UN and modern treaties on human rights, such as the International Covenant on Civil and Political Rights and the European Convention for the Protection of Human Rights and Fundamental Freedoms”, Corell wrote about the fisheries agreement in a new article in 2010[46].

It is, in the end, clear that the Saharawis do not benefit.

The nutritionists in the refugee camps can only observe that the fish will keep being absent from refugees' diet. Once a month, in average, do the refugees receive one small can of mackerel donated by a Swedish NGO[47]. The fish cans are labeled “Made in China”.

01.02.2011, Expelled after interviewing Saharawi on EU fisheries, http://www.wsrw.org/a204x1844; WSRW.org, 29.05.2011, WSRW forced to leave Western Sahara, http://www.wsrw.org/a204x1933; WSRW.org, 06.11.2012, Travelled to interview on EU fish deal – expelled from Western Sahara, http://www.wsrw.org/a214x2409.

45 EFE, 30 June 2010, http://www.abc.es/agencias/noticia.asp?noticia=438556.

46 Amb Hans Corell, Routes 4/2010, Western Sahara – status and resources, http://www.wsrw.org/a159x1747.

47 Parliamentarian Hans Linde, question in Swedish parliament, 14.02.2013, http://www.riksdagen.se/sv/Debatter--beslut/Interpellationsdebatter1/Debatt/?did=H010229&doctype=ip.

Awkward Arguments

The European Commission, the pro-fishing parliamentarians and Morocco itself worked actively on defending the agreement during the 4 years the agreement lasted. They had a lot to defend. A successful implementation of the fisheries partnership agreement would lay the grounds for a new one later. These were some of the arguments:

a) Don't ask us, as Morocco. "The UN Corell opinion confirms that [...] exploitation activities should be carried out 'for the benefit of the peoples of those Territories, on their behalf or in consultation with their representatives'. The Commission is of the view that it is Morocco's responsibility to ensure that this is the case", EU Fisheries Commissioner stated, as if the EU had no responsibility of the agreement[48].

b) Data will show the agreement is good. "The information on the economic impact of this agreement to the regions would only support the validity of this agreement"[49], EU ambassador Landáburu stated. This was before any data had yet been presented by Morocco to the EU, and while all evidence pointed to the opposite. In the end, no data was presented to answer to the prerequisites set by the European Parliament legal service.

c) Inventing legal support. In a press conference in Casablanca, the same EU ambassador to Morocco declared that "the legal services of the European Commission and all advices from independent institutions have shown that there is no problem with the international legality of the fisheries agreement with Morocco". After a number of letters had been sent to the ambassador and the Commission, his office finally replied that the independent legal opinions in fact were the two internal and confidential opinions from the European institutions themselves.

d) Claiming support from Parliament. "The EU fisheries partnership agreement with Morocco covers also Western Sahara. This was approved by the Commission and the European Parliament," the EU commissioner Joe Borg stated to a Swedish TV documentary in March 2010[50]. The correct is that the EU stated back then that it would be in "Moroccan waters" and that the same commissioner

48 Maria Damanaki, on behalf of the Commission, 21.06.2010, http://www.europarl.europa.eu/sides/getAllAnswers.do?reference=E-2010-2633&language=EN.

49 L'Economiste, republished in FisPros, 3.10.2010, Maroc/UE: l'accord dans l'impasse http://fishpros.purforum.com/t197-maroc-ue-l-accord-dans-l-impasse.

50 Commisisoner Joe Borg to Sveriges Television, Uppdrag Granskning, 03.03.2010, Det gränslösa fisket.

admitted several times before the vote that they had gone to great lengths to avoid mentioning it was in Western Sahara. The entire vagueness of the scope of the agreement even left it impossible for the Parliament's legal service to conclude on the legality of it.

e) Misrepresented the critique. "As for human rights, that's a horizontal problem. Why is this agreement the only pact where this is raised as an issue?", said parliamentarian Carmen Fraga[51]. The question was really never one of human rights, but of whether the EU should sign an agreement with the wrong government, in waters they never had claimed. In no other occasion would the EU sign agreement with the occupying power for fishing in occupied waters. As a parenthesis can be stated that human rights issues have been a main concern raised on other agreements.

f) If EU doesn't, someone else will. "A refusal would not mean the end of the use of maritime resources in the exclusive economic zone of the Western Sahara territory. Morocco could also conclude an FPA-style agreement with any other country seeking additional fishing resources. As a result, the FPA ensures that the demand for fish in the EU can be covered without fully exploiting or over-fishing the EU waters", German law firm Alber Geiger wrote in an email to a group of Parliamentarians 11 May 2011. The law firm was "representing Morocco's interest before the European Parliament."

g) *Told opponents misused the agreement for political purpose. The agreement "could* be used for political reasons, because that is the normal political game, but there is no problem", stated EU ambassador Landáburu[52].

The latter argument was repeatedly used, and is the key to the entire debate on the EU fisheries. Does it, or does it not have, a political dimension to fish in Western Sahara in partnership with the occupying power?

"Fishing in Former Sahara is apolitical"

The mentioned statement from the Moroccan government to the local media in Morocco, underlining that the fisheries agreement has a political dimension which is more important than the financial, should be enough to shoot down the EU ambassador's claims. Yet, both the Commission and the pro-fisheries lobby time and again argued that the agreement has no political significance.

---

51 Reuters, 8.06.2011, http://www.reuters.com/article/2011/06/08/ozabs-trade-morocco-fish-idAFJOE7570GI20110608.

52 ABC, 27.05.2010, La UE defiende la legalidad del acuerdo pesquero con Marruecos, http://www.abc.es/agencias/noticia.asp?noticia=397879.

"The Western Sahara issue will not be resolved here", stated a French, pro-Moroccan, parliamentarian in one of the debates in the Fisheries Committee.

"It is a polemic that tries to take political advantage of the media interest of an agreement", said the EU's chief negotiator for the EU-Morocco fisheries agreement, César Deben, shortly after the signing ceremony in 2006[53].

Ironically, in the same defense speech, Deben stated that Western Sahara waters had been "under Moroccan administration" since the Madrid Accords – the same accords that the 2002 legal opinion had found invalid.

> "There has always been a polemic regarding this, even during the previous agreements. An agreement with Morocco includes all waters and fishing zones of the Moroccan Kingdom. [...] I can say that Morocco has agreements with Russia, the Ukraine and other countries, and here have never been such polemics. The interest lies not in the fisheries activity in the waters of the former Sahara (*sic*), but that it is the EU that is negotiating it. But we are very confident, as the legal opinions both from the European Commission and the Parliament, as well as from the Council of Ministers have been unanimous – the agreement respect all prerequisites of communitarian and international law",

the negotiator said, misrepresenting the actual content of the Parliament's legal opinion[54].

'Former Sahara'? The statement from the former chief negotiator is clearly taking sides in the conflict, and appear in stark contrast to the UN terminology and to the foreign policies of the EU member states.

The claim that a fisheries accord covering the territory of occupied Western Sahara does not have political consequences is not only countered by the Moroccan minister of fisheries himself, as mentioned earlier, but also by Saharawis, Polisario, NGOs, scholars; all except the fish industry lobby.

"In order to find a solution [to the conflict], it is imperative that other actors do not behave in a manner that in fact risks undermining the efforts by the UN to find a solution. A particular responsibility rests with the members of the European Commission and in particular Spain", Ambassador Corell said about the agreement[55].

53 EuropaPress, 28.07.2005, El nuevo acuerdo pesquero entre la UE Marruecos incluye las aguas del Sáhara Occidental, http://www.fishelsewhere.eu/files/dated/2009-01-31/cesar_deben_statement_28.07.2005.pdf.

54 Canarias Ahora, 15.05.2006, Entrevista César Deben, http://www.fishelsewhere.eu/a170x971.

55 Amb Hans Corell, Routes 4/2010, Western Sahara – status and resources, http://www.wsrw.org/a159x1747.

The Norwegian government, not part of the EU, has labeled similar natural resources engagement in Western Sahara for "a particularly serious violation of fundamental ethical norms because it may strengthen Morocco's sovereignty claims and thus contribute to undermining the UN peace process"[56].

"It is extremely clear that Morocco only wants to keep the fisheries agreement with the EU for one reason – to legitimise Morocco's illegal occupation of Western Sahara by making the EU an accomplice", stated one of the many critics in the European Parliament, Isabella Lövin of the Swedish Green Party[57]. From 2011, a new document appeared that would shoot down the remaining arguments as to why the agreement should carry on. From then onwards, as all other arguments crumbled, even the pro-fishing lobby took to political arguments to defend the continued catches.

EU evaluation: all-time worst

At the time when EU fisheries agreements come to an end, the Commission is always obliged to contract an independent bureau to evaluate the implementation of the agreement. So too with the 2007-2011 EU-Morocco fisheries partnership agreement. The evaluation, done by a consultancy firm in Paris, did not go into details of the aspects of international law, the wishes of the Saharawi, or the political consequences that the Commission stated had been assessed. However, the report in detail studied and completely discredited the implementation of the agreement along two new fronts not much covered until then: the ecological destruction of Western Sahara waters and the financial loss to the EU[58].

The evaluation revealed that Morocco was unable to manage the fish stocks of Western Sahara in a sustainable manner. The 103 page evaluation report noted that the EU was co-responsible for the over-exploitation of the pelagic fish stocks and contributing to endanger threatened marine animals.

Of 11 demersal stocks fished in those waters, five appear overexploited, four are fully exploited, while two stocks were not sufficiently analysed due to lack of data. One of the priorities of the EU under the partnership was to have Morocco reduce unsustainable fisheries practices. In fact, the EU had during the entire agreement period requested that Morocco

56 Norwegian Ministry of Finance, 06.06.2005, Company Excluded from the Government Petroleum Fund, http://www.regjeringen.no/templates/Pressemelding.aspx?id=256359&epslanguage=EN-GB.

57 BBC, 15 Dec 2011, Morocco's fish fight: High stakes over Western Sahara, http://www.bbc.co.uk/news/world-africa-16101666.

58 WSRW.org, 05.03.2012, Here is the evaluation report of the Morocco fish deal, http://www.wsrw.org/a214x2261.

speed up the process of banning the use of driftnets, an unsustainable fisheries method banned by the EU. Morocco "is not doing enough" to stop the practice, stated EU fisheries commissioner Borg already in 2009[59]. The evaluation one year later revealed that the money destined for that purpose had not been used by Morocco at all.

The most surprising element of the evaluation was that the EU-Morocco fisheries agreement literally meant throwing money out of the window. The evaluation showed that "each euro spent by the EU only generated 83 cents turnover and 65 cents direct and indirect value added accruing to the EU [...] These are the lowest cost-benefit ratios of support to the European fleet across all ongoing bilateral agreements".

Said in other words: the information in the evaluation showed it would have been cheaper to just give the EU taxpayers' money directly to the fishermen in Spain, and not send them to Western Sahara to fish. Even in absence of an EU recession, such a deal would be nothing less than a squander. Tens of millions of Euros had been lost.

Finally, for those that claimed that the agreement was important for job creation for the local "Moroccan" economy, and as such important for the development of Morocco, also lost an argument: only 170 jobs were created under the agreement[60]. That's a whole lot of money for each job – not even taking into account whether they were Saharawis or not.

The leader of the Fisheries Committee, until then so defending of the agreement, was shocked about the findings. "The report is the most negative I have seen in my life", summarized Spanish Carmen Fraga, once the cat was out of the bag.[61]

So what arguments were left to support continued fisheries after that?

According to the EU institutions' own reports, the agreement was in violation of international law, it destroyed the environment, it hardly created any jobs and it was a waste of EU money. Leading experts on the Western Sahara issue said it also undermined the UN peace efforts, by allowing Morocco to score political points.

The 2011 extension

Half way through the 2007-2011 fisheries agreement, a large constitutional reform shook up the relations between the EU institutions.

---

59 EFEAGRO, 09.09.2009, La CE pide a Marruecos más esfuerzo para prohibir pescar con redes de deriva, http://www.efeagro.com/multimedia/la-ce-pide-a-marruecos-mas-esfuerzo-para-prohibir-pescar-con-redes-de-deriva/1-1043717.html.

60 Evaluation report, p. 91.

61 EFE, 02.09.2011, La Eurocámara critica los malos resultados del acuerdo con Marruecos, http://www.pesca2.com/informacion/desc_noticia.cfm?noticia=10686.

The so-called Lisbon Treaty gave increased power to the Parliament in certain areas, among them the ability to over-rule the Council of Ministers in matters such as fisheries agreements. Gaining these privileges led to a new power dynamic between the three EU institutions: The Parliament, the Council and the Commission. It is the Commission's role to answer to the development of the fisheries agreement. Observant parliamentarians were often frustrated that getting information from the Commission on the implementation of the agreement was just like talking to a wall. It seemed that the Lisbon Treaty which gave the Parliament increased powers, did not inspire the Commission to share all it knows, or doesn't know, about fishy deals as the one with Morocco.

Even just getting a clear answer from the Commission as to whether fishing took place in Western Sahara at all was for a long time seemingly impossible. The revelation about the EU actually fishing in Western Sahara came only after Members of the European Parliament had asked seven different written questions to the Commission, all with different wording and approach. The break-through came when a question was asked regarding the EU catch volumes under the current agreement reported from FAO's so-called fishing area 34.1.3, which is partially overlapping the Western Sahara waters[62].

Until then, when the Commission had been asked if EU vessels fished in the Western Sahara zone, the reply was normally that it was up to Morocco to define the area of application of the agreement.

"The lack of inter-institutional cooperation has obstructed the rapporteur's work through the entire process of preparing this draft recommendation", Finnish MEP Carl Haglund later stated as he was writing a report to the Fisheries Committee on the fisheries agreement. That is harsh language – particularly from a diplomatic parliamentarian as Haglund.

The lack of response and info-sharing was not due to a lack of knowledge. The Commission had constant dialogue with its Moroccan counterparts, and at all times would the Commission have full information of the whereabouts of its fleet. Modern tracking devices on the vessels give full traceability. Not only that. The Commission even made visits to the occupied territory.

"The original licences for both [...] vessels will be given in Dakhla on Monday morning by the Delegation of the European Commission and the Moroccan authorities to the vessel owner", stated a mail from the Commission to one of the member states in November 2007.

62 WSRW.org, 03.07.2008, EU Commission admits fishing in occupied Western Sahara, http://wsrw.org/a128x770.

The same lack of information appeared as the critical evaluation was completed. One would imagine that the Parliament would have access to all evaluations that analyses how the EU taxpayers' money is used. But no. For many months, it seemed that no one in the parliament even knew it had been written. When it was first known that it had been made, it was kept strictly confidential.

The evaluation report was only presented for a very limited circulation: It was only in French, only made available four months after it was made. And "available" is an exaggeration. Only the members of the parliament's Fisheries Committee could see it. The document was only accessible in a separate small room that was equipped with a table, a chair, and a light bulb. Laptops, mobile phones and even assistants of the parliamentarians were not allowed near the holy document. In the past, those same reports had been available for all MEPs upon a simple request, but not after the Lisbon Treaty.

As the news started to spread that the evaluation was truly slaughtering the agreement, the mood in the parliaments started to change.

As the 2007-2010 agreement came to an end 27 February 2011, a new 4 year agreement had not yet come in place as Spain had pushed for. Under intense pressure from the Spanish government, a provisional one year extension was initiated from the following day. Such an extension would also give the Commission one more year to study the benefits accruing from the agreement to the "local populations".

In order to be approved, the extension just had to be first passed in the Council of Ministers and then finally and formally approved by the Parliament in the autumn.

The debate in the European institutions during the whole year of 2011 was then whether or not to accept the 12 month continued fisheries which had already begun. The fish lobby would fail.

Growing opposition

On 13 December 2010, Morocco had for the first time forwarded information to the European Commission regarding how the EU funds had been used. The first impression was not too good. In a memo sent out from the Commission to the Council and Parliament on 16 February 2011, the content of the Moroccan report was diplomatically labeled as "some information" and "a step in the right direction". The Commission noted that "The socio-economic impacts on this region are assessed specifically and information provided tends to demonstrate that this region is benefitting in terms of job creation and additional turnover". However, a closer study of the Morocco's short, 44 slide PowerPoint presentation, would lead to a different conclusion[63]. The document neither mentions Western Sahara nor its population at all. As expected from a report requested from the Moroccan government, it did not take into account the Saharawis, including the half of the people that lives as refugees in Algeria.

One month later, 15 March 2011, still no more information had arrived the Commission, as the PowerPoint was sent out to the Council of Ministers.

The meager "benefit report", as it was named, proved to be crucial for many of the member states when they formulated their positions. It constituted the main argument for most of the Northern European countries, that all objected to extending the fisheries on such a shallow basis. But many small states are not enough to stop a vote in the European Council. A large EU member state or two are required to reach the sufficient qualified blocking minority. As the UK was negative to the fisheries from the beginning, and Spain, France and Poland were positive, it was clear that the call would be with the German government.

As the German officials reviewed the file, they concluded there was no evidence whatsoever as to whether the local population benefited. It seemed thus that the prolongation would remarkably be stopped by the Council, only a few months after the 12 months extension had begun. In the end, however, in the last minute before the final vote on 29 June 2011, Germany turned around. Without any new evidence having been placed on the table, Germany stated there was "overwhelming" evidence that there was local benefit. They never explained why they changed position.

Some speculate that the German U-turn was due to a political crisis in the relations with Madrid. German authorities had only four weeks before falsely claimed that Spanish cucumbers were responsible for an outbreak of E.coli bacteria in Europe. Others point to the German relations with Morocco's allies in France, relations that always have to be balanced carefully. With Germany's last minute turn-around, the Council could approve with necessary majority, and, in the wait of parliament's final approval later in the autumn, fisheries could still continue. No one appeared to challenge Berlin as to what information – after four years of frustrating Moroccan silence – had appeared out of the blue in order to make them turn. Applying the loss ratio explained by the evaluation report, the decision to extend the four year agreement with yet another year constituted a financial loss for the EU at a minimum 12.6 million Euros[64].

---

63 EuropeanVoice.com, 07.07.2011, Support for controversial Morocco fishing agreement, http://www.europeanvoice.com/article/imported/support-for-controversial-morocco-fishing-agreement-/71549.aspx.

64 35% loss of 36 million Euros, the annual payment under the protocol.

By the autumn 2011, five months later, it was the Parliament's turn to assess whether it would grant green light for what the Commission and the Council had already approved. Would they use their newly acquired Lisbon Treaty powers and actually stop an agreement that in either case would finish only two months later? The fisheries under the 1 year extension had by then already taken place for months. But there was discontent about the way it was extended despite of the flaws. "I am not happy that we had this sudden extension after asking for the Commission's views for a year", stated one parliamentarian[65].

The three committees – the Development Committee, the Budget Committee and the Fisheries Committee – would present its recommendations, but the fisheries would have most of the weight. It was the Fisheries Committee's recommendation that would be presented to the Plenary. In each committee, most controversial aspects of the agreement were debated, including the Sahara issue.

The Budget Committee was first out. Taking into account the evaluation report, the budget committee really had no choice but to recommend rejection of the one year extension.

"This agreement presents a double problem: it is not regular in legal terms, nor is it in line with the sustainable objectives that Parliament upholds […] Tax payers' money needs to be spent wisely and legally", the budget rapporteur French MEP François Alfonsi, remarked[66].

According to the rapporteur, the one single agreement with Morocco ate away a sizeable percentage of the entire budget that the EU has set aside for these types of bilateral fisheries agreements. "25% of the fisheries budget line is spent on this agreement – that is a lot", Alfonsi noted[67].

Surprisingly, even though it was documented as a spectacular financial loss for the union, it ended up in a close vote. And the voting procedure for this particular decision was apparently so confusing, that some parliamentarians ended up voting for the opposite of what they intended. As the turnout came negative to the prolonged agreement, a handful surprised Spanish socialists objected, but the chair of the meeting said that there would be no new vote.

Second out was the Development Committee – and they landed on the same conclusion. "The right way to go is not in neglecting international

---

65 European Voice, 09.06.2011, Morocco fishing deal "poor value for money". http://www.europeanvoice.com/article/imported/morocco-fishing-deal-poor-value-for-money-/71280.aspx.

66 WSRW, 21.10.2010, Budget rapporteur calls for rejection of fish pact, http://www.wsrw.org/a204x2134.

67 WSRW, 21.10.2010, Budget rapporteur calls for rejection of fish pact, http://www.wsrw.org/a204x2134.

law, principles of environmental sustainability or sound economics", the Development Committee's rapporteur, Swedish MEP Isabella Lövin stated.

Presenting her report in the Development Committee on 10 October 2011, the rapporteur strongly urged the Parliament to turn down the proposed one year extension of the Protocol[68].

The rapporteur stated how the sectoral support given under the fish agreement had been "a failure". Under the agreement, an annual 13.5 million Euro was earmarked for the development of the local fisheries sector of "Morocco". Only 15% of that money had been used. The rapporteur added that it was furthermore "unacceptable that Morocco has totally neglected the European Commission's questions on the benefits and the wishes of the Saharawi people"[69].

At that point, neither Morocco, nor the European Commission, had provided any proof that the Saharawi had been consulted or benefitted from the fish deal that the EU has signed with occupier Morocco. As mentioned, these were the prerequisites that the Parliament's legal services had mentioned in their legal opinion two years before.

Morocco's mentioned refusal of a delegation of Parliament's Fisheries Committee to check up on the implementation of the fish deal was not appreciated by the Development Committee. "Such tactics – not answering questions or allowing delegations – should not be awarded", stated Lövin.

As the decision came up for vote in the Development Committee, the negative report was passed with an overwhelming majority. Only some objected.

French MEP Maurice Ponga was one of them. Illustratively, Ponga deemed it important to support Morocco's "profound reforms" through approving the agreement. Morocco needed, according to the argument, to be rewarded for its alleged political achievements through the fisheries agreement[70]. Furthermore, "the fish have been caught and sold: we can't put them back in the water", he said. Ponga is himself from another non-self-governing territory, New Caledonia, and a fierce defender of the French control over the Melanesian archipelago.

To wrap it all up, the preparatory work in the committees ended with a splash in the Fisheries Committee. The rapporteur for the case in that committee, Finnish liberal Carl Haglund, issued a very critical report,

---

68 WSRW.org, 19.10.2011, Development rapporteur urges Parliament to thumb down fish deal, http://wsrw.org/a204x2123.

69 WSRW.org, 19.10.2011, Development rapporteur urges Parliament to thumb down fish deal, http://wsrw.org/a204x2123.

70 Fishelsewhere.eu, 07.11.2011, Two EU Parliament committees reject EU-Morocco Fish Pact, http://www.fishelsewhere.eu/a141x1344.

diplomatically outlining the problematic aspects of the evaluation. The report was a draft recommendation written for the Plenary to vote on after being dealt with in the Fisheries Committee.

The "Haglund report" underlined the main conclusions from the evaluation: How the agreement had resulted in a large financial loss for the European Union and destroyed the ecology of Western Sahara's and Morocco's ocean waters. The recommendation also noted that there were questions as to the legality of the agreement, since it is being applied to the waters off Western Sahara, and that there is no information that clarifies whether the Saharawi people benefit from the agreement.

But the draft report did not slide through as in the other two committees.

The main reason is to be found in the composition of the Committee. It only has members of fishing nations, each member representing its own national fisheries interests. The debates in the Committee normally thus follows the logic of parliamentarians overbidding each other in offering themselves generous concessions on their own fishing grounds, while the parliamentarians of other nationalities would not object – since their own respective interests are up for debate later. That mechanism of horse-trading threatened fish stocks are in itself one of the main explanations of why the EU has managed to destroy its own marine environment. Just to make the EU-Morocco debate even more problematic: A disproportionate number of the members are Spaniards and French – the two states with the closest relations to Rabat. All this led to a near impossible job to get Haglund' fisheries report approved: In the vote in the Fisheries Committee, it was thus decided to amend its concluding sentence.

The very critical report that was in the end presented before the entire European Parliament therefore appeared to, mildly speaking, be a bad joke. To summarise a long argument in few sentences, it stated something like this, once the amendment was made: "Because it is damaging to the environment, because it is a waste of taxpayers' money, because of the controversy over Western Sahara, because it has no development effect, the EU fisheries agreement *therefore* has to be continued". It was passed with a small majority. 12 for, eight against, one abstained[71].

"That went well", stated a smiling Spanish parliamentarian to the content Moroccan delegation in the back of the room as the meeting closed. The final vote would take place in Plenary three weeks later, and the recommendation was to continue the fisheries *because* it was damaging to the environment, the EU economy and international law.

71 Recommendation from Fisheries Committee, 29.11.2011, http://www.europarl.europa.eu/sides/getDoc.do?type=REPORT&reference=A7-2011-0394&language=EN&mode=XML.

Historical decision

"No fishing activity from the European fleet will be tolerated and all boats operating in the area of the fisheries agreement are asked to leave national territorial waters on Wednesday before midnight," the Moroccan foreign ministry said in a statement 14 December 2011. The Moroccan government underlined, half threatening, it would also do a "global reassessment of its partnership with the EU"[72].

The final vote in Strasbourg few hours earlier had come as a shock to most observers. It took the fisheries industry and the Moroccan government by complete surprise. 326 had voted in favour of ending the EU-Morocco fisheries protocol. 296 had voted against, while 58 abstained[73]. When the vote showed up on the screens in the parliament, spontaneous applause broke out in the room. The fisheries would end. It was the second time in the history of the European Union that a trade agreement was stopped by the European Parliament, and the first time ever for a fisheries agreement[74].

The surprise was, after all, maybe not that it was voted down. The peculiar thing was that in fact 296 Members of the European Parliament voted for the agreement. They didn't need to explain why. Most did it under the influence of the French and Spanish colleagues of the socialist and conservative blocks in the parliament.

There was, in the end, a lot at stake as the parliamentarians were requested to lay down their vote. The pressure on the members of parliament to accept a continuation of the fisheries had come mainly from three different fronts.

One was the Moroccan government itself with its main allies within the European Parliament. The Moroccan embassy to the EU had a large delegation consisting of lobbyists, parliamentarians and ambassadors seen strolling around in the corridors of the parliament. Morocco also commissioned a German law firm to represent them, a law firm that repeatedly contacted the parliamentarians.

The Moroccan ambassador several times met with his friends in a newly established EU-Morocco Friendship Committee at the parliament. The

---

72 AFP, 14.12.2011, EU lawmakers block Morocco-Western Sahara fishing deal, http://www.google.com/hostednews/afp/article/ALeqM5iTu3b_bhxlu74vJBkHlaiGnaeiVQ?docId=CNG.d1c14754f585e752b4e73771c6fc1b86.c61.

73 European Parliament, Press release, 14.12.2011, MEPs reject extension of the EU-Morocco fisheries agreement and call for a better deal, http://www.europarl.europa.eu/news/en/pressroom/content/20111213IPR34070/html/Extension-of-EU-Morocco-fisheries-agreement-rejected-call-for-a-better-deal.

74 First time the Parliament stopped an agreement was the Swift Agreement with the USA in February 2010. The third time was the Anti-Counterfeiting Trade Agreement (ACTA) in February 2012.

committee, a small group of mostly southern European parliamentarians, gathered with the ambassador a few times prior to the fisheries vote, and the main agenda was to agree how they could influence the mood in the European Parliament. The final touch to their arguments were developed and prepared by the embassy to its allies in this committee only a few days before the vote.

Hard copy documents written by the Moroccan government were circulated to the pigeon holes of Parliamentarians the day before the vote. The leaflets basically claimed that the findings of the Evaluation were erroneous, that the "political aspects of Western Sahara are not relevant to the EP's decision on the agreement"[75], and that Western Sahara is anyway part Morocco's "Southern regions".

The night before the vote, the president of the friendship committee, French MEP Gilles Pargneaux, without any underlying data, argued against the evaluation report, mailing to all other parliamentarians that the agreement is "economically profitable and ecologically responsible. […] I appeal to your critical discernment to reject those amendments which clearly exploit the issue of Western Sahara for well understood political ends, thus jeopardizing any future agreement between the EU and Morocco"[76]. The same Pargneaux would later "salute" the US for no longer demanding human rights monitoring in the mandate of the UN operation in Western Sahara, after the American suggestion had been blocked by the French government[77]. The pro-Moroccan parliamentary group consistently labels the territory "Moroccan Sahara", and has, as opposed to other European parliamentarians, travelled unimpeded to the occupied territory with their Moroccan hosts.

The second active group lobbying the Parliament consisted of the Spanish and Moroccan fisheries sector, in partnership with Parliamentarians that represented them, mainly in the parliament's Fisheries Committee. "In the Arab Spring, at a moment in which Morocco has begun a democratisation process, it would be a very negative message from the EU to reject this agreement", vice-chairman of the Fisheries Committee wrote to all the parliamentarians the night before the vote, at a time when dozens of mails went back and forth between the defenders and opponents of the agreement on the European Parliament's internal mailing lists.

---

75 Fishelsewhere.eu, 10.05.2013, Moroccan lobby arguments before the EP, http://fishelsewhere.eu/a202x1417.

76 Fishelsewhere.eu, 10.05.2013, Arguments sent to European Parliament FOR the fisheries, http://fishelsewhere.eu/a202x1418.

77 Groupe d'amitié UE-Maroc, 26.04.2013, Réaction à la résolution 2099 des Nations Unies, http://groupedamitieuemaroc.wordpress.com/.

"If we reject the agreement, it will send a negative signal to the region, in a time when it is going through a process of democratic renewal. Morocco is an important partner of the European Union, our support for Morocco must go beyond simply making statements and declarations – of which we make many – we have to provide practical support", the vice-chairman wrote[78].

Thirdly, there was the Commission itself, that had invested a whole lot in this particular agreement, the EU's largest fisheries agreement. The fisheries commissioner, warned two days before the vote that the Parliament "will be judged" in the light of the EU-Moroccan overall relations. "The winds of change that have affected the Southern Mediterranean and some countries beyond have touched Morocco too. So what is the commission's assessment about it? The Commission's assessment is that in Morocco, the authorities have launched a significant reform with elaboration of a new constitution, increasing democratic accountability, and the respect for Human Rights. […] The EU at all levels have welcomed these changes. […] This framework we have to have in mind in front of our decisions", Damanaki said[79].

Yet, despite the calls from the supporters of the agreement, the European Parliament turned it down. While objecting to the extension, the parliament at the same time called for a new protocol between the EU and Morocco, in which the environmental and financial aspects as well as the "benefits" to the local population in Western Sahara, were taken into account.

Commissioner for Fisheries and Maritime Affairs of the EU, Maria Damanaki, stated that "the EC will fully respect the European Parliament's vote today. […] We do not know if a new fisheries protocol with Morocco is possible. We will explore all the possible ways forward," she said as the result was clear[80].

The leading members of the Fisheries Committee had always stated that the Saharawi people's rights – or 'politics', as they said – had nothing to do in Fisheries Committee. Yet, suddenly the very same people had very strong opinions on the political importance of the fisheries agreements. It seemed it was the only argument left: Morocco is important to the EU.

---

78 MEP Cadec in European Parliament, 12.12.2011, Commission defends EU-Morocco fisheries agreement, http://news.bbc.co.uk/democracylive/hi/europe/newsid_9656000/9656559.stm.

79 Commissioner Maria Damanaki, in European Parliament, 12.12.2011, Commission defends EU-Morocco fisheries agreement, http://news.bbc.co.uk/democracylive/hi/europe/newsid_9656000/9656559.stm.

80 Fis.net, 15.11.2011, EP rejects extension of fisheries agreement with Morocco, http://fis.com/fis/worldnews/worldnews.asp?monthyear=&day=15&id=48505&l=e&special=&ndb=1%20target=.

Alain Cadec, vice-president of the Parliament's Fisheries Committee was in shock over the vote. "It is a very negative signal we are giving to Morocco in a time of Arab Spring", he stated[81]. The French parliamentarian had already stressed the importance of the "Moroccan fisheries all over the Moroccan territory"[82].

French former Minister of Justice, of Moroccan origin, called the Parliament's rejection a "provocation" and said Morocco instead need to be supported for the "courageous reforms" that the Moroccan government has carried out[83].

The Spanish government stated its regret of the Parliament's decision and said that they "don't agree" with the Parliament – without going into details on why they didn't. Both ship-owners associations and fishermen associations regretted the decision[84].

"It is now urgent to find all possible means, through a specific and immediate action of the EU, to compensate the serious consequences of the agreement disruption that will hit many enterprises and workers of the fishing industry", stated the president of the European association of national fisheries organizations. The group criticized Damanaki for not better defending the agreement in the European Parliament[85].

The Spanish government followed the demand from the sector and urged compensation from the EU for lost fisheries opportunities. By January 2012, the Spanish compensation demand to Brussels was at 16 million Euros[86]. That equals 1.6 times the amount of money that the EU aid organisation ECHO proudly donates every year to the Saharawi refugees – owners of the fish that the Spanish fishermen wanted to catch.

81 Les Echos, 15.12.2011, Le Parlement européen rejette un accord de pêche avec le Maroc, http://www.lesechos.fr/investisseurs/actualites-boursieres/reuters_00408556-le-parlement-europeen-rejette-un-accord-de-peche-avec-le-maroc-263143.php.

82 Map.ma, 26.11.2011, "Il est du devoir du PE de soutenir notre partenaire dans cette période de démocratisation dans le Monde arabe", estime Alain Cadec, http://mobile.lematin.ma/content/1322300352144517500/MatinActualite.

83 Le Maroc Hebdomadaire, 17-23.05.2013, Rachida Dati critique le Parlement européen, http://www.fishelsewhere.eu/a142x1426.

84 RTVE, 14.12.2011, El Gobierno rechaza el veto a la prórroga con Marruecos, negativo para pescadores y armadores, http://www.rtve.es/noticias/20111214/gobierno-rechaza-veto-prorroga-marruecos-muy-negativo-para-pescadores-armadores/481953.shtml.

85 16.12.2011, Indignation of the EU fishing shipowners following the rejection of the present protocol EU/Morocco by the European Parliament, http://www.fishupdate.com/news/fullstory.php/aid/16770/UE_FISHERIES:_Indignation_of_the_EU_fishing_shipowners_following_the_rejection_of_the_present_protocol_EU_Morocco_by_the_European_Parliament_.html.

86 Arn Digital, 11.01.2012, El Gobierno rebaja las compensaciones para los pescadores afectados por la ruptura del acuerdo UE-Marruecos, http://arndigital.com/articulo.php?idarticulo=784.

Also the ambassador of the EU to Morocco regretted the decision. "I am sorry for our relations with Morocco," the diplomat said. "Against the opinion of the Member States of the European Commission and Mrs. Ashton, EU High Representative for Foreign Affairs and Security Policy, the European Parliament voted against the proposed extension of the Protocol of the EU-Morocco fisheries agreement," Landáburu was quoted in the Moroccan state media[87].

Tomato side-effect

The Parliament's refusal of the fisheries agreement, and the following tension with Rabat, had a peculiar consequence. For years the Commission and Morocco had discreetly been negotiating another bilateral agreement, regarding free trade of agriculture and fisheries products.

The deal, which was an extension of the important EU-Morocco Association agreement from 2000, had already gone through the Council, and was up for vote in the Parliament on 16 February 2012, only two months after the European Parliament had thumbed down the fish pact. The agreement meant the trade liberalisation of a wide range of agriculture and fisheries products between the Moroccan and EU markets[88]. No mention whatsoever was done to Western Sahara or to the Saharawis.

Through the agreement, the EU would risk to give trade preferences to products from Western Sahara. The problem was identical to the one of the fisheries. What right did Morocco have to strike deals on natural resources in Western Sahara without taking into account the wishes and interests of the Saharawis? Could Moroccan importers claim that a tomato is from Morocco if it in fact is from occupied Western Sahara?

The question would in principle be rather easy to answer: No European state recognizes Moroccan claims to the territory. Other non-EU

---

87 MAP, 14.12.2011, Head of EU Delegation In Morocco Regrets EP Vote Against Extension Of Fisheries Agreement, http://www.moroccotomorrow.org/head-of-eu-delegation-in-morocco-regrets-ep-vote-against-extension-of-fisheries-agreement/.

88 European Parliament, 13.07.2011, Opinion of the Committee on Agriculture and Rural Development (PE 456.662v02-00) on the draft Council decision on the conclusion of an Agreement in the form of an Exchange of Letters between the European Union and the Kingdom of Morocco concerning reciprocal liberalisation measures on agricultural products, processed agricultural products, fish and fishery products, the replacement of Protocols 1, 2 and 3 and their Annexes and amendments to the Euro-Mediterranean Agreement establishing an association between the European Communities and their Member States, of the one part, and the Kingdom of Morocco, of the other part (15975/2010–C7-0432/2010–2010/0248(NLE)), http://www.europarl.europa.eu/committees/en/agri/draft-opinions.html?linkedDocument=true&ufolderComCode=AGRI&ufolderLegId=7&ufolderId=03838&urefProcYear=&urefProcNum=&urefProcCode=#menuzone.

countries, such as Norway, Switzerland or the US have clearly stated that trade preferences cannot be granted to goods from Western Sahara under their respective Free Trade Agreements with Morocco. In a recent case, a Norwegian importer was in fact imposed a 1.2 million Euro fine by the Norwegian government for importing goods from Western Sahara. The importer had falsely declared the goods as of Moroccan origin under Norway's free trade agreement with Morocco, and had thus incorrectly received tariff reduction on imported goods[89].

The EU tends, however, to go in the opposite direction: The EU has already approved the Moroccan government institution that issues origins of certificates for goods. That body has in turn offices located inside the occupied territories. Would the EU not violate its duty of non-recognition through such practice?

The vague geographical definition stirred debates. As the Parliament's agriculture committee looked into the agreement, it asked the Commission to identify whether Western Sahara goods would be included in the agreement or not. The Commission, unable to give a clear answer, invited the Moroccan ambassador himself for a hearing with the committee behind closed doors. "Let's start with the basics: Define your borders", the ambassador was challenged by the parliamentarians. After some time, the angry ambassador was observed departing the meeting room, slamming the doors.

An intense lobby was carried out on part of the Commission and the pro-Moroccan parliamentarians to avoid the same thing to happen to the trade agreement as what happened to the fisheries. In fact, the Parliament's rejection of the fisheries agreement in December 2011 was used as an argument to not vote against the new trade agreement also. Enough political damage had been caused on the relation with Rabat, was the argument. Yet, the problem was exactly the same:

> The agreement was scheduled to directly benefit companies that export fish and agricultural products from Morocco. But many of these businesses operated from occupied Western Sahara. A report from Western Sahara Resource Watch identified eleven agricultural plantations in the region around the town of Dakhla, owned either by the Moroccan king personally, or by French or Moroccan agriculture companies[90]. Similarly, a range of fish processing companies in Western Sahara and South Morocco utilize fish caught or landed in Western Sahara. These two sectors together are an important part of Morocco's strategy to cement the occupation, by employing Moroccan settlers in Western Sahara.

---

89 WSRW, 27.12.2010, Producer in Morocco stops purchases from Western Sahara, http://www.wsrw.org/a159x1764.

90 WSRW.org, 18.06.2012, Report: EU consumers unwittingly supporters of occupation, http://www.wsrw.org/a214x2321.

As the agriculture agreement was up for vote, many raised questions over why the EU left it to Morocco to determine the borders of its national territory. Two of the three Parliamentary rapporteurs appointed to examine the proposed agreement – the rapporteur of the Committee on Agriculture and Rural Development, and the one on International Trade – both recommended that Parliament withhold its consent[91]. The legal dilemmas resulting from the possible inclusion of Western Sahara in the territorial scope of the new agreement were part of their concern[92].

On 16 February 2012, under intense pressure from the European Commission, the European Parliament consented to the new agreement; 369 MEPs voted in favour, 225 against and 31 abstained. Many parliamentarians were in fact under the impression that agri-industry doesn't exist in Western Sahara and that the geographical definition debate, thus, was irrelevant. While there was a lot of knowledge in the Parliament over the EU-Morocco fisheries agreement, controversies of the trade deal, however, went under the radar of most parliamentarians.

And it is not strange the debate never got as heated as on the fisheries. "So far there is practically no agricultural activity in Western Sahara", wrote the Commissioner for Neighbourhood Policy in a 'fact sheet' to the parliamentarians few weeks before the parliamentarians voted[93]. The fact that Morocco had plans for massive boom of the sector in the occupied territory was not mentioned. Nor that the agreement also covers fisheries products.

The European Commission welcomed the vote of the European Parliament on the agreement with Morocco.

---

[91] 12. European Parliament, 1.02.2012, A70023/2012 Recommendation on the draft Council decision on the conclusion of an Agreement in the form of an Exchange of Letters between the European Union and the Kingdom of Morocco concerning reciprocal liberalisation measures on agricultural products, processed agricultural products, fish and fishery products, the replacement of Protocols 1, 2 and 3 and their Annexes and amendments to the Euro-Mediterranean Agreement establishing an association between the European Communities and their Member States, of the one part, and the Kingdom of Morocco, of the other part (15975/2010–C7-0432/2010–2010/0248(NLE)).

[92] 12. European Parliament, 1 February 2012, A70023/2012 Recommendation on the draft Council decision on the conclusion of an Agreement in the form of an Exchange of Letters between the European Union and the Kingdom of Morocco concerning reciprocal liberalisation measures on agricultural products, processed agricultural products, fish and fishery products, the replacement of Protocols 1, 2 and 3 and their Annexes and amendments to the Euro-Mediterranean Agreement establishing an association between the European Communities and their Member States, of the one part, and the Kingdom of Morocco, of the other part (15975/2010–C7-0432/2010–2010/0248(NLE)).

[93] European Parliament, Parliamentary Question E-002451/2012 of 2 March 2012, http://www.europarl.europa.eu/sides/getDoc.do?type=WQ&reference=E-2012-002451&format=XML&language=EN.

"As I said in the Plenary debate, this is an important agreement, not only in economic terms, but also in political terms", Commission Vice President Catherine Ashton stated to the EU lawmakers[94].

"To the extent that exports of products from Western Sahara are de facto benefitting from the trade preferences, international law regards activities related to natural resources undertaken by an administering power in a non-self-governing territory as lawful as long as they are not undertaken in disregard of the needs, interests and benefits of the people of that territory. The de facto administration of Morocco in Western Sahara is under a legal obligation to comply with these principles", stated Catherine Ashton[95]. The fact that Morocco does not view itself as the administering power of Western Sahara, does not behave as such in the UN institutions, and that the UN does not view Morocco as such, seems not to be part of the EU's analysis. The EU also went, as on the fish, against the UN legal opinion from 2002. "The EU recognises the Moroccan commercial rights in Western Sahara", one Moroccan newspaper interpreted Ashton's statements[96].

Alain Cadec, the same parliamentarian that lamented the turn-down of the fisheries activities in Western Sahara because Morocco positively had approached the Arab Spring, said the new trade deal was important since Morocco goes through a series of economic reforms[97].

The Moroccan ambassador to the EU called it "a great relief". "It is evidence of MEPs' confidence in the development and reform process in Morocco," he told the press[98]. His superior had told that the outcome was thanks to the work of the diplomatic service and Moroccan MPs[99].

The EU-Moroccan relations were back on track.

The new trade agreement, in the end, entered into force on 1 October 2012. Since then, some states have raised concerns regarding the application of it. Both Sweden and the Netherlands have so far stated that goods coming from Western Sahara cannot be given preferential tariffs

94 Europa.eu, 17.02.2012, EU-Morocco: Agricultural agreement sign of credibility, http://europa.eu/rapid/press-release_IP-12-143_en.htm.

95 14.06.2011, High Representative/Vice-President Ashton on behalf of the Commission, http://www.europarl.europa.eu/sides/getAllAnswers.do?reference=E-2011-002315&language=SL.

96 Yabiladi.com, 31.05.2011, http://www.yabiladi.com/articles/details/5677/l-ue-reconnait-droits-commerciaux-maroc.html.

97 Maghrebia, 21.02.2012, Morocco, EU adopt agriculture pact, http://magharebia.com/en_GB/articles/awi/features/2012/02/21/feature-04.

98 Maghrebia, 21.02.2012, Morocco, EU adopt agriculture pact, http://magharebia.com/en_GB/articles/awi/features/2012/02/21/feature-04.

99 Maghrebia, 21.02.2012, Morocco, EU adopt agriculture pact, http://magharebia.com/en_GB/articles/awi/features/2012/02/21/feature-04.

to the EU under the agreement[100]. The Commission again chose to look away from the Saharawi people's rights. The EU is split yet again.

Four more years

Back to the fisheries – the story hasn't ended. To the contrary. Immediately after the fish agreement had been voted down, and the fleet the was pulled out, the debate on EU fisheries in Western Sahara started all over again, from the very beginning. By the time of the December 2011 landslide, the former Commissioner for Fisheries, Maltese Joe Borg, had already been replaced by a more critical voice: Greek Maria Damanaki. As politically active against the former dictatorship in Greece, Damanaki is a keen defender of human rights – an, until then, not too much mentioned combination of words pronounced in the EU fisheries meetings.

Her first suggestion, supported by several states, was altogether to exclude Western Sahara from the new agreement with Morocco, and that this should be mentioned in her negotiation mandate.[101]

"Excluding Western Sahara waters would make it impossible for Morocco to reach to an agreement", stressed the president of the Spanish fisheries confederation, CEPESCA. He stated that because Western Sahara has been included in the deals before, they must be so again[102].

Together with its Moroccan partners, CEPESCA has for years carried out lobbying in the EU institutions. In CEPESCA's view, the suggestion to exclude Western Sahara, would not be a "viable" option for Rabat. Instead, CEPESCA underlined, Morocco would rather have to assure benefits accrued to the region – the same demand that the EU raised half a decade earlier, but which Morocco never bothered to report on.

After intense pressure from Spain, the Commission's suggestion to exclude Western Sahara was dropped from the draft negotiation mandate. Instead, a new suggestion was that the draft text would state clearly that the fishing zones covered by the envisioned agreement will include those "off the waters of the Non-Self Governing Territory of Western Sahara, south of 27°40N". A second specific mention stated that the Commission expected Morocco to guarantee it will fulfill its obligations

---

[100] WSRW, 13.03.2013, Dutch government repeats: Western Sahara products are not from Morocco, www.wsrw.org/a105x2541.

[101] FIS.com, 17.12.2010, EC proposes new fishing agreement with Morocco to exclude Saharan waters, http://www.fis.com/fis/worldnews/worldnews.asp?l=e&country=0&special=&monthyear=&day=&id=39784&ndb=1&df=0.

[102] EuropaPress, 07.12.2011, Pescadores marroquíes y españoles piden a la UE nuevo acuerdo de pesca con mismas condiciones pero mejoras técnicas, http://www.europapress.es/internacional/noticia-ue-pescadores-marroquies-espanoles-piden-ue-nuevo-acuerdo-pesca-mismas-condiciones-mejoras-tecnicas-20111207205307.html.

under international law which result from the "de facto administration of Western Sahara". According to the Commission, Morocco should regularly report on the geographical distribution of the socio-economic impact stemming from the support given under the agreement.

These two references to Western Sahara, however, stirred debates at the Council level for weeks. Spain and France, backed up by the fishing nations of Portugal, Latvia and Lithuania, demanded that any specific mention of Western Sahara be removed from the text, in order not to upset the Moroccan counterpart. On the other hand, countries like Sweden, the Netherlands, the UK and Germany favoured a clear reference[103].

The territory of "Western Sahara" was, in other words, considered by several governments as too political to mention. But apolitical if omitted. Obviously, the only party to take into account upon assessing the political controversy of the EU fishing in Western Sahara is, for some actors, the occupying power Morocco. With that in mind, the previous explanations of the apolitical nature of the fisheries agreement are placed in a whole new perspective. The Commissioner stressed back in 2006 that it respected international law and would not prejudice the Western Sahara issue. "He also noted that the agreement made no direct reference to the Western Sahara", wrote *Financial Times*[104].

So the negotiation mandate had to be changed: One could indeed fish, but just without mentioning where. As the reference to Western Sahara was in the end forced out of the negotiating mandate due to the mostly the Spanish pressure, Commissioner Damanaki instead introduced a clause on human rights as a precondition for a new agreement. But even the insistence on a human rights paragraph furiated the Moroccans and remained the main hindrance to the further negotiations. Even critics of the plans of a new agreement in Western Sahara questioned the insistence on human rights: The European Parliament had repeatedly condemned the Moroccan human rights track record in Western Sahara, while the UN Secretary General expressed his deep concern. If Human Rights were a precondition, would the terms not then already be broken the very same day that the agreement were to be signed?

While the negotiations took place, the European Parliament repeatedly stressed that the Human Rights in Western Sahara were violated. In February 2013 it stated that it

103 Fishelsewhere.eu, 26.01.2012, EU Council still split over reference to Western Sahara, http://www.fishelsewhere.eu/a140x1367.

104 Financial Times, 14.06.2006, EU fishing deal set to proceed despite Sahara dispute, http://www.ft.com/cms/s/0/7d092668-e380-11da-a015-0000779e2340.html.

> "Expresses its concern at the continued violation of human rights in Western Sahara; calls for the protection of the fundamental rights of the people of Western Sahara, including freedom of association, freedom of expression and the right to demonstrate; demands the release of all Sahrawi political prisoners; welcomes the establishment of a Special Envoy for the Sahel and stresses the need for international monitoring of the human rights situation in Western Sahara; supports a fair and lasting settlement of the conflict on the basis of the right to self-determination of the Sahrawi people, in accordance with the relevant United Nations resolutions"[105].

Summer of 2013, while all EU institutions were on summer break, a new agreement was reached between the Commission and the Government of Morocco[106]. No human rights clause was introduced, the first time to happen in a European fisheries partnership agreement since 2010[107]. Instead, a vague reference to the human rights clause in Association Agreement was made as a compromise with the Moroccans.

In parallel during the negotiations, the two states in the EU to lobby most fiercely for the Commission to enter into the agreement, Spain and France, prevented permanent UN monitoring of human rights. The UN Secretary-General Ban Ki-Moon has repeatedly urged the Security Council to introduce a permanent mechanism for human rights monitoring, which the US government suggested to the Security Council. The suggestion was shot down by the two states. Thus, it is unlikely that the gravity of the Moroccan violations will ever be documented well enough to have hte deal blocked.

The parliament approved that new agreement on Human Rights day, 2013. The EU community had achieved a cheaper agreement, but the international law violation in the new agreement was just as massive as in the past. That was enough change to give the Spanish fishing fleet – and the Moroccan government – its majority in the parliament.

Later that same day a dozen Saharawis were injured by Moroccan security forces in occupied Western Sahara as they protested the EU signing an illegal deal for the plunder of their fish stocks[108].

---

[105] European Parliament, Motion for Resolution in the 22nd Section of the UN Human Rights Council, http://www.europarl.europa.eu/sides/getDoc.do?type=MOTION&reference=B7-2013-0055&language=EN.

[106] WSRW.org, 24.07.2013, New EU-Morocco Fisheries Protocol signed today, http://www.wsrw.org/a217x2631.

[107] WSRW.org, 01.10.2013, Commission failed Council and Parliament instructions on human rights, http://www.wsrw.org/a217x2667.

[108] Associated Press, 10.12.2013, Western Saharans protest EU-Moroccan fishing accord, http://bigstory.ap.org/article/western-saharans-protest-eu-morocco-fishing-accord.

Conclusion: History

The voting down of the EU fisheries on in Western Sahara 14 December 2011 was a historical vote. It was the second time in the history of the European Union that the Parliament used its powers to stop an agreement.

The EU's own institutions, as well as the independent reports it had commissioned, documented that the EU fisheries agreement in Western Sahara was damaging the ecology, financially catastrophic for the EU, hardly creating any jobs – and violating international law. As the mood went against the deal, its defenders had fiercely tried all strategies to support the continued fisheries. They misrepresented the EU reports, they claimed the reports were wrong, and, most importantly, they argued for the political importance of Morocco.

The EU is an ally of Morocco – therefore the EU fleet must fish in Western Sahara. That was the logic during these hectic last days before the final vote. The same forces who so intensively argued for the apolitical nature of the EU fisheries practices in Western Sahara had switched to the other extreme. They argued with geopolitics to defend fisheries.

A completely new development might shake things up when it comes to the vague EU trade deals with Morocco. In February 2013 it was known that Frente Polisario had taken legal steps. The European Court of Justice has registered a complaint from Polisario to look into the legality of the EU's trade agreement with Morocco on fisheries and agricultural products[109]. In 19 March 2014, Polisario was to bring the new fisheries protocol to ECJ too[110].

These were the first times that legal measures are taken to stop EU's participation in the plundering of the territory. If the court agrees with Polisario, it could affect not only the agriculture agreement, but also put a halt to other EU plans to enter into dubious deals with Morocco in the territory which obviously is not part of Morocco.

The fish stocks offshore Western Sahara do not belong to Morocco, nor to the EU. The resources of Western Sahara belong to its people, the Saharawi.

---

[109] Official Journal of the European Union, 23.02.2012, Action brought on 19 November 2012 – Front Polisario vs. Council, Case T-512/12, http://eur-lex.europa.eu/LexUriServ/LexUriServ.do?uri=OJ:C:2013:055:0014:0015:EN:PDF.

[110] WSRW.org, 22.06.2014, Polisario asks for annulment of EU-Morocco illegal fish pact, http://www.wsrw.org/a105x2923.

The Principle of Sovereignty of Natural Resources and its Consequences

Hans CORELL

Former Under-Secretary-General for Legal Affairs, and the Legal Counsel of the United Nations

Introduction

I am speaking in my personal capacity. I have retired from public service. I am a senior citizen and therefore I am free to speak my mind as I do now.

On the 8th of December 1962, I started working as a law clerk in a court in my country – 52 years ago. And when I look at you I realize that I was maybe the same age as you are now. So I hope that what I am going to say now – among you, you will listen carefully and maybe carry with you some of the advices that I am going to include in my presentation.

I am also speaking as a neutral. What I mean by that is something I was taught in the courts. Ten years I served in the courts before I came to the Ministry of Justice for 13 years. And then I served in the Foreign Office as Ambassador and Head of the Legal Department for 9 years. And then I came to the United Nations where I was the Chief Legal Officer in the organization for 10 years, 3 years with Boutros Boutros-Ghali, and 7 years with Kofi Annan.

Also, when I talk about neutrality, I am referring to the analysis that the then Secretary-General Dag Hammarskjold made of the role of an international civil servant. This is a quote from him: "If the international civil servant knows himself to be free from such personal influences in his actions and guided solely by the common aims and rules laid down for, and by the organization he serves and by recognized legal principles, then he has done his duty, and then he can face the criticism which, even so, will be unavoidable. As I said, at the final last, this is a question of integrity, and if integrity in the sense of respect for law and respect for truth were to drive him into positions of conflict with this or that interest, then that conflict is a sign of his neutrality and not of his failure to observe neutrality, then it is in line, not in conflict with his duties as an international civil servant."

This has been a lodestar for me in my in my work as the Legal Counsel of the Organization for 10 years.

I intend to address five elements here. But I refer also to the abstract that is circulated where there are three important links to documents. The first element is my legal opinion from 2002; second the fisheries agreement from 2006-2007 when I discovered that; then the new fisheries agreement, the third element; the fourth element is King Mohammed VI speech in early November this year; the last is the Kosmos' oil drilling ship that you saw in the picture. Those are the five elements that I intend to address.

The Legal Opinion of 2002

As far as my legal opinion is concerned, it was a question that I was asked to respond to by the Security Council. This is rather unusual – that the Security Council asks the Legal Counsel to give an opinion in such a very important matter. But so they did. The question was whether oil prospecting contracts, given to two companies, Kerr McGee and TotalFina Elf, were legal under international law. I will not go into detail of my legal opinion because it is better that you read it by yourselves. There is a link to the document which has an acronym, S/2002/161. It is a very short document containing 25 paragraphs.

Now, I was asked to deliver an opinion on whether these contracts were legal under international law. And, of course, I had to analyze the situation in Western Sahara. This was not an opinion given by the Legal Office; it was given by the Legal Counsel, myself, that is a person who gives the opinion. But surely you must understand that I worked with a team, I had some 180 people in my department, in six different departments, one of these by the way dealing with the law of the sea, which we are actually looking at here. And I had a very good team to assist me in preparing this opinion. And when the opinion was delivered, I concluded that – and there was a quote earlier made here and often they only quote parts of my legal opinion because it is very important to read the very last sentence in the legal opinion. What was said in the opinion was:

> "The foregoing legal principles established in the practice of States and the United Nations pertain to economic activities in Non-Self-Governing Territories, in general, and mineral resource exploitation, in particular. It must be recognized, however, that in the present case, the contracts for oil reconnaissance and evaluation do not entail exploitation or the physical removal of the mineral resources, and no benefits have as of yet accrued. The conclusion is, therefore, that, while the specific contracts which are the subject of the Security Council's request are not in themselves illegal, if further exploration and exploitation activities were to proceed in disregard of the interests and wishes of the people of Western Sahara, they would be in

violation of the principles of international law applicable to mineral resource activities in Non-Self-Governing Territories."

It is very important when you read the analysis in the legal opinion to understand that we had to look at the situation in Western Sahara, realizing that this was a Non-Self-Governing Territory. But as a matter of fact there was no administering authority. Under the UN Charter it is a "sacred trust" to be an administering authority. That duty rested with Spain. But Spain just gave that responsibility away. They tried to invest it in Morocco and Mauritania. They had no legal authority whatsoever to do that. So the agreement concluded by Spain with Morocco and Mauritania is simply not valid under the UN Charter with respect to the rights of Western Sahara. So, by relinquishing this "sacred trust", Spain actually caused the situation that we are now experiencing in Western Sahara. And, as you know, the United Nations has been involved for a long time here. I will come back to the Security Council's actions. But my presentation here is much much broader in a sense than Western Sahara because it reflects some of the problems that we are facing in the world today. You are the young generation. You are the ones who are going to take over after us. What is the situation we are leaving behind for you to take care of? Could we not have done better, I am asking myself?

The whole issue actually points to one very important actor here, namely the Security Council of the United Nations. This situation has been going on and on and on and on. I gave the legal opinion almost 13 years ago. So much has happened since then, and I have been looking at other things in the meantime since I retired from public service in 2004. But when I am now getting familiar with this situation again, I am really quite astounded that the situation is as it is. In a sense it is a charade! Something has to be done here. And all the actors here, in particular since we are discussing the European Union, the Union should know better how to deal with this situation. I will come back to this when I come to the fisheries agreements. But it is very important to understand that if you are to use the resources of a Non-Self-Governing Territory for the benefit of the people, this is the first condition: it has to be for the benefit of the people, and you have to be able to prove that. You have to consult with them or their representatives, whoever it is depending on the situation in the decolonization as it were. And then you have to also realize that it has to be done either on behalf of or in consultation with representatives of the people. What do I mean by "on behalf of" that I draw from the resolutions by the General Assembly over the years? This means that they must have come so far in the decolonization process that they have a representative body that can decide to hand over and ask an administering power to deal with this matter and to sell for their benefit resources from the territory. And this is not the case in this particular situation.

Now, so far, my legal opinion that has been quoted many times. But I was quite taken aback when I saw how the European Commission had construed it from the beginning. It was nothing of the sort that I said. The last sentence is what counts: it has to be for the benefit of and in accordance with the will of the people of Western Sahara.

The EU-Morocco Fisheries Agreement

When we come to the second element, the fisheries agreement, I was invited to Pretoria, because they wanted to discuss Western Sahara as an example of processes of decolonization. When I saw the fisheries agreement I didn't believe my eyes. What is this? I mean, they are talking about Moroccan fisheries areas, and when I look to the coordinates… – And might I add that during my tenure as the Legal Adviser of the Foreign Office in Stockholm, I was involved in negotiating three delimitation agreements in the Baltic Sea: the one with the Soviet Union; then the one with Poland; and the one with Finland. So I am very familiar with delimitation in marine areas. And in the UN, I had to oversee the Division for Ocean Affairs and the Law of the Sea. So, I have been dealing extensively with sea matters. And I can read charts. I am actually a sailor! I was for 12 months; during the time when I was a student, I signed on ships. I sailed for 12 months in four summers.

So when I looked at the charts and saw the coordinates, I realized that these coordinates are actually referring to the whole area until it comes to the borderline of Mauritania. But there is no mention in the agreement about the fact that Western Sahara is a Non-Self-Governing Territory and that Morocco does not have jurisdiction in the true sense over that area. Not a whisper. So when I was invited to address this in Pretoria, I noted some elements here that I might share with you, namely the way in which it was described in the protocol. Let me reiterate what I said in Pretoria:

> "The Protocol to the Agreement refers to 'Morocco's resources' (art 4). With respect to the financial contribution, the Protocol provides that, subject to its article 6, 'the Moroccan authorities shall have full discretion regarding the use to which this financial contribution is put'. The Protocol also mentions 'the Moroccan fishing industry' (art 8). The Annex mentions the 'Moroccan Atlantic zone', 'Moroccan seamen' and 'Moroccan ports'. In Appendix 4, the limits of Moroccan fishing zones are indicated. Apart from some small-scale fishing between 34° 18' N and 35° 48' N off the coast of Morocco, the rest is indicated by 'The entire Atlantic' (apart from a limited area) for tuna fishing, and 'South of 29° 00' for demersal fishing and industrial pelagic fishing. What does 'South of 29° 00'mean? A tiny area southwards to 27°-28° N where the waters of Western Sahara commence, or all the waters southwards to where the waters of Mauritania meet at about 21° N?"

It is so obvious that this agreement concerns Western Sahara's waters. And there is not a whisper in this agreement about the fact that it concerns Western Sahara.

The New Fisheries Agreement

Now I come to the third element, the new fisheries agreement. I looked very carefully at that and basically it is the same all over again. When I looked in particular at the annex, first of all the agreement refers to "the Moroccan fishing zones". No distinction is made with respect to Western Sahara. And when I come to appendix 4 where the coordinates are included, again I meet the same. There are six areas here indicated and four of them are indicated exactly in the way which I quoted a while ago. South of 30°40', south of 29°00', all of the Atlantic apart from an area delimited by an irrelevant area here and then 6: industrial pelagic fishing south of 29°00'.

Not a whisper whether it is only a small portion, a few kilometers south to where Western Sahara starts, or whether it is the entire coast down there. So, if I met an agreement like this in a court of law, my indication would be: is this something signed in bad faith? This is how a judge would look at something of this nature.

The Speech of King Mohammed VI

Now we have the fourth element here; the speech of the King. If you read my legal opinion, I have quoted the General Assembly extensively when they adopted resolutions on self-determination. And here you will find actually that the General Assembly is warning those who administer territories that are subject to decolonization of plundering the resources of the peoples in those regions.

Let me quote from the speech of the King. He starts by saying that, this is a speech "on the occasion of the 39th anniversary of the glorious Green March". The glorious Green March when civilians from Morocco were sort of transferred into the area of Western Sahara. Is this a way of describing a violation of the Fourth Geneva Convention? Article 49, sixth paragraph of the Fourth Geneva Convention reads: "The occupying power shall not deport or transfer parts of its own civilian population into the territory it occupies."

And then there are actually now in the Rome Statute provisions that say that this kind of behavior could amount to a war crime under modern law. I say this since I had the honour of being Secretary-General Kofi Annan's representative at the Rome Conference for the negotiation of the Statute of the International Criminal Court back in 1998. It is very important to have this distinction clear. You are not allowed to transfer your population into an area that is occupied in this way.

Now, the King goes on to talk about "our southern provinces", he called them "the southern provinces", he is talking about "the nation's territorial integrity". And towards the end the King says, and I quote:

> "Let me say this, to reaffirm Morocco's position on the matter: We say 'No' to the attempt to change the nature of this regional conflict and to present it as a decolonization issue. Morocco is in its Sahara and never was an occupying power or an administrative power. In fact, it exercises its sovereignty over its territory."

The question I ask myself is: is this statement basis enough to renounce the fisheries agreement? This is very, very serious.

The Agreement between Morocco and Kosmos

And now I come to the Kosmos issue. The Kosmos ship is steaming northwest to start drilling off the coast off Western Sahara to see if there are oil resources there. In this agreement I just note that the company says that they are acting in conformity with my legal opinion. They are not! It is obvious that this agreement is also in violation of the manner in which the resources of Western Sahara should be administered. I also note that the agreement refers to Western Sahara as the "Southern provinces of the Kingdom of Morocco". Already signing an agreement of this nature would in my view violate the principles of corporate social responsibility and the Ruggie principles of Protect, Respect and Remedy. To sign an agreement where Western Sahara is referred in this manner is simply not acceptable.

Conclusions

Now, what are the conclusions here – because I do not want to take up too much time here. There have been so many speeches in the morning. What I would do now is to refer you to the broader aspect, namely: who is ultimately responsible here? Certainly we all have responsibilities, and I must say that as a European, as I said in Pretoria, I feel ashamed that the European Union has concluded an agreement of this nature with Morocco.

I have friends in many countries, but I have no connections whatsoever to the POLISARIO or to Morocco here and this is why I mentioned my neutrality here. I am speaking as a lawyer and a former judge, and I am trying my best to analyze the situation here and find a way forward. And as a matter of fact when I now got familiarized again with the situation in Western Sahara I am contemplating taking steps in my capacity as a former Legal Counsel of the United Nations.

What it boils down to is really something that is extremely important. And this is recognized by the United Nations. On the 24th of September 2012 the General Assembly adopted a global resolution on the rule of law. This, in my view, is the only way ahead. If you ask me, looking in the rear mirror from my years in the courts, the Justice Ministry, the Foreign Office, and the United Nations and now ten years after I left the UN – and I have been working for example for six years for Kofi Annan in relation to Kenya when he was asked to deal with the situation there after the terrible violence after the election in 2007 – it has been an extremely important learning experience. And I can tell you, and in particular the students, that you never cease to be a student. Sometimes when I address students I start by saying "fellow students" because you learn all the time. And I have the privilege again of learning all the time. And when I look in the rear mirror now, and I look at the conflicts in the world, anywhere where there is a conflict, you ask yourself the question: why is there a conflict? The answer is the same: no democracy, no rule of law!

In 2008, I was asked to give advice to an organization called the InterAction Council of Former Heads of State and Government. At the meeting all of a sudden Helmut Schmidt, 90 years old at the time, asked the question: do politicians understand their responsibility for the rule of law? By the way, I connect here to what I have said about the argument: "But this is a political issue, etc., etc.!" Never ever accept this argument! Look at it! Yes there are political issues, but also in a political context the politicians have to bow to the law. And parliament has to bow to the laws it has enacted itself. An international organization has to bow to the charter governing it. This is so important.

So, when I heard Helmut Schmidt, 90 years, putting this question I said: why do we not elaborate a guide for politicians on the rule of law at the national level and at the international level. So we did. A university institution in Sweden, the Raoul Wallenberg Institute and the Hague Institute for the Internationalisation of Law have now provided politicians in the world with this guide. Please take these words down: *Rule of Law – A guide for politicians*, and you will find it immediately on the web. It is now translated into 17 languages, Arabic, Bahasa Indonesia, Chinese, and so forth, and it is also translated into Italian. So I would advise you to read this guide, not only politicians but also journalists and lawyers could find some guidance in this guide.

So this would be my message to you. And this is where I use Western Sahara as an example of a situation where the law has not been followed properly. And I am not only referring to the European Union, I am referring to that the Security Council should have acted with more determination than they have done here. And this is where I come back to what I said about the United Nations.

The Security Council is the organization's most powerful organ, and yet it is sometimes its weakest link. How come that we have permanent members of the Security Council violating the Charter when it suits their interest. The attack on Iraq by the UK and the U.S. back in 2003, the attack on Georgia; and now the latest events in Ukraine – all by permanent members of the Security Council violating the very law they are set to supervise.

This is why it is so important that in the present situation, reading the Secretary-General's latest report, the Security Council really have to bring their act together and deal with Western Sahara in a proper manner.

Finally, since you are students, so many here: I challenged the students at Uppsala University a year ago when Kofi Annan visited with Jan Eliasson and they had a dialogue and I was invited to comment on the dialogue. In so doing, I challenged the students and said to them: why don't you, the new generation, challenge the Security Council – that they do their job in the proper manner. They have taken up this challenge. So now they have started STOP THE ILLEGITIMATE VETOES CAMPAIGN. If you google http://stopillegitimatevetoes.org/, you will find the report where they have analyzed the 33 vetoes cast in the Security Council after the fall of the Berlin Wall – 33 vetoes cast: none by France, none by the UK, 14 by the U.S., 11 by Russia and 8 by China. In this analysis, with a couple of exceptions, they come to the conclusion that they are almost all illegitimate vetoes.

One example: why did China veto a very, very important resolution on Guatemala? Because Guatemala had invited Taiwan to a ceremony in their country! I mean: is this a legitimate veto? I mean: are we looking at serious actors – the most powerful states in the world acting in the Security Council, the most powerful organ of the United Nations?

We have to see to it that they actually perform. Now just speaking as a lawyer here: there is no other way than abiding by the law. That will be my message, taking Western Sahara as an example; things could have been done much better here. Let us hope that the Council brings its act together and deals with the question of Western Sahara in the manner that it should do.

Legal Aspects of the European Union's Approach towards Western Sahara

Ricardo Passos

Director in the European Parliament Legal Service[1]

This paper will only focus on the legal issues and will not enter into political considerations of any kind concerning the Western Sahara conflict.

Concerning the Western Sahara, the European Parliament has acted through two approaches:

- one more general and indeed more political, through resolutions concerning the situation in Western Sahara, notably relating to human rights issues. These resolutions are prepared and elaborated by political groups and voted eventually in the Plenary. Not even committees are involved,
- the second approach concerns international agreements concluded by the Union. And, here, four agreements have been voted by the Plenary concerning Morocco: three fisheries agreements and one concerning a modification of the Association Agreement relating to reciprocal liberalisation measures on agricultural products.

Before analysing the position of the European Union in these fisheries agreements, let me first describe how the Union has considered the position of the Western Sahara in the context of the exploitation and exploration of its natural resources. I will then consider the evolution of the Fisheries Partnership Agreement with Morocco since 2006, in particular concerning the defence of the wishes and interests of the people of Western Sahara.

---

1 The views expressed in this article are purely personal and do not necessarily reflect those of the European Parliament or its Legal Service.

The position of the European Union concerning the status of Western Sahara and the responsibilities of Morocco

Status of Western Sahara in International Law

The European Union has acknowledged two main elements concerning the Western Sahara:

- Western Sahara is a Non-Self-Governing Territory within the meaning of Article 73 of the United Nations Charter[2]; despite the position taken by Morocco in its legal order, the territory of Western Sahara cannot under international law be considered as forming part of the territory of Morocco.

According to international law and to the General Assembly Resolutions (in particular Resolutions 1514 and 1541) the possibilities for Non-Self-Governing Territories are the following:

- emergence of a sovereign independent state;
- free association with an independent state; or
- integration with an independent state.

In any case, the consultation of the people of the territory awaiting decolonization is foreseen by the United Nations. In its resolution 2229 (XXI), the General Assembly "invites the administering Power to determine at the earliest possible date, [...] the procedures for the holding of a referendum under United Nations auspices with a view to enabling the indigenous population of the territory to exercise freely its right to self-determination..." (paragraph 4 of this resolution).

- Morocco, exercising *de facto* control over the territory of Western Sahara, has assumed itself the responsibilities for the administration of that territory. Yet, Morocco has never acquired the status of *de jure* administering power over that territory and is not listed as such in the list of United Nations of countries administrating a Non-Self-Governing Territory, in accordance with Article 73 (e) of the United Nations Charter.

---

2 Concerning Article 73 of the UN Charter, see M. Bedjaoui, *La Charte des Nations Unies, commentaire article par article*, eds. J.P. Cot, A. Pellet & M. Forteau, Economics, 3rd edition, 2012, p. 1752; see also U. Fastenrath, *The Charter of the United Nations, A commentary*, 3rd edition, 2012, Vol. II, p. 1829.

The responsibilities of Morocco concerning the exploration and exploitation of natural resources in Western Sahara

Two different approaches are possible:

- an approach, defended by some, based on the idea that the Western Sahara people has the right recognised by the United Nations to its self-determination and that Morocco has violated this right through armed force invasion of the territory in December 1975. In those circumstances, Morocco has violated a peremptory norm of general international law (*jus cogens*). According to this approach, the exploitation of Western Sahara's natural resources by Morocco is as such a violation of *jus cogens* and therefore illegal[3].
- another approach is to acknowledge the status of Western Sahara as a Non-Self-Governing Territory and to consider that Morocco is *de facto* assuming responsibilities for the administration of this territory and shall respect the principles enshrined in Article 73 of the Charter of United Nations according to which the interests of the inhabitants of Western Sahara are "*paramount*". In resolutions 48/46 of 10 December 1992 and 49/40 of 9 December 1994 the United Nations General Assembly reiterated that:

> "Any administering power that deprives the colonial people of Non-Self-Governing Territories of the exercise of their legitimate rights over their natural resources […] violates the solemn obligations it has assumed under the Charter of the United Nations".

The question is however, whether a distinction should not be made in this context between economic activities that are detrimental to the people of these territories and those directed to benefit them. This is the latest approach of the United Nations General Assembly (Resolution 50/33 of 6 December 1995), which acknowledges "the value of foreign economic investment undertaken in collaboration with the people of the Non-Self Governing Territories and in accordance with their wishes in order to make a valid contribution of the socio-economic development of the Territories".

This latter approach is the basis of the reasoning of Ambassador Corell in his legal opinion of 29 January 2002 as Legal Counsel of the United Nations to the President of the Security Council on the legality in international law on actions taken by Morocco concerning Western

---

3 See L. Hannikainen, *the case of Western Sahara from the perspective of jus cogens*, in K. Arts, P. Pinto Leite (ed.), *International Law and the Question of Western Sahara*, Leiden, IPJET, 2007, p. 59-108. See also V. Chapaux, "Le Sahara Occidental, 35 ans après l'avis de la Cour internationale de justice", in *Revue Belge de droit international*, Vol. XLIII, 1, 2010, p. 9.

Sahara consisting in the signing of contracts with foreign companies for the exploration of mineral resources in Western Sahara[4].

In his legal opinion, Mr Corell stated that

> "where resource exploitation activities are conducted in Non-Self-Governing Territories for the benefit of the people of those territories, on their behalf or in consultation with their representatives, they are considered compatible with the Charter obligations of the administering Power and in conformity with the General Assembly resolutions and the principles of "permanent sovereignty over natural resources" enshrined therein".

Concerning the contracts for oil reconnaissance under scrutiny concluded by the Moroccan authorities, Mr Corell noted that they did not entail exploitation or the physical removal of the mineral resources. The contracts were not deemed as illegal. Yet, he noted that (and I quote): "while the specific contracts are not in themselves illegal, if further exploration and exploitation activities were to proceed in disregard of the interests and wishes of the people of Western Sahara, they would be in violation of the principles of international law applicable to mineral resource activities in Non-Self-Governing Territories"[5].

From these two approaches, the European Union has definitively opted for the latter, in particular concerning the Fisheries Partnership Agreement (hereafter, FPA) concluded with Morocco. The European Parliament, for its part, always referred to the specific status of the Western Sahara and to the United Nations efforts to find a peaceful solution. In its resolution of 25 November 2010 on the situation of Western Sahara, the European Parliament noted that "several reports have shown that natural resources are being exploited without any benefit to the local population" and called "on the EU to demand that the Kingdom of Morocco abide by international law regarding the exploitation of the natural resources of Western Sahara"[6].

On 12 September 2012, the European Parliament:

> "urged Morocco and Fronte Polisario to continue negotiations for a peaceful and long-lasting solution of the Western Sahara conflict and reiterates the right of the Saharawi people to self-determination, and their right to decide on

---

4 Letter of 29.01.2002 from the Legal Counsel to the President of the Security Council, S/2002/161.

5 Following the release of the Corell opinion, both Kerr-McGee and TOTAL S.A. eventually abandoned exploration activities in the region after receiving negative publicity. See New York City Bar, *Report on legal issues involved in the Western Sahara Dispute: use of natural resources*, Committee on United Nations, April 2011, p. 11.

6 P7_TA(2010)0443, para. 11.

the status of Western Sahara through a democratic referendum, in accordance with the United Nations resolutions"[7].

The difficulty is however to assert eventually if the FPA, and its successive Protocols, concluded by the European Union are negotiated, concluded and implemented by Morocco in accordance with the wishes and interests of the people of Western Sahara. This is very complex to determine, given the difficulty to consult the people on such a matter[8].

In this respect, it is well known that since 29 April 1991 the Security Council (Resolution 690 (1991) decided to establish the United Nations mission for the referendum in Western Sahara (MINURSO), in accordance with a Secretary-General report containing a Settlement Plan. This plan provided for a transitional period during which the Special Representative of the Secretary-General would have exclusive responsibility over all matters relating to a referendum in which the people of Western Sahara would choose between independence and integration with Morocco. The transitional period was to begin with the coming into effect on the cease fire and end with the proclamation of the results of the referendum.

The Settlement Plan was accepted by the parties (Morocco and Fronte Polisario), but they diverge in particular on the criteria for eligibility to vote. Notwithstanding the divergences, the parties say they are committed to the Plan, and MINURSO has carried out its functions since 1991 until now. The last Resolution of the Security Council was adopted on 28 April 2015 (resolution 2218(2015). This is the last of a long series of resolutions extending for another year the mandate of MINURSO (now until 30 April 2016). This Decision calls upon the parties to continue negotiations with a view to achieving a just political solution, which will provide for the self-determination of the people of Western Sahara consistent with the principles of the Charter of the United Nations; it also recognises that "consolidation of the status quo is not acceptable, and noting further that progress in the negotiations is essential in order to improve the quality of life of the people of Western Sahara in all its aspects"[9].

---

7 P7_TA(2012)0334, para. 89. Parliament reiterated this request in its resolution of 4 February 2013 on the 22nd Session of the UN Human Rights Council, P7_TA(2013)0055, para. 21.

8 See in this regard, Parliamentary Assembly of the Council of Europe, report by Mrs Liliane Maury Pasquier, Parliamentary contribution to resolving the Western Sahara conflict, 6 June 2014, Doc. 13526.

9 This decision was taken on the basis of the report of the Secretary-General on the situation of Western Sahara of 13 April 2015. In his report the Secretary-General noted that Morocco and Fronte Polisario continue to diverge significantly in their interpretation of the MINURSO mandate. Morocco considers the mandate to be limited to ceasefire and military matters. Fronte Polisario considers that the organization of a referendum for self-determination remains its central element (see report, para 39).

This Resolution has the merit to show that the conflict is still pending before the instances of the United Nations for a possible positive outcome, even if the negotiations do not seem to evolve for the time being. Yet, the fact that there is a framework for continuing the negotiations has been used by the European Union as an argument to defend its neutrality in the conflict. This argument has sometimes been put forward regarding the criticism existing in some Member States and in some political groups in the European Parliament concerning the conclusion of the FPA with Morocco.

The Fisheries Partnerships Agreement with Morocco: the question of the defence of the wishes and interest of the people of Western Sahara

The Agreement of 2006 and it first protocol: a certain ambiguity

Since 1983 the European Union concluded several fisheries agreements with Morocco (1983, 1988 and 1995). As far as the European Parliament is concerned, curiously enough, the question concerning Western Sahara was not raised. Only in 2006 the Committee on Development (which had to give an opinion to the responsible committee, the Fisheries Committee) asked the Legal Service if the proposed Council regulation concluding an agreement with Morocco[10] that would allow European Union vessels to fish in the waters of the Western Sahara was compatible with international law.

At that time, it was not clear whether indeed the European Union vessels were fishing in the waters of Western Sahara. According to Article 2 of the Agreement "for the purposes of this Agreement, the Annex and the Protocol the "Moroccan fishing zone" is defined as "waters falling within the sovereignty or jurisdiction of the Kingdom of Morocco".

Moreover, the fishing zones indicated in the Annex to the Agreement (Chapter III) mention for some types of fishery (small-scale fishing, demersal fishing, tuna fishing and industrial pelagic fishing) "South of 30°40'00" and "South of 29°0'00", without laying down the latitudes of the fishing zones in the South. The question was therefore whether South of 29°0'00" means actually the waters of Western Sahara, which commence at 27-28°, until the waters of Mauritania, which commence at 21°. Besides, no mention whatsoever was made about Western Sahara people or territory.

This affects the credibility of the mission vis-à-vis the parties. In his recommendations, the Secretary-General stated that "in the light of increased interests in natural resources of Western Sahara, it is timely to call upon all relevant actors to recognize the principle that the interests of the inhabitants of these territories are paramount, in accordance with Chapter XI, Article 73 of the Charter of the United Nations" (para. 80).

10 COM (2005) of 23.12.2005.

Given this legal incertitude, the advice given to the political authorities in the Parliament was to seek clarification from the Commission and Council about the scope of the agreement and how the Moroccan authorities intended to implement the agreement and how they foresaw the benefits that it brings to the Saharawi People. It was eventually mentioned that in case Morocco disregarded manifestly its obligations stemming from international law, the question could be raised by the Commission in the Joint Committee (Article 10 of the Agreement) and the European Union could eventually enter into bilateral consultations with a view to suspending the agreement in conformity with its Article 15.

The FPA was concluded by the Council on 22 May 2006. It entered into force on 28 February 2007 with a duration of 4 years. The FPA provides only the framework for fishing activities. Allocation of fishing capacities and the financial compensation is set up in a Protocol, which forms integral part of the FPA. Without the Protocol in force or provisionally applied or initialled, the EU fishing activities may not take place, even if the FPA itself is in force. The first Protocol was concluded for a non-renewable period of four years (28.02.2007 – 28.02.2011). On 28 August 2010 the FPA was automatically renewed for another 4 years (until 27 February 2015) as neither party notified its intention to withdraw from the FPA. There was no question of not concluding the agreement or eventually seeking its suspension after its entry into force.

It should be noted in this context that in 2006 the European Parliament was merely consulted by the Council before the latter concluded the agreement. Its political influence was thus limited.

This situation changed dramatically with the Treaty of Lisbon, which foresees not a simple consultation of the European Parliament, but its consent (Article 218, § 6 of Treaty on the Functioning of the European Union (hereafter TFEU)). This modification of the Treaty had important consequences concerning the FPA with Morocco.

In the meantime, during 2008 and 2009, Members of the European Parliament put precise and specific written questions to the Commission about the FPA with Morocco, namely concerning its territorial scope and whether the agreement benefits the Saharawi people. It became clear from the answers that the European Union vessels were actually fishing in the Western Sahara waters[11]. Concerning the interests and wishes of the Saharawi people, the Commission indicated that the agreement foresaw the development of the fisheries industry in the territory and also that Saharawi seamen were hired to work in the crews of the European Union vessels[12].

[11] Reply of 12 March 2009 to written question No.67 by J. Holmes (H-0079/09).

[12] Reply of 12 September 2008 by Ms Ferrero-Waldner to written question E-4425/2008.

Finally, the Commission noted that the "EU considers that the issue of the international status of Western Sahara is a complex question that should be solved in a bilateral and multilateral context in the framework of the United Nations and that it is for this reason that the FPA does not include any reference to the status of Western Sahara"[13].

In the light of this information, which was not available before, the Legal Service of the European Parliament was requested in July 2009 to provide advice to the Committee on Development. This committee questioned whether the implementation of the FPA of 2006 was in conformity with the principles of international law.

The Legal Service examined the implementation of the FPA, in particular the programming measures[14]. It noted in substance that, even if some actions target port towns situated in the territory of Western Sahara, such as Laayoune, Dakhla and Boujdour, it is not demonstrated that the EU financial contribution is used for the benefit of the people of Western Sahara. It would be also the role of the Joint Committee to ensure that the agreement is implemented in accordance with the obligations stemming from international law concerning the rights of the Saharawi people over their natural resources. In case of doubts, the Union could envisage the suspension of the agreement or refrain from allowing EU vessels to fish in the waters of Western Sahara by requesting fishing licences only for fishing zones situated in the waters of Morocco.

The rejection by the European Parliament of the second protocol in 2011

As mentioned before, from 1st December 2009, with the Treaty of Lisbon in force, Parliament had the right of consent, in conformity with Article 218, § 6 TFEU.

A Second Protocol, similar to the first Protocol, was signed on 13 July 2011 concerning a one-year extension of the initial Protocol (from 28 February 2011 until 28 February 2012). The decision on the signature foresaw the provisional application until 28 February 2012. In the period of 28 February 2011 – 13 July 2011, the EU fishing activities in Moroccan fishing zones were continued in accordance with Article 9 of Council Regulation (EC) No. 1006/2008 of 29 September 2008 concerning authorisation for fishing activities of Community fishing vessels outside Community waters. This was possible because the Second Protocol was initialled before the First Protocol has expired.

---

13 Reply to question n° 67 by Jens Holmes.

14 Annexed to the 3rd and 4th Joint Committee meetings held on 17 and 18 March 2008, on 1st and 3rd April 2009 respectively.

On 29 September 2011, the Parliament considered a request by the Fisheries Committee with a view to obtaining an opinion by the European Court of Justice on the compatibility of the envisaged Second Protocol with the Treaties, in particular concerning the question whether fishing in the Western Sahara waters was in conformity with the international law principles. The Parliament rejected this recommendation and decided not to request an opinion of the Court of Justice, in conformity with Article 218(11) TFEU (221 votes in favour, 302 against – mainly EPP and S&D – and 30 abstentions).

Subsequently, on 14 December 2011, the Parliament rejected the Second Protocol[15] and its provisional application was immediately terminated. The rejection was motivated mainly by economic, environmental and political reasons. The refusal of consent to the Second Protocol does not imply that the FPA will not continue in force but a new Protocol has to be adopted to enable fishing activities.

During the debates before the vote declining consent, many Members of Parliament, in particular the rapporteur of the Fisheries Committee, Carl HAGLUND, showed concern on the compatibility of the Protocol with international law. He stated in his report that the relevant documentation concerning the Protocol does not clarify the sensitive question whether it benefits directly the Saharawi people[16]. (The rapporteur was not followed by the Fisheries Committee, which recommended to the Parliament to give consent).

He wrote in his report:

> "After many requests from the Commission about benefits to the "local population", Morocco responded on 13 December 2010 with a PowerPoint document on the outcome of some investment programmes divided into 4 different regions – the "South" includes the Western Sahara as well as other territory. The document does not show whether the people of Western Sahara have benefitted socio-economically from the agreement. Although the document claims that jobs are created in all areas, it is highly likely that the agreement mainly benefits Moroccan settlers, transferred into occupied territory in violation of Article 49 of the IV Geneva Convention of 1949. Regrettably, the document does not support any EU conclusion on benefits for either the local population or for the Saharawi people. The document fails entirely to address the prerequisite whether the agreement has been concluded in accordance with the wishes of the people of Western Sahara"[17].

15 326 votes in favour, 296 against and 58 abstentions, P7_TA(2011)0569.

16 Report form the Fisheries Committee, PE 472.260, 04-00, p. 8.

17 Report from the Committee on Development, PE 472.260, 04-00, p. 11, 12.

Following this vote, Parliament adopted, on the same day (14 December 2011), a resolution on the future Protocol setting out the fishing opportunities and financial compensation provided for in the Fisheries Agreement with Morocco[18]. In this resolution, Parliament presented in a way its *"conditions"* for giving consent to a future Protocol.

Concerning the political and legal issues relating to the local populations in Western Sahara, the resolution – without mentioning this territory – considered that the Protocol "fully respects international law and benefits all the local population groups affected". In this context, it insisted on having effective oversight mechanisms to ensure that funds earmarked for development, and in particular for infrastructure improvements in the fisheries sector, are used properly.

The third protocol of December 2013: evaluation of its implementation

The substance

The Commission negotiated a Third Protocol claiming that it took into account the main three concerns expressed by the Parliament. It improved significantly the cost-benefit ratio, increasing the fishing opportunities and at the same time reducing the amount of the EU annual financial contribution, from 36.1 to 30 Mio EUR (16 Mio is linked with the access and 14 Mio for the development and implementation of the Moroccan fisheries policy)[19]. It also indicated that the fishing activities are depending on sound and scientific advice. Finally, concerning the delicate issue of Western Sahara, the new text requires Morocco to provide regular, detailed reports on the use of the financial contribution for the fisheries sector, including the economic and social benefits on a geographical basis, and providing for a mechanism for the possible suspension of the Protocol, including in the event of violations of human rights and democratic principles.

Article 1, second paragraph states that:

> "The Protocol is implemented in accordance with Article 1 of the Association Agreement on developing dialogue and cooperation and Article 2 of the same Agreement concerning the respect for democratic principles and fundamental human rights."

---

18 Resolution of 14 December 2011, P7_TA(2011)0573.

19 It should however be mentioned that 10 Mio EUR are moreover paid by the fishing licenses by the EU vessel owners.

According to Article 6, paragraph 5

"Morocco shall draw up a progress report on projects implemented with sectoral support as provided for by this Protocol, which shall be submitted to and examined by the Joint Committee."

Moreover, paragraph 6 mentions that:

"Depending on the nature of the projects and the duration of their implementation, Morocco shall submit a report to the Joint Committee on the implementation of projects that have been completed with sectoral support as provided for by this Protocol; the report shall include information on any social and economic consequences, particularly the impact on employment, investment and any other quantifiable repercussions of the measures taken, together with their geographical distribution."

Finally, paragraph 7 states that:

"Morocco shall also submit, prior to the expiry of this Protocol, a final report on the implementation of the sectoral support provided for by this Protocol, including the elements referred to in the paragraphs above."

The Third Protocol was initialled on 24 July 2013, followed by the Council Decision of 15 November 2013 on its signature. Taking on board the recommendation of the Parliament, no provisional application of the Protocol was foreseen before its final conclusion after the Parliament's consent.

On 10 December 2013, Parliament gave consent to the new text of the Third Protocol[20]. This time, three parliamentary committees (Fisheries, Development and Budgets) made the same proposal, even if within some political groups (in particular the Greens, GUE and ALDE) there was still a strong reluctance to accept the protocol. The Rapporteur, Carmen Fraga, considered that, even though there are some aspects that the fisheries sector hopes to modify in the Joint Committee established in the Agreement, the new protocol contains huge improvements and highlights the efforts made to respond to Parliament's concerns, in particular from an economic and financial point of view, and in terms of social and environmental sustainability.

In order to respond to the criticism made regarding a lack of sufficient control of the implementation of the agreement, including on the financial benefits to the local Saharawi population, the resolution entails the following paragraph:

20 310 in favour, 204 against and 4 abstentions, Resolution P7_TA(2013)0522 of 10 December 2013, and minutes of the sitting of that day, Annex 1, results of votes, item 4.

"Recalls the European Parliament's right to be kept punctually and fully informed about the application of the Protocol and its results, and therefore insists once again that representatives of the European Parliament should have the opportunity to attend meetings of the Joint Committee provided for in Article 10 of the Fisheries Agreement as observers. Further calls for Parliament to be provided with documentation on the guidelines, objectives and indicators concerning the chapter relating to support for the fisheries sector in Morocco, and all information necessary for the proper monitoring of the aspects included in Article 6 of the Protocol[21], including the final report that Morocco is to submit on the implementation of the sectoral support programme. Also reiterates its request to the Commission that it submit a full report on the results and operation of the current Protocol to the European Parliament, before opening negotiations on a new protocol"[22].

The Council adopted a decision on the conclusion of the Third Protocol on 16 December 2013[23] [24].

Evaluation of its implementation

The question remains whether the Protocol will be implemented in a way which could be considered as compatible with the principles of international law given the specific status of the Western Sahara in international law. This issue is not clearly dealt with neither in the FPA nor in this Third Protocol, which do not explicitly mention the waters of Western Sahara (some MEPs were rather in favour of excluding completely fishing in the Western Sahara waters). However, the Parliament has accepted that, even if this territory is not mentioned explicitly in

21 According to this provision, Morocco is required to provide regular and detailed reports on the use of the financial contribution for the fisheries sector development, including in respect of the economic and social benefits for the local population on a geographic basis.

22 Resolution P7_TA(2013)0522 of 10 December 2013, para. 2.

23 Council Decision on the conclusion, on behalf of the European Union, of the Protocol between the European Union and the Kingdom of Morocco setting out the fishing opportunities and financial contribution provided for in the Fisheries Partnership Agreement in force between the two parties, OJ L349 [21.12.2013], p. 1.

24 On 14 March 2014, the Front Polisario lodged an action before the General Court of the European Union against the Council seeking the annulment of Council Decision of 16 December 2013 (Case T-180/14 *Front Polisario v Council*). The Front Polisario contests the legality of the act. It alleges *inter alia* that the decision breaches the UNCLOS, in so far as it allows the entry into force of a protocol by which the EU and Morocco set fishing quotas for waters not under their sovereignty and authorise the EU vessels to exploit fisheries resources under the sole sovereignty of the Saharawi people. It claims also an infringement of Article 73 of the Charter of UN, because it was not consulted. The Commission intervened in support of the Council. This case is pending.

Article 6 of the Protocol, Morocco has to provide information to the Joint Committee on the impact of the financial contributions allocated for specific projects, taking into account also their geographical contribution. Moreover, it was advanced as an argument to accept the agreement that, in case the implementation of the Protocol raises difficulties, the latter can be suspended "if the dispute between the two parties is deemed to be serious and if the consultations held within the Joint Committee [...] have not resulted in an amicable settlement" (Article 8(2) of the Protocol). In this regard, the Parliament insisted, as mentioned before, on being fully informed about the application of the Protocol and its results, and that its representatives could attend the meetings of the Joint Committee. This is new and was put forward as a condition to accept the Protocol. Another condition was the obligation to implement the Protocol in accordance with the respect for democratic principles and fundamental human rights (Article 1, second paragraph of the Protocol).

The Third Protocol entered into force only on 15 July 2014, following the ratification by Morocco.

The fishing activities were launched in September 2014 after the licences were granted by the Moroccan authorities.

The Joint Committee (foreseen in Article 10 of the FPA) met on 4 and 5 September 2014. Several projects were adopted which concern the territory of Western Sahara, for example: building of a new market in Dakhla, building of housing for seamen in the port of Boujdour, building of places to stock material in Dakhla, Boujdour and Laayoune, construction of a laboratory in Dakhla or purchase of a ship for training in Boujdour. However, no specific indication is provided specifying in which way these programs directly benefit the population of Western Sahara. No reference at all to the Saharawi people is to be found in the documentation.

The European Parliament has not sent one of its Members as observer to this meeting, but was provided by the Commission with documentation on the guidance and indicators concerning the chapter relating to support for the fisheries sector in Morocco and the information necessary for the proper monitoring of the aspects, included in Article 6 of the Protocol, including the final report that Morocco is to submit on the implementation of the sectorial support programme.

It results from the foregoing that it remains an obligation for the EU institutions to abide by international law in determining how the Protocol is implemented, and in particular to what extent it benefits the Saharawi people. This has to be submitted by the Morocco authorities and monitored by the Joint Committee established in Article 10 of the FPA. The institutions may then assume their responsibility on the way the EU should implement the agreement in the light of the information provided. This is important not only as far as the current Third Protocol is concerned, but also concerning the evaluation that the EU has to make about the possible adoption of a new Protocol in 2018.

The 2013 Fisheries Protocol between the EU and Morocco
Fishing 'too South' Continues...

Enrico Milano

Associate Professor of International Law, University of Verona[1]

Background

On 10 December 2013 the European Parliament approved the Protocol between the European Union and the Kingdom of Morocco setting out the fishing opportunities and financial contribution provided for in the Fisheries Partnership Agreement between the European Union and the Kingdom of Morocco[2] (hereinafter "the Protocol") with 310 votes in favour, 204 against and 49 abstentions. The Protocol establishes the fishing opportunities and the economic counterpart already envisaged in the Fisheries Partnership Agreement (hereinafter "FPA") concluded between the EC and the Kingdom of Morocco in 2006[3]. The Protocol has entered into force in February 2014, upon ratification by the Parliament in Rabat. It extends for four more years the FPA, entered into force in February 2007 and provisionally extended from February to December 2011 on the basis of a protocol that was later rejected by the European Parliament. The current Protocol grants to EU fishing vessels access to Moroccan fishing areas, with a view to contributing to the development of the Moroccan fishing industry; the EU contributes 30 million Euros net per year (for a period of 4 years), plus 10 million Euros per year for fishing licenses to be released by Moroccan authorities.

1 The present chapter is an English translation and updated version of the article "Il nuovo Protocollo di pesca tra Unione europea e Marocco e i diritti del popolo sahrawi sulle risorse naturali", appeared in *Diritti umani e diritto internazionale*, No.2, Il Mulino, 2014, pp. 505-512.

2 OJ L 328 of 12 July 2013.

3 Council Regulation (EC) No 764/2006 of 22 May 2006, in *Official Journal of the European Union*, L 141 (2006), OJ L 144 of 29 May 2006.

As anticipated, a first protocol extending the FPA had been rejected by the Parliament in 2011 as it had been deemed too expensive for the EU, environmentally unsustainable, and not in compliance with the rights of the population of Western Sahara under international law. As to the latter concern, in the resolution stating the dismissal of the Protocol, the Parliament had called on the Commission "to ensure that the future Protocol fully respects international law and benefits all the local population groups affected"[4].

The rejection of the protocol in point was the direct consequence of the dispute concerning the territorial scope of application of the FPA, namely whether the latter extended to the waters off the coast of Western Sahara, hence prompting the question of its compatibility with international law. Already in May 2006, Sweden had voted against the approval by the Council of the FPA following the consideration that the agreement did not take "into full consideration that Western Sahara is not a part of the territory of Morocco under international law [...]"; and that "all concerned [were] not ensured to benefit from the implementation of this agreement in accordance with the will of the people of Western Sahara, as provided by international law". Similar concerns, regarding in particular the implementation of the FPA, had been put forward by Finland and the Netherlands in their statement of abstention[5]. The decision of the Council to eventually approve the 2006 FPA, and the positive opinion expressed by the Parliament, had been significantly influenced by the positive legal advices of the respective Legal Services. According to the Parliament's Legal Service, the agreement did not exclude, nor include, the waters of Western Sahara, and, in any case, it would be the duty of Morocco to comply with its international obligations *vis-à-vis* the people of Western Sahara; the Community could eventually enter into consultations with a view to suspending the agreement, should the implementation by Morocco have disregarded the interests of the local population[6].

In 2009, following numerous questions submitted by MEPs, the Commission "disclosed" the first data revealing that the fishing licenses issued by the Moroccan authorities, and distributed to the fishing operators through the Delegation of the European Commission in Rabat, extended also to fishing areas off Western Sahara's shores. After this revelation, the Committee on development of the EU Parliament asked

---

4 Doc. 2011/2949(RSP), para. 9.

5 The full text of the declarations can be found in E. Milano, *The New Fisheries Partnership Agreement between the European Community and Morocco*, "Anuario español de derecho internacional", vol. XXII, 2006, p. 413-428, footnote 61.

6 Legal Opinion of the Legal Service of the European Parliament, 20 February 2006, SJ-0085/06, para. 45.

the Parliament's Legal Service for a new legal opinion. In the document, issued on 13 July 2009, the Legal Service acknowledged the extension of the scope of application of the FPA to the waters of Western Sahara, and yet it denied that the declaration of the Sahrawi Arab Democratic Republic (SADR) establishing an exclusive economic zone could produce any legal consequence under international law, due to the lack of effectiveness of the SADR and given the status of the territory concerned as "non-self-governing" in accordance with Art. 73 of the UN Charter. However, the Legal Service maintained that there was no evidence that the EU financial contribution had been used for the benefit of the Sahrawi population. As the EU (back then European Community) is bound by the principle of permanent sovereignty over natural resources, the EU should have resorted to the implementation mechanisms envisaged by the EC-Morocco joint committee in order to ensure that the local population would actually take advantage from the European financial contribution. Had these conditions not been met, the EC should have refrained from requesting further fishing licenses in the waters of Western Sahara or should have suspended the FPA[7]. The legal opinion in point has certainly been decisive in inducing the Parliament to dismiss the provisional protocol in December 2011. Within the Council, Sweden, Denmark and the Netherlands decided to cast a negative vote against the Protocol, while United Kingdom, Cyprus, Austria and Finland abstained, because of the potential breaches of international law.

As far as the 2013 Protocol is concerned, the Commission has followed through the invitation of the Parliament to negotiate and draft a new protocol in full compliance with international law, in particular through the strengthening of implementation mechanisms concerning the European financial contribution outreach in regard to the development of fishing industry and of the coastal population in general[8]. For that purpose Art. 1 of the Protocol sets out a new provision: the Protocol shall be implemented in compliance with the democratic conditionality clause and with human rights, as provided for by Art. 2 of the Association Agreement between the EU and Morocco[9].

---

7 Legal Opinion of the Legal Service of the European Parliament, 13 July 2009, SJ 0269/09.

8 Opinion of the Committee for Development to the Committee on Fisheries on the proposal for a Council Decision on the conclusion of the Protocol between the European Union and the Kingdom of Morocco setting out the fishing opportunities and financial contribution provided for in the Fisheries Partnership Agreement in force between the two Parties, 5 November 2013, COM (2013)0648 – C7 – 2013/0315(NLE).

9 Euro-Mediterranean Agreement establishing an association between the European Communities and their Member States, of the one part, and the Kingdom of Morocco, of the other part, Art. 2, OJ L 70 of 18 March 2000.

These ameliorations, once again, have not been found fully persuasive by some States within the Council: Sweden and Denmark have voted against; Finland, the United Kingdom and the Netherlands abstained. The declaration of the Dutch representative is particularly meaningful in this regard: "The protocol does not explicitly refer to the Western Sahara, but allows for its application to maritime areas adjacent to the Western Sahara that are not under the sovereignty or jurisdiction of Morocco. Morocco, as the administering power of the Western Sahara, may not disregard the interests and wishes of the people of the Western Sahara, when applying the protocol to such maritime areas. The Netherlands notes that the protocol does not contain any provision ensuring that Moroccan authorities will use the amount paid for access to the resource in accordance with their obligations under international law owed to the people of Western Sahara. The Netherlands considers that, under international law, a proportionate share of this amount should benefit the people of the Western Sahara. Compliance with international law will therefore depend on the implementation of the protocol by Moroccan authorities". As to the position of Sweden, the representative has justified its negative vote as follows: "Sweden has been questioning whether the EU's fisheries partnership agreement with Morocco is compatible with international law for some time. Since Western Sahara is not part of Moroccan territory, international law requires that its fishery resources should be used for the benefit of the Sahrawi people in Western Sahara and in accordance with their interests and wishes. Sweden notes the efforts made by the Commission and by Morocco to guarantee a better allocation of the revenue from the agreement within the region. Despite some progress in the right direction, Sweden's view is that the changes made are insufficient to ensure that the obligations of international law are fulfilled in relation to the Sahrawi people in Western Sahara. This overall assessment is the reason why Sweden cannot support the protocol to the fisheries partnership agreement and will vote against all three proposal relating to the new protocol, i.e. the proposals on the signing and conclusion of the new protocol, and on the allocation of fishing opportunities"[10].

In the latest development, in proceedings initiated by POLISARIO, the General Court of the European Union has annulled the 2012 EU/Morocco on liberalisation of trade in agricultural and fish products, arguing that the agreement is applied to the territory of Western Sahara and it does not ensure that the economic and social benefits resulting therefrom are shared by the local population. While the 2012 agreement is distinct from the Protocol, the same contentious international legal issues have been considered by the General Court and, to that extent, the outcome of the

---

[10] Doc. 17194/13, ADD 1 LIMITE PECHE 590, 10 December 2013.

current appeal before the Court of Justice may turn decisive for the future of the Protocol.[11]

The legal regime of exploitation of natural resources in Non-Self-Governing Territories

We shall now assess whether the reluctance and opposition towards the FPA and related protocols are justified under international law, with particular regard for the latest Protocol. The starting point – as well as sticking point in the arguments variably employed by the Commission, by States and by MEPs in presenting their position in favour, or, alternatively, against the FPA and its protocols – is the 2002 legal opinion rendered by the UN Legal Counsel concerning the exploitation of natural resources in non-self governing territories, in particular in Western Sahara. The legal advice was issued upon request by the UN Security Council on the matter of the legality of the actions taken by the Moroccan authorities consisting in the offering and signing of contracts with foreign companies for the exploration of mineral resources in the seabed off the coast of Western Sahara. The UN Legal Counsel pointed to the significant evolution of international law on the matter, exemplified by a series of General Assembly (GA) resolutions, highlighting the shift from a general prohibition of exploitation of natural resources in non-self-governing territories towards a regime where international law only prohibits "those economic activities which are not undertaken in accordance with the interests and wishes of the people of the territory and deprive them of their legitimate rights over their natural resources" (emphasis added)[12]. Since 2002, the GA has adopted a series of resolutions on the regime regulating of economic activities in non-self governing territories that corroborate the conclusions drawn by the UN Legal Office in 2002. Lately, in the resolution adopted on 5 December 2014, the GA has re-affirmed "the value of foreign economic investment *undertaken* in collaboration with the peoples of the Non-Self-Governing Territories and in accordance with their wishes in order to make a valid contribution to the socioeconomic development of the Territories, especially during times of economic and financial crisis" and "its concern about any activities aimed at the

11 Judgment of the General Court of the European Union (Eighth Chamber) of 10 December 2015 (Case T-512/12), in which the Court has annulled Council Decision 2012/297/EU of 8 March 2012 approving the Agreement in the form of an Exchange of Letters between the European Union and the Kingdom of Morocco concerning reciprocal liberalisation measures on agricultural products, processed agricultural products, fish and fishery products.

12 Letter dated 29 January 2002 from the Under-Secretary-General for Legal Affairs, the Legal Counsel, addressed to the President of the Security Council, UN doc. S/2002/161, para. 19.

exploitation of the natural resources that are the heritage of the peoples of the Non-Self-Governing Territories [...] to the detriment of their interests, and in such a way as to deprive them of their right to dispose of those resources" (emphasis added)[13].

From a joint reading of the FPA and of the 2013 Protocol it is strikingly evident the absence of any reference to Western Sahara and to its population. If this absence was the result of the Parties' intention, in particular of the EU, to exclude the waters of Western Sahara from the scope of application of the agreements, one would be reassured. Yet, after the Commission has revealed the practice of the first four years of application of the agreements, a wholly different picture has emerged. In fact, the inclusion of the waters of Western Sahara has been made possible by the provision of Art. 2, lett. a) of the FPA, according to which the "Moroccan fishing area" is delimited by the "waters falling within the sovereignty or the jurisdiction of the Kingdom of Morocco". The 2013 Protocol, as well as the former protocols, identifies the southern limit of the fishing area with the zone situated below the 29th parallel, that cuts across the Moroccan coast, close to the borders between Morocco and Western Sahara. Thus the relevant provisions are ambiguous for the purpose of determining the exact territorial scope of application of the agreements; it is necessary to rely on the subsequent practice of the parties, in accordance with Art. 31, par. 3, lett. b) of the Vienna Convention on the Law of Treaties. The relevant practice has clearly extended the licences to the whole sea area within the *de facto* jurisdiction of Moroccan authorities, including Western Sahara. Exactly on the basis of the implementing practice, the General Court has annulled the 2012 EU/Morocco agreement on the liberalisation of trade in agricultural and fish products as far as Western Sahara is concerned: according to the General Court, in order to interpret a treaty, the general context has to be considered and, in that respect, the practice of the parties was clearly inclusive of the territory of Western Sahara.[14] Finally, one may also note that the EU has paid, and keeps paying, a financial contribution to fish in international waters, considering that Morocco has never delimited an exclusive economic zone over the waters off the coast of Western Sahara.

Leaving aside the question of the applicability of the law of occupation to the exploitation of natural resources in Western Sahara[15], it can certainly

---

13 GA Res. 69/98, paras. 2 and 4.

14 The Court employes context, rather than subsequent practice, as interpretative tool, but the end result is identical. See Judgment of the General Court of the European Union, 10 December 2015, cit. paras. 89-104.

15 On this question see C. Ruiz Miguel, *El acuerdo de pesca UE-Marruecos o el intento español de considerar a Marruecos como "Potencia administradora" del Sahara occidental*, in "Anuario español de derecho internacional", Vol. XXII, 2006, p. 395.

be maintained that, *de minimis*, Morocco is bound by the obligations provided for in Art. 73 of the UN Charter and binding for administering powers of non-self-administering territories. This is supported by the legal opinion of the UN Legal Office. If that is the case, we cannot but notice a first interpretive and argumentative twist by EU institutions and by Member States, in that they emphasize the element of the "benefits" for the population of Western Sahara, totally neglecting the need to hold consultations with the legitimate representatives of Sahrawi people, stemming from the obligation to ensure that economic activities are "in accordance with their wishes". The Legal Service of the Parliament, in the latest legal advice rendered to the Committee on Fisheries in November 2013, has underlined the obligation under international law that the FPA and related protocols are implemented in a way that will bring about *benefits* for the Sahrawi population[16]. In the joint declaration of vote issued by Austria, Germany and Ireland, the three countries have asked the Commission to inform the Council on the income resulting for the population of Western Sahara from the application of the agreement and to ensure that an appropriate quota is dedicated to that effect in line with the interests of the local population[17]. During the debate in the parliament regarding the vote on the Protocol, the Commissioner on fisheries, Maria Damanaki, has stated the following:

> "I would like to make one point very clear: no legal authority until now – including the United Nations, the European Court of Justice or the Legal Services of any of the EU institutions (Commission, Council and Parliament) – has ever said that an agreement with Morocco covering Western Sahara is illegal. Nobody. What they do say – and rightly so – is that such an agreement must fulfil certain conditions; in particular, referring to the fisheries agreement, that fishing activities must benefit the local population" (emphasis added)[18].

Irrelevant, at least for European institutions, has become the opposition to the agreement and to the protocols expressed by the legitimate representatives of the SADR and of the Frente Polisario. This has clearly emerged also form the UN Secretary General (SG) report of 10 April 2014, concerning the situation in Western Sahara. The document states that "Moroccan and international investments in the part of the Territory under Moroccan control, as well as in the territorial waters adjacent to Western Sahara, were the subject of contention between Morocco and the Frente Polisario, given the longstanding status of Western Sahara as a Non-Self-Governing Territory. A new Protocol of the Fisheries Partnership

16 Legal Opinion of the Legal Service of the European Parliament, 3 November 2013, SJ 0665-13.

17 Doc. 17194/13, *supra* n. 8.

18 European Parliament, Debates, CRE 09/12/2013 – 20.

Agreement between the European Union and the Kingdom of Morocco was signed in the final quarter of 2013 and came into effect in February 2014, following ratification by Morocco. The Secretary-General of the Frente Polisario wrote to me repeatedly to condemn Morocco's exploitation of the Territory's resources and publicly announced his intention to consider a possible judicial appeal against the Agreement" (emphasis added)[19]. Moreover, the SG mentions information received from Frente Polisario about the extension of the contracts between Morocco and foreign oil companies to explore the continental shelf of Western Sahara, recalling the 2002 legal opinion and hence quoting the passage regarding the need to respect the interests and wishes of the people[20].

The selective reading of the 2002 legal opinion given by the European institutions has been confirmed by a sort of authoritative and authentic interpretation given by the former Under-Secretary-General for Legal Affairs, Hans Corell. In a public speech in 2008, Corell has criticised the misuse of the opinion by the Commission to justify the legality of the agreement under international law. Corell has declared: "I find it incomprehensible that the Commission could find any such support in the legal opinion, unless, of course, it had established that the people of Western Sahara had been consulted, had accepted the agreement, and the manner in which the profits from the activity were to benefit them. However, an examination of the agreement leads to a different conclusion"[21]. Corell has also underlined the need to hold consultations and to find an agreement with the representatives of the population. It thus seems that the current Protocol, despite the reference to the clause of humanitarian and democratic conditionality and notwithstanding the strengthening of the monitoring mechanisms over the use of natural resources by Morocco, is not in compliance with international law, namely with the right of the Sahrawi population to decide on the use of and to benefit from their own natural resources. The Sahrawi legitimate representatives have been excluded from negotiations and from the functioning of the implementation mechanisms. This constitutes a breach of their right granted under international law, irrespective of any eventual and effective benefit that may derive from the implementation of the agreement for the Saharawi population living along the coast (besides, such a benefit has never been proved in the four years of implementation from 2007 to 2011). Eventually, it must be noted that the rights over

---

19 UN doc. S/2014/258, para. 11.

20 *Ibid.*, para. 12.

21 H. Corell, *The Legality of Exploring and Exploiting Natural Resources in Western Sahara*, Conference on Multilateralism and International Law with Western Sahara as a Case Study, Pretoria, 5 December 2008, available at www.havc.se/res/SelectedMaterial/20081205pretoriawesternsahara1.pdf, at p. 242.

natural resources derive from *erga omnes* norms and, as such, they bind the EU as a subject of international law that takes advantages from the agreement and that actively participates in the procedure to issue fishing licenses through the Commission Delegation in Rabat.[22] Accordingly, one cannot endorse the emphasis put by the EU Legal Service, and by the European institutions too, on the obligation incumbent on the Moroccan authorities to grant the rights of the Sahrawi population following a proportionate distribution of EU financial resources. The EU has an own duty to exploit natural resources, through its fishing vessels on the basis of the FPA and of the Protocol, in a way consistent with the right of the Sahrawi people: for example by consulting their representatives in the procedures to issue fishing licenses on Western Sahara waters, and by promoting the employment of Sahrawi inhabitants in the fishing activities of EU vessels. It is exactly to these international obligations towards the people of Western Sahara that the General Court has pointed in its recent judgment of 12 December 2015 concerning the EU/Morocco liberalization agreement.[23]

The obligations of non-recognition

A further critical aspect of compatibility of the Protocol with international law lies with the tentative violation of the obligation of non-recognition by the EU. In other words, the conclusion of the Protocol and the renewal of the FPA would imply the acknowledgement of the legality of the Moroccan annexation and administration of Western Sahara. Corell himself, in its comments to the conclusion of the FPA, had concluded: "As a European, I feel embarrassed. Surely, one would expect Europe and the European Commission – most of all – to set an example by applying the highest possible international legal standards in matters of this nature. Under all circumstances, I would have thought

22 Annex to the Protocol, Conditions Governing Fishing Activities by EU Vessels in the Moroccan Fishing Zone, point A, para. 4.

23 As far as the EU responsibility as "third party" is concerned, it is worth quoting the following passage of the Court's judgment: "Given the fact, *inter alia*, that the sovereignty of the Kingdom of Morocco over Western Sahara is not recognised by the European Union or its Member States, or more generally by the UN, and the absence of any international mandate capable of justifying Moroccan presence on that territory, the Council, in the examination of all the relevant facts of the present case, with a view to exercising its wide discretion as to whether or not to conclude an agreement with the Kingdom of Morocco which may also apply to Western Sahara, should have satisfied itself that there was no evidence of an exploitation of the natural resources of the territory of Western Sahara under Moroccan control likely to be to the detriment of its inhabitants and to infringe their fundamental rights. The Council cannot merely conclude that it is for the Kingdom of Morocco to ensure that no exploitation of that nature takes place." (Judgment of the General Court, 10 December 2015, cit., para. 241).

that it was obvious that an agreement of this kind that does not make a distinction between the waters adjacent to Western Sahara, and the waters adjacent to the territory of Morocco, would violate international law" (emphasis added)[24]. Corell's nipping comment clearly underlines that the conclusion of an international agreement regarding a NSGT should specify the "differentiated regime" of that territory: differently, the parties would seem to implicitly recognise the Moroccan authority over Western Sahara. The alternative should be represented by the explicit exclusion through a dedicated clause or by an interpretative declaration (as the US and Norway have done with regard to the implementation of the respective free trade agreements with the Kingdom of Morocco), or by an implicit exclusion resulting from practice.

That the EU's conduct may constitute a violation of the obligations of non-recognition enshrined in Arts. 40 and 41 of the ILC Draft Articles on the Responsibility of States (DARS) and in Arts. 41 and 42 of the Draft Articles on the Responsibility of International Organizations (DARIO) is confirmed by the letter of the commentary to Art. 41 of the DARS. In fact, the commentary specifies that the duty not to recognize as lawful a situation created by serious breaches of peremptory norms of general international law "applies to 'situations' [...] such as, for example, attempted acquisition of sovereignty over territory through denial of self-determination. It not only refers to the formal recognition of these situations, but also prohibits acts which would imply such recognition" (emphasis added)[25]. Moreover, in the *Namibia* advisory opinion, the ICJ covered the issue of the explicit and implicit recognition of the South African authority over a not-yet-decolonised territory, namely Namibia. The Court specified the extent of the obligation of non-recognition, stating that third parties shall abstain from entering into treaty relations with the State responsible for the violation in all cases in which the government purports to act on behalf of or concerning the annexed or occupied territory[26]. The commentary to Art. 42 DARIO further specifies that "[...] these obligations were considered to apply to international organizations when a breach was allegedly committed by a State"[27].

---

24 H. Corell, *The Legality of Exploring and Exploiting Natural Resources in Western Sahara*, cit., p. 243.

25 International Law Commission, *Draft articles on the responsibility of States, with commentaries,* 2001, UN Doc. A/56/10.

26 International Court of Justice, *Legal Consequences for States of the Continued Presence of South-Africa in Namibia (South-West Africa) notwithstanding Security Council Resolution 276 (1970),* Advisory Opinion, I.C.J. Reports 1971, 16.

27 International Law Commission, Draft articles on the responsibility of international organizations, with commentaries, 2011, UN Doc. A/66/10.

Concluding remarks

Whilst reasonable doubts may be raised over the conformity of customary practice related to NSGTs with the above rule of conduct, it is equally clear that in an age in which general international law is moving away from its traditional customary conception to increasingly appear as an "argumentative space", one remains with the impression that the spaces in which the EU is making its legal cases are extremely narrow. We believe that an international organization should not operate in such narrow spaces, especially when its mission is to "contribute to peace, security, the sustainable development of the Earth, solidarity and mutual respect among peoples, free and fair trade, eradication of poverty and the protection of human rights, in particular the rights of the child, as well as to the strict observance and the development of international law, including respect for the principles of the United Nations Charter"[28]. Our hope is that the EU will implement the Protocol consistently with its mission and its founding principles, thus abstaining from seeking fishing licences in the waters of Western Sahara. The recent judgment of the General Court on the agreement on liberalisation of trade indeed marks an important judicial development, with potential implications also for the future of the Protocol.

28 Treaty on European Union, 2012/C 326/01, Art. 2, para. 5.

Appendix

Documents

United Nations

1. Committee on Economic, Social and Cultural Rights, 22 October 2015, Concluding Observations on the Fourth Periodic Report of Morocco, E/C.12/MAR/CO/4.

UNITED NATIONS **E/C.12/MAR/CO/4***
ECONOMIC AND SOCIAL COUNCIL

Distr.: General
22 October 2015
Original: French

Committee on Economic, Social and Cultural Rights

Concluding observations on the fourth periodic report of Morocco

1. The Committee on Economic, Social and Cultural Rights considered the fourth periodic report of Morocco on the implementation of the International Covenant on Economic, Social and Cultural Rights (E/C.12/MAR/4) ...*omissis*...

C. Principal subjects of concern and recommendations

Self-determination and natural resources

5. While taking note of the Moroccan Extended Autonomy Initiative, the Committee reiterates its concern about the failure to find a solution to the issue of the right to self-determination of the Non-Self-Governing Territory of Western Sahara. Likewise, the Committee remains concerned about the precarious situation, upon their return, of the Sahraouis refugees displaced by the conflict in Western Sahara, particularly women and children. It is also concerned that the Sahraouis' right to participate in the use and exploitation of natural resources is still not respected (arts. 1 and 25).

6. The Committee recommends that the State party:

(a) Strengthen its efforts, under the auspices of the United Nations, to find a solution to the issue of the right to self-determination for Western

Sahara, as established in article 1 of the Covenant, which recognizes the right of all peoples to freely determine their political status and freely pursue their economic, social and cultural development. The Committee recalls that States parties to the Covenant are obligated to promote the realization of the right of self-determination in Non-Self-Governing Territories and to respect that right, in conformity with the provisions of the Charter of the United Nations;

(b) Take measures to ensure that the rights of Sahraouis refugees are respected upon their return. It further recommends that the State party guarantee respect for the principle of the prior, free and informed consent of the Sahraouis, and thus that they are able to exercise their right to enjoy and utilize fully and freely their natural wealth and resources.

The Berm

7. While acknowledging the security concerns invoked by the State party, the Committee is deeply concerned that the Berm, which is fortified by anti-personnel mines and was built by the State party to separate the Moroccan-controlled part of Western Sahara from the rest of the territory, is preventing the Sahraouis from fully enjoying their rights under the Covenant.

8. The Committee recommends that the State party take appropriate steps to enable the Sahraouis to access their land and natural resources and rejoin their families. It also urges the State party to expedite its mine clearance programme along the Berm. The Committee asks the State party to provide, in its next periodic report, detailed information on the enjoyment, by the Sahraouis, of all the rights set out in the Covenant.

...omissis...

2. UN Security Council, Under-Secretary-General for Legal Affairs, Legal Counsel, Letter dated 29 January 2002 addressed to the President of the Security Council, New York, 12 February 2002, S/2002/161.

UNITED NATIONS **S/2002/161**
SECURITY COUNCIL

Distr.: General
12 February 2002

Original: English

Letter dated 29 January 2002 from the Under-Secretary-General for Legal Affairs, the Legal Counsel, addressed to the President of the Security Council

1. In a letter addressed to me on 13 November 2001, the President of the Security Council requested, on behalf of the members of the Council, my opinion on "the legality in the context of international law, including relevant resolutions of the Security Council and the General Assembly of the United Nations, and agreements concerning Western Sahara of actions allegedly taken by the Moroccan authorities consisting in the offering and signing of contracts with foreign companies for the exploration of mineral resources in Western Sahara".

2. At my request, the Government of Morocco provided information with respect to two contracts, concluded in October 2001, for oil-reconnaissance and evaluation activities in areas offshore Western Sahara, one between the Moroccan Office National de Recherches et d'Exploitations Petrolières (ONAREP) and the United States oil company Kerr McGee du Maroc Ltd., and the other between ONAREP and the French oil company TotalFinaElf E&P Maroc. Concluded for an initial period of 12 months, both contracts contain standard options for the relinquishment of the rights under the contract or its continuation, including an option for future oil contracts in the respective areas or parts thereof.

3. The question of the legality of the contracts concluded by Morocco offshore Western Sahara requires an analysis of the status of the Territory of Western Sahara, and the status of Morocco in relation to the Territory. As will be seen, it also requires an analysis of the principles of international law governing mineral resource activities in Non-Self-Governing Territories.

4. The law applicable to the determination of these questions is contained in the Charter of the United Nations, in General Assembly resolutions pertaining to decolonization, in general, and economic activities in Non-Self-Governing Territories, in particular, and in agreements concerning the status of Western Sahara. The analysis of the applicable law must also reflect the changes and developments which have occurred as international law has been progressively codified and developed, as well as the jurisprudence of the International Court of Justice and the practice of States in matters of natural resource activities in Non-Self-Governing Territories.

A. The status of Western Sahara under Moroccan administration

5. A Spanish protectorate since 1884, Spanish Sahara was included in 1963 in the list of Non-Self-Governing Territories under Chapter XI of the Charter (A/5514, annex III). Beginning in 1962, Spain as administering Power transmitted technical and statistical information on the Territory under Article 73 *e* of the Charter of the United Nations. This information was examined by the Special Committee on the Situation with regard to the Implementation of the Declaration on the Granting of Independence to Colonial Countries and Peoples ("the Special Committee"). In a series of General Assembly resolutions on the question of Spanish/Western Sahara, the applicability to the Territory of the Declaration on the Granting of Independence to Colonial Countries and Peoples (General Assembly resolution 1514 (XV)) was reaffirmed.

6. On 14 November 1975, a Declaration of Principles on Western Sahara was concluded in Madrid between Spain, Morocco and Mauritania ("the Madrid Agreement"), whereby the powers and responsibilities of Spain, as the administering Power of the Territory, were transferred to a temporary tripartite administration. The Madrid Agreement did not transfer sovereignty over the Territory, nor did it confer upon any of the signatories the status of an administering Power, a status which Spain alone could not have unilaterally transferred. The transfer of administrative authority over the Territory to Morocco and Mauritania in 1975 did not affect the international status of Western Sahara as a Non-Self-Governing Territory.

7. On 26 February 1976, Spain informed the Secretary-General that as of that date it had terminated its presence in Western Sahara and relinquished its responsibilities over the Territory, thus leaving it in fact under the administration of both Morocco and Mauritania in their respective controlled areas. Following the withdrawal of Mauritania from the Territory in 1979, upon the conclusion of the Mauritano-Sahraoui agreement of 19 August 1979 (S/13503, annex I), Morocco has

administered the Territory of Western Sahara alone. Morocco, however, is not listed as the administering Power of the Territory in the United Nations list of Non-Self-Governing Territories, and has, therefore, not transmitted information on the Territory in accordance with Article 73 *e* of the Charter of the United Nations.

8. Notwithstanding the foregoing, and given the status of Western Sahara as a Non-Self-Governing Territory, it would be appropriate for the purposes of the present analysis to have regard to the principles applicable to the powers and responsibilities of an administering Power in matters of mineral resource activities in such a Territory.

B. The law applicable to mineral resource activities in Non-Self-Governing Territories

9. Article 73 of the Charter of the United Nations lays down the fundamental principles applicable to Non-Self-Governing Territories. Members of the United Nations who assumed responsibilities for the administration of these Territories have thereby recognized the principle that the interests of the inhabitants of these Territories are paramount, and have accepted as a sacred trust the obligation to promote to the utmost the well-being of the inhabitants of these Territories. Under Article 73 *e* of the Charter, they are required to transmit regularly to the Secretary-General for information purposes statistical and other information of a technical nature relating to economic, social, and educational conditions in the Territories under their administration.

10. The legal regime applicable to Non-Self-Governing Territories was further developed in the practice of the United Nations and, more specifically, in the Special Committee and the General Assembly. Resolutions of the General Assembly adopted under the agenda item entitled "Implementation of the Declaration on the Granting of Independence to Colonial Countries and Peoples" called upon the administering Powers to ensure that all economic activities in the Non-Self-Governing Territories under their administration did not adversely affect the interests of the peoples of such Territories, but were instead directed towards assisting them in the exercise of their right to self-determination. The Assembly also consistently urged the administering Powers to safeguard and guarantee the inalienable rights of the peoples of those Territories to their natural resources, and to establish and maintain control over the future development of those resources (resolutions 35/118 of 11 December 1980, 52/78 of 10 December 1997, 54/91 of 6 December 1999, 55/147 of 8 December 2000 and 56/74 of 10 December 2001).

11. In the resolutions adopted under the agenda item entitled "Activities of foreign economic and other interests which impede the

implementation of the Declaration on the Granting of Independence to Colonial Countries and Peoples in Territories under colonial domination", the General Assembly reiterated that "the exploitation and plundering of the marine and other natural resources of colonial and Non-Self-Governing Territories by foreign economic interests, in violation of the relevant resolutions of the United Nations, is a threat to the integrity and prosperity of those Territories", and that "any administering Power that deprives the colonial peoples of Non-Self-Governing Territories of the exercise of their legitimate rights over their natural resources… violates the solemn obligations it has assumed under the Charter of the United Nations" (resolutions 48/46 of 10 December 1992 and 49/40 of 9 December 1994).

12. In an important evolution of this doctrine, the General Assembly, in its resolution 50/33 of 6 December 1995, drew a distinction between economic activities that are detrimental to the peoples of these Territories and those directed to benefit them. In paragraph 2 of that resolution, the General Assembly affirmed "the value of foreign economic investment undertaken in collaboration with the peoples of the Non-Self-Governing Territories and in accordance with their wishes in order to make a valid contribution to the socio-economic development of the Territories". This position has been affirmed by the General Assembly in later resolutions (resolutions 52/72 of 10 December 1997, 53/61 of 3 December 1998, 54/84 of 6 December 1999, 55/138 of 8 December 2000 and 56/66 of 10 December 2001).

13. The question of Western Sahara has been dealt with both by the General Assembly, as a question of decolonization, and by the Security Council, as a question of peace and security. The Council was first seized of the matter in 1975, and in its resolutions 377 (1975) of 22 October 1975 and 379 (1975) of 2 November 1975 it requested the Secretary-General to enter into consultations with the parties. Since 1988, in particular, when Morocco and the Frente Popular para la Liberacíon de Saguia el-Hamra y del Río de Oro (Frente POLISARIO) agreed, in principle, to the settlement proposals of the Secretary-General and the Chairman of the Organization of African Unity, the political process aiming at a peaceful settlement of the question of Western Sahara has been under the purview of the Council. For the purposes of the present analysis, however, the body of Security Council resolutions pertaining to the political process is not relevant to the legal regime applicable to mineral resource activities in Non-Self-Governing Territories and for this reason is not dealt with in detail in the present letter.

14. The principle of "permanent sovereignty over natural resources" as the right of peoples and nations to use and dispose of the natural resources

in their territories in the interest of their national development and well-being was established by the General Assembly in its resolution 1803 (XVII) of 14 December 1962. It has since been reaffirmed in the 1966 International Covenants on Economic, Social and Cultural Rights and on Civil and Political Rights, as well as in subsequent General Assembly resolutions, most notably, resolution 3201 (S-VI) of 1 May 1974, entitled "Declaration on the Establishment of a New International Economic Order", and resolution 3281 (XXIX) of 12 December 1974, containing the Charter of Economic Rights and Duties of States. While the legal nature of the core principle of "permanent sovereignty over natural resources", as a corollary to the principle of territorial sovereignty or the right of self-determination, is indisputably part of customary international law, its exact legal scope and implications are still debatable. In the present context, the question is whether the principle of "permanent sovereignty" prohibits any activities related to natural resources undertaken by an administering Power (cf. para. 8 above) in a Non-Self-Governing Territory, or only those which are undertaken in disregard of the needs, interests and benefits of the people of that Territory.

C. The case law of the International Court of Justice

15. The question of natural resource exploitation by administering Powers in Non-Self-Governing Territories was brought before the International Court of Justice in the case of *East Timor (Portugal v. Australia)* and the case concerning *Certain Phosphate Lands in Nauru (Nauru v. Australia)*. In neither case, however, was the question of the legality of resource exploitation activities in Non-Self-Governing Territories conclusively determined.

16. In the case of *East Timor*, Portugal argued that in negotiating with Indonesia an agreement on the exploration and exploitation of the continental shelf in the area of the Timor Gap, Australia had failed to respect the right of the people of East Timor to permanent sovereignty over its natural wealth and resources, and the powers and rights of Portugal as the administering Power of East Timor. In the absence of Indonesia's participation in the proceedings, the International Court of Justice concluded that it lacked jurisdiction.

17. In the *Nauru Phosphate case*, Nauru claimed the rehabilitation of certain phosphate lands worked out before independence in the period of the trusteeship administration by Australia, New Zealand and the United Kingdom of Great Britain and Northern Ireland. Nauru argued that the principle of permanent sovereignty over natural resources was breached in circumstances in which a major resource was depleted on grossly inequitable terms and its extraction involved the physical reduction of the

land. Following the judgment on the Preliminary Objections, the parties reached a settlement and a judgment on the merits was no longer required.

D. The Practice of States

18. In the recent practice of States, cases of resource exploitation in Non-Self-Governing Territories have, for obvious reasons, been few and far apart. In 1975, the United Nations Visiting Mission to Spanish Sahara reported that at the time of the visit, four companies held prospecting concessions in offshore Spanish Sahara. In discussing the exploitation of phosphate deposits in the region of Bu Craa with Spanish officials, the Mission was told that the revenues expected to accrue would be used for the benefit of the Territory, that Spain recognized the sovereignty of the Saharan population over the Territory's natural resources and that, apart from the return of its investment, Spain laid no claim to benefit from the proceeds (A/10023/Rev.1, p. 52).

19. The exploitation of uranium and other natural resources in Namibia by South Africa and a number of Western multinational corporations was considered illegal under Decree No.1 for the Protection of the Natural Resources of Namibia, enacted in 1974 by the United Nations Council for Namibia, and was condemned by the General Assembly (resolutions 36/51 of 24 November 1981 and 39/42 of 5 December 1984). The case of Namibia, however, must be seen light of Security Council resolution 276 (1970) of 30 January 1970, in which the Council declared that the continued presence of South Africa in Namibia was illegal and that consequently all acts taken by the Government of South Africa were illegal and invalid.

20. The case of East Timor under the United Nations Transitional Administration in East Timor (UNTAET) is unique in that, while UNTAET is not an administering Power within the meaning of Article 73 of the Charter of the United Nations, East Timor is still technically listed as a Non-Self-Governing Territory. By the time UNTAET was established in October 1999, the Timor Gap Treaty was fully operational and concessions had been granted in the Zone of Cooperation by Indonesia and Australia, respectively. In order to ensure the continuity of the practical arrangements under the Timor Gap Treaty, UNTAET, acting on behalf of East Timor, concluded on 10 February 2000 an Exchange of Letters with Australia for the continued operation of the terms of the Treaty. Two years later, in anticipation of independence, UNTAET, acting on behalf of East Timor, negotiated with Australia a draft "Timor Sea Arrangement" which will replace the Timor Gap Treaty upon the independence of East Timor. In concluding the agreement for the exploration and exploitation of oil and natural gas deposits in the continental shelf of East Timor, UNTAET, on

both occasions, consulted fully with representatives of the East Timorese people, who participated actively in the negotiations.

E. Conclusions

21. The question addressed to me by the Security Council, namely, "the legality…of actions allegedly taken by the Moroccan authorities consisting in the offering and signing of contracts with foreign companies for the exploration of mineral resources in Western Sahara", has been analysed by analogy as part of the more general question of whether mineral resource activities in a Non-Self-Governing Territory by an administering Power are illegal, as such, or only if conducted in disregard of the needs and interests of the people of that Territory. An analysis of the relevant provisions of the Charter of the United Nations, General Assembly resolutions, the case law of the International Court of Justice and the practice of States supports the latter conclusion.

22. The principle that the interests of the peoples of Non-Self-Governing Territories are paramount, and their well-being and development is the "sacred trust" of their respective administering Powers, was established in the Charter of the United Nations and further developed in General Assembly resolutions on the question of decolonization and economic activities in Non-Self-Governing Territories. In recognizing the inalienable rights of the peoples of Non-Self-Governing Territories to the natural resources in their territories, the General Assembly has consistently condemned the exploitation and plundering of natural resources and any economic activities which are detrimental to the interests of the peoples of those Territories and deprive them of their legitimate rights over their natural resources. The Assembly recognized, however, the value of economic activities which are undertaken in accordance with the wishes of the peoples of those Territories, and their contribution to the development of such Territories.

23. In the cases of *East Timor* and *Nauru*, the International Court of Justice did not pronounce itself on the question of the legality of economic activities in Non-Self-Governing Territories. It should be noted, however, that in neither case was it alleged that mineral resource exploitation in such Territories was illegal *per se*. In the case of *East Timor*, the conclusion of an oil exploitation agreement was allegedly illegal because it had not been concluded with the administering Power (Portugal); in the *Nauru* case, the illegality allegedly arose because the mineral resource exploitation depleted unnecessarily or inequitably the overlaying lands.

24. The recent State practice, though limited, is illustrative of an opinion juris on the part of both administering Powers and third States: where resource exploitation activities are conducted in Non-Self-Governing

Territories for the benefit of the peoples of those Territories, on their behalf or in consultation with their representatives, they are considered compatible with the Charter obligations of the administering Power and in conformity with the General Assembly resolutions and the principle of "permanent sovereignty over natural resources" enshrined therein.

25. The foregoing legal principles established in the practice of States and the United Nations pertain to economic activities in Non-Self-Governing Territories, in general, and mineral resource exploitation, in particular. It must be recognized, however, that in the present case, the contracts for oil reconnaissance and evaluation do not entail exploitation or the physical removal of the mineral resources, and no benefits have as of yet accrued. The conclusion is, therefore, that, while the specific contracts which are the subject of the Security Council's request are not in themselves illegal, if further exploration and exploitation activities were to proceed in disregard of the interests and wishes of the people of Western Sahara, they would be in violation of the principles of international law applicable to mineral resource activities in Non-Self-Governing Territories.

3. Fisheries Partnership Agreement between the European Community and the Kingdom of Morocco[1]

FISHERIES PARTNERSHIP AGREEMENT
between the European Communities and the Kingdom of Morocco

THE EUROPEAN COMMUNITY,

hereinafter referred to as 'the Community', and

THE KINGDOM OF MOROCCO,

hereinafter referred to as 'Morocco',

Hereinafter referred to as the 'parties',

CONSIDERING the close working relationship between the Community and Morocco, particularly in the context of the Euro Mediterranean Agreement establishing an association between the European Communities and their Member States, of the one part, and the Kingdom of Morocco, on the other part, and their mutual desire to intensify that relationship,

HAVING REGARD TO the United Nations Convention on the Law of the Sea,

AWARE OF the importance of the principles established by the Code of conduct for responsible fisheries adopted at the FAO Conference in 1995,

DETERMINED to cooperate, in their mutual interest, in promoting the introduction of responsible fisheries to ensure the long-term conservation and sustainable exploitation of marine living resources, and in particular by implementing a control system covering fishing activities as a whole, in order to ensure the effectiveness of the measures for the development and conservation of fishery resources,

---

1 Adopted by Council Regulation (EC) No.764/2006, 22 May 2006, in *Official Journal of the European Union*, L 141, 2006, p. 1 ff.

CONVINCED that such cooperation must take the form of initiatives and measures which, whether taken jointly or separately, are complementary and ensure consistent policies and synergy of effort,

DECIDED, to these ends, to contribute, within the framework of Morocco's sectoral fisheries policy, to promoting the development of a partnership with a view in particular to identifying the most appropriate means of ensuring that this policy is effectively implemented and that economic operators and civil society are involved in the process,

DESIROUS of establishing terms and conditions governing the fishing activities of Community vessels in Moroccan fishing zones and Community support for the introduction of responsible fishing in those fishing zones,

RESOLVED to pursue closer economic cooperation in the fishing industry and related activities through the setting up and development of investments involving companies from both parties,

HEREBY AGREE AS FOLLOWS:

Article 1

Purpose

This Agreement establishes the principles, rules and procedures governing:

- economic, financial, technical and scientific cooperation in the fisheries sector with a view to introducing responsible fishing in Moroccan fishing zones to guarantee the conservation and sustainable exploitation of fisheries resources and develop the Moroccan fisheries sector,
- the conditions governing access by Community fishing vessels to Moroccan fishing zones,
- the arrangements for policing fisheries in Moroccan waters with a view to ensuring that the above rules and conditions are complied with, the measures for the conservation and management of fish stocks are effective, and illegal, undeclared or unregulated fishing is prevented,
- partnerships between companies aimed at developing, in the common interest, economic and related activities in the fisheries sector.

Article 2

Definitions

For the purposes of this Agreement, the Protocol and the Annex:

(a) 'Moroccan fishing zone' means the waters falling within the sovereignty or jurisdiction of the Kingdom of Morocco;

(b) 'Moroccan authorities' means the Ministry of Agriculture, Rural Development and Sea Fisheries – Sea Fisheries Department;

(c) 'Community authorities' means the European Commission;

(d) 'Community vessel' means a fishing vessel flying the flag of a Member State of the Community and registered in the Community;

(e) 'Joint Committee' means a committee made up of representatives of the Community and Morocco whose functions are described in Article 10 of this Agreement.

Article 3

Principles and objectives underlying this Agreement

1. The parties hereby undertake to promote responsible fishing in the Moroccan fishing zones based on the principle of non-discrimination between the different fleets fishing in those waters.

2. The parties undertake to establish the principles of dialogue and of prior consultations, *omissis*...

3. The parties shall also cooperate in carrying out *ex ante*, ongoing and *ex post* evaluations, both jointly and unilaterally, of measures, programmes and actions implemented on the basis of this Agreement.

4. The parties hereby undertake to ensure that this Agreement is implemented in accordance with the principles of good economic and social governance.

...*omissis*...

Article 5

Access by Community vessels to fisheries in Moroccan fishing zones

1. Morocco hereby undertakes to authorise Community vessels to engage in fishing activities in its fishing zones in accordance with this Agreement, including the Protocol and Annex thereto.

2. The fishing activities governed by this Agreement shall be subject to the laws and regulations in force in Morocco. The Moroccan authorities shall notify the Commission of any amendments to that legislation. Without prejudice to any provisions which might be agreed between the parties, Community vessels shall comply with this legislation within one month.

3. Morocco shall ensure the effective implementation of the fisheries monitoring provisions in the Protocol. Community vessels shall cooperate with the Moroccan authorities responsible for carrying out such monitoring.

4. The Community undertakes to take all the appropriate steps required to ensure that its vessels comply with this Agreement and the legislation governing fisheries in the waters over which Morocco has jurisdiction, in accordance with the United Nations Convention on the Law of the Sea.

Article 6

Conditions governing fishing activities

1. Community vessels may fish in Moroccan fishing zones only if they are in possession of a fishing licence issued under this Agreement. The exercise of fishing activities by Community vessels shall be subject to the holding of a licence issued by the competent Moroccan authorities at the request of the competent Community authorities.

...omissis...

Article 7

Financial contribution

1. The Community shall grant Morocco a financial contribution in accordance with the terms and conditions laid down in the Protocol and Annexes. This contribution shall be composed of two related elements, namely:

(a) a financial contribution for access by Community vessels to Moroccan fishing zones, without prejudice to the fees due by Community vessels for the licence fee;

(b) Community financial support for introducing a national fisheries policy based on responsible fishing and on the sustainable exploitation of fisheries resources in Moroccan waters.

...omissis...

Article 10

Joint Committee

1. A Joint Committee shall be set up between the two parties to monitor the implementation of this Agreement. The Joint Committee shall also perform the following functions:

(a) supervise the implementation, interpretation and smooth operation of the application of the Agreement;

...omissis...

(d) act as a forum for the amicable settlement of any disputes regarding the interpretation or application of the Agreement;

...omissis...

Article 11

Area of application

This Agreement shall apply, on the one hand, to the territories in which the Treaty establishing the European Community applies, under the conditions laid down in that Treaty and, on the other, to the territory of Morocco and to the waters under Moroccan jurisdiction.

...omissis...

4. Protocol between the European Union and the Kingdom of Morocco setting out the fishing opportunities and financial contribution provided for in the Fisheries Partnership Agreement between the European Union and the Kingdom of Morocco[1].

PROTOCOL

between the European Union and the Kingdom of Morocco setting out the fishing opportunities and financial contribution provided for in the Fisheries Partnership Agreement between the European Union and the Kingdom of Morocco

Article 1

General Principles

This Protocol, together with its Annex and Appendices, form an integral part of the Fisheries Partnership Agreement between the European Union and the Kingdom of Morocco, dated 28 February 2007, hereinafter referred to as the 'Fisheries Agreement' – which forms part of the euro-Mediterranean Agreement establishing an association between the European Union and the Kingdom of Morocco dated 26 February 1996 – hereinafter referred to as the 'Association Agreement'. It helps to meet the general objectives of the Association Agreement and aims to ensure the viability of fisheries resources from ecological, economic and social points of view.

The Protocol is implemented in accordance with Article 1 of the Association Agreement on developing dialogue and cooperation and Article 2 of the same Agreement concerning the respect for democratic principles and fundamental human rights.

Article 2

Period of application, duration and fishing opportunities

From the application of this Protocol and for a period of four years, the fishing opportunities granted under Article 5 of the Fisheries Agreement shall be those stated in the table attached hereto.

The first subparagraph above shall apply subject to the provisions of Articles 4 and 5 of this Protocol.

Under Article 6 of the Fisheries Agreement, vessels flying the flag of a Member State of the European Union (EU) may engage in fishing

1 Adopted by Council decision 2013/785/EU, 16 December 2013, in *OJEU*, L 349/1, 21 December 2013.

activities in the Moroccan fishing zone only if they are in possession of a fishing licence issued under this Protocol and in accordance with the provisions of the Annex hereto.

Article 3

Financial contribution

1. The estimated total annual value of the Protocol is EUR 40,000,000 for the period referred to in Article 2,

...omissis...

5. Subject to the provisions of Article 6 of this Protocol, the Moroccan authorities shall have full discretion regarding the use to which this financial contribution is put.

Article 4

Coordination in the scientific area and in exploratory fishing

1. In accordance with Article 4(1) of the Agreement, the parties undertake to organise, on a regular basis and when needed, scientific meetings to discuss scientific questions raised by the Joint Committee for the management and technical monitoring of this Protocol. The mandate, composition and running of these scientific meetings are to be established by the Joint Committee referred to in Article 10 of the Fisheries Agreement.

2. The two parties hereby undertake to promote responsible fishing in the Moroccan fishing zone based on the principle of non-discrimination between the different fleets fishing in those waters.

3. Pursuant to Article 4(2) of the Fisheries Agreement, the two parties, on the basis of the conclusions of the Scientific Committee's meetings, shall consult each other within the Joint Committee referred to in Article 10 of the Fisheries Agreement in order to adopt, where necessary and by mutual agreement, measures to ensure the sustainable management of fisheries resources.

4. For research purposes and to advance scientific knowledge, exploratory fishing may be carried out in the Moroccan fisheries zone at the request of the Joint Committee. The methods for doing so shall be decided in accordance with the provisions in Chapter IV of the Annex to this Protocol.

Article 5

Review of fishing opportunities

1. The fishing opportunities referred to in Article 2 may be reviewed by the Joint Committee by mutual agreement, provided that this review is designed to ensure the durability of Moroccan fisheries resources.

2. In the event of an increase, the financial contribution referred to in Article 3(1)(a)(i) shall be increased proportionally to the fishing opportunities and *pro rata temporis*. The total amount of the financial contribution made by the EU may not, however, exceed twice the amount indicated in Article 3(1)(a)(i) as a result of this adjustment. If the parties agree to a reduction in the fishing opportunities provided for in Article 2, the financial contribution shall be reduced proportionally to the fisheries opportunities and *pro rata temporis*.

3. The allocation of the fishing opportunities among the various categories of vessels may also be reviewed by mutual agreement between the two parties, taking into account the durability of stock which may be affected by such redistribution. The parties shall agree on the corresponding adjustment of the financial contribution should the redistribution of fishing opportunities so warrant.

Article 6

Support for sectoral fisheries policy in Morocco

1. The financial contribution referred to in Article 3(1)(a)(ii) of this Protocol will help to develop and implement Morocco's sectoral fisheries policy as part of the 'Halieutis' strategy for developing the fisheries sector.

2. The contribution shall be allocated and managed by Morocco on the basis of the setting up by the two parties, by mutual agreement within the Joint Committee, of the objectives to be met and of the relevant annual and multi-annual programme, in accordance with the 'Halieutis' strategy and based on an estimation of the anticipated impact of the projects to be carried out.

3. For the first year of application of the Protocol, the allocation by Morocco of the contribution referred to in paragraph 1 shall be notified to the EU as soon as the guidelines, objectives, criteria and evaluation indicators have been approved by the Joint Committee. For each of the following years, Morocco shall present this allocation to the EU no later than 30 September of the previous year.

4. Any amendment to these guidelines, objectives, criteria and evaluation indicators shall be approved by the two parties within the Joint Committee.

5. Morocco shall draw up a progress report on projects implemented with sectoral support as provided for by this Protocol, which shall be submitted to and examined by the Joint Committee.

6. Depending on the nature of the projects and the duration of their implementation, Morocco shall submit a report to the Joint Committee on the implementation of projects that have been completed with

sectoral support as provided for by this Protocol; the report shall include information on any social and economic consequences, particularly the impact on employment, investment and any other quantifiable repercussions of the measures taken, together with their geographical distribution. This information is to be prepared on the basis of indicators to be defined in greater detail by the Joint Committee.

7. Morocco shall also submit, prior to the expiry of this Protocol, a final report on the implementation of the sectoral support provided for by this Protocol, including the elements referred to in the paragraphs above.

8. The two parties shall, if necessary, continue to monitor the implementation of the sectoral support beyond the expiry of this Protocol or, as the case may be, in the event of its suspension in accordance with the provisions of this Protocol.

9. The specific financial contribution provided for by Article 3(1)(a)(ii) of this Protocol will be paid in instalments, on the basis of an approach where the analysis of the results of the implementation of the sectoral support and the needs identified at the planning stage are taken into account.

10. The framework for operational implementation shall be established by the Joint Committee.

Article 7

Economic integration of EU operators in the Moroccan fisheries sector

In accordance with the legislation and regulations currently in force, the two parties shall promote contacts and help ensure cooperation between economic operators in the following areas:

- development of subsidiary industry related to fisheries, particularly naval construction and repair and the manufacturing of fishing gear and materials;
- promoting exchange of professional expertise and training of managers for the maritime fishing sector;
- sale of fishery products;
- marketing;
- aquaculture.

Article 8

Suspension of the Protocol on the grounds of a dispute as regards interpretation or application

1. Any dispute between the parties over the interpretation of this Protocol or its application shall be the subject of consultations between

the parties within the Joint Committee provided for in Article 10 of the Fisheries Agreement, in a special meeting if necessary.

2. The application of this Protocol may be suspended at the initiative of one party if the dispute between the two parties is deemed to be serious and if the consultations held within the Joint Committee mentioned in paragraph 1 above have not resulted in an amicable settlement.

3. Suspension of application of the Protocol shall require the interested party to notify its intention in writing at least three months before the date on which suspension is due to take effect.

4. In the event of suspension, the parties shall continue to consult each other with a view to finding an amicable settlement to their dispute. The Protocol shall once again be applied once the dispute has been resolved. The amount of the financial contribution shall be reduced proportionately and pro rata temporis to the period during which application of the Protocol was suspended.

Article 9

Non-compliance with technical obligations arising under the Protocol

In accordance with the provisions of this Protocol and legislation currently in force, Morocco reserves the right to apply penalties as provided for in the Annexes in the event of non-compliance with the provisions of and obligations arising under the implementation of this Protocol.

Article 10

Electronic data exchange

Morocco and the EU undertake to set up as soon as possible the systems necessary for ensuring the electronic exchange of all information and documents relating to the technical management of this Protocol, such as data on catches, the VMS positions of vessels and notifications of entry into and exit from the zone.

Article 11

Applicable provisions of national law

The activities of vessels operating under this Protocol and its Annex, in particular regarding transhipment, the use of port services and the purchase of supplies, etc., shall be governed by the applicable laws of Morocco.

...*omissis*...

ANNEX

CONDITIONS GOVERNING FISHING ACTIVITIES BY EU VESSELS IN THE MOROCCAN FISHING ZONE

CHAPTER I

PROVISIONS GOVERNING APPLICATIONS FOR AND ISSUING OF LICENCES

A. Licence applications

1. Only eligible vessels may obtain a licence to fish in the Moroccan fishing zone.

2. In order for a vessel to be eligible, neither the owner, the master nor the vessel itself must be prohibited from fishing in Morocco, nor must the vessel be legally listed as an IUU vessel.

3. They must be in order vis-à-vis the Moroccan administration in so far as they must have fulfilled all prior obligations arising from their fishing activities in Morocco under fisheries agreements concluded with the European Union.

4. The competent EU authorities (hereinafter referred to as the 'Commission') shall submit to the Ministry of Agriculture and Sea Fisheries – Sea Fisheries Department (hereinafter referred to as 'Department') the lists of vessels applying to engage in fishing activities within the limits laid down in the datasheets annexed to the Protocol at least 20 days before the licences requested are due to become valid. These lists shall be sent electronically in a format compatible with the software used by the Department.

These lists shall state the number of vessels for each fishing category and zone and, for each vessel, its main characteristics, payments broken down by heading and the gear to be used during the period in question.

...omissis...

CHAPTER III

FISHING ZONES

Morocco shall inform the EU, prior to the date of application of the Protocol, of the geographical coordinates of the baselines, its fishing zone and all zones within it which are closed to fishing, other than the Mediterranean zone of Morocco situated east of 35°47′18″N – 5°55′33″W (Cape Spartel), which is excluded from this Protocol.

The fishing zones for each category in Morocco's Atlantic zone are defined in the datasheets (Appendix 2).

CHAPTER IV

DETAILS OF IMPLEMENTATION OF EXPLORATORY FISHING

The two parties shall decide jointly on (i) which European operators may practice exploratory fishing, (ii) the most favourable period for such fishing and (iii) the conditions applicable. To facilitate exploratory work by vessels, the Department shall forward any available scientific data and other basic data. The two parties shall agree on the scientific protocol to be used as a basis for such exploratory fishing, and which shall be forwarded to the operators concerned.

The Moroccan fishing sector shall be closely involved (coordination and dialogue on the conditions for implementing exploratory fishing).

The duration of the campaigns will be a minimum of three months and maximum of six months, unless modified by the parties by mutual agreement.

The Commission shall communicate requests for licences for exploratory fishing to the Moroccan authorities. It shall provide a technical dossier specifying:

- the technical characteristics of the vessel;
- the level of expertise of the vessel's officers as regards such fishing;
- the proposal for the technical parameters of the campaign (length, gear, exploration regions, etc.);
- the form of funding.

If necessary, the Department shall organise a dialogue regarding technical and financial aspects with the Commission, and possibly with the shipowners concerned.

Before the start of the exploratory fishing campaign, the EU vessel shall report to a Moroccan port for inspections such as those provided for in points 1.1 and 1.2 of Chapter IX of this Annex.

Before the start of the campaign, vessel owners shall submit the following to the Department and to the Commission:

- a declaration of the catches already on board;
- the technical characteristics of the fishing gear to be used during the campaign;
- an assurance that they will comply with Moroccan fisheries legislation.

During the campaign, the owners of the vessels concerned shall:

- send to the Department and to the Commission a weekly report on catches made per day and by haul, including a description of the campaign's technical parameters (position, depth, date and time, catches and other observations or comments);

- communicate the vessel's position, speed and heading by VMS;
- ensure the presence on board of a Moroccan scientific observer or an observer chosen by the Moroccan authorities. The role of the observer will be to gather scientific information from the catches, as well as to sample the catches. Observers shall be treated in the same way as a ship's officer, and the shipowner shall cover their living costs during their stay on the vessel. The decision on the observer's time on board, the length of their stay and the boarding and landing harbour will be fixed in agreement with the Moroccan authorities. Unless there is agreement between the parties to the contrary, the vessel will never be obliged to put into harbour more than once per two months,
- submit their vessel to inspection before it leaves the Moroccan fishing zone if the Moroccan authorities so request,
- comply with Morocco's fisheries legislation.

The catches, including by-catches, made during the scientific campaign shall remain the property of the shipowner, provided they comply with the provisions made to this end by the Joint Committee and the provisions of the scientific protocol.

The Department shall appoint a contact person responsible for addressing any unforeseen problems that might hinder the development of the exploratory fishing.

CHAPTER V

PROVISIONS APPLICABLE TO SATELLITE MONITORING OF EU FISHING VESSELS OPERATING IN THE MOROCCAN FISHING ZONES ON THE BASIS OF THIS AGREEMENT

General provisions

1. Moroccan regulations governing the operation of satellite tracking and positioning devices apply to EU vessels operating or intending to operate in the Moroccan fishing zone under this Protocol. The flag State shall ensure that vessels flying its flag comply with the provisions of those regulations.

2. For the purposes of satellite monitoring, the Moroccan authorities shall communicate to the EU the coordinates (latitudes and longitudes) of the Moroccan fishing zone, as well as any area in which fishing is prohibited.

(i) The Department shall forward this information to the Commission prior to the date of application of this Protocol;

(ii) This information shall be transmitted in electronic form, in decimal form N/S DD.dddd (WGS84);

(iii) Any changes to these coordinates must be notified immediately.

3. The flag State and Morocco shall each designate a VMS correspondent who will act as the point of contact.

(i) The Fisheries Monitoring and Control Centres (CSCP) of the flag State and of Morocco shall communicate, prior to the date of application of the Protocol, the coordinates (name, address, telephone, telex, e-mail) of their respective VMS correspondent.

(ii) Any changes to the contact details of the VMS correspondent must be notified immediately.

...omissis...

CHAPTER VI
CATCH DECLARATIONS

1. Logbook

1. Masters of vessels shall use the logbook specially designed for fishing in Morocco's fishing zone, a template for which is provided in Appendix 7 of the Annex. They shall keep this logbook up-to-date in accordance with the provisions of the explanatory note for that logbook.

2. Shipowners shall forward a copy of the logbook to their competent authorities no later than 15 days after catches have been landed. These authorities shall forward copies to the Commission without delay, who shall be responsible for forwarding to the Department.

3. Failure by shipowners to comply with the obligations provided for in paragraphs 1 and 2 above shall entail automatic suspension of the fishing licence until such obligations have been met. The Commission shall be informed without delay of any such decision.

2. Quarterly catch declarations

1. By the end of the third month of each quarter the Commission shall notify the Department of the quantities caught by all EU vessels in the previous quarter, in accordance with the templates provided in Appendices 8 and 9 of this Annex.

2. This information shall be broken down monthly and by category for each vessel and each species specified in the logbook.

3. The information shall also be sent to the Department in a computer file in a format compatible with software used by the Ministry.

3. Reliability of data

The information in the documents referred to in points 1 and 2 above must reflect the actual fishing situation in order to constitute one of the bases for monitoring changes in stocks.

4. Transition to an electronic system

Both parties have established a protocol for the electronic exchange of all information relating to catches and declarations ('Electronic Reporting System'), referred to as 'ERS data', set out in Appendix 11. Both parties will make provision for the implementation of this protocol and the replacement of the paper version of the catch declaration by ERS data, from the implementation by Morocco of the equipment and software required.

5. Landings outside Morocco

Shipowners shall send the landing declarations for catches made under this Protocol to their competent authorities no later than 15 days after the landing. These authorities shall forward copies to the Delegation without delay, who shall be responsible for forwarding.

CHAPTER VII
EMBARKATION OF MOROCCAN SEAMEN

1. Shipowners who have been awarded fishing licences under this Agreement shall take on board, for the duration of their presence in the Moroccan fishing zone, Moroccan seamen, as provided for in the datasheets contained in Appendix 2.

2. The shipowners will choose the seamen who they take on board their vessels from the official list of successful candidates of maritime training schools transmitted by the Department to the Commission and communicated by the latter to the flag States concerned. The list is updated every year on 1 February. The shipowners are free to select the candidates from the list of successful applicants who have the best expertise and most suitable experience.

...omissis...

CHAPTER VIII

MONITORING AND OBSERVATION OF FISHING

A. Observation of fishing

1. Vessels authorised to fish in the Moroccan fishing zone under this Protocol shall take on board the observers appointed by Morocco on the terms set out below.

...omissis...

4. The observer shall be taken on board at a port chosen by the shipowner at the beginning of the first trip in the Moroccan fishing zone after notification of the list of designated ships.

...omissis...

9. Observers shall be treated on board as officers. They shall carry out the following tasks:

9.1. observe the fishing activities of the vessels;

9.2. verify the position of vessels engaged in fishing operations;

9.3. perform biological sampling in the context of scientific programmes;

9.4. note the fishing gear used;

9.5. verify the catch data for the Moroccan fishing zone recorded in the logbook;

9.6. verify the percentages of by-catches and estimate the quantity of discards of species of marketable fin-fish, crustaceans and cephalopods;

9.7. report fishing data by fax or by radio, including the quantity of catches and by-catches on board.

10. The master shall do everything in their power to ensure the physical safety and welfare of the observer during the performance of their duties.

11. The observer shall be offered every facility needed to carry out their duties. The master shall facilitate their access to the means of communication needed for the discharge of their duties, to documents directly concerned with the vessel's fishing activities, in particular the logbook and the navigation log, and to those parts of the vessel necessary to facilitate the exercise of their tasks as observer.

12. While on board, the observer shall:

1. take all appropriate steps to ensure that the conditions of their boarding and presence on the vessel neither interrupt nor hamper fishing operations,

2. take care of the material and equipment on board and respect the confidentiality of all documents belonging to the vessel.

13. At the end of the observation period and before leaving the vessel, the observer shall draw up an activity report to be transmitted to the competent authorities in Morocco, with a copy to the Delegation. He/she shall sign it in the presence of the master, who may add or cause to be added to it any observations considered relevant, followed by the master's signature. A copy of the report shall be handed to the master when the observer is put ashore.

...omissis...

17. Failure by the shipowner to comply with the obligations laid down in point 4 shall entail automatic suspension of the fishing licence until such obligations have been met. The Delegation shall be informed without delay of any such decision.

B. Joint monitoring of fishing

1. The contracting parties shall set up a system of joint monitoring and observation of checks on landings, with the aim of improving the effectiveness of such checks so as to ensure compliance with the provisions of this Protocol.

2. The parties shall prepare an annual schedule for joint monitoring, covering all fishing categories provided for in this Protocol.

3. To this end, the competent authorities of each contracting party shall designate a representative to attend checks on landings and observe the arrangements for conducting such checks, notifying their name to the other contracting party.

4. The representative of the Moroccan authority shall attend, as an observer, inspections on landings by vessels which have operated in the Moroccan fishing zone carried out by the national inspection authorities of the Member States.

5. The representative shall accompany national inspection officials in their visits to ports, on board vessels, in dock, to auctions, fish wholesalers' shops, coldstores and other premises for landing fish before it is placed on the market, and shall have access to the documents which are the subject of these inspections.

6. The representative of the Moroccan authority shall draw up and submit a report detailing the inspections attended. A copy of the report shall be sent to the Delegation.

7. The Department shall invite the Delegation to attend inspection visits scheduled in the ports of landing, giving one month's notice.

8. At the Commission's request, EU fishing inspectors may attend as observers inspections carried out by the Moroccan authorities on landing operations by EU vessels in Moroccan ports.

9. The practical arrangements for these operations will be laid down by mutual agreement between the competent authorities of the two parties.

CHAPTER IX
MONITORING

1. Technical inspection

1.1. Once a year and after any change to their technical characteristics or following a request for a change in fishing category necessitating the use of a different type of fishing gear, EU vessels holding a licence under this Protocol shall report to a Moroccan port to undergo the inspections required by the legislation in force. Such inspections shall take place within 48 hours of the vessel's arrival in port.

1.2. Once the inspection has been completed satisfactorily, the master of the vessel shall be issued with a certificate having the same period of validity as the licence, and which shall be automatically extended in the case of vessels renewing their licence within the year. However, the maximum validity may not exceed one year. This certificate must be kept on board at all times.

1.3. The purpose of the technical inspection is to establish the compliance of the vessel's technical characteristics and gear, to check the operation of the satellite tracking and positioning device installed on board and ensure that the provisions relating to its Moroccan crew have been complied with.

1.4. The cost of the inspection shall be borne by the shipowner at the rates laid down by Moroccan law. It may not be greater than the amount normally paid by other vessels for the same services.

1.5. Failure by the shipowner to comply with points 1.1 and 1.2 above shall result in automatic suspension of the fishing licence until such obligations have been met. The Delegation shall be informed without delay of any such decision.

2. Entering and leaving the zone

2.1. EU vessels holding a licence under this Protocol shall notify the Department, at least six hours in advance, of their intention to enter or leave the Moroccan fishing zone, together with the following information:

2.1.1. date and time of transmission;

2.1.2. the vessel's position, in accordance with point 5 of Chapter V;

2.1.3. the weight in kilograms and catches per species on board, as identified using the 3-alpha code;

2.1.4. messages such as 'catches on entry' (COE) and 'catches on exit' (COX).

2.2. This information should preferably be communicated by fax or, for vessels not equipped with a fax, by radio (in this respect, see the information provided in Appendix 10).

2.3. In the case of vessels falling under the category 'industrial pelagic fishing', the final exit from the Moroccan fishing zone shall be subject to the Department's prior authorisation. This authorisation shall be issued within 24 hours of the request being made by the ship's master or agent, with the exception of a request arriving on the day before a weekend where the authorisation has to be issued on the following Monday. If authorisation is withheld, the Department shall notify the owner of the vessel and the Commission without delay of the reasons for such refusal.

2.4. A vessel found to be fishing without having informed the Department shall be regarded as a vessel without a licence.

2.5. The fax and telephone numbers of the vessel and the master's e-mail address are to be indicated by the owner on the fishing licence application form.

3. Monitoring procedures

3.1. Masters of EU fishing vessels holding a licence under this Protocol shall allow and facilitate boarding and the discharge of their duties by any Moroccan official responsible for the inspection and monitoring of fishing activities.

3.2. These officials shall not remain on board for longer than is necessary for the discharge of their duties.

3.3. Once the inspection and monitoring has been completed, a certificate shall be issued to the master of the vessel.

4. Boarding

4.1. The Department shall inform the Delegation as soon as possible and within no more than 48 hours of all boardings of and penalties imposed on EU vessels in the Moroccan fishing zone.

4.2. The Commission shall at the same time receive a brief report of the circumstances and reasons leading to the boarding.

5. Statement of boarding

5.1. After the Moroccan authorities responsible for inspection have drawn up a statement, the master of the vessel shall sign it.

5.2. This signature shall not prejudice the master's rights or any defence which he or she may make to the alleged infringement.

5.3. The master shall take the vessel to the port indicated by the Moroccan authorities responsible for inspection. A vessel in breach of the applicable Moroccan sea fishing legislation shall be kept in port until completion of the usual administrative formalities relating to boarding.

6. Settlement of infringements:

6.1. Before any judicial procedure, an attempt shall be made to resolve the presumed infringement by means of an amicable settlement. This procedure shall end no later than three working days after the boarding.

6.2. In the event of an amicable settlement, the amount of the fine shall be determined in accordance with Moroccan fisheries legislation.

6.3. If the case cannot be settled by amicable procedure and has to be brought before a competent judicial body, a bank security set to take account of the boarding costs and the fines and compensation payable by the parties responsible for the infringement shall be paid by the shipowner into a bank account specified by the competent Moroccan authority.

6.4. The bank security shall be irrevocable until the legal proceedings have been concluded. It shall be released once legal proceedings end without a conviction. Similarly, in the event of a conviction leading to a fine of less than the security lodged, the balance shall be released by the competent Moroccan authorities.

6.5. The vessel shall be authorised to leave the port:

– once the obligations arising under the amicable settlement have been fulfilled; or

– when the bank security referred to in point 6.3 above has been lodged and accepted by the competent Moroccan authority, pending completion of the legal proceedings.

7. Transhipment

7.1. Any transhipment at sea of catches shall be prohibited in the Moroccan fishing zone. However, EU industrial pelagic trawlers that have been granted a licence in accordance with the provisions of this Protocol and wish to tranship catches in Moroccan waters may do so in a Moroccan port or other place designated by the competent Moroccan authorities, after authorisation by the Department. Such transhipment shall take place under the supervision of the observer or of a representative of the maritime fisheries delegation and the control authorities. Any person infringing this provision shall be liable to the penalties provided for by Moroccan law.

7.2. Before any transhipment, the owners of these vessels must notify the following information to the Department at least 24 hours in advance:

- the names of the transhipping fishing vessels;
- the name of the cargo vessel, its flag, registration number and call sign;
- the tonnage by species to be transhipped;
- the destination of catches;
- the date and day of transhipment.

7.3. Morocco reserves the right to refuse transhipment if the carrier vessel has carried out illegal, undeclared or unregulated fishing inside or outside the Moroccan fishing zone.

7.4. Transhipment shall be considered as an exit from the Moroccan fishing zone. Vessels must therefore submit their catch declarations to the Department and state whether they intend to continue fishing or leave the Moroccan fishing zone.

7.5. Masters of EU industrial pelagic trawlers that have been granted a licence in accordance with the provisions of this Protocol engaged in landing or transhipment operations in a Moroccan port shall allow and facilitate the inspection of such operations by Moroccan inspectors. Once the inspection and control have been completed in the port, a certificate shall be issued to the master of the vessel.

...omissis...

Appendices

(1) Licence application form

(2) Datasheets

(3) Communication of VMS messages to Morocco, position report

(4) Coordinates of fishing zones

(5) Contact details of the Moroccan CSCP

(6) ICCAT logbook for tuna fishing

(7) Logbook (other fisheries)

(8) Catch declaration form (industrial pelagic fisheries)

(9) Catch declaration form (fisheries other than industrial pelagic and tuna)

(10) Characteristics of the radio station of the Moroccan Sea Fisheries Department

(11) ERS protocol

...omissis...

Appendix 2

The fishing conditions for each category shall be agreed each year before the issue of licences.

Fishing datasheet No 1

Small-scale fishing in the north: pelagic

Number of vessels authorized	20
Authorised gear	Seine Maximum authorised dimensions corresponding to the conditions in the zone: 500 m × 90 m. Ban on fishing with lampara nets.
Type of vessel:	< 100 GT
Fees	EUR 75 per GT per quarter
Geographical limit of the authorised zone	North of 34°18′00″ An extension of up to latitude 33°25′00″ is permitted for five vessels at once, operating on a rotation system, subject to scientific observation. Beyond 2 nautical miles
Target species	Sardine, anchovy and other small pelagic species
Requirement to land in Morocco	30% of declared catches
Biological recovery	Two months: February and March.
Requirement to embark	Three Moroccan seamen per vessel
Comments	The fact that the activity of the five seiners is extended to south of latitude 34°18′00″N will be the subject of assessment one year after application in order to establish the result of any interaction with the national fleet and impact on resources.

Fishing datasheet No 2

Small-scale fishing in the north

Number of vessels authorized	35
Authorised gear	Bottom-set longline Cat. (a): < 40 GT – Maximum number of hooks per longline: 10,000 hooks armed, mounted and ready for use, with a maximum of five bottom-set longlines. Cat. (b): ≥ 40 GT and < 150 GT – 15,000 hooks armed, mounted and ready for use, with a maximum of eight bottom-set longlines.
Type of vessel:	(a) < 40 GT: 32 licences (b) ≥ 40 GT and < 150 GT: 3 licences
Fees	EUR 67 per GT per quarter

Geographical limit of the authorised zone	North of 34°18′00″N. An extension of up to latitude 33°25′00″ is permitted for four vessels at once[2], operating on a rotation system, subject to scientific observation. Beyond 6 nautical miles.
Target species	Scabbardfish, sparidae and other demersal species
Requirement to land in Morocco	Voluntary landing
Biological recovery	From 15 March to 15 May
By-catches	0% of swordfish and surface sharks
Requirement to embark:	< 100 GT: Voluntary ≥ 100 GT: One Moroccan seaman
Comments	The fact that the activity of the four seiners will be extended to south of latitude 34°18′00″N will be the subject of assessment one year after application in order to establish the result of any interaction with the national fleet and impact on resources.

Fishing datasheet No 3
Small-scale fishing/south

Number of vessels authorized	10
Authorised gear	Rods and lines
Type of vessel	< 80 GT
Fees	EUR 67 per GT per quarter
Geographical limit of the authorized zone	South of 30°40′00″N Beyond 3 nautical miles
Target species	Croaker and sparidae
Requirement to land in Morocco	Voluntary landing
Biological recovery	–
Seine nets authorised for catching live bait	Mesh of 8 mm for catching live bait Seine used beyond 3 nautical miles
By-catches	0% of cephalopods and crustaceans 5% of other demersal species
Requirement to embark	Two Moroccan seamen per vessel

2 After one year, if the situation is favourable and based on the opinion of the Joint Committee, the number of vessels which may operate in the extended zone may be revised.

Fishing datasheet No 4
Demersal fishing

Number of vessels authorized	16 vessels, 5 trawlers and 11 longliners
Authorised gear	– For trawlers: – bottom trawl: – Cod end mesh size: 70 mm – Doubling of the cod-end is prohibited. – Doubling of the twine forming the cod-end is prohibited. – For longliners: – bottom longline: – maximum de 20 000 hameçons par navire
Type of vessel:	Trawlers: – maximum tonnage: 600 GT per vessel; Longliners: – maximum tonnage: 150 GT per vessel.
Fees	60 EUR per GT per quarter
Geographical limit of the authorized zone	South of 29° N Beyond the isobath of 200 m for trawlers; Beyond 12 nautical miles for longliners
Target species	Black hake, scabbardfish, leerfish/bonito
Requirement to land in Morocco	30% of catches per journey
Biological recovery	–
By-catches	0% of cephalopods and crustaceans, 5% of deep-sea sharks.
Requirement to embark	Four Moroccan seamen for longliners Seven Moroccan seamen for trawlers

Fishing datasheet No 5
Tuna fishing

Number of vessels authorized	27
Authorised gear	Troll pole and line
Geographical limit of the authorized zone	Beyond 3 miles All of Morocco's Atlantic zone, apart from a protected area east of a line from 33°30′N/7°35′W to 35°48'N/6°20′W
Target species	Tunas
Requirement to land in Morocco	25% of declared catches comprising skipjack (*Katsuwonus pelamis*), bonito (*Sarda sarda*) and frigate mackerel (*Auxis thazard*) per journey
Biological recovery	–
Seine nets authorized for catching live bait	8 mm seine mesh for catching live bait, with seiners used beyond 3 nautical miles.
Fees	EUR 35 per tonne fished
Advance	A flat-rate advance of EUR 7,000 is to be paid when applying for annual licences
Requirement to embark	Three Moroccan seamen per vessel

Fishing datasheet No 6
Industrial pelagic fishing

Number of vessels authorised	18
Authorised gear	Pelagic or semi-pelagic
Quota allocated	80,000 tonnes per year, – with a maximum 10,000 tonnes per month for the whole fleet. – except for the months of August to October, when the monthly maximum for catches is increased to 15,000 tonnes.
Type of vessel	Industrial pelagic trawler
Number of vessels authorized	Distribution of vessels authorised to fish: – Ten vessels with a tonnage of more than 3,000 GT – Three vessels with a tonnage of between 150 and 3,000 GT – Five vessels with a tonnage of less than 150 GT
Authorised maximum tonnage of vessel	7,765 GT, taking into account the structure of the European Union's fishing fleet.
Geographical limit of the authorised zone	South of 29°N, – beyond 15 nautical miles for freezer trawlers – beyond 8 nautical miles for RSW trawlers
Target species	Sardine, sardinella, mackerel, horse mackerel and anchovy
Composition of catches (per group of species):	– horse mackerel/mackerel/anchovies: 65% – sardine/sardinella: 33% – by-catches: 2% This composition may be changed by the Joint Committee.
Requirement to land in Morocco	25% of catches per journey
Biological recovery	Authorised fishing vessels must observe all biological recovery periods laid down by the Department in the authorised fishing zone and stop any fishing activity there[3].

3 The Department will notify this decision to the Commission in advance, specifying the period or periods for which there is a prohibition on fishing, and the areas concerned

Authorised net	The minimum size of the stretched mesh of the pelagic or semi-pelagic trawl is 40 mm. The bag of the pelagic or semi-pelagic trawl may be strengthened with a piece of netting with a minimum mesh size of 400 mm of stretched mesh and by straps placed at least 1.5 metres apart, except for the strap at the back of the trawl which may not be placed less than 2 metres from the window in the bag. The strengthening or doubling of the bag for any other means is prohibited and the trawl may in no case target species other than the small pelagic species authorised.
By-catches	Maximum of 2% of other species. The list of permitted by-catch species is stipulated by the Moroccan regulations on 'small pelagic fisheries in the South Atlantic'.
Industrial processing	Industrial processing of catches into fishmeal and/or fish oil is strictly prohibited. However, damaged or spoiled fish and the waste resulting from handling catches may be processed into fishmeal or fish oil without exceeding the maximum threshold of 5% of total allowable catches.
Fees	For industrial pelagic freezer trawlers: – EUR 100/tonne payable in advance on a monthly basis. For industrial pelagic trawlers operating with non-freezer vessels: – EUR 35/tonne payable in advance on a monthly basis. Fees will be increased if authorised catches are exceeded by a factor of 3.
Requirement to embark:	Tonnage of vessel < 150 GT: – Two Moroccan seamen 150 GT ≤ vessel tonnage < 1,500 GT: – Four Moroccan seamen 1,500 GT ≤ vessel tonnage < 5,000 GT: – Eight Moroccan seamen 5,000 GT ≤ vessel tonnage < 7,765 GT: – 16 Moroccan seamen

…omissis…

Appendix 4

Coordinates of Fishing Zones

Data sheet	Category	Fishing zone (latitude)	Distance from the coast
1.	Small-scale fishing in the north: pelagic	34°18′00″N – 35°48′00″N (extended to 33°25′00″N, as indicated in datasheet No 1)	Beyond 2 miles
2.	Small-scale fishing in the north: longline	34°18′00″N – 35°48′00″N (extended to l 33°25′00″N, as indicated in datasheet No. 2)	Beyond 6 miles
3.	Small-scale fishing in the south	South of 30°40′00″	Beyond 3 miles
4.	Demersal fishing	South of 29°00′00″	Longliners: beyond 12 miles
			Trawlers: beyond the 200 metre isobath
5.	Tuna fishing	All of the Atlantic apart from the area delimited by: 35°48′N; 6°20′W/ 33°30′N; 7°35′W	Beyond 3 miles and 3 miles for bait
6.	Industrial pelagic fishing	South of 29°00′00″	Beyond 15 miles (freezers)
			Beyond 8 miles (RSW vessels)

Prior to entry into force, the Department will notify the Commission of the geographical coordinates of the Moroccan base line, the Moroccan fishing zone and areas in which navigation and fishing is prohibited. The Department will also notify, at least one month in advance, any change to these delimitations.

...omissis...

5. Agreement in the form of an Exchange of Letters between the European Union and the Kingdom of Morocco concerning reciprocal liberalisation measures on agricultural products, processed agricultural products, fish and fishery products, the replacement of Protocols 1, 2 and 3 and their Annexes and amendments to the Euro-Mediterranean Agreement establishing an association between the European Communities and their Member States, of the one part, and the Kingdom of Morocco, of the other part[1].

AGREEMENT

in the form of an Exchange of Letters between the European Union and the Kingdom of Morocco concerning reciprocal liberalisation measures on agricultural products, processed agricultural products, fish and fishery products, the replacement of Protocols 1, 2 and 3 and their Annexes and amendments to the Euro-Mediterranean Agreement establishing an association between the European Communities and their Member States, of the one part, and the Kingdom of Morocco, of the other part

A. *Letter from the Union*

Dear Sir/Madam,

I have the honour to refer to the negotiations which took place in accordance with the Euro-Mediterranean Roadmap for agriculture (Rabat Roadmap) adopted on 28 November 2005, by the Ministers for Foreign Affairs at the Euro-Mediterranean conference, for the acceleration of liberalisation of trade in agricultural products, processed agricultural products, fish and fishery products under Articles 16 and 18 of the Euro-Mediterranean Agreement establishing an association between the European Communities and their Member States, of the one part, and the Kingdom of Morocco, of the other part (hereinafter the 'Association Agreement'), in force since 1 March 2000, which provides for the gradual implementation of greater liberalisation of reciprocal trade in agricultural products, processed agricultural products, fish and fishery products.

At the end of the negotiations the European Union and the Kingdom of Morocco agreed upon the following amendments to the Association Agreement:

---

1 Adopted by Council decision 2012/497/EU, 8 March 2012, in *OJEU*, L 241/2, 7 September 2012.

(1) the text of Article 7 shall be replaced by the following text:

'The provisions of this Chapter shall apply to products originating in the European Union or in Morocco other than those listed in Chapters 1 to 24 of the Combined Nomenclature (CN) and those listed in Annex 1, paragraph 1, (ii) of the WTO Agreement on Agriculture;

(2) Article 10 is deleted;

(3) the title of Chapter II shall be replaced by the following:

'AGRICULTURAL PRODUCTS, PROCESSED AGRICULTURAL PRODUCTS, FISH AND FISHERY PRODUCTS';

(4) the text of Article 15 shall be replaced by the following text:

'The expressions "agricultural products" "processed agricultural products" and "fish and fishery products" refer to the products listed in Chapters 1 to 24 of the Combined Nomenclature (CN) and those listed in Annex 1, paragraph 1, (ii) of the WTO Agreement on Agriculture.';

(5) the text of Article 17 shall be replaced by the following text:

'1. Agricultural products, processed agricultural products, fish and fishery products originating in Morocco listed in Protocol No 1 shall be subject to the arrangements set out in that Protocol on importation into the European Union.

The provisions of this chapter shall not preclude the retention by the European Union of an agricultural component on imports of fructose (CN code 1702 50 00) originating in Morocco.

This agricultural component reflects the gaps between the prices on the market of the European Union of agricultural products considered as used in the production of fructose and the price of imports of such products from third countries.

2. Agricultural products, processed agricultural products, fish and fishery products originating in the European Union listed in Protocol No 2 shall be subject to the arrangements set out in that Protocol on importation into Morocco.

The provisions of this chapter shall not preclude the separate specification by Morocco of an agricultural component in the import duties in force on the products listed in subchapter HS 1902 (pasta) and included in list 3 attached to Protocol No 2.';

(6) the text of Article 18(1) shall be replaced by the following text:

'1. The parties shall meet no later than three years from the date of entry into force of this agreement to consider the possibility of granting each other further preferential concessions, taking into account the agricultural policy, sensitivity and specific characteristics of each product concerned.';

(7) Protocols 1, 2 and 3 and their Annexes shall be replaced by those set out in Annexes I and II attached to this exchange of letters.

This Agreement in the form of an exchange of letters shall enter into force on the first day of the third month following the date of deposit of the last instrument of approval.

I would be grateful if you could confirm the agreement of your Government to the above.

Please accept, Sir/Madam, the assurance of my highest consideration.

...omissis...

ANNEX I

PROTOCOL No 1

concerning the arrangements applicable to the importation into the European Union of agricultural products, processed agricultural products, fish and fishery products originating in the Kingdom of Morocco

Imports into the European Community of agricultural products, processed agricultural products, fish and fishery products originating in Morocco shall be subject to the conditions set out below.

TITLE I

GENERAL PROVISIONS

Article 1

1. With a view to accelerating the liberalisation of bilateral trade in agricultural products, processed agricultural products, fish and fishery products between the Kingdom of Morocco and the European Union, new provisions and concessions shall be established by both parties, in accordance with the terms of the 2005 Euro-Mediterranean Rabat Roadmap, established for the liberalisation of trade in agricultural products, processed agricultural products, fish and fishery products.

2. These new provisions and concessions, as set out in the specific provisions cited below, shall govern the bilateral trade in agricultural products, processed agricultural products, fish and fishery products, of the two parties.

TITLE II

SPECIAL PROVISIONS

Article 2

Tariff provisions

1. On the date of entry into force of this Protocol, customs duties (*ad valorem* and specific) applicable on imports into the European Union of agricultural products, processed agricultural products, fish and fishery products originating in Morocco shall be eliminated, except if otherwise provided for in paragraphs 2 and 3 for the agricultural products and in Article 5 for the processed agricultural products.

...omissis...

B. *Letter from the Kingdom of Morocco*

Dear Sir/Madam,

I have the honour to acknowledge receipt of your letter of today's date which reads as follows:

'I have the honour to refer to the negotiations which took place in accordance with the Euro-Mediterranean Roadmap for agriculture (Rabat Roadmap) adopted on 28 November 2005, by the Ministers for Foreign Affairs at the Euro-Mediterranean conference, for the acceleration of liberalisation of trade in agricultural products, processed agricultural products, fish and fishery products under Articles 16 and 18 of the Euro-Mediterranean Agreement establishing an association between the European Communities and their Member States, of the one part, and the Kingdom of Morocco, of the other part (hereinafter the "Association Agreement"), in force since 1 March 2000, which provides for the gradual implementation of greater liberalisation of reciprocal trade in agricultural products, processed agricultural products, fish and fishery products.

At the end of the negotiations the European Union and the Kingdom of Morocco agreed upon the following amendments to the Association Agreement:

(1) the text of Article 7 shall be replaced by the following text:

"The provisions of this Chapter shall apply to products originating in the European Union or in Morocco other than those listed in Chapters 1 to 24 of the Combined Nomenclature (CN) and those listed in Annex 1, paragraph 1, (ii) of the WTO Agreement on Agriculture.";

(2) Article 10 is deleted;

(3) the title of Chapter II shall be replaced by the following:

"AGRICULTURAL PRODUCTS, PROCESSED AGRICULTURAL PRODUCTS, FISH AND FISHERY PRODUCTS";

(4) the text of Article 15 shall be replaced by the following text:

"The expressions 'agricultural products', 'processed agricultural products' and 'fish and fishery products' refer to the products listed in Chapters 1 to 24 of the Combined Nomenclature (CN) and those listed in Annex 1, paragraph 1, (ii) of the WTO Agreement on Agriculture.";

(5) the text of Article 17 shall be replaced by the following text:

"1. Agricultural products, processed agricultural products, fish and fishery products originating in Morocco listed in Protocol No 1 shall be subject to the arrangements set out in that Protocol on importation into the European Union.

The provisions of this chapter shall not preclude the retention by the European Union of an agricultural component on imports of fructose (CN code 1702 50 00) originating in Morocco.

This agricultural component reflects the gaps between the prices on the market of the European Union of agricultural products considered as used in the production of fructose and the price of imports of such products from third countries.

2. Agricultural products, processed agricultural products, fish and fishery products originating in the European Union listed in Protocol No 2 shall be subject to the arrangements set out in that Protocol on importation into Morocco.

The provisions of this chapter shall not preclude the separate specification by Morocco of an agricultural component in the import duties in force on the products listed in subchapter HS 1902 (pasta) and included in List 3 attached to Protocol No 2";

(6) the text of Article 18(1) shall be replaced by the following text:

"1. The parties shall meet no later than three years from the date of entry into force of this agreement to consider the possibility of granting each other further preferential concessions, taking into account the agricultural policy, sensitivity and specific characteristics of each product concerned.";

7) Protocols 1, 2 and 3 and their Annexes shall be replaced by those set out in Annexes I and II attached to this exchange of letters.

This Agreement in the form of an exchange of letters shall enter into force on the first day of the third month following the date of deposit of the last instrument of approval.

I would be grateful if you could confirm the agreement of your Government to the above.'

I have the honour to confirm the agreement of my Government with the contents of this letter.

Please accept, Sir/Madam, the assurance of my highest consideration.

...*omissis*...

6. Council of the European Union, Legal Service, Opinion on the Currently Negotiated Partnership Fisheries Agreement between the EC and the Kingdom of Marocco, Brussels, 22 February 2006, 6664/06[1].

COUNCIL OF THE EUROPEAN UNION

Brussels, 22 February 2006

6664/06

LIMITE

DOCUMENT PARTIALLY ACCESSIBLE TO THE PUBLIC

JUR 74
PECHE 52
MA 3

OPINION OF THE LEGAL SERVICE (*)

Subject: The currently negotiated Partnership Fisheries Agreement between the EC and the Kingdom of Morocco
– Compatibility with international Law

---

1. At its meeting on 19 January 2006, the Working Party on External Fisheries Policy asked the Council Legal Service for a written opinion on the following question:

Is the currently negotiated text of the Partnership Fisheries Agreement between the European Community and the Kingdom of Morocco that would allow Community vessels to fish in waters of the Western Sahara compatible with international Law?

---

1 Other opinions were issued by the European Parliament's Legal Service in 2009 and 2013 but they are classified as confidential. Hence, they could not be reported here.

(*) This document contains legal advice protected under Article 4(2) of Regulation (EC) No. 1049/2001 of the European Parliament and of the Council of 30 May 2001 regarding public access to European Parliament, Council and Commission documents, and not released by the Council of the European Union to the public. The Council reserves all its rights in law as regards any unauthorised publication.

I. Background

2. The previous Partnership Fisheries Agreement between the European Community and Morocco[2] which came into force on 1 December 1995 expired on 30 November 1999.

After long negotiations to conclude a new agreement with Morocco, the European Community recognized on March 2001 that an Agreement could not be reached. Following the suspension of the negotiations a fund scheme for the restructuring of the Community fleet which had operated under the previous fisheries agreement and was forced to stop its fishing activities (basically located in Spain and Portugal) was approved[3].

3. The Commission resumed its negotiations with Morocco in the first half of 2005 on the basis of the mandate granted by the Council on 15 October 1999 for the previous set of negotiations; the Council updated the negotiating Directives on 18 July 2005. The Commission initialled with Morocco on 25 July 2005 a Fisheries Partnership Agreement (hereinafter referred to as the Agreement) together with a Protocol and Annex setting out the technical and financial conditions governing the fishing activities of Community vessels.

4. The Agreement, as currently drafted, provides Community fishermen with fishing opportunities in Moroccan fishing zones for a period of four years from its entry into force in exchange for a financial contribution of 144,400,000 € that the Community commits to grant to Morocco. As has been the practice under previous fisheries agreements with Morocco, Community vessels would have access to fishing stocks situated in Western Sahara waters, although the agreement does not expressely refer to Western Sahara waters.

5. At present, the sovereignty of the territory and maritime waters of Western Sahara is contested between the Kingdom of Morocco (which largely controls this region, including the almost totality of the coast areas, and claims full sovereignty over the territory and maritime waters of Western Sahara) and the Frente Popular para la Liberación de Saguia el-Hamra y de Río de Oro (Frente Polisario) a movement which claims the full independence and right to self-determination of Western Sahara.

...omissis...

---

2 Council Regulation (EC) No. 150/97 of 12 December 1996 on the conclusion of an Agreement on cooperation in the sea fisheries sector between the European Community and the Kingdom of Morocco and laying down provisions for its implementation (OJ L 030, 31.01.1997, p. 1).

3 Council Regulation (EC) No 2561/2001 of 17 December 2001 aiming to promote the conversion of fishing vessels and of fishermen that were, up to 1999, dependent on the fishing agreement with Morocco (OJ L 344, 28.12.2001, p. 0017.).

African Union

7. African Union Commission, Office of the Legal Counsel and Directorate for Legal Affairs of the African Union, Legal Opinion on the Legality in the Context of International Law, Including the Relevant United Nations Resolutions and OAU/AU Decisions, of Actions Allegedly Taken by the Moroccan Authorities or Any Other State, Group of States, Foreign Companies or Any Other Entity in the Exploration and/or Exploitation of Renewable and Non-Renewable Natural Resources or Any Other Economic Activity in Western Sahara, Addis Abeba, 14 October 2015.

AFRICAN UNION

UNION AFRICAINE

الاتحاد الأفريقي

UNIÃO AFRICANA

LEGAL OPINION

ON THE LEGALITY IN THE CONTEXT OF INTERNATIONAL LAW, INCLUDING THE RELEVANT UNITED NATIONS RESOLUTIONS AND OAU/AU DECISIONS, OF ACTIONS ALLEGEDLY TAKEN BY THE MOROCCAN AUTHORITIES OR ANY OTHER STATE, GROUP OF STATES, FOREIGN COMPANIES OR ANY OTHER ENTITY IN THE EXPLORATION AND/OR EXPLOITATION OF RENEWABLE AND NON-RENEWABLE NATURAL RESOURCES OR ANY OTHER ECONOMIC ACTIVITY IN WESTERN SAHARA

BY

THE OFFICE OF THE LEGAL COUNSEL AND DIRECTORATE FOR LEGAL AFFAIRS OF THE AFRICAN UNION COMMISSION

A. INTRODUCTION

1. The Government of the Saharawi Arab Democratic Republic (SADR), through a letter dated 25 February 2015, addressed to the Chairperson of the Commission, Dr. Nkosazana Dlamini Zuma, requesting a legal opinion from the Office of the Legal Counsel (OLC) on "the Illegality of the exploitation of the natural resources of Western Sahara by the Kingdom of Morocco, the occupying force, and any other entity, company or group." The issue, as submitted, already presupposed the illegality of the exploitation of natural resources by the Kingdom of Morocco.

2. The Permanent Mission of Saharawi Arab Democratic Republic in a note verbale under reference number 44/2015 dated 03 April 2015, however, modified the issue to "the legality in the context of international law, including the relevant UN resolutions and OUA/AU decisions, of actions allegedly taken by the Moroccan authorities or any other State, group of States, foreign companies or any other entity consisting in the exploration and/or exploitation of renewable and non-renewable natural resources or any other economic activities in Western Sahara."

3. It should be recalled that in February 2002, the UN Under-Secretary-General for Legal Affairs and Legal Counsel delivered a legal opinion to the United Nations Security Council on almost an identical issue, "the legality in the context of international law, including relevant resolutions of the Security Council and the General Assembly of the United Nations, and agreements concerning Western Sahara of actions allegedly taken by the Moroccan authorities consisting in the offering and signing of contracts with foreign companies for the exploration of mineral resources in Western Sahara"[1].

4. Since the issues concerning the Saharawi Republic are multidimensional, for purposes of this legal opinion, the OLC will restrict itself to the issue as contained in the note verbale from the Permanent Mission of SADR dated 3 April 2015.

---

1 The European Parliament Legal Service has also delivered legal opinions in respect of the Fisheries Partnership Agreement between the European Community and the Kingdom of Morocco in 2006 and 2009. The unofficial copies of the opinions are available on the website. See http://www.arso.org/LegalopinionUE200206.pdf accessed on 22.04.15 at 10.00; http://www.fisheiswhere.eu/a140x1077 accessed on 22.04.15 at 11:23 and Report on Legal Issues Involved in the Western Sahara Dispute: Use of Natural Resources available at http://www.nycbar.org/pdf/report/uploads/20072089ReportonLegalIssuesInvolvedintheWesternSaharaDispute.pdf, accessed on 20.04.15 at 14:25.

B. FACTUAL BACKGROUND[2]

5. The Territory of Western Sahara became a Spanish colony in 1884. During the time when the territory was a colony of Spain, it was known as Spanish Sahara.

6. The territory borders Morocco in the North, Mauritania in the South and East, Algeria in the East and the Atlantic Ocean in the West.

7. In 1963, Western Sahara was included on the list of non-self-governing territories under Article 73 of the UN Charter and Spain was the administering power[3]. The General Assembly had demanded that Spain should undertake immediate steps to guarantee the exercise of self-determination by the people of Western Sahara. This underscored the right to a referendum on self-determination under UN General Assembly Resolution 1514 (XV) adopted in 1960. The General Assembly has always maintained that the people of Western Sahara are entitled to the right to self-determination.

8. The International Court of Justice (ICJ) issued an advisory opinion on the status of Western Sahara on 16 October 1975 at the request of the UN General Assembly. In the opinion, the ICJ dismissed the sovereignty claims by Morocco and Mauritania. After the ICJ delivered its opinion, Spain entered into a secret agreement with Morocco and Mauritania (Madrid Accords) which purported to authorize Spain's withdrawal from the Territory of Western Sahara and permit the occupation by Morocco and Mauritania.

9. On 31 October 1975, Morocco invaded Western Sahara on the pretext of claiming the territory, despite the ICJ's advisory opinion on the issue, that clearly stated that there were no legal ties between either Morocco or Mauritania with the Western Sahara. In response to the ICJ Advisory Opinion, King Hassan II of Morocco in November 1975 ordered a "Green March" of over 350,000 Moroccans into Western Sahara, disregarding a formal call from the Security Council to put an end forthwith to the declared march into Western Sahara[4].

10. As a result of pressure, Spain negotiated a secret settlement on 14 November, 1975 with Morocco and Mauritania, under the Madrid Tripartite Accords, which resulted in Spain's withdrawal from what was then called the Spanish Sahara on 26 February 1976.

---

2 The facts generally have been gathered from a number of Reports of the Commission on Western Sahara.

3 UNGA Resolution 2072 (XX) of 17 December 1965.

4 UN Security Council Resolution 379 (1975).

11. Spain withdrew after it had notified the Secretary-General of the UN. This was immediately followed by a unilateral proclamation of the Saharawi Arab Democratic Republic (SADR) by the Polisario Front on 27 February 1976 filling the legal and administrative vacuum that Spain unilaterally created when it withdrew from its colony without finishing the process of decolonization that the UN entrusted it with.

12. Before Spain's withdrawal as the administering power, the General Assembly had demanded that Spain should undertake immediate steps to guarantee the exercise of self-determination by the people of Western Sahara[5].

13. Following the Madrid Accords, Moroccan and Mauritanian armed forces invaded Western Sahara. This invasion led to a war by Moroccan and Mauritanian forces on the one hand against the Polisario Front, on the other. The Polisario Front is a liberation movement fighting for the independence of Western Sahara. Mauritania withdrew its forces in 1979 and renounced its sovereignty claims. Mauritania also decided to recognize SADR as the legitimate authority in Western Sahara[6]. The war between Morocco and the Polisario Front continued until it reached a stalemate in 1988. Later that year, the United Nations and the Organization of African Unity persuaded the parties to agree to a cease-fire and a settlement plan. Under the settlement plan, the issue of sovereignty over the Territory of Western Sahara would have to be settled by a referendum.

14. The war stopped in 1991 and the UN Mission for the Referendum of Western Sahara (MINURSO) was established by UN Security Council resolution 690 of 29 April 1991. The referendum was planned to take place within 6 months and the Saharawi people were to choose between independence or integration with Morocco. The referendum has not been held up to now.

C. THE STATUS OF THE WESTERN SAHARA/SADR

i) African Union

15. The SADR[7] became a Member State of the Organization of African Unity (OAU) in 1982. It should be recalled that membership to the OAU was open to any independent sovereign African State[8]. The admission

---

5 UNGA Resolutions 2229 (XXI of 20 December 1966, and 2354 (XXII) of 19 December 1967.

6 A/34/427-S/13503, Annex I and II, Official Record of the Security Council, Thirty-Fourth Year, Supplement for July, August and September 1979.

7 SADR was proclaimed by the Polisario Front on 27 February, 1976.

8 Article XXVIII (1) of the OAU Charter.

of SADR to the membership of OAU in 1982 signified that more than half of Member States of the OAU recognized Western Sahara as an independent sovereign African State[9]. It should also be recalled that one of the purposes of the OAU was to eradicate all forms of colonialism from Africa[10]. Accordingly, the SADR is one of the founders and a member of the African Union, the successor organization to OAU.

16. Notwithstanding the membership of SADR to both OAU and AU, there is recognition that the people of Western Sahara are not fully liberated. The SADR controls only a part of Western Sahara[11]. To this end, both the OAU and AU have undertaken efforts to conduct a referendum for self-determination of the people of Western Sahara. A year after the admission of SADR as member of the OAU, the Assembly of Heads of State and Government of the OAU urged the Kingdom of Morocco and the Polisario Front "to undertake direct negotiations with a view of bringing about a ceasefire to create the necessary condition for a peaceful and fair referendum for self-determination of the people of Western Sahara, a referendum without any administrative or military constraints…"[12]. The right of the people of Western Sahara to a referendum for self-determination has been discussed regularly and reaffirmed by the Assembly of the African Union[13]

17. It should be noted that in the plan of action adopted at the AU Special Session on the Consideration and Resolution of Conflicts in Africa, held in Tripoli, Libya in August 2009, the Assembly of the African Union resolved to support the efforts of the UN to overcome the impasse on Western Sahara. The Assembly also recalled relevant UN Security Council resolutions which called for direct negotiations without preconditions and in good faith, which would provide for the self determination of the people of Western Sahara in the context of arrangements consistent with the principles and purposes of the Charter of the UN[14].

18. The debate on the referendum for the right to self-determination of the people of Western Sahara reached its climax during the celebration of the 50th Anniversary of the African Union in May 2013. The Executive

---

9 Admission is based on decision by simple majority of Member States. See Article XXVIII (2).

10 Article II (1) (d) of the OAU Charter.

11 The rest is occupied by the Kingdom of Morocco.

12 Resolution AHG/Res.104 (XIX) adopted in June, 1983.

13 See AU Special Session of the Assembly on the Consideration and Resolution of Conflicts, Tripoli, Libya; Assembly/AU/Dec.559 (XXIV) adopted in January 2015; EX.CL/Dec.758 (XXII) adopted in January 2013.

14 Progress Report of the Chairperson of the Commission on the situation in Western Sahara (EX.CL/788 (XXIII)-Rev-1.

Council reiterated the call to the two parties, namely, the Kingdom of Morocco and Polisario Front, to undertake direct negotiations, with a view of achieving a just, lasting and mutually acceptable political solution, which would provide for the self-determination of the people of Western Sahara[15] The Assembly of the African Union also reiterated the call of the United Nations Security Council to the parties[16].

19. The Peace and Security Council of the African Union at its 496th meeting held in Addis Ababa, Ethiopia on 27 March 2015 recalled that the Western Sahara remained an issue in the completion of the decolonization process of Africa and urged the UN Security Council to take all necessary decisions to ensure progress in search for a solution to the conflict in Western Sahara and appealed for an enhanced and coordinated international action towards the early organization of a referendum for the self-determination of Western Sahara, in compliance with relevant OAU/AU decisions and UN resolutions[17].

20. As can be seen from the above, the African Union has continued to call for a referendum of self-determination of the people of Western Sahara within the acknowledged principles of international law.

21. It should be noted that the African Union considers Western Sahara to be under colonial occupation by Morocco[18]. The occupation is against the spirit of the founding objectives and principles of both the OAU and the AU.

ii) United Nations

22. The SADR is not a member of the UN.

23. As far back as 1963, the Territory of Western Sahara[19] was listed among Non-Self-Governing Territories as recognized in the UN General Assembly resolution 1514 (XV) of 14 December 1960 that contained the Declaration on the Granting of Independence to Colonial Countries and Peoples. It should be recalled that under Resolution 1514 (XV), the General Assembly, declared inter alia, that all peoples have the right to self-determination, and that by virtue of that right, they should freely determine their political status and freely pursue their economic, social and

15 Para. 3 of EX.CL/Dec.773 (XXIII). The same call was repeated by the Assembly in Assembly/AU/Dec.559 (XXIV).

16 Assembly/AU/Dec.559 (XXIV).

17 Para. 7 (i) and (ii) of Communique for the 496th PSC Meeting, PSC/PR/COMM/1. (CDXCVI)

18 SOLEMN DECLARATION ON THE 50th ANNIVERSARY OF THE OAU/AU (Assembly/AU/Decl.3.(XXI), adopted by the twenty first AU Summit held from 26-27 May 2013 in Addis Ababa, Ethiopia.

19 Then Spanish Sahara.

cultural development[20]. In this regard, the right of the people of Western Sahara to a referendum for self-determination has been reaffirmed by both the General Assembly and the UN Security Council as well as by the International Court of Justice[21].

24. Chapter XI of the UN Charter deals with Non-Self-Governing Territories. Article 73 of the Charter provides that Member States of the UN which have or assumed responsibilities for the administration of Non-Self-Governing Territories must recognize the principle that the interests of the inhabitants of these territories are paramount, and must accept as a sacred trust the obligation to promote to the utmost, the well-being of the inhabitants of these territories. In addition, Article 73 (e) requires the administering Power to transmit to the UN Secretary General, statistical and other information of a technical nature relating to economic, social and educational conditions in the Non-Self-Governing Territory.

25. However, from the UN perspective, Western Sahara does not have any administering power, as Spain had withdrawn from the territory on 26 February 1976[22].

26. In the implementation of Article 73 of the Charter, the UN General Assembly elaborated some principles that must be adhered to, namely that:

a) All States should comply with the resolutions of the General Assembly on the activities of foreign economic and financial interests *and to refrain from helping to perpetuate the colonial situation in the Territory by means of investments (emphasis added)*[23]. States must therefore avoid any economic activity that adversely affects the interests of the peoples of the Non-Self-Governing Territories[24].

---

20 Para. 2 of UNGA Resolution 1514 (XV).

21 See UNGA Resolution 2983 (XXVII) on the Question of Spanish Sahara adopted on 14 December 1972; UNGA resolution 61/123 adopted on 14 December 2006 on Economic and other activities which affect the interests of the peoples of the Non-Self-Governing Territories; UNSC Resolution 1979 (2011) adopted on 27 April 2011; ICJ Advisory Opinion on Western Sahara of 16 October 1975.

22 http://www.un.org/en/decolonization/nonselfgovterritories.shtml accessed on 20.4.15 at 10:00 hrs. It is indicated that on 26 February 1976, Spain informed the Secretary-General that as of that date it had terminated its presence in the Territory of the Sahara and deemed it necessary to place on record that Spain considered itself thenceforth exempt from any responsibility of any international nature in connection with the administration of the Territory, in view of the cessation of its participation in the temporary administration established for the Territory. In 1990, the General Assembly reaffirmed that the question of Western Sahara was a question of decolonization which remained to be completed by the people of Western Sahara.

23 UNGA Resolution 2983 (XXVII) on the Question of Western Sahara, para. 6.

24 UNGA resolution 61/123 adopted on 14 December 2006 on Economic and other activities which affect the interests of the peoples of the Non-Self-Governing Territories.

Accordingly, investments that may constitute an obstacle to the liberation of a territory should not be promoted by States[25].

b) The territory of a colony or other Non-Self-Governing Territory, has under the UN Charter, a status separate and distinct from the territory of the state administering it and that the separate and distinct status shall exist until the right to self-determination has been fully exercised[26].

c) Sovereignty over natural resources is a basic constituent of the right to self-determination[27].

d) Natural resources are a heritage of the peoples of the non-self-governing territories and that exploitation and plundering of the marine and other natural resources of Non-Self-Governing Territories, in violation of the relevant resolutions of the UN, is a threat to the integrity and prosperity of the Non-Self-Governing Territories[28].

27. In addition, Resolution III of the UN Conference on the Law of the Sea, took into account the provisions of the Charter of the UN, in particular Article 73 and declared that:

> In the case of a territory whose people have not attained full independence or other self-governing status recognized by the United Nations, or a territory under colonial domination, provisions concerning rights and interests under the Convention *shall be implemented for the benefit of the people of the territory with a view to promoting their well-being and development (emphasis added)*[29].

---

25 Article 16 (2) of the Charter of Economic Rights and Duties of States.

26 UNGA Resolution 2625 (XXV) on the Declaration on Principles of International Relations and Cooperation among States in accordance with the Charter of the United Nations, paragraph on the principle of equal rights and self-determination of peoples.

27 UNGA Resolution 1314 (XIII) on the Recommendations concerning International respect for the right of peoples and nations to self-determination; UNGA Resolution 1803 (XVII) on the Permanent Sovereignty over natural resources, preambular paragraph 2; UNGA48/46 (1993) on the Activities of foreign and other economic interests which impede the implementation of the Declaration on the Granting of Independence of Colonial Countries and Peoples in Territories under Colonial domination; UNGA resolution 49/40 (1994) on the Activities of foreign and other economic interests which impede the implementation of the Declaration on the Granting of Independence of Colonial Countries and Peoples in Territories under Colonial domination.

28 UNGA resolution 61/123 adopted on 14 December 2006 on Economic and other activities which affect the interests of the peoples of the Non-Self-Governing Territories, paragraph 7; UNGA resolution 48/46 (1993); UNGA resolution 49/40 (1994).

29 http://www.un.org/depts/los/convention_agreements/texts/final_act_eng.pdf accessed on 24.04.15 at 15:36.

D. MOROCCO AND THE STATUS OF WESTERN SAHARA

28. Despite the fact that it occupies a large part of the Territory of Western Sahara, Morocco has never acquired the status of an administering Power of the territory in terms of Article 73 of the UN Charter. The UN list of non-self-governing territories confirms that after the withdrawal and abandonment of responsibilities by Spain on 26 February 1976, Western Sahara has not had any other administering power[30]. Morocco has also never complied or purported to comply with the requirements of Article 73 of the UN Charter, in particular the transmission of statistical and other information.

29. With regard to Morocco's claims of sovereignty over the Territory of Western Sahara. It should be recalled that on 16 October 1975, the International Court of Justice (ICJ) issued an Advisory Opinion denying the claims of Morocco and Mauritania and affirming the right of the Saharawi to self-determination under international law. One of the issues on which the Court was requested to provide an Advisory Opinion by the UN General Assembly was the legal ties between Western Sahara and both Morocco and Mauritania[31]. The ICJ found that both Morocco and Mauritania never displayed any effective and exclusive activity in Western Sahara[32]. Both countries therefore failed to establish any tie to territorial sovereignty over the Territory of Western Sahara. The Court concluded that it had "not found legal ties of such a nature as might affect the application of resolution 1514 (XV) in the decolonization of Western Sahara and, in particular, of the principle of self-determination through the free and genuine expression of the will of the people of the Territory"[33]. Accordingly, the UN Security Council called upon Morocco to withdraw from Western Sahara when[34] it occupied the Territory on 31st October 1975.

30. It should be noted, as indicated by the UN Legal Counsel in his opinion to the Security Council[35], that "the Madrid Agreement did not transfer sovereignty over the Territory, nor confer upon any of the signatories the status of an administering power, a status which Spain alone could not have unilaterally transferred".

---

30 http://www.un.org/en/decolonization/nonselfgovterritories.shtml accessed on 20.4.15 at 10:00 hrs.

31 UNGA Resolution 3292 (XXIX, UN Doc. A /9631 (1974).

32 ICJ opinion at 49 and 68.

33 ICJ opinion at 60.

34 UN Security Council Resolution 379 (1975).

35 Para. 6 of the Legal Opinion.

31. In its resolution of 28 April 2015, the UN Security Council called upon the parties "to continue negotiations under the auspices of the UN Secretary-General without preconditions and in good faith, with a view to achieving a just, lasting, and mutually acceptable political solution, which will provide for the self-determination of the people of the Western Sahara in the context of arrangements consistent with the principles and purposes of the Charter of the United Nations…[36]".

32. It should be noted that the issue of Western Sahara is dealt with by the Fourth Committee of the UN General Assembly, which addresses issues relating to decolonization.

E. RELEVANT INSTRUMENTS ON THE ISSUE OF EXPLORATION OR EXPLOITATION OF NATURAL RESOURCES FROM WESTERN SAHARA

i) International and Regional Instruments

33. Several international and regional instruments have recognized the right of peoples to self-determination and the right of peoples to permanent sovereignty over their natural resources. These include the following :

34. **Convention IV respecting the Laws and Customs of War on Land and its Annex, the Hague Convention of 1907**: Under the Convention and other rules of international humanitarian law, the occupying Power may not change the legal, institutional and political status of the occupied territory. This is because occupation is only a temporary status and the occupying Power should not introduce permanent changes in the occupied territory. The occupying power, may however, take measures to restore and ensure public order and safety in the occupied territory[37]. Article 47 of the Convention also formally forbids pillage.

35. It should be noted that the UN General Assembly characterized Morocco as the occupying Power in Western Sahara in 1979 and 1980. However, Morocco denies the applicability of such law as it considers Western Sahara under its own sovereignty even though this claim had been dismissed by the ICJ.

36. **The 4th Geneva Convention of 1949**: Article 33 of the Convention prohibits pillage of natural resources.

37. **The two International Covenants on Civil and Political Rights and on Economic, Social and Cultural of 1966 (entered into force**

---

36 UNSC Resolution 2218 (2015).

37 Article 43 of the IV Hague Convention.

in 1976): Article 1 of both Covenants provides that all peoples have a right to self-determination and to freely determine their political status and to freely pursue their economic, social and cultural development. In addition, the Article provides that all peoples also have a right to freely dispose of their natural wealth[38]. Accordingly, States Parties to the Covenant, including those having responsibility for the administration of Non-Self-Governing and Trust Territories, must promote the realization of the right of self-determination and respect that right, in conformity with the provisions of the Charter of the United Nations[39].

38. **UN Charter of Economic Rights and Duties of States of 1974**: Article 16 (2) provides that "*No state has the right to promote or encourage investments that may constitute an obstacle to the liberation of a territory occupied by force*".

39. **The African Charter on Human and Peoples' Rights of 1981**: Article 20 of the African Charter on Human and Peoples' Rights provides that:

All peoples shall have the right to existence. They shall have the unquestionable and inalienable right to self-determination. They shall freely determine their political status and shall pursue their economic and social development according to the policy they have freely chosen.

40. Article 21 provides that all peoples shall freely dispose of their wealth and natural resources and that in case of spoliation, the dispossessed people shall have the right to the lawful recovery of their property as well as to an adequate compensation.

41. **UN Convention on the Law of the Sea of 1982**: While Western Sahara is not a Party to the UN Convention on the Law of the Sea, Resolution III of the UN Conference on the Law of the Sea declared that "in the case of territory whose people have not attained full independence or other self-governing status recognized by the United Nations, or a territory under colonial domination, provisions concerning rights and obligations under the Convention shall be implemented for the benefit of the people of the territory…".

ii) The case law of the International Court of Justice:

42. In the case of *Democratic Republic of Congo (DRC) v Uganda (Armed Activities on the Territory of the Congo)*, the ICJ dealt with the question of natural resource exploitation and made reference to Articles

38 The same is contained in Article 1 of the International Covenant on Economic, Social and Cultural Rights.

39 Article 1 (3) of the International Covenant on Civil and Political Rights and the International Covenant on Economic, Social and Cultural Rights.

43 and 47 of the Hague Convention and Article 33 of the 4th Geneva Convention of 1949 relating to the prohibition of pillage. The ICJ also observed that both DRC and Uganda are both Parties to the African Charter on Human and Peoples' Rights. The Court then referred to Article 21 (2) of the African Charter which provides that "in case of spoliation the dispossessed people shall have the right to the law full recovery of its property as well as to an adequate compensation". The Court concluded that the occupying Power is internationally responsible for acts of looting, plundering, and exploitation of natural resources in the occupied territories.

43. There were other two cases in which it was argued that the principle of permanent sovereignty over natural resources was violated but the ICJ never issued any judgment on the merits[40].

F. LEGAL OPINION BY THE UN UNDER-SECRETARY FOR LEGAL AFFAIRS AND LEGAL COUNCIL, 12 FEBRUARY 2002

44. As already indicated in paragraph 3 of this opinion, the UN Under-Secretary for Legal Affairs and Legal Counsel delivered a legal opinion at the request of the UN Security Council. The request was made on 13 November, 2001 and the issue that he was asked to address was "the legality in the context of international law, including relevant resolutions of the Security Council and the General Assembly of the United Nations, and agreements concerning Western Sahara of actions allegedly taken by the Moroccan authorities consisting in the offering and signing of contracts with foreign companies for the exploration of mineral resources in Western Sahara"[41].

45. The UN Legal Counsel after examining Article 73 of the UN Charter, the resolutions of the UN General Assembly and practices States noted that "while the legal nature of the core principle of permanent sovereignty over natural resources, as a corollary to the principle of territorial sovereignty or the right to self-determination, is indisputably part of customary international law, its exact legal scope and implications are still debatable"[42].

46. The Legal Counsel then analyzed the issue of mineral resource exploitation by analogy and concluded that mineral resources exploitation

40 In the case of *East Timor v Portugal*, the Court concluded that it lacked jurisdiction while in the *Nauru Phosphate Case*, the Parties reached a settlement following a judgment on preliminary objections.

41 Para. 1 of the Legal Opinion.

42 Para. 14 of the Legal Opinion.

in Non-Self-Governing Territories is not illegal per se, but illegal if it is conducted in disregard of the needs and interests of the people of that territory[43]. Regrettably, under this approach, the UN Legal Counsel did not consider the question of whether Morocco should be considered as an occupying or administering Power of Western Sahara under provisions of the UN Charter. The UN Legal Counsel also did not consider any UN Security Council and General Assembly resolutions relating to the status or occupation of Morocco of Western Sahara.

47. Using the analogy of mineral resource activities conducted in Non-Self-Governing Territories, the UN Legal Counsel concluded that:

> "...the contracts for oil reconnaissance and evaluation do not entail exploitation or the physical removal of the mineral resources, and no benefits have as of yet accrued. The conclusion is, therefore, that while the specific contracts which are the subject of the Security Council's request are not in themselves illegal, *if further exploitation and exploitation activities were to proceed in disregard of the interests and wishes of the people of Western Sahara, they would in violation of the international law principles applicable to mineral resource activities in Non-Self-Government Territories (emphasis added)*".

48. The former UN Legal Counsel has acknowledged in his latter presentations on the matter that Morocco does not have the status of administering Power with respect to Western Sahara. He has indicated that matters concerning the status of Western Sahara are sensitive[44]. He has also decried statements by Morocco claiming sovereignty over Western Sahara as being incompatible with UN Security Council resolutions and the 1975 ICJ Advisory Opinion[45].

G. LEGAL ANALYSIS

49. The first issue to be addressed is whether Morocco can explore and exploit renewable and non-renewable natural resources in the Territory of Western Sahara.

50. The issue can only be fully addressed first by analyzing the status of Morocco on Western Sahara. Western Sahara is a Non-Self-Governing Territory under Article 73 of the UN Charter. As a Non-Self-Governing Territory, Western Sahara retains its separate and distinct status until the right to self-determination by its people has been fully exercised through

---

43 Para. 21 of the Legal Opinion.

44 See the Legality of exploring and exploiting natural resources in Western Sahara, paper presented by Ambassador Hans Corell, former UN Legal Counsel http://www.unisa.ac.za/contents/faculties/law/docs/14corell.pdf, accessed on 27.04.2015 at 07:55.

45 See http://www.judicialmonitor.org/current/specialcommentary.html, accessed on 24.04.15 at 14:00.

a referendum. It should be recalled that Morocco has never acquired the status of administering Power over the Territory of Western Sahara in terms of Article 73 of the UN Charter.

51. In addition, the ICJ, in its Advisory Opinion of 1975 on Western Sahara dismissed any sovereignty claims over Western Sahara by both Morocco and Mauritania.

52. It should be recalled that as indicated in Article II (d) of the OAU Charter, one of the objectives of the Organization of the African Unity was to rid the continent from the vestiges of colonialism.

53. The UN, the African Union and all Member States of the UN have never recognized the sovereignty claims of Morocco over Western Sahara nor approved Morocco's occupation of Western Sahara.

54. Regarding the political settlement on Western Sahara, the UN and the OAU/AU have recognized the unquestionable and inalienable right of the people of Western Sahara to a referendum for self-determination. Accordingly, both the UN and the AU has called on the two parties to reach a solution which will provide for the self-determination of the people of Western Sahara.

55. Furthermore, the UN, the AU and the ICJ have recognized the permanent sovereignty of the people of Western Sahara over their natural resources. The natural resources of Western Sahara are owned by the people of Western Sahara. The natural resources of Western Sahara forms part of the heritage of the people of Western Sahara.

56. The right of Self-determination and the right of people and sovereignty over their natural resources are peremptory norms (Jus Cogens) and Erga Omnes rights under international law as defined in article 53 of The Vienna Convention on the Law of Treaties of 1969[46], and as States cannot derogate from these norms.

57. Accordingly, Morocco has no legal right under the UN Charter and international law to occupy or govern the Territory of Western Sahara. It should be recalled that the UN Security Council called upon Morocco to withdraw from the Territory of Western Sahara after it had occupied the territory soon after the ICJ's Advisory Opinion. In this regard, Morocco has no right to explore and exploit any natural resources, renewable or non-renewable located in the occupied territories of Western Sahara or to enter into agreements with third parties concerning those resources.

46 "...a peremptory norm of general international law is a norm accepted and recognized by the international community of States as a whole as a norm from which no derogation is permitted and which can be modified only by a subsequent norm of general international law having the same character", article 53 of the Vienna convention on the law of Treaties.

58. In addition, any exploration and exploitation of the natural resources by Morocco in Western Sahara seriously undermines the efforts and negotiations, for a peaceful settlement, which have been ongoing for over four decades. The exploration and exploitation also undermines both the UN and AU principles and resolutions/decisions particularly the right of the people of Western Sahara to self-determination through a referendum and the right over their natural resources.

59. Member States of the UN are under an obligation from the UN Charter and other UN Resolutions to refrain from helping to perpetuate or to legitimize the colonial situation by means of investments or exploitation of natural resources in the Non-Self-Governing Territory.

60. In view of the foregoing, any exploration and exploitation of natural resources by Morocco, any other State, group of States, or foreign companies engaged by Morocco in Western Sahara is illegal since they violate international law and resolutions of the UN and the AU. The exploitation of natural resources is also a threat to the integrity and prosperity of the people of Western Sahara. In this regard, foreign companies and any other State or group of States entering into arrangements of agreements/contracts with Morocco for exploitation of natural resources in Western Sahara are aiding and abetting an illegal situation and such agreements/contracts are invalid[47].

61. Both the UN Security Council and the AU Peace and Security Council should exercise their responsibilities and put pressure on Morocco to ensure that the illegal exploration and exploitation of Western Sahara natural resources should cease until a just, lasting solution is achieved by the parties through a referendum for self-determination.

62. The second issue deals with the circumstances under which exploration or exploitation of the natural resources of Western Sahara should take place. It is only on this point that we agree with the opinion of the former UN Legal Counsel which he delivered to the UN Security Council. Western Sahara is a Non-Self-Governing Territory and therefore all activities must be undertaken in strict compliance with the provisions of Article 73 of the UN Charter as elaborated by various resolutions of the UN Security Council and the General Assembly. An extra margin of caution should be applied if the State concerned is not the administering Power over the territory as in the case of Morocco.

63. It should be recalled that the former Legal Counsel of the UN had concluded thus:

---

47 See UNSC Resolution 276 (1979) where the UN Security Council declared the continued presence of South African in Namibia illegal and that consequently all acts taken by the Government of South Africa were illegal and invalid.

> "…if further exploration and exploitation activities were to proceed in disregard of the interests and wishes of the people of Western Sahara, they would be in violation of the international law principles applicable to mineral resource activities in Non-Self-Governing Territories."

64. We reiterate the fact that only the people of Western Sahara, as a Non-Self-Governing Territory, have the right to permanent sovereignty over their natural resources. To be legal, economic activities for exploration and exploitation of natural resources in Western Sahara must benefit the people of Western Sahara and respect their wishes. The people of Western Sahara and their legitimate representatives (Polisario Front)[48] and Saharawi Republic Government should not only be consulted but must directly be involved in any arrangement or agreement regarding the exploitation or exploration of natural resources in in their territory.

65. In this regard, if Morocco has entered into agreements for the exploration and exploitation of natural resources in Western Sahara, the UN Security Council should ensure that Morocco scrupulously accounts for such activities and transfer all benefits that have accrued to the people of Western Sahara through a transparent and independent mechanism supervised by the UN and AU. There might be need for the UN and AU to appoint a Joint independent panel to verify Morocco's account.

H. CONCLUSIONS AND RECOMMENDATIONS

66. From the analysis above, it is evident that both the UN and AU must exercise their responsibilities and put pressure on Morocco to comply with principles of the UN and relevant international law on the right to self-determination and exploitation of natural resources. The uncertainty that has marked the issue of Western Sahara for over four decades cannot be allowed to continue.

67. Morocco is not an administering Power over Western Sahara's territory under Article 73 of the UN Charter. Morocco also does not have sovereignty over Western Sahara; therefore Western Sahara question remains a pending issue of decolonization and should therefore be resolved in accordance with UN General Assembly resolution 1514 (XV) of 14 December 1960 on the Granting of Independence to Colonial Countries and Peoples.

68. Morocco has no right to explore and exploit any natural resources, renewable or non-renewable located in the occupied territories of Western Sahara or to enter into agreements/contracts with third parties concerning these resources.

---

[48] UNGA resolution 34/37 (1979).

69. Thus, AU through the African Union Commission and other relevant organs must appeal to the UN Security Council to ensure that exploration and exploitation of natural resources in Western Sahara is undertaken under the following framework:

a) Morocco should not enter into any agreements with any other State, group of States or foreign companies for exploration or exploitation of renewable or non-renewable natural resources over the Territory of Western Sahara. In this regard, Agreements entered into by Morocco should be limited exclusively to its territory internationally recognized under its sovereignty (which does not include Western Sahara);

b) Any exploration or exploitation of natural resources in Western Sahara must be for the benefit of the people of Western Sahara and in accordance with their wishes;

c) Accordingly, the people of Western Sahara and their legitimate representatives[49] must not only be consulted but they must consent and effectively participate in reaching any agreement that involves the exploitation of natural resources in the Territory of Western Sahara.

d) Morocco and any other entity should be held accountable for agreements/contracts entered into for exploration and/or exploitation of renewable or non-renewable natural resources in the Territory of Western Sahara and ensure that all benefits accrue to the people of Western Sahara in accordance with international law. In this regard, the UN and AU should consider appointing a joint independent panel to verify Morocco's account.

70. The UN Security Council and AU Peace and Security Council must also inform all Member States of the UN and AU accordingly that any agreements/contracts for the exploration and/or exploitation of renewable or non-renewable natural resources over Western Sahara in disregard of the interests and wishes of the people of Western Sahara without consultations with their legitimate representatives violates principles of international law on self-determination and exploitation of natural resources in Non-Self-Governing Territories, such agreements/ contracts are null and therefore illegal.

71. Since Saharawi Republic (SADR) is a Member State of the African Union, all Member States of the African Union must bear in mind the principles and objectives of the African Union particularly on the need to defend the sovereignty and territorial independence of SADR. The African Union concerns on the illegal exploration and exploitation

49 The Polisario Front. See UNGA Resolution 34/37/1979.

of natural resources in Western Sahara must be transmitted by the African Union Commission and other relevant AU organs and offices to other international, regional organizations and partners. Therefore, the issue should be included in the agenda for discussion with the partners involved in the illegal exploration and/or exploitation of renewable or non-renewable natural resources in Western Sahara.

72. Member States of the UN and their companies are under obligation according to international law, UN Charter and other UN resolutions to refrain from helping in the perpetuation or legitimization of the colonial situation in Western Sahara by means of investments or exploration and/or exploitation of renewable or non-renewable natural resources and other economic activities in the Non-Self-Governing Territory, and should therefore refrain from entering into agreements/contracts with Morocco as the occupying Power in accordance to the UNGA Resolution 2711 of 1970.

73. The UN, the AU and the ICJ have recognized the unalienable right of the Saharawi people to self-determination and their permanent sovereignty over their natural resources. The latter are owned by the people of Western Sahara and form part of their heritage. UN Member States should make the necessary political and legal arrangements and inform their companies about the legal status of Western Sahara and the illegality of exploration and/or exploitation of renewable or non-renewable natural resources and other economic activities in this territory.

74. Any exploration and exploitation of renewable or non-renewable natural resources by Morocco, any other State, group of States or foreign companies in Western Sahara is contrary to the UN Charter, customary international law and therefore illegal as it violates international law.

75. The exploitation and exploration of renewable or non-renewable natural resources in the current situation of occupation is also a threat to the integrity and prosperity of the people of Western Sahara and to the peace and stability in the North Africa. This is in accordance to the UNGA Resolution 2983(XXVII) of 1972.

76. The UN should assume its political and legal responsibilities and protect the Sahrawi's renewable or non-renewable natural resources as it did in East Timor and Namibia till the people of the territory express their will and chose their destiny through a free and fair referendum.

77. All States or foreign companies shall refrain from importing Saharawi's products or investing in the occupied areas of Western Sahara as these activities are in violation of international law.

78. Any exploration and exploitation of natural resources by Morocco is illegal as it violates international law and resolutions of the UN and the

AU relating to the right to self-determination and permanent sovereignty of the people of Western Sahara over their natural resources. In addition, the exploration and exploitation seriously undermines the efforts and negotiations for a just and peaceful settlement over Western Sahara.

79. The African Union Commission should elaborate a comprehensive strategy aimed at Morocco, any other State, group of States or foreign Companies involved in the illegal exploration or exploitation of Western Sahara's renewable or non-renewable natural resources in compliance with the AUPSC communiqué 496 adopted in 27 March 2015.

United States

8. Executive Office of the President, The United States Trade Representative, Letter to the Honorable J.R. Pitts, U.S. House of Representatives concerning the Free Trade Agreement (FTA) between the United States and Morocco, Washington, 20 July 2004.

EXECUTIVE OFFICE OF THE PRESIDENT
The United States Trade Representative
Washington, D.C. 20508

20 July 2004

The Honorable J.R. Pitts,
U.S. House of Representatives
Washington, DC 20151

Dear Congressman Pitts:

Thank you for your letter of July 19, 2004, concerning our Free Trade Agreement (FTA) with Morocco and the status of Western Sahara.

The Administration's position on Western Sahara is clear: sovereignty of Western Sahara is in dispute, and the United States fully supports the United Nations' efforts to resolve this issue. The United States and many other countries do not recognize Moroccan sovereignty over Western Sahara and have consistently urged the parties to work with the United Nations to resolve the conflict by peaceful means.

The FTA will cover trade and investments in the territory of Morocco as recognized internationally, and will not include Western Sahara. As our Harmonized Tariff Schedule makes clear, for U.S. customs purposes, the United States treats imports from Western Sahara and Morocco differently. Nothing in the FTA will require us to change this practice. The Administration will draft the proclamation authorized in the legislation implementing the FTA (H.R. 4842) to provide preferential tariff treatment for goods from the territory of Morocco. Preferential tariff treatment will not be provided to goods from Western Sahara.

I hope this letter addresses your question regarding the FTA and the status of Western Sahara. I encourage you to support the FTA. It will create economic opportunities for U.S. manufacturing and service firms, workers, and farmers, and will support economic reform and foreign investment in Morocco.

Thank you again for your letter. Please feel free to contact me should you have further questions.

Sincerely,
Robert B. Zoellick

Non-Governmental Associations

9. New York City Bar Association, Committee on United Nations, Report on Legal Issues Involved in the Western Sahara Dispute: Use of Natural Resources, New York, April 2011.

NEW YORK
CITY BAR

REPORT ON LEGAL ISSUES INVOLVED IN THE WESTERN SAHARA DISPUTE:
USE OF NATURAL RESOURCES

Committee on United Nations
APRIL 2011

NEW YORK CITY BAR ASSOCIATION
42 WEST 44TH STREET, NEW YORK, NY 10036

REPORT ON LEGAL ISSUES INVOLVED IN THE WESTERN SAHARA DISPUTE: USE OF NATURAL RESOURCES

ABSTRACT

The present report, issued by the Association of the Bar of the City of New York (the "Association") and prepared by the Association's United Nations Committee, examines the legal issues involved in the use by Morocco of the natural resources within the territory of Western Sahara. The report is the result of more than 16 months of research, fact gathering and analysis. While acknowledging the well-known dispute as to the legal status of Morocco's presence within Western Sahara, the report concludes that assuming the legal status most favorable to the Moroccan position – that is, treating Morocco as an administering power in the territory – to the extent Morocco is using natural resources located within the territory of Western Sahara, unless such use is in consultation with and to the direct benefit of the people of Western Sahara, Morocco's use of the natural resources of the territory constitutes a violation of international law.

...omissis...

II. LEGAL STATUS OF MOROCCO'S USE OF THE NATURAL RESOURCES OF WESTERN SAHARA

A. Factual Background

When Morocco entered Western Sahara in the 1970s, the major resources being exploited in the territory were the phosphate reserves in the Bou Craa mines[1] and the fisheries contained in Western Sahara's coastal waters[2]. More recently, commercial interests in the region have also focused on oil exploration in the waters off the coast of Western

---

1 Morocco is the single largest exporter of phosphates (used primarily in fertilizers) in the world, and Western Sahara contains large phosphate deposits, most notably at Bou Craa. According to the United Nations Environment Programme (UNEP), Morocco jointly operates the mine with Spanish interests. While the mine amounts to only two or three per cent of Morocco's phosphate production, the reserves are valuable because of the uranium that can be extracted from them (http://www.na.unep.net/atlas/webatlas.php?id=369, accessed on 16.05.2010). Reports indicate that two American fertilizer companies may have received up to one-third of all the phosphates extracted from the Bou Craa mines (C. Wilson, Foreign Companies Plundering Western Sahara Resources: Who is Involved and What is Being Done to Stop This?, International Law and the Question of Western Sahara, The Hague, 2006 at 270).

2 U.S. Geological Survey, 2008 Minerals Yearbook: Morocco and Western Sahara [Advance Release], February 2010 at 5 (http://minerals.usgs.gov/minerals/pubs/country/2008/myb3-2008-mo-wi.pdf, accessed on 16.05.2010).

Sahara. A summary of the facts pertaining to the legal issues surrounding Morocco's use of the natural resources of Western Sahara is set forth below[3].

1. Oil and Gas Resources

a. Oil Exploration in Western Sahara's Waters

Western Sahara's territory and coastal region sit primarily on the Aaiun Basin, a sedimentary basin that extends for almost 1100km from northern Mauritania, north through Western Sahara into southern Morocco[4]. The Aaiun Basin consists of two discrete sub-basins: the Boujdour sub-basin to the north, and the Dakhla sub-basin to the south (see Figure 1.1.). According to representatives of the government of the Sahrawi Arab Democratic Republic ("SADR"), all the key elements–reservoir, source, seal and trap–necessary for the successful exploration and exploitation of oil and gas resources are present within certain regions of the Aaiun Basin, which is believed to be one of the last frontier sedimentary basins remaining in Africa[5]. Although the amount of oil and gas contained in the Aaiun Basin is not known, it is believed to be vast, making its potential value great in a world of increasing competition for ever dwindling energy resources.

---

[3] The Committee's conclusions are based on its understandings from publicly available documentary evidence. The Committee is mindful that it is not in a position to make factual findings as to the situation in the territory of Western Sahara as it has not conducted any first-hand investigation into the facts addressed in this report. Nevertheless, there is significant, independent documentary evidence of the activities detailed in this report. In drafting this report the Committee has relied on these independent sources, as well as on interviews with representatives of both sides of this issue.

[4] Sahrawi Arab Democratic Republic Oil and Gas Exploration, Geological Summary (http://sadroilandgas.com/geosum.htm, accessed on 28.11.2010).

[5] *Id.*

Figure 1.1

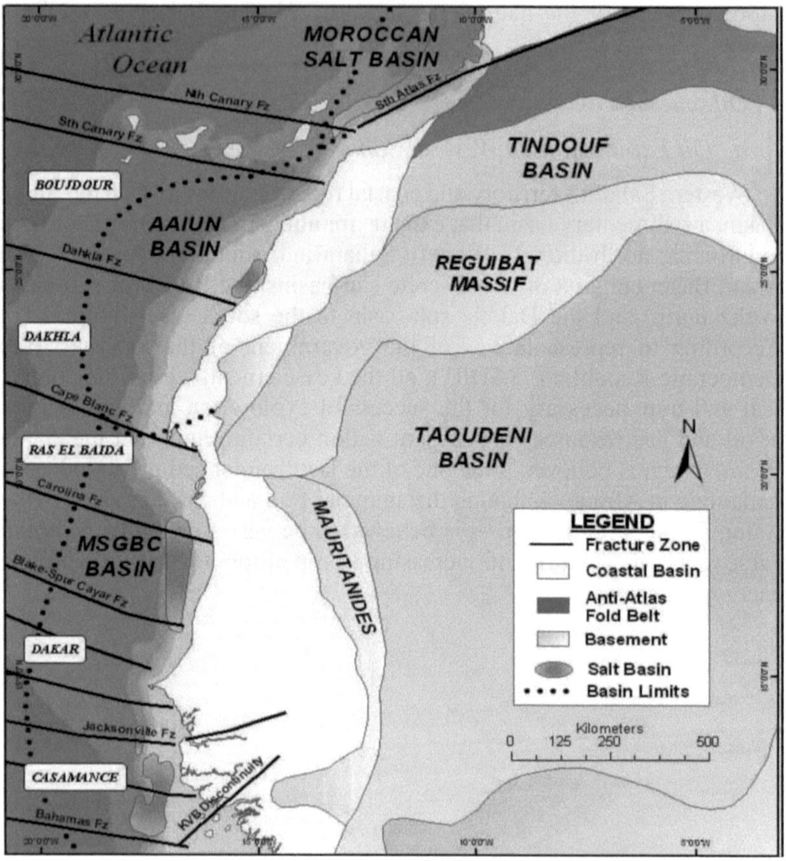

b. Activities by Morocco and International Business Interests

In October 2001, the Moroccan state oil company, ONHYM[6], entered into agreements with an American company, the Kerr-McGee Corporation[7] ("Kerr-McGee"), and a French company, TotalFinaElf S.A. ("TotalFinaElf"), to engage in pre-exploration activities in the oil reserves off the coast of Western Sahara[8]. The agreement with Kerr-McGee would

6 Office National des Hydrocarbures et des Mines (http://www.onhym.com).

7 In 2006, the Kerr-McGee Corporation was purchased by the Houston-based Anadarko Petroleum Corporation.

8 BBC News Online, Oil: Western Sahara's Future, March 4, 2003 (http://news.bbc.co.uk/2/hi/business/2758829.stm, accessed on 16.05.2010); Petroleum Exploration Society of Australia, Fusion provides 200,000 km2 study for new African acreage

have allowed the company to explore approximately 110,000 square kilometers of deep water off the coast of Western Sahara, while the agreement with TotalFinaElf was for exploration of a 115,000 square kilometer area off the coast of the Dakhla region.

At the request of the UN Security Council, Hans Corell, UN Legal Counsel and Under-Secretary-General for Legal Affairs, conducted a legal analysis of the agreements that resulted in an Advisory Opinion, dated February 12, 2002, on the legality of the October 2001 exploration contracts under international law (the "Corell Opinion")[9]. In conducting his analysis Corell did not address the issue of whether Morocco should be considered an "occupying" or "administering" power under international law. Rather, he analyzed the issue under the assumption that Morocco possessed the most expansive rights possible under the circumstances. The Corell Opinion concluded that:

> [...] the contracts for oil reconnaissance and evaluation do not entail exploitation or the physical removal of the mineral resources, and no benefits have as of yet accrued. The conclusion is, therefore, that, while the specific contracts which are the subject of the Security Council's request are not in themselves illegal, if further exploration and exploitation activities were to proceed in disregard of the interests and wishes of the people of Western Sahara, they would be in violation of the principles of international law applicable to mineral resource activities in Non-Self-Governing Territories[10].

The principles of law outlined by the Corell Opinion have been supported by the General Assembly in a number of resolutions, most recently A/RES/61/123, of December 14, 2006 in which *inter alia*, the General Assembly stated that it:

> "1. *Reaffirms* the right of peoples of Non-Self-Governing Territories to self-determination ... as well as their right to the enjoyment of their natural resources and their right to dispose of those resources in their best interest;
>
> 2. *Affirms* the value of foreign economic investment undertaken in collaboration with the peoples of the Non-Self-Governing Territories and in accordance with their wishes..."

Following the release of the Corell Opinion, both Kerr-McGee and Total S.A. (successor to TotalFinaElf) engaged in research and evaluation

---

chance, April/May 2003, at 5-6 (http://www.pesa.com.au/publications/pesa_news/april_03/sahara.htm, accessed on 13.05.2010).

9 Letter dated 29 January 2002 from the Under-Secretary-General for Legal Affairs, the Legal Counsel, addressed to the President of the Security Council, S/2002/161, dated February 12, 2002.

10 *Id.* at para. 25.

work in the territory, including geological and geophysical studies[11]. However, as reported in the press, both companies eventually abandoned exploration activities in the region after receiving negative publicity[12]. The withdrawal of Kerr-McGee in particular came after the Norwegian Government's Petroleum Fund, one of the largest investment funds in the world, liquidated its $52 million investment in the company on the basis of the conclusion of the Fund's Council on Ethics that Kerr-McGee's activities in Western Sahara "constitute[d] an unacceptable risk for contributing to other particularly serious violations of fundamental ethical norms"[13].

At the present time, several companies are involved in oil and gas exploration off the coast of Western Sahara. According to the website of ONHYM, as of October 2010, it had at least four corporate partners engaged in exploratory activities in regions that include Western Saharan territory[14]:

- In 2004, U.S.-based Kosmos Energy and its affiliate Kosmos Energy Offshore Morocco (collectively, "Kosmos") purchased

---

[11] Petroleum Exploration Society of Australia, Fusion provides 200,000 km² study for new African acreage chance, April/May 2003, at 5-6 (http://www.pesa.com.au/publications/pesa_news/april_03/sahara.htm, accessed on 13.05.2010). Kerr McGee du Maroc Ltd., a subsidiary of Kerr McGee Corporation, entered into a reconnaissance permit with ONHYM for the Boujdour area offshore from the portion of Western Sahara currently occupied by Morocco. The permit was renewed on several occasions and the contract was valid through 2006. See C. Wilson, *supra*, n. 15, at 254. In its 2006 SEC filing, the company listed the Boujdour block as being part of Moroccan territory and within its exploration plans.

[12] See, e.g., Le Journal Hebdomadaire, Kerr-McGee Folds, January 12, 2005; SADR Petroleum Authority, Press Release dated May 3, 2006 (http://www.sadroilandgas.com/pdfs/kerr_mcgee_withdrawl.pdf, accessed on 16.05.2010); Afrol News, "No oil off Sahara" says withdrawing Total, November 29, 2004 (http://www.afrol.com/articles/14879, accessed on 06.05.2010).

[13] Recommendation on Exclusion from the Government Petroleum Fund's Investment Universe of the Company Kerr-McGee Corporation, Petroleum Fund's Council on Ethics, Ministry of Finance, Norway, April 12, 2005 (http://www.regjeringen.no/nb/dep/fin/tema/statens_pensjonsfond/ansvarlige-investeringer/tilradninger-og-brev-fra-etikkradet/Recommendation-on-Exclusion-from-the-Government-Petroleum-Funds-Investment-Universe-of-the-Company-Kerr-McGee-Corporation.html?id=419582).

[14] ONHYM, Liste des sociétés partenaires de l'ONHYM au 10.15.2010 (http://www.onhym.com/en/HYDROCARBURES/PartenariatetCoop%C3%A9rationP%C3%A9trole/Listedespartenaires/tabid/325/language/en-US/Default.aspx?Cat=30, accessed on 28.11.2010); see also ONHYM Activity Report 2008 (http://www.onhym.com/ONHYM/pdf/ONHYM_2008_Ang.pdf, accessed on 29.11.2010). As detailed below, company websites for Kosmos Energy, San Leon Energy, Longreach Oil & Gas Ventures, and DVM International seem to indicate that they continue to hold exploration interests in on- and offshore territory in Moroccan-occupied Western Sahara.

a 30% interest in the Boujdour sub-basin from ONHYM[15]. In 2006, Kosmos entered into a Petroleum Agreement with ONHYM granting it a 75% interest in the Boujdour sub-basin[16]. These projects are still in the exploratory phase.

- In 2008, the Irish energy firm, San Leon Energy Plc ("SLE"), through its subsidiary, San Leon Morocco Ltd, entered into 8-year licenses with ONHYM regarding the Zag Basin and Tarfaya Onshore basins[17]. These projects are still in the exploratory phase.
- In 2008 and 2009, U.K.-based Longreach Oil & Gas Ventures Ltd. entered into licenses with ONHYM relating to the exploration of the Zag Basin and Tarfaya Onshore block[18]. These projects are still in the exploratory phase.
- In February 2010, Australian-based DVM International, Ltd. acquired a 75% working interest and operatorship in the Tarfaya Offshore Block[19]. This project is still in exploratory phase.

---

15 ONHYM Activity Report 2005 (http://www.onhym.com/ONHYM/pdf/Rapport-Annuel-Anglais-2005.pdf, accessed on 29.11.2010); Kosmos Energy Presentation, 5th Maghreb and Mediterranean Conference, May 2007 (www.kosmosenergy.com/pres/Maroc5-2007.pdf, accessed on 28.11.2010).

16 Kosmos Energy, Our Assets: Morocco, Boujdour Offshore Block (http://www.kosmosenergy.com/morocco.html, accessed on 16.05.2010); Kosmos Energy Presentation, 5th Maghreb and Mediterranean Conference, May 2007 (www.kosmosenergy.com/pres/Maroc5-2007.pdf, accessed on 28.11.2010).

17 San Leon Energy, Moroccan Operational Update, February 25, 2009 (http://www.sanleonenergy.com/sanleon/communications/Moroccan_Operational_Update.php?ln=en, accessed on 16.05.2010); see also San Leon Energy, Press Release: Award of full Exploration license in Sag, Morocco, July 19, 2009 (http://www.sanleonenergy.com/sanleon/communications/Award_of_full_Exploration_licence_in_Zag_Morocco.php?ln=en, accessed on 16.05.2010); San Leon Energy Presentation, May 2010, pp. 11-17 (available at http://www.wsrw.org/files/dated/2010-04-07/san-leon_presentation_march_2010.pdf, accessed on 28.11.2010).

18 Longreach Oil and Gas Ventures, Ltd. Operations (http://www.longreachoilandgas.com/operations.php, accessed on 28.11.2010).

19 DVM International, Tarfaya Offshore Block, Morocco, Large Prospects – Low Risk (http://www.dvminternational.com/projects/tarfaya.shtml, accessed on 28.11.2010); DVM International, Ltd. Press Release dated February 8, 2010 (http://www.dvminternational.com.au/pdf/2010/2010.02.08_Acquisition%20of%20Tarfaya%20Offshore%20Morocco.pdf, accessed on 28.11.2010).

c. *Activities by SADR/Polisario*

In the early 2000s, SADR announced an oil and gas licensing initiative for offshore exploration adjacent to Western Sahara[20]. SADR divided the area into onshore and offshore blocks. (See Figure 1.2.)

Figure 1.2

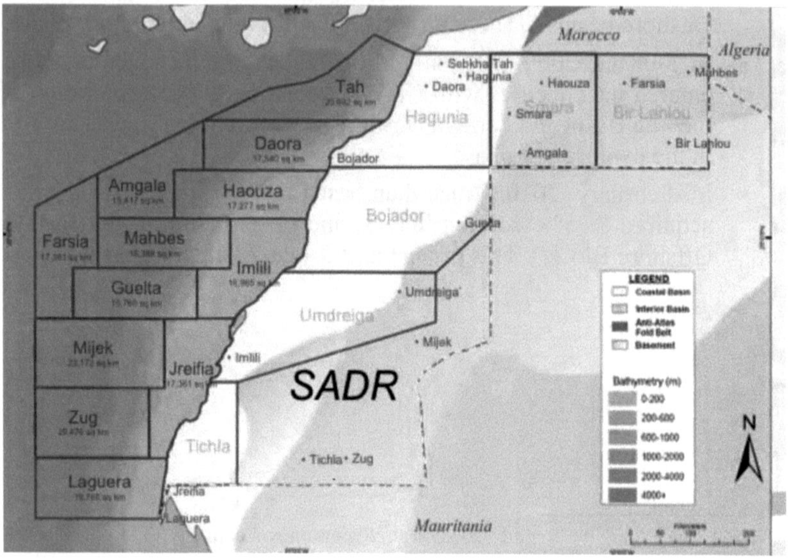

In 2006, SADR commenced a similar licensing initiative for onshore oil and gas exploration in the territory of Western Sahara[21]. This latter initiative related to the Aaiun and Tindouf basins, which had been relatively unexplored since Spanish colonial occupation[22].

In late 2007, SADR launched a second round of petroleum and natural gas licensing for nine offshore and onshore blocks in Western Sahara, most of which were located in the relatively unexplored Mesozoic and

20 SADR Petroleum Authority, Press Release dated May 17, 2005 (http://www.sadroilandgas.com/press_releases/Media%20Pack%20-%20Press%20Release%20English.pdf, accessed on 16.05.2010).

21 SADR Petroleum Authority, Press Release dated January 17, 2006 (http://www.sadroilandgas.com/pdfs/SADR%202006%20Onshore%20Oil%20Gas%20License%20Offering.pdf, accessed on 16.05.2010).

22 *Id.*

Tertiary Aaiun Basin[23]. SADR extended the closing date of the second licensing offering to March 31, 2009[24].

An Australian oil and gas exploration company, Fusion Oil & Gas NL, in contracting with SADR, stated that it entered into a "technical co-operation agreement" pending issuance of licenses[25]. Under the terms of the SADR licensing initiatives, any contracts issued will not come into force until the political status of Western Sahara is resolved[26]. On January 21, 2009, SADR issued Law 03/2009, which declared a 200-mile "Exclusive Economic Zone (EEZ)" for maritime areas in and off Western Sahara with the intent to assert exclusive jurisdiction over offshore natural resources, including mineral and petroleum seabed resources[27].

2. *Fisheries*

In addition to oil and gas exploration, in recent years the Moroccan government appears to have engaged in commercial fishing activity in waters off the coast of Western Sahara. Evidence of this activity can be found in an examination of the fisheries treaties with Morocco entered into by the European Union ("EU") and its predecessors, the European Economic Community ("EEC") and the European Community "(EC").

a) Treaty Obligations

Since Morocco entered Western Sahara in the 1970s, the EU, EEC, and EC have been parties to several fisheries agreements with Morocco, pursuant to which financial contributions to Morocco have been a key component. In 1985, the EEC undertook to assume responsibility for

---

23 This second licensing round consisted of six offshore blocks (Tah, Zug, Jreifia, Farsia, Imlili, and Amgala) and three onshore blocks (Umdreiga, Smara, and Tichla) (U.S. Geological Survey, 2008 Minerals Yearbook: Morocco and Western Sahara [Advance Release], February 2010 at 5).

24 U.S. Geological Survey, 2008 Minerals Yearbook: Morocco and Western Sahara [Advance Release], February 2010 at 5; SADR Petroleum Authority, Press Release dated November 14, 2008 (http:www.sadroilandgas.com/pdfs/08_11_18_saharawi_arab.pdf, accessed on 16.05.2010).

25 Petroleum Exploration Society of Australia, Fusion provides 200,000 km^2 study for new African acreage chance, April/May 2003 (http://www.pesa.com.au/publications/pesa_news/april_03/sahara.htm, accessed on 13.05.2010).

26 *Id.* [USGS at 5]; SADR Petroleum Authority, Frequently Asked Questions dated June 8, 2005 (http://www.sadroilandgas.com/pdfs/FAQ.pdf, accessed on 16.05.2010); CIA World Factbook – Western Sahara, updated November 22, 2010 (https://www.cia.gov/library/publications/the-world-factbook/geos/wi.html, accessed on 29.11.2010).

27 Law No. 03/2009 of 21 January 2009, Establishing the Maritime Zones of the Sahrawi Arab Democratic Republic (http://www.sadroilandgas.com/pdfs/09_04_28_eez_law.pdf, accessed on 16.05.2010); SADR Petroleum Authority, Press Release dated April 28, 2009 (http://www.sadroilandgas.com/pdfs/09_04_28_eez_media.pdf, accessed on 16.05.2010).

existing fisheries agreements by Spain (entered into in 1983) and Portugal (entered into in 1976) with Morocco, as part of the conditions of the two countries' accession to the EEC[28]. Thereafter, the EEC entered into its own fisheries sector agreements with Morocco in 1988 and 1992, to provide "fishing opportunities for fishermen of the enlarged Community in the waters over which Morocco has sovereignty or jurisdiction"[29]. The protocol to the 1988 agreement provided for the EEC to make financial contributions to Morocco, including direct disbursements to its Ministry of Maritime Fishing and Merchant Navy[30]. Articles 2 and 6 of the 1992 agreement provide for financial contributions to Morocco to build up scientific research, and develop Morocco's human resources and training facilities for the maritime industry[31].

The EC entered into a new fisheries agreement with Morocco in 1995. The scope of the agreement also expressly covered waters "of which the Kingdom of Morocco has sovereignty or jurisdiction" (Article 1); it does not mention Western Sahara, but contains direct references to benefits and direct financial contributions to Morocco[32].

In 2006, Morocco and the EU signed a four-year agreement allowing European vessels to fish off the coast of Morocco, which, according to the U.S. Central Intelligence Agency, included waters off the coast of Western Sahara[33]. The Fisheries Partnership Agreement ("FPA")[34] sets forth a scheme in which the government of Morocco shall receive direct financial contributions from the EU in exchange for issuing fishing licenses for EU vessels. Article 2 provides that the "Moroccan fishing zone" governed by the agreement "means the waters falling within the sovereignty or jurisdiction of the Kingdom of Morocco"; there is no

28 OJ L 302, November 15, 1985, p. 128; OJ L 232, August 19, 1987, p. 18-19; OJ L 346, December 10, 1987, p. 35.

29 OJ L 99, April 16, 1988, p. 45. See also *id.* at 47, 61; OJ L 181, July 12, 1988, pp. 1-17; OJ L 218, August 1, 1992, pages 137-138; OJ L 407, December 31, 1992, at pp. 3-14.

30 OJ L 99, April 16, 1988, p. 61.

31 OJ L 407, December 31, 1992, at pp. 3-14.

32 OJ L 306, December 19, 1995, at pp. 7-43. For example, Article 3 provides that the parties shall undertake the sustainable development of Morocco's fisheries sector, including "development of port infrastructure and the improvement of conditions for the reception of fishing fleets in Moroccan ports"; Article 4 provides for a financial contribution for "Morocco's needs in the matter of vocational training of seamen."

33 CIA World Factbook – Western Sahara, updated April 20, 2010 (https://www.cia.gov/library/publications/the-world-factbook/geos/wi.html, accessed on 13.05.2010).

34 The agreement can be linked to here: http://eur-lex.europa.eu/LexUriServ/LexUriServ.do?uri=OJ:L:2006:141:0004:0037:EN:PDF. OJ L 141, May 29, 2006, p. 4 et seq., adopted pursuant to Council Regulation (EC) No. 764/2006 (OJ L 141, May 29, 2006, at 1).

reference to Western Sahara or the Sahrawis in the FPA. Article 7(1) of the Agreement and Article 2 of its Protocol provides that the EU will pay Morocco 144.4 million Euros for the four-year contract term, both as compensation for access to the fishing zones and to support a sustainable national fisheries policy. Morocco has "full discretion" regarding the use of the funds[35].

The text of the FPA does not describe the boundary of the maritime areas covered in the agreement[36]. The current list of ports and fishing companies accepted under the agreement, which were devised for the prior 1995 EC-Morocco fisheries agreement, includes companies operating out of Sahrawi ports, including Dakhla, Boujdour, and Laayoune[37]. In February 2006, the European Parliament Legal Service issued an unpublished opinion cautioning that, given the lack of clarity in the text of the agreement as to whether fishing would take place in waters off Western Sahara, implementation of the FPA should be carefully monitored to ensure compliance with international law[38]. The opinion had been requested by the European Parliament's Development Committee, which had assumed that the FPA would allow EU vessels to fish off of Western Sahara[39]. In its analysis of the FPA's compatibility with international law, the Legal Service relied on two points: (1) that Western Sahara has the status of a non-self-governing territory under Article 73 of the UN Charter and that Morocco was its *de facto* administrator; and (2) that Western Sahara "enjoys the right to the natural resources of the territory, in the sense that economic activities concerning those resources shall not be carried out in disregard of the interests and wishes of the local population"[40]. On the second point, the Legal Service adopted the

35 OJ L 141, pp. 6 and 9.

36 *See* Legal Opinion of the European Parliament Legal Service, SJ-0085/06, dated February 20, 2006, para. 45, at 9 (available by unofficial copy at http://www.arso.org/LegalopinionUE200206.pdf, accessed on 16.05.2010); San Martin, Pablo, EU-Morocco Fisheries Agreement: The Unforeseen Consequences of a Very Dangerous Turn, Colaboraciones del Grupo de Estudios Estrategicos (GEES), No. 1013 (http://www.gees.org/articulos/eu_morocco_fisheries_agreement_the_unforeseen_consequences_of_a_very_dangerous_turn_2601, accessed on 16.05.2010).

37 Annex B to European Community Decision 95/30/EC, amended DU 08.07.2005.

38 *See* Legal Opinion of the European Parliament Legal Service, SJ-0085/06, dated February 20, 2006, para. 45, at 9 (available by unofficial copy at http://www.arso.org/LegalopinionUE200206.pdf, accessed on 16.05.2010); see also the report, dated May 4, 2006, of the European Parliament Committee on Fisheries, A6-0163/2006 (http://www.europarl.europa.eu/sides/getDoc.do?language=EN&reference=A6-0163/2006, accessed on 29.11.2010).

39 Legal Opinion of the European Parliament Legal Service, *supra* note 52 at para. 1.

40 *Id.* at para. 37.

analysis of the UN Legal Counsel in the Corell Opinion[41]. It also noted that this approach to the principle of sovereignty over natural resources was consistent with the United Nations Conference on the Law of the Sea (UNCLOS) and general principles of public international law[42].

The Legal Service concluded that the FPA's compliance with international law would depend on the way in which the Moroccan authorities implemented the agreement and the extent to which it foresaw benefits to the people of Western Sahara, noting that such information would need to be obtained from Morocco[43].

Most recently, on February 11, 2011, the European Commission recommended that the European Council grant it a mandate to renew the fisheries protocol with Morocco, which expired on February 27, 2011, for a one year period, without including any provisions dealing with the legal issues raised by the fishing occurring in Western Saharan waters, while it "assesses" information about Morocco's compliance with international law that was provided to it by Morocco on December 13, 2010[44]. The one-year extension has been initialed by the Commission, thus allowing current fishing activities to continue for up to six months pending a final decision by the Council on whether to extend the protocol[45].

b) Implementation of the Treaty and Current Fishing Activities

The FPA went into effect in 2007, and issues raised in the 2006 European Parliament Legal Service opinion have repeatedly been the subject of inquiry within the European Parliament. First, a series of written Parliamentary questions and answers with the Committee on Fisheries confirms that, according to data reported under the FPA, EU member states have declared that catches are taking place in areas (subdivision 34.1.3) off the coast of Western Sahara[46].

In addition, there has been significant Parliamentary discussion regarding the EU's pursuit of information from Morocco, within the context of the Joint Committee under the FPA, about the socioeconomic effects of the fishing activities and the industry support provided by the

---

41 *Id.* at para. 16-21.

42 *Id.* at para. 21 and 37(b).

43 *Id.* at para. 49, Conclusions (b)-(d).

44 *See* SEC/2011/0170, available at http://eur-lex.europa.eu/LexUriServ/LexUriServ.do?uri=SEC:2011:0170:FIN:EN:PDF.

45 *See* "Fisheries: EU initials extension of the fisheries protocol with Morocco", European Parliament Press Release, dated February 28, 2011, available at http://ec.europa.eu/fisheries/news_and_events/press_releases/2011/20110228/index_en.htm#.

46 *See* written questions E-1073/08 of March 4, 2008, E-4295/08 of July 25, 2008, and E-0717/10 of February 16, 2010, and the written answers thereto by Commissioner Borg.

EU under the terms of the agreement[47]. According to the Commission, it "has used every possible official and unofficial occasion to solicit relevant information from the Moroccan authorities"[48]. It has also stated that measures such as suspension of the agreement or negotiation of additional protocols might be required when the information became available, but that its opinion was that it is Morocco's responsibility to ensure compliance with the rights of the people of Western Sahara under international law[49].

As discussed above, SADR's January 2009 resolution declaring an EEZ also claims jurisdiction over fisheries resources in the 200-nautical mile area off Western Sahara[50]. In February 2010, the European Parliament Legal Service issued a second legal opinion concerning the legality of the EEZ and an assessment of whether the implementation of the FPA to date was in compliance with international law[51].

As a preliminary matter, the opinion found that "EU-flagged vessels [appear to] have fished in the waters off Western Sahara"[52]. Further, the Legal Service concluded that (1) SADR's declaration of an EEZ had no legal effect on the FPA; and (2) as it is not in a position to establish the "facts on the ground," an assessment of whether acts carried out under the FPA "actually benefit the people of Western Sahara" and otherwise

---

47 *See* written questions E-1758/10 of March 22, 2010, E-2633/10 of April 20, 2010, and E-5723/10 of July 22, 2010, and the written answers thereto by Commissioner Damanaki.

48 *See* written answer E-5723/10.

49 *See* written answer E-2633/10.

50 Law No. 03/2009 of 21 January 2009, Establishing the Maritime Zones of the Sahrawi Arab Democratic Republic (http://www.sadroilandgas.com/pdfs/09_04_28_eez_law.pdf, accessed on 16.05.2010); SADR Petroleum Authority, Press Release dated April 28, 2009 (http://www.sadroilandgas.com/pdfs/09_04_28_eez_media.pdf, accessed on 16.05.2010). It should be noted that the Polisario strongly opposes the FPA. See also Polisario statement regarding EU-Morocco FPA, statement made by Mohamed Sidati, Polisario Minister Delegate for Europe, May 22, 2006 (http:/groups.yahoo.com/group/Sahara-Update/message/1757, accessed on 29.11.2010).

51 Associated Press (Brussels), EU assembly report questions Morocco fishing deal, February 23, 2010 (http://finance.yahoo.com/EU-assembly-report-questions-apf-3855611862.html?x=0&.v=1, accessed on 16.05.2010); *see also* the written Parliamentary question to the Commission on Fisheries, confirming the content of the legal opinion (E-1758/10, dated March 22, 2010). A leaked, unofficial copy of this Legal Services opinion, which is dated July 13, 2009, can be accessed at http://www.wsrw.org/index.php?parse_news=single&cat=105&art=1346 (accessed on 16.05.2010).

52 Legal Services opinion, dated July 13, 2009, at para. 5; *see also* para. 15 ("Not only can this be deducted from the data provided by the Member States to the [European] Commission pursuant to their obligations established by Community legislation on 'control,' but also it has been explicitly acknowledged in several Commission declarations") (internal footnote omitted).

comply with international law should be carried out under the auspices of the Joint Committee established in the FPA to monitor compliance[53].

In reaching its conclusion in (2) above, the Legal Service analyzed the provisions related to the implementation of a sectoral fisheries policy in Article 7(1) (b) of the FPA and Articles 6 and 7 of its Protocol. It concluded that it could not be demonstrated that the financial contributions under the FPA are being used for the benefit of the people of Western Sahara because the sectoral fisheries policy's matrix of objectives and results did not contain "specific actions explicitly foreseen with a view to benefit the population of Western Sahara"; nor were actions foreseen to target Western Sahara ports such as Laayoune, Dakhla, and Boujdour sufficient, because those ports were "undisputed" to be in territory controlled by Morocco and the demography of those regions had been substantially modified due to Moroccan settlement and lack of integration of the Saharawi population[54].

It should be noted that in this 2009 opinion, the European Parliament Legal Service (as it did in its 2006 opinion) adopted the approach taken by the UN Legal Counsel in the Corell Opinion, finding that activities under the FPA would be prohibited under international law so long as "those activities are carried out in disregard of the interests and of the wishes of the people" of Western Sahara[55].

B. Morocco's Status in Western Sahara

Morocco's legal status in Western Sahara is disputed. Formerly a Spanish colony, and now a territory claimed by both the Kingdom of Morocco and the SADR government, its legal status, according to the UN, is as a non-decolonized territory and it is included on the UN's list of non-self-governing territories. For the past 35 years, parts of Western Sahara have been under the de facto control of Morocco (Mauritania entered into a peace treaty with SADR in 1979 and withdrew from the territory that same year), while another section of the territory, known as the Free Zone, has been administered by the SADR. A UN-monitored cease-fire has been in effect since September 1991. In order to resolve the sovereignty issue, the UN has attempted to hold a referendum through the United Nations Mission for the Referendum in Western Sahara (MINURSO), which to date, despite the efforts of a number of special envoys including James Baker, former U.S. Secretary of State, and despite efforts at direct talks undertaken by current envoy Christopher Ross, has not been successful.

53 Legal Services opinion, dated July 13, 2009, at para. 38(7)-(9).

54 *Id.* at para. 25-29.

55 *Id.* at para. 18.

At the present time the Committee does not take a position with respect to the sovereignty dispute or Morocco's present status in the territory. Instead, the Committee sets forth below a legal analysis of Morocco's use of the natural resources of Western Sahara under the status most favorable to the Moroccan position, that of an administering power in the territory. The analysis concludes that Morocco may use the natural resources of Western Sahara only in the best interests and to the benefit of the Sahrawis themselves[56].

(a) Legal Precedent

Although there is limited authority under international law addressing the use of natural resources by an administering power, the Correll Opinion offers guidance for assessing Morocco's activities with respect to natural resources in the territory of Western Sahara. According to the Corell Opinion, administering powers are obligated "to ensure that all economic activities in the Non-Self-Governing Territories under their administration do not adversely affect the interests of the peoples of such territories, but are instead directed to assist them in the exercise of their right to self-determination"[57].

In coming to this legal conclusion, the Corell Opinion examined both traditional and "soft law" sources of international law. Corell noted

---

[56] If Morocco is ever recognized as having sovereign rights over Western Sahara, there would appear to be no limits under international law on Morocco's exploration and exploitation of the natural resources of Western Sahara. The principle of permanent sovereignty over natural resources would apply without limitation in such circumstances. *See* "Declaration of Permanent Sovereignty over Natural Resources," UNGA Resolution 1803 (XVI), 14 December 1962; Article 1(2) of the International Covenant on Civil and Political Rights (1976) and Article 1(2) of the International Covenant on Economic, Social and Cultural Rights (1976); United Nations Council for Namibia, "Decree No. 1 for the Protection of Natural Resources of Namibia," adopted in UNGA Res. 3295, 13 December 1974, and UNGA Res. 57/132, 25 February 2003. For a further discussion of this right, see Catriona Drew, "The East Timor Story: International Law on Trial", 12 *European Journal of International Law*, 2001, at 651-684, and Stephanie Koury, *The European Community and Member States' Duty of Non-Recognition under the EC-Morocco Association Agreement: State Responsibility and Customary International Law, International Law and the Question of Western Sahara* (The Hague 2006), at 170-172. We do not analyze, and take no position on, whether Morocco can be an occupying power. Article 55 of the Hague Regulations, reflecting customary international law, provides that an occupying power "shall be regarded only as administrator and usufructuary of public buildings, real estate, forests, and agricultural estates belonging to the hostile State, and situated in the occupied country. It must safeguard the capital of these properties, and administer them in accordance with the rules of usufruct."

[57] Corell Opinion, citing GA res. 35/118 of 11 Dec. 1980; 52/78 of 10 Dec. 1997; 54/91 of 6 Dec. 1999; 55/147 of 8 Dec. 2000; and 56/74 of 10 Dec. 2001. The full text of the Corell Opinion is attached hereto as Exhibit TK.

that the rights of "administering powers" are limited; that they have the obligation "to ensure that all economic activities in the Non-Self-Governing Territories under their administration do not adversely affect the interests of the peoples of such territories, but are instead directed to assist them in the exercise of their right to self-determination"[58]. Corell also noted the resolutions declaring that "the exploitation and plundering of the marine and other natural resources of colonial and Non-Self-Governing Territories by foreign economic interests, in violation of the relevant resolutions of the United Nations, is a threat to the integrity and prosperity of these Territories" and that "any administering Power that deprives the colonial peoples of Non-Self-Governing Territories of the exercise of their legitimate rights over their natural resources... violates the solemn obligations it has assumed under the Charter of the United Nations"[59].

After concluding that the case law of the ICJ was inconclusive on the extent to which "administering powers" may utilize natural resources during their period of occupation in the two cases in which that issue had been presented[60], he then referred to the practice of States and noted that such precedent was also inconclusive: in the case of Namibia, the exploitation of uranium and other natural resources by South Africa was condemned[61], whereas in the case of East Timor an arrangement with

---

58 Citing GA res. 35/118 of 11 December 1980; 52/78 of 10 December 21997; 54/91 of 6 December 1999; 55/147 of 8 December 2000; and 56/74 of 10 December 2001.

59 Citing GA res. 48/46 of 10 December 1992 and 49/40 of 9 December 1994.

60 In the Case of East Timor, Portugal argued that in negotiating with Indonesia an agreement on the exploration and exploitation of the continental shelf in the area of the Timor Gap, Australia had failed to respect the right of the people of East Timor to permanent sovereignty over its natural wealth and resources, and the powers and rights of Portugal as the administering power of East Timor. In the absence of Indonesia's participation in the proceedings, however, the ICJ concluded that it lacked jurisdiction. In the Nauru Phosphate Case, Nauru claimed the rehabilitation of certain phosphate lands worked out before independence in the period of the Trusteeship administered by Australia, New Zealand and the United Kingdom. Nauru argued that the principle of permanent sovereignty over natural resources was breached in circumstances in which a major resource was depleted on grossly inequitable terms and its extraction involved the physical reduction of the land. Following the Judgment on the Preliminary Objections, the parties reached a settlement and a Judgment on the merits was no longer required.

61 Corell noted that the exploitation of uranium and other natural resources in Namibia by South Africa and a number of Western multinational corporations was considered illegal under Decree No. 1 for the Protection of the Natural Resources of Namibia, enacted in 1974 by the United Nations Council for Namibia, and was condemned by the General Assembly (GA res. 36/51 of 24 November 1981, and 39/42 of 5 December 1984). He suggested, however, that the case of Namibia "must be seen in the light of Security Council resolution 278 (1970) of 30 January 1970, which declared that the continued presence of South Africa in Namibia was illegal and that consequently all acts taken by the Government of South Africa were illegal and invalid."

Australia for the exploitation of oil and natural gas deposits was approved on the basis that representatives of the East Timorese people had actively participated in the arrangement[62].

Despite the inconclusive nature of State practice concerning this issue, Corell nevertheless distilled certain legal principles from existing law: where resource exploitation activities are conducted for the benefit of the peoples of Non-Self-Governing territories, on their behalf, or in consultation with their representatives, those activities are considered compatible with the UN Charter obligations of the administering power and in conformity with the General Assembly resolutions and the principle of permanent sovereignty over natural resources enshrined therein. On the other hand, when such activities are conducted in disregard of the needs and interests of the people of the Non-Self-Governing Territories and without the participation of those people, those activities are illegal under international law.

Addressing Morocco's activities in relation to the natural resources of Western Sahara in 2002, the Corell Opinion stated that the specific contracts then under consideration (namely, Morocco's contracts for oil reconnaissance and evaluation with Kerr-McGee and TotalFinaElf) were not in themselves illegal because they "do not entail exploitation or the physical removal of the mineral resources, and no benefits have as of yet accrued"[63]. However, he considered that should

> further exploration and exploitation activities … proceed in disregard of the interests and wishes of the people of Western Sahara, those activities would be in violation of the international law principles applicable to mineral resource activities in Non-Self-Governing Territories.

(b) Legal Analysis

The Committee agrees with the analysis of the legal issues and the conclusions reached in the Corell Opinion. As discussed above, as of the end of 2010, Morocco had at least four corporate partners engaged in oil

62 Corell suggested that the case of East Timor under the United Nations Transitional Administration in East Timor (UNTAET) was "unique" in that it involved the decisions of a UN body, not an "administering power." By the time UNTAET was established in October 1999, the Timor Gap Treaty was fully operational and concessions had been granted in the Zone of Cooperation by Indonesia and Australia. In order to ensure the continuity of the practical arrangements under this Treaty, UNTAET concluded an Exchange of Letters with Australia for the continued operation of the terms of the Treaty. Two years later, in anticipation of independence, UNTAET negotiated with Australia a draft "Timor Sea Arrangement" which was to replace the Treaty. On both occasions, according to Corell, UNTAET "consulted fully" with representatives of the East Timorese people, who "participated actively" in the negotiations.

63 *Id.* at para. 25.

and gas exploration in regions that include Western Saharan territory. As it appears from publicly available information that, to date, such activities remain exploratory, these relationships with corporate partners arguably are consistent with Morocco's obligations as an administering power under international law. Should these agreements be expanded to include, or should new agreements be concluded for, the extraction of oil and/ or gas from the territory of Western Sahara, such exploitation of natural resources would be unlawful, unless it resulted from consultation with and involvement of the people of Western Sahara and was done for their benefit.

In addition, to the extent Morocco may have received payments or accrued benefits under any of the above-mentioned oil reconnaissance and evaluation contracts separate and apart from actual exploitation and extraction – for instance, if any contracting parties provided Morocco payments or provided resources for oil exploration or infrastructure development – in the absence of the participation of and benefit to the people of Western Sahara, Morocco may be considered to have violated international law. A decisive conclusion would require more information regarding any such payments or accrued benefits.

Certain of Morocco's commercial fishing activities in waters off the coast of Western Sahara may be in violation of the State's obligations under international law. In particular, the EU-Morocco FPA currently in force grants Morocco complete discretion with respect to the use of funds paid by the EU to Morocco in part as compensation for access to territorial waters including those adjacent to Western Sahara. The Committee is unable to ascertain any information regarding Morocco's use of sums received under the FPA; indeed, the European Commission has also been unable to obtain this information[64]. The Committee is of the opinion that retention by Morocco of any portion of those sums relating to fishing activities in Western Sahara's territorial waters, or disbursement of such funds without consideration for the interests of Western Sahara or the Sahrawi people, would violate international law. Further, to the extent commercial fishing activities are currently taking place in Western Saharan waters, such activities must be done in consultation with the Sahrawi population and any benefits from the activities must flow to the Sahrawi people.

In this regard, the Committee notes with approval the approach taken in certain free trade agreements concluded with Morocco in recent years. The 2004 United States-Morocco Free Trade Agreement excludes Western

64 *See* written questions E-1758/10 of March 22, 2010, E-2633/10 of April 20, 2010, and E-5723/10 of July 22, 2010, and the written answers thereto by Commissioner Damanaki.

Sahara from its scope[65]. In particular, as exemplified in a letter submitted by the U.S. Trade Representative's Office to Congressman Joseph R. Pitts of the U.S. House of Representatives and dated July 20, 2004, detailing the Bush Administration's position with respect to Western Sahara, because "the United States [does] not recognize Morocco's sovereignty over Western Sahara," the U.S. Free Trade Agreement with Morocco explicitly "will not include Western Sahara"[66].

The EU fisheries agreement, by contrast, appears to include products from Western Sahara. If that is the case, it is incumbent upon the EU to ensure that the agreement does not condone or permit its member states to benefit from violations of international law. This would require, at a minimum, that any future agreement between the EU and Morocco include a clause providing that the agreement shall be in conformity with international law and that Morocco shall have the duty to provide evidence that the agreement, to the extent it involves fisheries resources from Western Saharan waters, inures primarily to the benefit of the Sahrawis and meets with their approval[67].

If such evidence is not forthcoming, we suggest that the EU, at a minimum, follow the advice of its Legal Service and refrain from allowing vessels to fish in the waters off Western Sahara by requesting fisheries licenses only for fishing zones that are situated in the waters off Morocco. We would also suggest that the EU prohibit the importation of fisheries resources coming from Moroccan vessels operating in the waters of Western Sahara[68].

---

65 Congressional Record, 108th Congress (2003-2004), UNITED STATES-MOROCCO FREE TRADE AGREEMENT IMPLEMENTATION ACT – (House of Representatives – July 22, 2004), Page H6627 (http://thomas.loc.gov/cgi-bin/query/C?r108:./temp/~r108jDzL9J, accessed on 29.11.2010).

66 *See* Letter dated July 20, 2004, from U.S. Trade Representative Robert B. Zoelick to Congressman Joseph R. Pitts.

67 For additional consideration of this matter, see the legal opinion entitled "Western Sahara and the EU-Morocco Fisheries Partnership Agreement (FPA)," dated 16 February 2011 and issued by seven professors of international law Swedish universities in Uppsala, Gothenburg, Stockholm, and Lund, available at http://www.wsrw.org/index.php?parse_news=single&cat=105&art=1860. The opinion warns that "[a] renewed FPA may make the EU and its member states liable for a violation of international law, namely as a recognition of and assistance to serious breaches of international law by Morocco." *Id.* Among the conclusions reached in the opinion is that "[a]n FPA with Morocco that covers waters outside Western Sahara must conform with the following conditions: The agreement should make clear that it does not cover Western Sahara as a part of the territory of Morocco [and] the agreement must be in accordance with the wishes and interests of the people of Western Sahara".

68 In the report it issued in 2009 the Legal Service found "[i]n the event that it could not be demonstrated that the FPA was implemented in conformity with the principles of international law concerning the rights of the Sahrawi people over their natural

III. CONCLUSION

The present report is intended as an assessment under international law of Morocco's use of the natural resources within the territory of Western Sahara. Such an assessment, of course, is related to and dependent upon the legal status of Morocco's presence in Western Sahara. At the present time the Committee does not take a position with respect to this urgent and important question. However, as borne out in the analysis set forth in this report, because even under the most generous interpretation of Morocco's legal status in Western Sahara – that is, treating Morocco as an administering power in the territory – Morocco may use the natural resources within the territory only in so far as such use is with the participation of and in the best interests and for the benefit of the Sahrawi people; any use by Morocco of those resources that is not in the benefit of the Sahrawi people constitutes a violation of international law.

Based on the information available to the Committee, it appears that, to date, Morocco's activities relating to oil and gas exploration are only exploratory and have not become exploitative. To the extent this is the case, such activities are arguably consistent with Morocco's obligations as an administering power or an occupying power under international law. However, should these activities be expanded to include, or should new agreements be concluded for, the extraction of oil and/or gas from the territory of Western Sahara, such exploitation of natural resources would be unlawful, unless it resulted from consultation with and involvement of the people of Western Sahara and was done for their benefit. Further, to the extent Morocco may have received payments or accrued benefits under any of the existing oil reconnaissance and evaluation contracts separate and apart from actual exploitation and extraction–for instance, if any contracting parties provided Morocco payments or provided resources for oil exploration or infrastructure development–in the absence of the participation of and benefit to the people of Western Sahara, Morocco may be considered to have violated international law.

With respect to certain of Morocco's commercial fishing activities in waters off the coast of Western Sahara, some of these activities may be in violation of Morocco's obligations as an administering or occupying power under international law. In particular, the EU-Morocco FPA currently in force grants Morocco complete discretion with respect to the use of funds paid by the EU to Morocco in part as compensation for access to territorial waters including those adjacent to Western Sahara.

resources, principles which the Community is bound to respect, the Community should refrain from allowing vessels to fish in the waters off Western Sahara by requesting fisheries licenses only for fishing zones that are situated in the waters off Morocco." Legal Services opinion, *supra*, note 81, at para. 37.

From our review of available information, commercial fishing activities may be occurring in waters off of the coast of Western Sahara. While the Committee has been unable to ascertain any information regarding Morocco's use of sums received under the FPA, it is of the opinion that retention by Morocco of any portion of those sums relating to fishing activities in Western Sahara's territorial waters, or disbursement of such funds without consideration for the interests of Western Sahara or the Sahrawi people, would violate international law. To the extent commercial fishing activities are currently taking place in Western Saharan waters, such activities must be in consultation with the Sahrawi population and any benefits from the activities must flow to the Sahrawi people. If they are not, such activities are illegal under international law.

Finally, with respect to the use of the phosphates extracted from the Bou Craa mines in Western Sahara, while the U.S. Trade Representative has confirmed that the free trade agreement entered into by Morocco and the United States excludes the territory of Western Sahara, such exclusion does not necessarily prevent the importation of products and resources extracted from Western Sahara into the United States. To the extent Bou Craa phosphates are declared on U.S. customs declarations to be from Morocco, such importation may be in violation of both international law and U.S. customs regulations. In any event, unless and until the U.S. Congress promulgates laws or the President issues executive decisions that explicitly prohibit such imports into the United States, it is unclear whether U.S. companies can, in the absence of enabling legislation or executive order, be prosecuted for what would constitute a violation of international law.

There is much that is not known about Morocco's activities relating to the resources of Western Sahara. The United Nations has issued its legal opinion regarding the responsibilities of Morocco as a de facto administering power but has not followed this opinion with a further investigation and evaluation of whether Morocco is operating consistently with the legal opinion. We urge the United Nations to investigate and evaluate whether the local population has actually benefited from the exploitation of Western Sahara resources by Morocco and whether Morocco is fulfilling its responsibilities in this regard.

...omissis...

10. Group of Jurists, Western Sahara and the Protocol to the EU-Morocco Fisheries Partnership Agreement (FPA) of 2013 – A Legal Analysis, 2 December 2013.

2 December, 2013

Western Sahara and the Protocol to the EU-Morocco Fisheries Partnership Agreement (FPA) of 2013 – a Legal Analysis

1. Summary

- A new Protocol to the FPA may make the EU and its member states liable for a violation of international law, namely recognition of and assistance to serious breaches of international law by Morocco, amounting to aggression and denial of the right of self-determination, including the right to freely dispose of their natural wealth and resources.
- An agreement with Morocco that covers waters outside Western Sahara must conform with the following conditions:
  - The agreement should make clear that it does not cover Western Sahara as a part of the territory of Morocco, but only as an occupied, non-self-governing territory.
  - The agreement must be in accordance with the wishes and interests of the people of Western Sahara.
- The current Protocol falls far short of these requirements and is therefore in violation of international law.

2. Legal background

2.1 The legal status of Western Sahara

...omissis...

The people of Western Sahara (the Saharawis) have a right to self-determination, which can be fulfilled through the creation of a fully sovereign state, if they so choose. Under that principle, they also have the right to "freely dispose of their natural wealth and resources"[1]. The Moroccan occupation and annexation of the territory is a serious breach of International Law. Western Sahara is not a part of Morocco and Morocco

[1] Common Article 1 of the International Covenant on Civil and Political Rights and the International Covenant on Economic, Social and Cultural Rights.

has no legal title or claim on the territory. Morocco has an obligation to respect the right of the people of Western Sahara to self-determination and to end its illegal annexation and occupation of Western Sahara.

2.2 Duties of third states, such as the EU and its member states

In case of an illegal situation, third states have the following duties, as summed up by the ICJ regarding the wall (or barrier) in Occupied Palestinian Territory:

> "All States are under an obligation not to recognize the illegal situation resulting from the construction of the wall and not to render aid or assistance in maintaining the situation created by such construction; all States parties to the Fourth Geneva Convention relative to the Protection of Civilian Persons in Time of War of 12 August 1949 have in addition the obligation, while respecting the United Nations Charter and international law, to ensure compliance by Israel with international humanitarian law as embodied in that Convention[2]."

These principles apply to the current situation as well, meaning that the EU and its member states shall not recognize the annexation of Western Sahara and that they shall not assist in the continued occupation and annexation. Further, they should cooperate to bring an end to the illegal situation. Hence, it is illegal to enter into an agreement with Morocco, which explicitly or implicitly recognizes the annexation of Western Sahara; any such agreement that covers Western Sahara would have to clarify that the territory is not under Moroccan sovereignty. Further, any such agreement should not strengthen the Moroccan occupation, and should hence not support measures that strengthen Moroccan control or that facilitate Morocco's transfer of settlers into the territory.

It should be pointed out in this context that this Moroccan responsibility is in addition to liability that individual Moroccan officials bear for acts in Western Sahara, which entail individual criminal responsibility, including for aggression, war crimes and possibly also crimes against humanity. Such liability may attach also to individuals in third countries that assist or in other ways take part in those crimes.

2.3 Use of natural resources

Since Morocco has no legal right to govern the territory, she has no legal title to the natural resources of Western Sahara. Consequently, Morocco has no right as a sovereign to dispose of such natural resources for her own purposes. Furthermore, any agreement that Morocco enters into with other countries cannot cover Western Sahara as a part of Morocco.

---

2 Legal Consequences of the Construction of a Wall in the Occupied Palestinian Territory, ICJ Reports 2004, para. 163.

Since the annexation is illegal it is null and void and Morocco is therefore an occupying power. The basic principles of belligerent occupation are: the occupying power may not change the legal and political framework; it should proceed from the premise that the occupation is temporary and that the occupying power may not introduce permanent changes into the occupied territory. Furthermore, Western Sahara is a non-self-governing territory, and its people has a right to permanent sovereignty over its natural resources and the right to "freely dispose of their natural wealth and resources", as provided in Article 1(2) of the two UN Covenants on Human Rights.

Nevertheless, Morocco may under some circumstances use the natural resources of the territory. Under the law of occupation, as set out in the IV Hague Convention on Land Warfare, Morocco has a responsibility to uphold order as well as the "vie publique" – public life and welfare (Article 43)[3]. This means that Morocco must offer basic public goods to the population of Western Sahara, which entails that there must be income to pay for these goods. Consequently, Morocco may make arrangements with regard to the resources of Western Sahara, provided that they benefit the people of Western Sahara. This would be particularly appropriate with regard to renewable resources, like sustainable fishing. The principle of self-determination further requires that the people of Western Sahara should be able to influence how this is done.

...omissis...

In several statements and analyses from various EU institutions, the last requirement [*Any such agreement must be for the benefit of the people of Western Sahara and according to the wishes of that people, in accordance with the right of a people to freely dispose of their natural wealth and resources*] has been watered down to "benefit the local population". However, this formula fails in two ways to respond to what international law requires:

1) It uses the term "population" instead of "people". "Local population" excludes a very large proportion of the people of Western Sahara, who live in refugee camps beyond Moroccan control. It further includes Moroccan settlers, introduced into Western Sahara in violation of Article 49 of the IV Geneva Convention.
2) It omits the requirement that the agreement be in accordance with the wishes of the people, *omissis...*

3 See also a number of provisions in the IV Geneva Convention (1949) which indicate positive obligations for the occupying power, such as Articles 50, 55 and 56.

3. The Fisheries Partnership Agreement (FPA)

On 22 May 2006, the EU Council of Ministers adopted the FPA with Morocco with one negative vote (Sweden) and one abstention (Finland). During the course of the negotiations, serious concerns with regard to Western Sahara had been voiced also by Denmark, Ireland and the Netherlands. While the FPA does not say so explicitly, it was meant to cover, and has indeed covered, also the waters outside of Western Sahara, which provide an important part of the total fisheries allocated to the EU[4].

The FPA entered into force on 28 February but the relevant protocol to the FPA expired on 27 February 2011. A new protocol was negotiated and adopted by a divided Council of Ministers in 2011 but was rejected by Parliament, partly due to the problems mentioned above. The Commission has now negotiated yet another Protocol, which was adopted by the Council in mid-November and will be voted upon in Parliament in December. Unfortunately, the relevant changes in the protocol compared to 2011 are cosmetic, at best.

The explanatory memorandum to the proposal for a Council decision claims that one of the reasons for why the 2011 Protocol was rejected was "that it did not respect international law insofar as it did not prove that the local populations would benefit from the economic and social benefits of that Protocol". As explained above, this is a misrepresentation of the problem, since international law requires that the agreement is to the benefit of *and in accordance with the wishes of the people* (not "the local population"). The alleged remedy to this misrepresented problem is that the new Protocol is:

> "requiring Morocco to provide regular, detailed reports on the use of the financial contribution for the fisheries sector, including the economic and social benefits on a geographical basis, and providing for a mechanism for the possible suspension of the Protocol, including in the event of violations of human rights and democratic principles."

This remedy fails to address the problem even in the diminished and misrepresented form quoted above. The concrete provisions which the memorandum alludes to are set out in Articles 6 and 8:

According to Article 6, the EU's financial contribution shall be used "to develop and implement Morocco's sectoral fisheries policy as part of the [Moroccan] 'Halieutis' strategy for developing the fisheries sector" "on the basis of the setting up by the two parties, by mutual agreement within the Joint Committee, of the objectives to be met and of the relevant annual and multi-annual programme". Morocco shall report including by providing

4 See para. 29, the Legal opinion.

"information on any social and economic consequences, particularly the impact on employment, investment and any other quantifiable repercussions of the measures taken, together with their geographical distribution".

This provision does not prevent an implementation of the Protocol in accordance with international law. However, neither does it do much to secure such an implementation. In fact, it is highly unlikely that Morocco would accept "in mutual agreement" an implementation in accordance with the "wishes and interests of the people of Western Sahara". Neither is it likely that the European Commission would be able to (or even try to) press the Moroccan authorities to implement the agreement in this fashion, in particular since the reporting requirement is far too general to secure reporting on the impact on the people of Western Sahara.

With respect to human rights, the Protocol hence adds nothing to what was already in place. The clause on general principles in Article 1 and the suspension clause (Article 8) refer to the human rights clause in the Association agreement and the suspension clause in the FPA. There are no reports of this clause ever having been used for the protection of the rights of the people of Western Sahara during the thirteen years that have passed since the Agreement entered into force in 2000.

4. Conclusion

The conclusion is that the 2013 Protocol still does not address the failure to conform with international law that was one of the reasons that the European Parliament rejected the Protocol in 2011.

In the 2013 legal opinion to the European Parliament, the Parliament's legal service cited its own previous opinion of 2009. The legal service here found that "compliance with international law requires that economic activities related to the natural resources of a Non-Self-Governing Territory are carried out for the benefits of the people of such Territory, and in accordance with their wishes." Further, "[i] n the event that it could not be demonstrated that the FPA was implemented in conformity with the principles of international law concerning the rights of the Saharawi people over their natural resources, principles which the Community is bound to respect, the Community should refrain from allowing vessels to fish in the waters off Western Sahara by requesting fisheries licenses only for fishing zones that are situated in the waters off Morocco". Since there are no records of this having been the case, before or after 2009, Parliament should reject this Protocol and let it be known to the Commission that it expects the Commission to negotiate a new agreement which fully respects international law[5].

5 See paras. 5 e) and 5 i), Legal opinion.

Oscar Abalde Cantero, Professor of Public International Law, Universidad del País Vasco

Lennart Aspegren, Former UN Judge

Nathaniel Berman, Rahel Varnhagen Professor of International Affairs, Law, and Modern Culture, Brown University

Maria Dolores Bollo Arocena, Professor of Public International Law, Universidad del País Vasco

Ove Bring, Professor Emeritus in International Law, Stockholm University & Swedish National Defence College

Candelaria Carrera Asturiano, Miembro de AIODH (Asociación Internacional para la Observación de los Derechos Humanos), Abogados de Badajoz Law School

Tony Carty, Sir Y K Pao Chair in Public Law, Hongkong University

Ola Engdahl, Associate Professor of International Law Swedish National Defence College

David Fisher, Professor of International Law, Faculty of Law, Stockholm University

Andres Marin Garcia, Miembro de AIODH, Abogados de Badajoz Law School

Matthew Happold, Professor of Public International Law, Université du Luxembourg 4

Frederik Harhoff, Professor of International Law, Syddansk Universitet i Odense

Iñigo Iruretagoiena Agirrezabalaga, Professor of Public International Law, Universidad del País Vasco

Francisco Javier Quel Lopez, Professor of Public International Law, Universidad del País Vasco

Mark Klamberg, LL.D. and senior lecturer in Public International Law at Uppsala University

David Langlet, Associate Professor, Stockholm University, Stockholm Centre Oxford Fellow, Faculty of Law, University of Oxford

Nicolás Alonso Moreda, Professor of Public International Law, Universidad del País Vasco

Frédéric Mégret PhD, Associate Professor at the Faculty of Law, McGill University, and the holder of the Canada Research Chair in the Law of Human Rights and Legal Pluralism.

Jarna Petman, Senior Lecturer/Professor a.i. in International Law, Helsinki University

Juan Soroeta Liceras, Professor of Public International Law, Universidad del País Vasco and President of AIODH

Pål Wrange, Professor of Public International Law at Stockholm University

Case-Law

European Union

11. Court of Justice of the EU, case C-565/13, Criminal proceedings against Ove Ahlström and Others (2014), not yet reported.

JUDGMENT OF THE COURT (Third Chamber)

9 October 2014 (*)

(Reference for a preliminary ruling – External relations – Fisheries Partnership Agreement between the European Community and the Kingdom of Morocco – Exclusion of any possibility for Community vessels to carry out fishing activities in Moroccan fishing zones on the basis of a licence issued by the Moroccan authorities without the intervention of the competent European Union authorities)

In Case C-565/13,

REQUEST for a preliminary ruling under Article 267 TFEU from the Hovrätten för Västra Sverige (Sweden), made by decision of 31 October 2013, received at the Court on 4 November 2013, in the criminal proceedings against:

Ove Ahlström,

Lennart Kjellberg,

Fiskeri Ganthi AB,

Fiskeri Nordic AB,

...*omissis*...

Judgment

1. This request for a preliminary ruling concerns the interpretation of the Fisheries Partnership Agreement between the European Community and the Kingdom of Morocco, approved on behalf of the Community by Council Regulation (EC) No 764/2006 of 22 May 2006 (OJ 2006 L 141, p. 1) ('the Fisheries Agreement').

2. The request has been made in the context of criminal proceedings instituted against Mr Ahlström and Mr Kjellberg and against Fiskeri Ganthi AB ('Fiskeri Ganthi') and Fiskeri Nordic AB ('Fiskeri Nordic'), who are accused of having carried out unauthorised fishing activities in Moroccan fishing zones between April 2007 and May 2008 inclusive.

...omissis...

The dispute in the main proceedings and the questions referred for a preliminary ruling

17. It is apparent from the decision making the reference that Mr. Ahlström, who is the legal representative of Fiskeri Ganthi, owner of the vessel Aldo, and Mr. Kjellberg, who is the legal representative of Fiskeri Nordic, owner of the vessel Nordic IV, are being prosecuted, under Paragraphs 24 and 40 of the Law on fisheries, and Chapter 3, Paragraph 1, and Chapter 4, Paragraph 3, of the Fiskeriverket regulatory provisions, for having, over the period between April 2007 and May 2008 inclusive, intentionally or through serious negligence, carried out professional fishing activities off the coast of Western Sahara with those vessels registered in the Swedish vessels register, although they did not possess and hold on board the necessary permits issued by the Fiskeriverket, namely the general professional fishing permits and the specific permits for fishing in the waters in question in accordance with the Fisheries Agreement.

18. In the alternative, the Kammaråklagaren (public prosecutor) has based those prosecutions on Paragraph 40 of the Law on fisheries, on Article 3 of Commission Regulation (EC) No 1281/2005 of 3 August 2005 on the management of fishing licences and the minimal information to be contained therein (OJ 2005 L 203, p. 3), and on Article 22(1)(a) of Council Regulation (EC) No 2371/2002 of 20 December 2002 on the conservation and sustainable exploitation of fisheries resources under the Common Fisheries Policy (OJ 2002 L 358, p. 59), in conjunction with Article 6 of the Fisheries Agreement.

19. In support of the abovementioned prosecutions, the Kammaråklagaren contended, inter alia, that those vessels, the crew of which was made up of Swedish and Moroccan fishermen, carried out on an ongoing basis trawl fishing, generating a total income amounting to at least 14 million Swedish crowns (SEK) in 2007 and SEK 6 million in 2008. He classified the offences as serious by reason of the fact that they were committed in a systematic manner over a protracted period of time, that they involved a particularly important activity and that the catches were of a significant value.

20. Mr Ahlström and Mr Kjellberg deny the facts of which they are accused and contest their criminal liability. They claim that the fishing vessels Aldo and Nordic IV were leased, by a charter arrangement known as a 'bareboat' charter, to the Moroccan company Atlas Pelagic, which has its own fishing rights in Moroccan territorial waters as well as fishing rights of other Moroccan persons. As part of its activity, that company leased the two vessels and used them itself. According to Mr Ahlström and Mr Kjellberg, the authorisation of the Swedish authorities or of any other European authority was not required for carrying out that activity, since the Fiskeriverket regulatory provisions do not apply to leasing activities undertaken by Fiskeri Ganthi and Fiskeri Nordic. No breach of EU law was committed, they argue, since Article 6(1) of the Fisheries Agreement, in the same way as that agreement as a whole, does not apply to the facts of the main proceedings.

21. In the view of the Hovrätten för Västra Sverige (Court of Appeal for Western Sweden), before which an appeal has been brought against a judgment of the Göteborgs tingsrätt (District Court, Gothenburg), it is unclear whether EU law and the Fisheries Agreement exclude fishing activities by Community vessels in Moroccan waters without the authorisation of the European Union or of one of its Member States.

22. The referring court essentially takes the view that Article 6(2) of the Fisheries Agreement could be interpreted as meaning that there is such an exclusion. However, it notes that, according to certain authors, that provision would allow an interpretation to the effect that a Community vessel may carry out fishing under a private licence issued by a third country. It adds that, in the main proceedings, it is argued that the competent Moroccan authorities were of the view that the fishing activities of the two vessels in question were carried out in accordance with the Fishing Agreement and that they had issued the authorisations necessary for that purpose.

23. It was in those circumstances that the Hovrätten för Västra Sverige decided to stay the proceedings and to refer to the Court the following questions for a preliminary ruling:

> "(1) Can Article 6(1) of the [Fisheries Agreement] be regarded as an exclusionary provision in the sense that it excludes the possibility for Community vessels to carry out fishing activities in Moroccan fishing zones on the basis of licences issued exclusively by the competent Moroccan authorities to Moroccan owners of fishing quotas?
>
> (2) Can Article 6(1) of the [Fisheries Agreement] be regarded as an exclusionary provision in the sense that it excludes the possibility of leasing Community vessels to Moroccan companies, by a "bareboat" charter arrangement (in accordance with the standard "Barecon 2001" BIMCO

standard Bareboat Charter form), so that they can carry out fishing activities in Moroccan fishing zones on the basis of licences issued exclusively by the competent Moroccan authorities to Moroccan owners of fishing quotas?

(3) Would the answer to Question 2 be different if the lessor also provides the Moroccan company with expertise in the form of administration and crewing as well as technical assistance?

(4) Does the [Fisheries Agreement] provide that the Kingdom of Morocco is to develop and perform that agreement in tandem with its own national pelagic fishing industry to the south of the 29th parallel north? If that is the case, does that agreement grant the Kingdom of Morocco the right to lease fishing vessels flying the flag of a Member State of the [European Union] or to issue licences directly to those vessels for its own national fishing activities, without the [European Union's] authorisation?"

Consideration of the questions referred for a preliminary ruling

24. By its questions, which should be examined together, the referring court is essentially asking whether the Fisheries Agreement, in particular Article 6 thereof, must be interpreted as excluding any possibility for Community vessels to carry out fishing activities in Moroccan fishing zones on the basis of a licence issued by the Moroccan authorities without the intervention of the competent European Union authorities.

25. The referring court seeks guidance, in particular, on the question whether the Fisheries Agreement excludes the possibility, for the purpose of carrying out fishing activities in those fishing zones, of leasing a Community vessel, by a 'bareboat' charter arrangement, to a Moroccan company which holds only a licence issued by the competent Moroccan authorities to Moroccan owners of fishing quotas. The referring court is also unsure whether the same applies in the case where the lessor also provides that company with expertise and technical assistance.

26. It should be noted that the parties to the Fisheries Agreement gave expression, in the preamble to that agreement, to their desire to establish terms and conditions governing the fishing activities of Community vessels in Moroccan fishing zones. The purpose of that agreement, as defined in Article 1 thereof, is to establish the principles, rules and procedures covering, inter alia, the conditions governing access by those vessels to the fishing zones referred to. Since the agreement does not provide for any exception to those conditions, all Community vessels – which, according to Article 2(d) of the Fisheries Agreement, are vessels flying the flag of a Member State of the Community and registered in the Community – that wish to carry out fishing activities in those zones are consequently subject to that agreement.

27. Thus, Article 6 of the Fisheries Agreement, concerning the conditions governing fishing activities, provides, in paragraph 1 thereof, that Community vessels may fish in Moroccan fishing zones only if they are in possession of a fishing licence issued under that Fisheries Agreement.

28. According to the actual wording of that provision, the exercise of fishing activities by Community vessels in Moroccan fishing zones is subject to the holding of a licence issued by the competent authorities of the Kingdom of Morocco at the request of the competent European Union authorities. Article 6(2) of the Fisheries Agreement, moreover, provides that licences may be granted to Community vessels by the Moroccan authorities for categories of fishing not covered by the protocol, but that, within the spirit of partnership established by the Fisheries Agreement, the granting of such licences 'remains dependent on a favourable opinion from the European Commission'.

29. It follows that an intervention of the competent European Union authorities is always required in order for a Community vessel to be authorised to carry out fishing activities in Moroccan fishing zones and, consequently, that such a vessel cannot carry out such activities in those zones under a licence issued by the competent Moroccan authorities in the absence of such intervention.

...omissis...

31. It must also be stated that granting Community vessels the possibility of accessing Moroccan fishing zones in order to carry out fishing activities there by dispensing with the intervention of the competent European Union authorities would run contrary to the objective of the Fisheries Agreement, which seeks, as is apparent from its preamble and from Articles 1 and 3, to introduce responsible fishing in those fishing zones in order to ensure the long-term conservation and sustainable exploitation of fisheries resources, in particular by implementing a control system covering fishing activities as a whole, in order to ensure the effectiveness of the measures for the conservation and management of those resources. Such a possibility might be liable to increase access by Community vessels to those fishing zones and to intensify their exploitation of those resources there, and that without the control of the competent European Union authorities.

32. Likewise, access by Community vessels to Moroccan fishing zones outside of the scope of the Fisheries Agreement would not be in keeping with the basis and purpose of the financial contribution granted by the European Union to the Kingdom of Morocco pursuant to Article 7 of that agreement, which consists, according to that article, of providing financial compensation for access by Community vessels to Moroccan

fishing zones and of providing financial support for introducing a national fisheries policy based on responsible fishing and on the sustainable exploitation of fisheries resources in Moroccan waters.

33. Consequently, it cannot be accepted that Community vessels should be able to access Moroccan fishing zones in order to carry out fishing activities there through the conclusion, for that purpose, of a 'bareboat' charter arrangement with a Moroccan company holding a licence issued by the Moroccan authorities to Moroccan owners of fishing quotas or by using any other legal instrument in order to access those fishing zones for the purpose of carrying out such activities there outside the scope of the Fisheries Agreement and, consequently, without the intervention of the competent European Union authorities.

...omissis...

On those grounds, the Court (Third Chamber) hereby rules:

The Fisheries Partnership Agreement between the European Community and the Kingdom of Morocco, approved on behalf of the Community by Council Regulation (EC) No 764/2006 of 22 May 2006, in particular Article 6 of that agreement, must be interpreted as excluding any possibility for Community vessels to carry out fishing activities in Moroccan fishing zones on the basis of a licence issued by the Moroccan authorities without the intervention of the competent European Union authorities.

...omissis...

12. Court of Justice of the EU, General Court (Eighth Chamber), Case T-512/12, Front populaire pour la libération de la saguia-el-hamra et du rio de oro (Front Polisario) v. Council of the European Union (2015), not yet reported.

ARRÊT DU TRIBUNAL (huitième chambre)

10 décembre 2015 (*)

"Relations extérieures – Accord sous forme d'échange de lettres entre l'Union et le Maroc – Libéralisation réciproque en matière de produits agricoles, de produits agricoles transformés, de poissons et de produits de la pêche – Application de l'accord au Sahara occidental – Front Polisario – Recours en annulation – Capacité à agir – Affectation directe et individuelle – Recevabilité – Conformité avec le droit international – Obligation de motivation – Droits de la défense".

Dans l'affaire T-512/12,

Front populaire pour la libération de la saguia-el-hamra et du rio de oro (Front Polisario), représenté initialement par Mes C.-E. Hafiz et G. Devers, puis par Me Devers, avocats,

partie requérante,

contre

Conseil de l'Union européenne, représenté par Mme S. Kyriakopoulou, M. Á. de Elera-San Miguel Hurtado, Mmes A. Westerhof Löfflerová et N. Rouam, en qualité d'agents,

partie défenderesse,

soutenu par

Commission européenne, représentée initialement par MM. F. Castillo de la Torre, E. Paasivirta et D. Stefanov, puis par MM. Castillo de la Torre et Paasivirta, en qualité d'agents,

partie intervenante,

ayant pour objet une demande d'annulation de la décision 2012/497/UE du Conseil, du 8 mars 2012, concernant la conclusion de l'accord sous forme d'échange de lettres entre l'Union européenne et le Royaume du Maroc relatif aux mesures de libéralisation réciproques en matière de produits agricoles, de produits agricoles transformés, de poissons et de produits de la pêche, au remplacement des protocoles nos 1, 2 et 3 et de leurs annexes et aux modifications de l'accord euro-méditerranéen établissant une association entre les Communautés européennes et leurs États membres, d'une part, et le Royaume du Maroc, d'autre part (JO L 241, p. 2),

...omissis...

Arrêt

Antécédents du litige

...omissis...

Sur la décision attaquée et ses antécédents

17. L'accord euro-méditerranéen établissant une association entre les Communautés européennes et leurs États membres, d'une part, et le Royaume du Maroc, d'autre part (JO 2000, L 70, p. 2, ci-après "l'accord d'association avec le Maroc") a été conclu à Bruxelles le 26 février 1996.

18. En vertu de son article 1er, il établit une association entre, d'une part, la Communauté européenne et la Communauté européenne du charbon et de l'acier (désignées ensemble dans l'accord d'association avec le Maroc comme étant la "Communauté") ainsi que leurs États membres et, d'autre part, le Royaume du Maroc. L'accord d'association avec le Maroc est subdivisé en huit titres relatifs, respectivement, à la libre circulation des marchandises, au droit d'établissement et aux services, aux "[p]aiements, [aux] capitaux, [à la] concurrence et [aux] autres dispositions économiques", à la coopération économique, à la coopération sociale et culturelle, à la coopération financière et, enfin, aux dispositions institutionnelles générales et finales. L'accord d'association avec le Maroc comporte également sept annexes dont les six premières énumèrent les produits visés par certaines dispositions de ses articles 10, 11 et 12 (qui figurent tous sous le titre afférent à la libre circulation des marchandises), alors que la septième est relative à la propriété intellectuelle, industrielle et commerciale. En outre, sont annexés à l'accord d'association avec le Maroc cinq protocoles, relatifs, respectivement, au régime applicable à l'importation dans la Communauté des produits agricoles originaires du Maroc, au régime applicable à l'importation dans la Communauté des produits de la pêche originaires du Maroc, au régime applicable à l'importation au Maroc des produits agricoles originaires de la Communauté, à la définition de la notion de "produits originaires" et aux méthodes de coopération administrative et, enfin, à l'assistance mutuelle en matière douanière entre les autorités administratives. Les protocoles nos 1, 4 et 5 comportent leurs propres annexes, qui, dans le cas du protocole n° 4 relatif à la définition de la notion de "produits originaires", sont très volumineuses.

19. L'accord d'association avec le Maroc, les protocoles qu'il comporte en tant qu'annexes ainsi que les déclarations et échanges de lettres annexés à l'acte final ont été approuvés au nom de la Communauté

européenne et de la Communauté européenne du charbon et de l'acier par la décision 2000/204/CE, CECA du Conseil et de la Commission, du 24 janvier 2000, relative à la conclusion de l'accord d'association avec le Maroc (JO L 70, p. 1).

20. En vertu de la décision 2012/497/UE du Conseil, du 8 mars 2012, concernant la conclusion de l'accord sous forme d'échange de lettres entre l'Union européenne et le Royaume du Maroc relatif aux mesures de libéralisation réciproques en matière de produits agricoles, de produits agricoles transformés, de poissons et de produits de la pêche, au remplacement des protocoles nos 1, 2 et 3 et de leurs annexes et aux modifications de l'accord d'association avec le Maroc (JO L 241, p. 2, ci-après la "décision attaquée"), le Conseil de l'Union européenne a approuvé, au nom de l'Union européenne, l'accord sous forme d'échange de lettres entre l'Union et le Royaume du Maroc relatif aux mesures de libéralisation réciproques, au remplacement des protocoles nos 1 à 3 et de leurs annexes et aux modifications de l'accord d'association avec le Maroc.

21. Le texte de l'accord approuvé par la décision attaquée, qui a été publié au *Journal officiel de l'Union européenne*, supprime l'article 10 de l'accord d'association avec le Maroc, qui fait partie de son titre II, relatif à la libre circulation des marchandises, et apporte des modifications aux articles 7, 15, 17 et 18 du même titre ainsi qu'à l'intitulé du chapitre II qui figure également sous ce titre. En outre, l'accord approuvé par la décision attaquée remplace le texte des protocoles nos 1 à 3 de l'accord d'association avec le Maroc.

Procédure et conclusions des parties

...omissis...

29. Le requérant conclut à l'annulation de la décision attaquée "et [,] par voie de conséquence, à tous actes d'application".

30. Toutefois, lors de l'audience, le représentant du requérant a indiqué que la référence à "tous actes d'application" résultait d'une erreur de plume et qu'il convenait de comprendre les conclusions du requérant en ce sens qu'il demandait uniquement l'annulation de la décision attaquée. Il a été pris acte de cette déclaration au procès-verbal de l'audience.

...omissis...

32. Le Conseil conclut à ce qu'il plaise au Tribunal :

– rejeter le recours comme irrecevable ;
– si le Tribunal devait juger le recours recevable, rejeter le recours comme non fondé ;
– condamner le requérant aux dépens.

33. La Commission soutient les conclusions du Conseil tendant au rejet du recours comme irrecevable ou, à défaut, comme non fondé et conclut, en outre, à la condamnation du requérant aux dépens.

Sur la recevabilité

Sur la capacité d'ester en justice du Front Polisario

34. Aux termes de l'article 263, quatrième alinéa, TFUE, toute personne physique ou morale peut former, dans les conditions prévues aux premier et deuxième alinéas, un recours contre les actes dont elle est le destinataire ou qui la concernent directement et individuellement, ainsi que contre les actes réglementaires qui la concernent directement et qui ne comportent pas de mesures d'exécution.

35. L'article 44, paragraphe 5, du règlement de procédure du Tribunal du 2 mai 1991, qui était d'application au moment du dépôt de la requête, prévoyait ce qui suit:

> "Si le requérant est une personne morale de droit privé, il joint à sa requête :
>
> a) ses statuts ou un extrait récent du registre de commerce, ou un extrait récent du registre des associations ou toute autre preuve de son existence juridique ;
>
> b) la preuve que le mandat donné à l'avocat a été régulièrement établi par un représentant qualifié à cet effet".

36. En outre, aux termes de l'article 44, paragraphe 6, du règlement de procédure du 2 mai 1991, si la requête n'est pas conforme aux conditions énumérées aux paragraphes 3 à 5 du même article, le greffier fixe au requérant un délai raisonnable aux fins de régularisation de la requête ou de production des pièces mentionnées auxdits paragraphes.

37. Dans la requête, le requérant relève qu'il est "un sujet de droit international, qui dispose de la personnalité juridique internationale reconnue aux mouvements nationaux de libération en droit international". Il fait en outre valoir, en invoquant plusieurs textes qu'il a joints à la requête, qu'il a été "reconnu comme représentant du peuple sahraoui… par les instances de l'ONU, de l'Union européenne et par le (Royaume du) Maroc, pour les négociations". Il ajoute que tant le Conseil de sécurité que l'Assemblée générale de l'ONU ont reconnu la validité de l'accord de paix qu'il avait conclu avec la Mauritanie en août 1979 (voir point 13 ci-dessus). Enfin, il invoque le fait que, dans deux résolutions, le Parlement européen lui a demandé ainsi qu'au Royaume du Maroc de coopérer pleinement avec le Comité international de la Croix-Rouge ainsi qu'avec l'ONU.

38. Le requérant n'avait pas joint à sa requête de documents tels que ceux prévus à l'article 44, paragraphe 5, du règlement de procédure du 2 mai 1991. À la suite de la fixation d'un délai par le greffe aux fins de régularisation de la requête, il a produit des extraits de ses statuts, un mandat à son avocat établi par une personne habilitée à cet effet par lesdits statuts, à savoir par son secrétaire général, ainsi que la preuve de l'élection de ce dernier. En revanche, il n'a pas produit de documents additionnels pour prouver qu'il disposait de la personnalité juridique.

39. C'est dans ces conditions que le Tribunal a adopté la mesure d'organisation de la procédure mentionnée au point 23 ci-dessus.

40. En réponse aux questions du Tribunal, le requérant a déclaré ce qui suit:

> "Le Front Polisario n'est constitué en personne morale selon le droit d'aucun État internationalement reconnu ou pas. Pas plus qu'un État étranger ou que l'Union européenne elle-même, le Front Polisario ne saurait tirer son existence légale du droit interne d'un État."

41. Il a en outre affirmé qu'il était "un sujet du droit international public" et il a ajouté:

> "[L]e Front Polisario n'a en aucune manière à rapporter la preuve de sa constitution selon le droit interne d'un État internationalement reconnu. Incarnation de la souveraineté du peuple sahraoui, il ne saurait faire dépendre son existence de l'ordre juridique de l'ancienne puissance coloniale, le Royaume d'Espagne, qui manque à tous ses devoirs internationaux depuis quarante ans, et encore moins [de] la puissance occupante, le Maroc, qui impose son ordre juridique par un usage illégal de force armée [...]"

42. Le Conseil fait valoir que le requérant "n'a pas prouvé l'existence de sa capacité juridique à former le présent recours". Selon lui, le requérant semble assimiler sa qualité de représentant du peuple du Sahara occidental à l'existence de la personnalité juridique de plein droit au regard du droit international, qui est propre aux États souverains. Le Conseil conteste que ces deux concepts soient assimilables et que le requérant puisse être assimilé à un État.

43. Le Conseil ajoute que, à supposer même que le requérant ait été reconnu en tant que mouvement de libération nationale et qu'il dispose, de ce fait, de la personnalité juridique, cela n'implique pas automatiquement une capacité procédurale à agir devant les juridictions de l'Union. Selon le Conseil, la reconnaissance du requérant par l'ONU en tant que représentant du peuple du Sahara occidental lui donne tout au plus la capacité de participer aux négociations concernant le statut du Sahara occidental qui sont conduites par l'ONU et d'être, avec le Royaume du Maroc, son interlocuteur à cette fin. En revanche, cette reconnaissance

ne lui conférerait pas de locus standi devant les cours et tribunaux qui se trouvent en dehors du contexte de l'ONU et auxquels il n'appartient pas de résoudre le différend international l'opposant au Royaume du Maroc.

44. La Commission déclare ne pas contester "la qualité de représentant du peuple sahraoui dont jouit le Front Polisario et qui lui a été reconnue par l'Assemblée générale de l'ONU".

45. Elle ajoute, toutefois:

> "[L]a personnalité juridique du Front Polisario est douteuse. En tant que représentant du peuple sahraoui il est censé tout au plus disposer d'une personnalité juridique fonctionnelle et transitoire."

46. Au regard des arguments des parties, tout d'abord, il convient de préciser que, en l'espèce, il ne s'agit de déterminer ni si le Front Polisario peut être qualifié de "mouvement national de libération", ni même si une telle qualification, à la supposer exacte, suffit à lui conférer la personnalité juridique. La question que le Tribunal est appelé à trancher est celle de savoir si le Front Polisario peut ester en justice devant lui afin de demander, en vertu de l'article 263, quatrième alinéa, TFUE, l'annulation de la décision attaquée.

47. Ensuite, il y a lieu de relever qu'il ressort du libellé de l'article 263, quatrième alinéa, TFUE que seules les personnes physiques et les entités dotées de la personnalité juridique peuvent former un recours en annulation en vertu de cette disposition. Ainsi, dans son arrêt du 27 novembre 1984, *Bensider e.a./Commission* (50/84, Rec, EU:C:1984:365, point 9), la Cour de justice de l'Union européenne a rejeté comme irrecevable un recours en ce qu'il avait été introduit par une société commerciale qui, au moment de l'introduction dudit recours, n'avait pas encore acquis la personnalité juridique.

48. Cependant, dans son arrêt du 28 octobre 1982, *Groupement des Agences de voyages/Commission* (135/81, Rec, EU:C:1982:371, point 10), la Cour de justice a relevé que la notion de "personne morale", telle qu'elle figure à l'article 263, quatrième alinéa, TFUE, ne coïncidait pas nécessairement avec celles propres aux différents ordres juridiques des États membres. Ainsi, dans l'affaire ayant donné lieu à cet arrêt, la Cour de justice a admis la recevabilité d'un recours introduit par une "association occasionnelle de dix agences de voyages regroupées pour répondre ensemble à un appel d'offres" contre une décision de la Commission d'écarter cette association d'un appel d'offres. La Cour de justice a relevé à cet égard que la Commission avait admis elle-même la recevabilité de l'offre introduite par l'association en cause et l'avait rejetée après un examen comparatif de l'ensemble des soumissionnaires. Par conséquent, selon la Cour de justice, la Commission ne pouvait pas contester la capacité d'ester

en justice d'une entité qu'elle avait admise à participer à un appel d'offres et à laquelle elle avait adressé une décision négative après un examen comparatif de l'ensemble des soumissionnaires (arrêt *Groupement des Agences de voyages/Commission*, précité, EU:C:1982:371, points 9 à 12).

49. De même, dans ses arrêts du 8 octobre 1974, *Union syndicale – Service public européen e.a./Conseil* (175/73, Rec, EU:C:1974:95, points 9 à 17) et *Syndicat général du personnel des organismes européens/Commission* (18/74, Rec, EU:C:1974:96, points 5 à 13), la Cour de justice a énuméré un certain nombre d'éléments, à savoir, premièrement, le fait que les fonctionnaires de l'Union jouissent du droit d'association et peuvent notamment être membres d'organisations syndicales ou professionnelles, deuxièmement, le fait que les requérants dans ces deux affaires étaient des syndicats regroupant un nombre important de fonctionnaires et d'agents des institutions de l'Union, troisièmement, le fait que leurs statuts et leur structure interne étaient de nature à leur assurer l'autonomie nécessaire pour agir comme des entités responsables dans les rapports juridiques et, quatrièmement, le fait que la Commission les avait reconnus comme interlocuteurs à l'occasion de négociations, pour conclure qu'on ne saurait leur nier la capacité d'agir en justice devant les juridictions de l'Union, en formant un recours en annulation dans le respect des conditions de l'article 263, quatrième alinéa, TFUE.

50. Enfin, il convient également de rappeler que, dans son arrêt du 18 janvier 2007, *PKK et KNK/Conseil* (C-229/05 P, Rec, EU:C:2007:32, points 109 à 112), la Cour de justice a admis la recevabilité d'un recours en annulation introduit par une entité ayant fait l'objet des mesures restrictives dans le cadre de la lutte contre le terrorisme, sans s'interroger sur la question de savoir si cette entité disposait de la personnalité juridique. Rappelant la jurisprudence selon laquelle l'Union est une Union de droit, la Cour de justice a relevé que, si le législateur de l'Union avait estimé que l'entité en question avait une existence suffisante pour faire l'objet des mesures restrictives en cause, la cohérence et la justice imposaient de reconnaître à cette entité la capacité de contester cette décision. Toute autre conclusion aurait pour résultat qu'une organisation pourrait être incluse dans la liste en question sans pouvoir former un recours contre cette inclusion.

51. Toutefois, si la jurisprudence citée ci-dessus démontre que les juridictions de l'Union peuvent admettre la capacité d'ester en justice devant elles d'une entité qui ne dispose pas d'une capacité juridique analogue à celle que confère le droit d'un État membre ou d'un État tiers, voire qui ne dispose pas de la personnalité juridique au regard de ce droit, il convient de relever que, dans son ordonnance du 14 novembre 1963, *Lassalle/Parlement* (15/63, Rec, EU:C:1963:47, p. 97, 100), la

Cour de justice a relevé que les éléments qui constituaient la base de la capacité d'ester en justice devant les juridictions de l'Union comportaient notamment une autonomie et une responsabilité, même restreintes, et elle a rejeté une demande d'intervention présentée par le comité du personnel du Parlement lequel, selon elle, ne satisfaisait pas à ces critères. Cette considération est également reflétée dans la jurisprudence citée au point 49 ci-dessus, dans la mesure où elle explique la constatation de la Cour de justice, selon laquelle les statuts et la structure interne des syndicats ayant introduit les recours dans les affaires en cause leur assuraient l'autonomie nécessaire pour agir comme des entités responsables dans les rapports juridiques.

52. Au regard de cette jurisprudence, il convient de conclure que, dans certains cas particuliers, une entité qui ne dispose pas de la personnalité juridique selon le droit d'un État membre ou d'un État tiers peut néanmoins être considérée comme une "personne morale", au sens de l'article 263, quatrième alinéa, TFUE, et être admise à former un recours en annulation sur le fondement de cette disposition (voir, en ce sens, arrêts *Groupement des Agences de voyages/Commission*, point 48 *supra*, EU:C:1982:371, points 9 à 12, et *PKK et KNK/Conseil*, point 50 *supra*, EU:C:2007:32, points 109 à 112). Tel est notamment le cas lorsque, dans leurs actes ou agissements, l'Union et ses institutions traitent l'entité en question comme étant un sujet distinct, qui peut posséder des droits qui lui sont propres ou être soumis à des obligations ou à des restrictions.

53. Cela présuppose toutefois que l'entité en question dispose de statuts et d'une structure interne lui assurant l'autonomie nécessaire pour agir comme entité responsable dans les rapports juridiques (voir, en ce sens, ordonnance *Lassalle/Parlement*, point 51 *supra*, EU:C:1963:47, p. 100 ; arrêts *Union syndicale – Service public européen e.a./Conseil*, point 49 *supra*, EU:C:1974:95, points 9 à 17, et *Syndicat général du personnel des organismes européens/Commission*, point 49 *supra*, EU:C:1974:96, points 5 à 13).

54. En l'espèce, il convient de constater que les conditions mentionnées au point 53 ci-dessus sont remplies en ce qui concerne le Front Polisario. En effet, celui-ci possède ses propres statuts, dont il a produit une copie, ainsi qu'une structure interne fixe, disposant notamment d'un secrétaire général qui a donné mandat à son conseil aux fins de l'introduction du présent recours. De toute apparence, cette structure lui permet d'agir comme entité responsable dans les rapports juridiques, et ce d'autant plus que, ainsi qu'en témoignent les divers textes invoqués par lui, il a participé à des négociations sous l'égide de l'ONU et a même signé un accord de paix avec un État internationalement reconnu, à savoir la République islamique de Mauritanie.

55. S'agissant des considérations mentionnées au point 52 ci-dessus, il est certes exact que le Front Polisario n'a pas fait l'objet d'actes de l'Union ou de ses institutions de nature analogue à ceux en cause dans les affaires ayant donné lieu aux arrêts *Groupement des Agences de voyages/Commission*, point 48 *supra* (EU:C:1982:371), et *PKK et KNK/Conseil*, point 50 *supra* (EU:C:2007:32). Les deux résolutions du Parlement invoquées par lui (voir point 37 ci-dessus) sont de nature différente, ne produisant pas, à tout le moins à son égard, des effets de droit obligatoires.

56. Il n'en est pas moins exact que, ainsi qu'il ressort des informations résumées aux points 1 à 16 ci-dessus, le Sahara occidental est un territoire dont le statut international est à l'heure actuelle indéterminé. Tant le Royaume du Maroc que le requérant le revendiquent et l'ONU œuvre depuis longtemps en vue d'une résolution pacifique de ce différend. Ainsi qu'il ressort des écrits du Conseil et de la Commission, tant l'Union que ses États membres s'abstiennent de toute intervention et de prise de parti dans ce différend et, le cas échéant, accepteront toute solution décidée conformément au droit international, sous l'égide de l'ONU. À cet égard, la Commission ajoute qu'elle soutient les efforts déployés par le Secrétaire général de l'ONU en vue de parvenir à une solution politique juste, durable et mutuellement acceptable, qui permette l'autodétermination du peuple du Sahara occidental. Elle poursuit en relevant que, "[e]n attendant, le Sahara occidental reste un territoire non autonome administré de facto par le Royaume du Maroc".

57. Premièrement, il convient ainsi de constater que le requérant est une des parties au différend concernant le sort de ce territoire non autonome et, en tant que partie à ce différend, il est nominativement évoqué dans les textes y afférents, y compris les résolutions du Parlement mentionnées au point 37 ci-dessus.

58. Deuxièmement, il convient également de constater que, à l'heure actuelle, il est impossible au Front Polisario de se constituer formellement en personne morale du droit du Sahara occidental, ce droit étant encore inexistant. S'il est exact que, comme le relève la Commission, le Royaume du Maroc administre de facto pratiquement l'ensemble du territoire du Sahara occidental, il s'agit d'une situation de fait à laquelle le Front Polisario s'oppose et qui est, précisément, à l'origine du différend entre lui et le Royaume du Maroc, que l'ONU tend à résoudre. Il serait certainement possible au Front Polisario de se constituer en personne morale conformément au droit d'un État tiers, mais il ne saurait pas davantage être exigé de lui qu'il le fasse.

59. Troisièmement, enfin, il y a lieu de rappeler que le Conseil et la Commission reconnaissent eux-mêmes que le statut international et la situation juridique du Sahara occidental présentent les particularités

mentionnées au point 58 ci-dessus et considèrent que le statut définitif de ce territoire et, partant, le droit qui y est applicable doivent être fixés dans le cadre d'un processus de paix sous les auspices de l'ONU. Or, c'est précisément l'ONU qui considère le Front Polisario comme un participant essentiel d'un tel processus.

60. Compte tenu de ces circonstances fort particulières, il convient de conclure que le Front Polisario doit être considéré comme une "personne morale", au sens de l'article 263, quatrième alinéa, TFUE, et qu'il peut introduire un recours en annulation devant le juge de l'Union, quand bien même il ne disposerait pas de la personnalité juridique selon le droit d'un État membre ou d'un État tiers. En effet, ainsi que cela a été relevé ci-dessus, il ne saurait disposer d'une telle personnalité que conformément au droit du Sahara occidental qui n'est toutefois, à l'heure actuelle, pas un État reconnu par l'Union et ses États membres et ne dispose pas de son propre droit.

Sur l'affectation directe et individuelle du Front Polisario par la décision attaquée

...omissis...

67. Il convient de rappeler que l'article 263, quatrième alinéa, TFUE prévoit deux hypothèses dans lesquelles la qualité pour agir est reconnue à une personne physique ou morale pour former un recours contre un acte dont elle n'est pas le destinataire. D'une part, un tel recours peut être formé à condition que cet acte la concerne directement et individuellement. D'autre part, une telle personne peut introduire un recours contre un acte réglementaire ne comportant pas de mesures d'exécution si celui-ci la concerne directement (arrêts du 19 décembre 2013, *Telefónica/Commission*, C-274/12 P, Rec, EU:C:2013:852, point 19, et du 27 février 2014, *Stichting Woonlinie e.a./Commission*, C-133/12 P, Rec, EU:C:2014:105, point 31).

...omissis...

71. En l'espèce, ainsi qu'il ressort de son préambule, la décision attaquée a été adoptée suivant la procédure définie à l'article 218, paragraphe 6, sous a), TFUE, qui prévoit que le Conseil, sur proposition du négociateur, en l'occurrence la Commission, adopte la décision de conclusion de l'accord après approbation du Parlement. Cette procédure répond aux critères définis à l'article 289, paragraphe 2, TFUE et constitue, par conséquent, une procédure législative spéciale.

72. Il s'ensuit que la décision attaquée est un acte législatif et, de ce fait, ne constitue pas un acte réglementaire. C'est donc la première des deux hypothèses envisagées au point 67 ci-dessus qui est pertinente en l'espèce. Partant, et compte tenu du fait que le requérant n'est pas destinataire de

la décision attaquée, afin que le présent recours soit recevable, il doit être démontré que ladite décision le concerne directement et individuellement.

73. Pour examiner cette question, il convient de déterminer si l'accord dont la conclusion a été approuvée par la décision attaquée s'applique ou non au territoire du Sahara occidental, dans la mesure où le requérant est susceptible d'être affecté directement et individuellement par l'acte attaqué en raison de sa qualité de partie impliquée dans le processus de règlement du sort du territoire en question (voir point 57 ci-dessus) et de sa prétention à être le représentant légitime du peuple sahraoui (voir point 61 ci-dessus).

74. À cet égard, le Conseil et la Commission font valoir que, aux termes de son article 94, l'accord d'association avec le Maroc s'applique au territoire du Royaume du Maroc. Selon le Conseil, puisque cet article ne définit pas le territoire du Royaume du Maroc, l'accord d'association avec le Maroc ne préjuge pas du statut juridique du Sahara occidental et n'entraîne aucune reconnaissance formelle des droits que le Royaume du Maroc revendique à l'égard de ce territoire. Aucune disposition de la décision attaquée, ou de l'accord approuvé par elle, ne prévoirait que le champ d'application de ce dernier s'étendrait aussi au Sahara occidental.

75. La Commission rappelle à cet égard les termes de la déclaration relative aux principes du droit international touchant aux relations amicales et à la coopération entre les États conformément à la charte des Nations unies, approuvée par la résolution 2625 (XXV) de l'Assemblée générale de l'ONU, du 24 octobre 1970, selon laquelle "[l]e territoire d'une colonie ou d'un autre territoire non autonome possède, en vertu de la (charte des Nations unies), un statut séparé et distinct de celui du territoire de l'État qui l'administre" et selon laquelle "ce statut séparé et distinct en vertu de la (dite) charte existe aussi longtemps que le peuple de la colonie ou du territoire non autonome n'exerce pas son droit à disposer de lui-même conformément à la charte (des Nations unies) et, plus particulièrement, à ses buts et principes". Il en découle, selon la Commission, qu'un territoire non autonome ne fait pas partie de la puissance l'administrant, mais possède un statut distinct au regard du droit international. Les accords internationaux conclus par la puissance administrant un territoire non autonome ne s'appliqueraient pas sur ce territoire, sauf extension expresse. La Commission fait ainsi valoir que, en l'espèce, en l'absence d'une telle extension, l'accord d'association avec le Maroc ne s'applique qu'aux produits originaires du Royaume du Maroc, État qui, en droit international, ne comprend pas le Sahara occidental.

76. Le Front Polisario rétorque que le Royaume du Maroc n'administre pas le Sahara occidental en vertu de l'article 73 de la charte des Nations unies, mais l'occupe militairement. Du point de vue de l'ONU, le Royaume d'Espagne serait toujours la puissance exerçant

l'administration du Sahara occidental. Le Royaume du Maroc serait une puissance occupante, au sens du droit international humanitaire.

77. Le Front Polisario ajoute que le Royaume du Maroc appliquerait au Sahara occidental les accords conclus avec l'Union, y compris l'accord d'association avec le Maroc. Il s'agirait d'un fait notoire, connu tant du Conseil que de la Commission. Le Front Polisario invoque plusieurs éléments à l'appui de cette affirmation.

78. Premièrement, il invoque la réponse commune donnée par la haute représentante de l'Union pour les affaires étrangères et la politique de sécurité, vice-présidente de la Commission, Mme Catherine Ashton, au nom de la Commission aux questions écrites posées par les députés au Parlement et portant les références E-001004/11, P-001023/11 et E-002315/11 (JO 2011, C 286 E, p. 1).

79. Deuxièmement, il fait valoir que, comme l'indiquent plusieurs documents disponibles sur le site Internet de la direction générale (DG) "Santé et sécurité alimentaire" de la Commission, après la conclusion de l'accord d'association avec le Maroc, l'Office alimentaire et vétérinaire, qui relève de cette DG, a effectué plusieurs visites au Sahara occidental pour s'assurer du respect par les autorités marocaines des normes sanitaires établies par l'Union.

80. Troisièmement, il fait valoir que la liste des exportateurs marocains agréés au titre de l'accord d'association avec le Maroc, publiée sur le site Internet de la Commission, comporte, au total, 140 entreprises qui sont implantées au Sahara occidental.

81. Invité, dans le cadre d'une mesure d'organisation de la procédure, à présenter ses observations sur les allégations susvisées du Front Polisario, le Conseil a relevé qu'il soutenait pleinement les efforts de l'ONU aux fins de trouver une solution stable et durable à la question du Sahara occidental et qu'aucune institution de l'Union n'avait jamais reconnu ni de facto ni de jure une quelconque souveraineté marocaine sur le territoire du Sahara occidental.

82. Néanmoins, selon le Conseil, les institutions de l'Union ne peuvent pas ignorer la réalité des faits, c'est-à-dire que le Royaume du Maroc est la puissance exerçant de facto l'administration du Sahara occidental. S'agissant donc du territoire du Sahara occidental, cela signifierait que l'Union doit s'adresser aux autorités marocaines, seules autorités qui pourraient donner suite aux dispositions de l'accord dans ce territoire, dans le respect des intérêts et des droits du peuple sahraoui. Ce fait n'entraînerait aucune reconnaissance, ni de facto ni de jure, d'une quelconque souveraineté du Royaume du Maroc sur le territoire du Sahara occidental.

...omissis...

85. Selon la Commission, sauf à vouloir exclure toute exportation à partir du Sahara occidental, le Front Polisario ne peut sérieusement prétendre que, en matière de santé publique au Sahara occidental, l'Office alimentaire et vétérinaire devrait l'avoir comme interlocuteur exclusif. Le Front Polisario n'exercerait aucun pouvoir réel sur le territoire concerné et ne serait pas à même de s'assurer que les exportations respectent les règles de santé publique.

...omissis...

87. Au surplus, lors de l'audience, tant le Conseil que la Commission ont indiqué, en réponse à une question du Tribunal, que l'accord visé par la décision attaquée était appliqué de facto au territoire du Sahara occidental. Il a été pris acte de cette déclaration au procès-verbal de l'audience.

88. Il convient de remarquer que la question posée au point 73 ci-dessus exige, en définitive, une interprétation de l'accord dont la conclusion a été approuvée par la décision attaquée.

...omissis...

90. En outre, conclu entre deux sujets de droit international public, l'accord visé par la décision attaquée est régi par le droit international et, plus particulièrement, du point de vue de son interprétation, par le droit international des traités (voir, en ce sens, arrêt *Brita*, point 89 *supra*, EU:C:2010:91, point 39).

91. Le droit international des traités a été codifié, en substance, dans la convention de Vienne sur le droit des traités, du 23 mai 1969 (Recueil des traités des Nations unies, vol. 1155, p. 331) (ci-après la "convention de Vienne").

92. Les règles contenues dans la convention de Vienne s'appliquent à un accord conclu entre un État et une organisation internationale, tel que l'accord visé par la décision attaquée, dans la mesure où ces règles sont l'expression du droit international général de nature coutumière (voir, en ce sens, arrêt *Brita*, point 89 *supra*, EU:C:2010:91, point 41). L'accord visé par la décision attaquée doit, par conséquent, être interprété suivant ces règles.

...omissis...

94. Aux termes de l'article 31 de la convention de Vienne, un traité doit être interprété de bonne foi suivant le sens ordinaire à attribuer aux termes du traité dans leur contexte et à la lumière de son objet et de son but. À cet égard, il doit être tenu compte, en même temps que du contexte, de toute règle pertinente de droit international applicable dans les relations entre les parties.

95. Dans l'arrêt *Brita*, point 89 *supra* (EU:C:2010:91, points 44 à 53), la Cour de justice a jugé qu'un accord d'association entre l'Union et l'État d'Israël applicable, selon ses termes, "au territoire de l'État d'Israël" devait être interprété en ce sens qu'il ne s'appliquait pas aux produits originaires de la Cisjordanie, un territoire qui est situé en dehors du territoire de l'État d'Israël, tel qu'il est internationalement reconnu, mais qui comporte des colonies de peuplement israéliennes, contrôlées par l'État d'Israël.

96. Toutefois, la Cour de justice est parvenue à cette conclusion en prenant en considération, d'une part, le principe de droit international général de l'effet relatif des traités, selon lequel les traités ne doivent ni nuire ni profiter à des sujets tiers (*pacta tertiis nec nocent nec prosunt*), qui, selon la Cour de justice, trouve une expression particulière dans l'article 34 de la convention de Vienne, en vertu duquel un traité ne crée ni obligations ni droits pour un État tiers sans son consentement (arrêt *Brita*, point 89 *supra*, EU:C:2010:91, point 44), et, d'autre part, le fait que l'Union avait également conclu un accord d'association avec l'Organisation de libération de la Palestine (OLP) agissant pour le compte de l'Autorité palestinienne de la Cisjordanie et de la bande de Gaza, ce dernier accord étant notamment applicable, selon ses termes, au territoire de la Cisjordanie (arrêt *Brita*, point 89 *supra*, EU:C:2010:91, points 46 et 47).

97. Les circonstances de la présente affaire sont différentes, dans la mesure où, en l'espèce, l'Union n'a conclu un accord d'association portant sur les produits originaires du Sahara occidental ni avec le Front Polisario ni avec un autre État ou une autre entité.

98. L'accord dont la conclusion a été approuvée par la décision attaquée doit dès lors être interprété conformément à l'article 31 de la convention de Vienne (voir point 94 ci-dessus).

99. Conformément à cet article, il convient de tenir compte notamment du contexte dans lequel s'insère un traité international tel que l'accord visé par la décision attaquée. L'ensemble des éléments mentionnés aux points 77 à 87 ci-dessus font partie de ce contexte et démontrent que les institutions de l'Union étaient conscientes de l'application, par les autorités marocaines, des dispositions de l'accord d'association avec le Maroc également à la partie du Sahara occidental contrôlée par le Royaume du Maroc et ne se sont pas opposées à cette application. Au contraire, la Commission a coopéré, dans une certaine mesure, avec les autorités marocaines en vue de cette application et en a reconnu les résultats, en incluant des entreprises établies au Sahara occidental parmi celles inscrites sur la liste mentionnée au point 74 ci-dessus.

100. Il y a lieu également de rappeler qu'il existe une divergence entre les thèses respectives de l'Union et du Royaume du Maroc quant au statut international du Sahara occidental. Si la thèse de l'Union est

suffisamment et correctement résumée par le Conseil et la Commission (voir points 74 et 75 ci-dessus), il est constant que le Royaume du Maroc a une conception des choses totalement différente. Selon lui, le Sahara occidental fait partie intégrante de son territoire.

101. Ainsi, à l'article 94 de l'accord d'association avec le Maroc, la référence au territoire du Royaume du Maroc était susceptible d'être comprise par les autorités marocaines comme incluant le Sahara occidental ou, du moins, sa partie la plus importante contrôlée par le Royaume du Maroc. Bien que les institutions de l'Union fussent, ainsi que cela a été relevé, conscientes de cette thèse soutenue par le Royaume du Maroc, l'accord d'association avec le Maroc n'inclut aucune clause interprétative et aucune autre disposition qui aurait comme résultat d'exclure le territoire du Sahara occidental de son champ d'application.

102. Il convient également de tenir compte du fait que l'accord visé par la décision attaquée a été conclu douze ans après l'approbation de l'accord d'association avec le Maroc et alors que cet accord avait été mis en œuvre pendant l'ensemble de cette période. Si les institutions de l'Union souhaitaient s'opposer à l'application au Sahara occidental de l'accord d'association, tel que modifié par la décision attaquée, elles auraient pu insister afin d'inclure, dans le texte de l'accord approuvé par cette décision, une clause excluant une telle application. Leur omission sur ce point démontre qu'elles acceptent, du moins implicitement, l'interprétation de l'accord d'association avec le Maroc et de l'accord approuvé par la décision attaquée, selon laquelle ces accords s'appliquent également à la partie du Sahara occidental contrôlée par le Royaume du Maroc.

103. Dans ces conditions, il convient de conclure que l'accord dont la conclusion a été approuvée par la décision attaquée, replacé dans son contexte tel qu'il a été défini ci-dessus, s'applique également au territoire du Sahara occidental ou, plus précisément, à la plus grande partie de ce territoire, contrôlée par le Royaume du Maroc.

104. C'est en tenant compte de cette conclusion qu'il convient d'apprécier l'affectation directe et individuelle du Front Polisario par la décision attaquée.

105. S'agissant de l'affectation directe, il ressort d'une jurisprudence constante que la condition selon laquelle une personne physique ou morale doit être "directement concernée" par l'acte faisant l'objet du recours requiert la réunion de deux critères cumulatifs, à savoir que la mesure contestée, en premier lieu, produise directement des effets sur la situation juridique de la personne concernée et, en second lieu, ne laisse aucun pouvoir d'appréciation à ses destinataires qui sont chargés de sa mise en œuvre, celle-ci ayant un caractère purement automatique et découlant

de la seule réglementation de l'Union, sans application d'autres règles intermédiaires (voir arrêt du 10 septembre 2009, *Commission/Ente per le Ville Vesuviane* et *Ente per le Ville Vesuviane/Commission*, C-445/07 P et C-455/07 P, Rec, EU:C:2009:529, point 45 et jurisprudence citée).

106. À cet égard, il y a lieu de relever que le fait, invoqué par le Conseil (voir point 63 ci-dessus), que la décision attaquée concerne la conclusion d'un accord international entre l'Union et le Royaume du Maroc n'exclut pas qu'elle produise des effets juridiques par rapport à des tiers.

107. En effet, selon une jurisprudence constante, une stipulation d'un accord conclu par l'Union et ses États membres avec des États tiers doit être considérée comme étant d'effet direct lorsque, eu égard à ses termes ainsi qu'à l'objet et à la nature de cet accord, elle comporte une obligation claire et précise qui n'est subordonnée, dans son exécution ou dans ses effets, à l'intervention d'aucun acte ultérieur (voir arrêt du 8 mars 2011, *Lesoochranárske zoskupenie*, C-240/09, Rec, EU:C:2011:125, point 44 et jurisprudence citée).

108. En l'espèce, force est de constater que l'accord sous forme d'échange de lettres conclu en vertu de la décision attaquée contient des dispositions comportant des obligations claires et précises, non subordonnées, dans leur exécution ou dans leurs effets, à l'intervention d'actes ultérieurs. Il convient de mentionner, à titre d'exemple, que le protocole n° 1 de l'accord d'association avec le Maroc, relatif aux régimes applicables à l'importation dans l'Union de produits agricoles, de produits transformés, de poissons et de produits de la pêche originaire du Royaume du Maroc, comporte un article 2, remplacé en vertu de l'accord visé par la décision attaquée, qui prévoit, à son paragraphe 1, que les droits de douane, applicables aux importations dans l'Union de produits agricoles, de produits agricoles transformés, de poissons et de produits de la pêche originaires du Maroc, sont éliminés, sauf dispositions contraires reprises aux paragraphes 2 et 3 du même article pour les produits agricoles et à l'article 5 du même protocole pour les produits agricoles transformés. Il convient également de mentionner que le protocole n° 2 de l'accord d'association avec le Maroc, relatif aux régimes applicables à l'importation dans le Royaume du Maroc de produits agricoles, de produits transformés, de poissons et de produits de la pêche originaires de l'Union, comporte un article 2, remplacé en vertu de l'accord approuvé par la décision attaquée, qui contient des dispositions tarifaires spécifiques, applicables aux importations dans le Royaume du Maroc des produits agricoles, des produits agricoles transformés, des poissons et des produits de la pêche originaires de l'Union.

109. Ces dispositions produisent des effets sur la situation juridique de l'ensemble du territoire sur lequel s'applique l'accord (et, partant, sur

le territoire du Sahara occidental contrôlé par le Royaume du Maroc), en ce sens qu'elles déterminent les conditions dans lesquelles des produits agricoles et de la pêche peuvent être exportés de ce territoire vers l'Union ou peuvent être importés de l'Union dans le territoire en question.

110. Or, ces effets concernent directement non seulement le Royaume du Maroc mais également le Front Polisario, dans la mesure où, comme il ressort des éléments mentionnés aux points 1 à 16 ci-dessus, le statut international définitif de ce territoire n'a pas encore été déterminé et doit être déterminé dans le cadre d'une procédure de négociations, sous l'égide de l'ONU, entre le Royaume du Maroc et, précisément, le Front Polisario.

111. Pour le même motif, le Front Polisario doit être regardé comme étant individuellement concerné par la décision attaquée.

...omissis...

Sur le fond

115. À l'appui du recours, le Front Polisario invoque onze moyens, tirés :

- le premier, de l'insuffisance de motivation de la décision attaquée ;
- le deuxième, du non-respect du "principe de consultation" ;
- le troisième, de la violation des droits fondamentaux ;
- le quatrième, de la "violation du principe de cohérence de la politique de l'Union, par le non-respect du principe de...souveraineté" ;
- le cinquième, de la "violation des valeurs fondant l'Union...et des principes présidant son action extérieure" ;
- le sixième, du "manquement à l'objectif de développement durable" ;
- le septième, de la "contrariété" de la décision attaquée "aux principes et objectifs de l'action extérieure de l'Union dans le domaine de la coopération au développement" ;
- le huitième, de la violation du principe de protection de la confiance légitime ;
- le neuvième, de la "contrariété" de la décision attaquée "avec plusieurs accords conclus par l'Union" ;
- le dixième, de la "contrariété" de la décision attaquée avec le "droit international général" ;
- et, enfin, le onzième, du "droit de la responsabilité internationale en droit de l'Union".

116. À titre liminaire, il convient de constater qu'il ressort de l'argumentation avancée par le Front Polisario à l'appui de l'ensemble

de ses moyens que son recours tend à l'annulation de la décision attaquée en ce que celle-ci a approuvé l'application, au Sahara occidental, de l'accord visé par elle. En effet, ainsi qu'il ressort des considérations exposées ci-dessus, au sujet de l'affectation directe et individuelle du Front Polisario par la décision attaquée, c'est précisément du fait que cet accord trouve à s'appliquer également au Sahara occidental que le Front Polisario est directement et individuellement concerné par la décision attaquée.

117. Il convient également de constater que le Front Polisario invoque plusieurs moyens, parmi lesquels les deux premiers portent sur la légalité externe de la décision attaquée, alors que les autres portent sur sa légalité interne. En substance, le requérant invoque une illégalité de la décision attaquée, au motif qu'elle violerait le droit de l'Union ainsi que le droit international. L'ensemble des moyens du recours posent en réalité la question de l'existence ou non d'une interdiction absolue de conclusion, au nom de l'Union, d'un accord international susceptible d'être appliqué à un territoire contrôlé dans les faits par un État tiers, sans toutefois que la souveraineté de cet État sur ce territoire ne soit reconnue par l'Union et ses États membres ou, plus généralement, par tous les autres États (ci-après un "territoire disputé"), ainsi que, le cas échéant, la question de l'existence d'un pouvoir d'appréciation des institutions de l'Union à cet égard, des limites de ce pouvoir et des conditions de son exercice.

118. Ces précisions faites, il y a lieu d'examiner, tout d'abord, les deux premiers moyens qui, comme le relève le requérant lui-même, portent sur la légalité externe de la décision attaquée.

...omissis...

Sur le deuxième moyen

128. Le Front Polisario fait valoir que la décision attaquée est "frappée de nullité pour violation d'une formalité substantielle", dès lors que le Conseil ne l'a pas consulté avant la conclusion de l'accord visé par cette décision, bien qu'il soit le seul "représentant légitime du peuple sahraoui".

129. Le Front Polisario considère que l'obligation du Conseil de le consulter découle de l'article 41 de la charte des droits fondamentaux de l'Union européenne. Il invoque, dans le même contexte, l'article 220, paragraphe 1, TFUE, lequel prévoit ce qui suit:

> "L'Union établit toute coopération utile avec les organes des Nations unies et de leurs institutions spécialisées, le Conseil de l'Europe, l'Organisation pour la sécurité et la coopération en Europe et l'Organisation de coopération et de développement économiques.

L'Union assure, en outre, les liaisons opportunes avec d'autres organisations internationales."

130. Enfin, il invoque une "obligation de consultation d'origine internationale" que, selon lui, le Conseil avait à son égard.

131. Le Conseil et la Commission contestent les arguments du requérant, faisant notamment valoir que le principe du contradictoire ne s'applique pas aux procédures de caractère normatif.

132. Il y a en effet lieu de rappeler que, si l'article 41, paragraphe 1, de la charte des droits fondamentaux prévoit que toute personne a le droit de voir ses affaires traitées impartialement, équitablement et dans un délai raisonnable par les institutions, organes et organismes de l'Union, l'article 41, paragraphe 2, sous a), de la charte des droits fondamentaux prévoit que ce droit comporte notamment le droit de toute personne d'être entendue avant qu'une mesure individuelle qui l'affecterait défavorablement ne soit prise à son encontre. Ainsi, le libellé de cette disposition ne vise que les mesures individuelles.

133. Par ailleurs, le Tribunal a jugé à de nombreuses reprises que la jurisprudence relative au droit d'être entendu ne saurait être étendue au contexte d'une procédure législative aboutissant à l'adoption de mesures normatives ou de portée générale qui impliquent un choix de politique économique et s'appliquent à la généralité des opérateurs concernés (arrêts du 11 décembre 1996, *Atlanta e.a./CE*, T-521/93, Rec, EU:T:1996:184, point 70 ; du 11 septembre 2002, *Alpharma/Conseil*, T-70/99, Rec, EU:T:2002:210, point 388, et du 11 juillet 2007, *Sison/Conseil*, T-47/03, EU:T:2007:207, point 144).

134. La circonstance que l'intéressé est directement et individuellement concerné par la mesure normative ou de portée générale en cause ne saurait modifier cette conclusion (voir arrêt *Alpharma/Conseil*, point 133 *supra*, EU:T:2002:210, point 388 et jurisprudence citée).

...*omissis*...

137. Il s'ensuit que, la décision attaquée ayant été adoptée à la suite d'une procédure législative spéciale pour approuver la conclusion d'un accord de portée et d'application générale, le Conseil n'était pas obligé de consulter le Front Polisario préalablement à son adoption, contrairement à ce que fait valoir ce dernier.

138. Par ailleurs, une obligation de consulter le Front Polisario avant l'adoption de la décision attaquée ne résulte pas davantage du droit international. À cet égard, il y a lieu de relever que le requérant n'a fourni aucune précision quant à l'origine et la portée de "l'obligation de consultation d'origine internationale" dont il se prévaut et qu'il évoque vaguement dans ses écrits.

139. Partant, il convient d'écarter le deuxième moyen comme étant non fondé.

Sur les autres moyens

140. Les troisième à onzième moyens du Front Polisario portent tous sur la légalité interne de la décision attaquée. Ainsi que cela a déjà été relevé au point 117 ci-dessus, le Front Polisario fait valoir, en substance, que, dans la mesure où il a approuvé la conclusion d'un accord avec le Royaume du Maroc qui trouve à s'appliquer également sur la partie du Sahara occidental contrôlée par ce dernier, en dépit de l'absence de reconnaissance internationale des prétentions marocaines sur ce territoire, le Conseil a entaché la décision attaquée d'une illégalité. Cette illégalité résulterait de la violation tant du droit de l'Union, pour les motifs avancés dans le cadre des troisième à huitième moyens, que du droit international, pour les motifs avancés dans le cadre des neuvième à onzième moyens.

141. Partant, il convient d'examiner si et, le cas échéant, sous quelles conditions l'Union peut conclure avec un État tiers un accord tel que celui approuvé par la décision attaquée, qui trouve également à s'appliquer sur un territoire disputé.

Sur l'existence d'une interdiction absolue de conclusion d'un accord susceptible d'être appliqué à un territoire disputé.

142. Il convient, tout d'abord, de déterminer si les moyens et arguments invoqués par le Front Polisario permettent de conclure qu'il est en toute hypothèse interdit au Conseil d'approuver la conclusion avec un État tiers d'un accord susceptible d'être appliqué à un territoire disputé.

– Sur le troisième moyen

143. Dans le cadre de son troisième moyen, le requérant se réfère aux dispositions et à la jurisprudence relatives au respect des droits fondamentaux par l'Union pour faire valoir que, en décidant "de publier un accord qui bafoue le droit à l'autodétermination du peuple sahraoui, et qui a pour effet immédiat d'encourager la politique d'annexion conduite par le Maroc, puissance occupante, le Conseil viole les principes de liberté, de sécurité et de justice, tournant le dos au respect des droits fondamentaux et des systèmes juridiques des États membres".

144. Selon le Front Polisario, "il y a atteinte à la liberté, car la liberté d'un peuple est ignorée, et pire, combattue par cette décision, qui encourage la domination économique, et tend à modifier les structures de la population pour rendre toujours plus complexe la perspective du référendum d'autodétermination". Le Front Polisario invoque également

une “atteinte à la sûreté et à la sécurité juridique”, faisant référence aux prétendues violations des “droits individuels” du “peuple sahraoui” par “un régime annexionniste” ainsi qu’à l’absence de valeur, selon lui, des certificats d’origine qui seront émis par les autorités marocaines pour l’exportation des produits en provenance du Sahara occidental. Enfin, il invoque une “atteinte aux libertés, qu’il s’agisse de la liberté collective du peuple sahraoui [...] ou par le non-respect de la propriété, de la liberté d’aller et venir, de la liberté d’expression, des droits de la défense et du principe de dignité”.

145. Il y a lieu de relever que, certes, comme le rappelle le Front Polisario, l’article 6 TUE prévoit que l’Union reconnaît les droits, les libertés et les principes énoncés dans la charte des droits fondamentaux, alors que, aux termes de l’article 67 TFUE, l’Union constitue un espace de liberté, de sécurité et de justice dans le respect des droits fondamentaux et des différents systèmes juridiques des États membres.

146. Toutefois, il ne découle ni de ces dispositions ni de celles de la charte des droits fondamentaux une interdiction absolue pour l’Union de conclure un accord avec un État tiers concernant des échanges économiques en matière de produits agricoles, de produits agricoles transformés, de poissons et de produits de la pêche, lequel serait susceptible d’être appliqué également à un territoire contrôlé par cet État tiers sans que sa souveraineté sur ce territoire ne soit internationalement reconnue.

147. La question de savoir sous quelles conditions un tel accord peut être conclu sans violer l’obligation de l’Union de reconnaître les droits fondamentaux est examinée, avec les autres arguments du requérant ayant trait à la mise en œuvre et au respect par les institutions de l’Union de leur pouvoir d’appréciation, aux points 223 et suivants ci-après.

148. Sous réserve de cet examen, il convient de rejeter le troisième moyen, pour autant qu’il reproche au Conseil la violation d’une prétendue interdiction absolue de conclusion d’un accord tel que celui en cause en l’espèce.

– Sur le quatrième moyen

149. Par son quatrième moyen, le Front Polisario fait valoir que la décision attaquée doit être annulée, car elle est contraire au principe de cohérence des politiques de l’Union prévu par l’article 7 TFUE, aux termes duquel “[l]’Union veille à la cohérence entre ses différentes politiques et actions, en tenant compte de l’ensemble de ses objectifs “. Selon lui, la décision attaquée “avalise une souveraineté de fait du [Royaume du] Maroc sur le territoire du Sahara Occidental” et “apporte un soutien politique et économique au [Royaume du] Maroc, qui viole le droit de l’ONU et le principe de souveraineté”, alors qu’aucun État européen n’a

reconnu la souveraineté du Royaume du Maroc sur le Sahara occidental et que l'Union a été acceptée comme membre observateur de l'ONU.

150. Le Front Polisario considère par conséquent que le "principe de cohérence" interdit à l'Union d'adopter des actes qui ont pour effet direct de violer le droit à l'autodétermination, alors même que les États membres respectent ce droit, en refusant de reconnaître la souveraineté du Royaume du Maroc sur le Sahara occidental.

151. Enfin, le Front Polisario fait valoir "qu'une autre incohérence est manifeste". Selon lui, l'Union "ne peut sanctionner certaines violations des droits, comme elle l'a fait par exemple pour la Syrie, et en avaliser d'autres, surtout quand il s'agit de normes du jus cogens".

152. Dans la réplique, le Front Polisario invoque une "troisième incohérence de la part de l'Union". Il soutient que le service d'aide humanitaire de la Commission octroie des aides substantielles aux réfugiés sahraouis installés dans des camps (voir point 16 ci-dessus), alors que, en même temps, le Conseil, avec l'adoption de la décision attaquée, "contribue à renforcer la mainmise du (Royaume du) Maroc sur le Sahara occidental, et *in fine* à fabriquer des réfugiés sahraouis".

153. Il convient de constater que l'article 7 TUE ne saurait servir d'appui aux arguments du Front Polisario. Les différentes politiques de l'Union relèvent toutes de différentes dispositions des traités constitutifs et des actes adoptés en application de ces dispositions. La prétendue "incohérence" d'un acte avec la politique de l'Union dans un domaine déterminé implique nécessairement que l'acte en cause soit contraire à une disposition, à une règle ou à un principe qui régit cette politique. Ce seul fait, s'il était démontré, serait suffisant pour entraîner l'annulation de l'acte en cause, sans qu'il soit nécessaire d'invoquer l'article 7 TUE.

154. En l'espèce, pour faire valoir la violation du principe de cohérence, le Front Polisario part de la prémisse selon laquelle l'approbation par la décision attaquée de l'accord en cause entre l'Union et le Royaume du Maroc "avalise" la "souveraineté" de ce dernier sur le Sahara occidental. Cette prémisse est toutefois erronée : aucune clause ayant un tel effet ne figure dans l'accord en question et le seul fait que l'Union admette l'application des termes de l'accord par le Royaume du Maroc à l'égard des produits agricoles ou de la pêche exportés vers l'Union à partir de la partie du territoire du Sahara occidental que celui-ci contrôle, ou aux produits qui sont importés dans ce territoire, n'équivaut pas à une reconnaissance de la souveraineté marocaine sur ce territoire.

155. S'agissant de l'argument selon lequel l'Union violerait le "droit de l'ONU" ou le *jus cogens*, il n'a aucun rapport avec la violation alléguée de l'article 7 TFUE. Il ne fait que réitérer les arguments avancés à l'appui du dixième moyen, qui est examiné ci-après.

156. L'argument tiré de l'adoption par l'Union de mesures restrictives au regard de la situation dans d'autres pays ne suffit pas davantage à démontrer une prétendue "incohérence" de la politique de l'Union. Il y a lieu de rappeler que, comme il découle notamment de la jurisprudence relative aux mesures restrictives adoptées à l'égard de la situation en Syrie, le Conseil dispose d'un pouvoir discrétionnaire d'appréciation en la matière (voir, en ce sens, arrêt du 13 septembre 2013, *Makhlouf/ Conseil*, T-383/11, Rec, EU:T:2013:431, point 63). Partant, il ne saurait lui être reproché une incohérence du fait qu'il a adopté des mesures restrictives au regard de la situation dans un pays, et non dans un autre.

157. Enfin, pour ce qui est de la "troisième incohérence" invoquée par le Front Polisario dans la réplique, il convient de constater que le fait que l'Union apporte un soutien aux réfugiés sahraouis installés dans des camps en même temps qu'elle conclut, avec le Royaume du Maroc, des accords tels que celui approuvé par la décision attaquée, loin de constituer une incohérence dans sa politique, démontre, au contraire, qu'elle ne souhaite pas prendre parti dans le différend qui oppose le requérant au Royaume du Maroc, tout en soutenant les efforts de l'ONU en vue d'un règlement juste et durable de ce différend par des négociations.

158. Par conséquent, il convient de rejeter le quatrième moyen.

– Sur le cinquième moyen

159. À l'appui de son cinquième moyen, le Front Polisario invoque l'article 2 TUE, l'article 3, paragraphe 5, TUE et l'article 21 TUE ainsi que l'article 205 TFUE. Il fait valoir que la décision attaquée est contraire aux valeurs fondamentales de l'Union qui président à son action extérieure. Selon lui, en approuvant la conclusion de l'accord visé par la décision attaquée, le Conseil "bafoue les résolutions de l'ONU et l'accord intervenu entre le (Royaume du) Maroc et le Front Polisario pour l'organisation du référendum d'autodétermination, en encourageant la politique illicite d'annexion du (Royaume du) Maroc". Il considère qu'il "suffisait de geler l'accord", dès lors que le Conseil "[savait] parfaitement que le développement économique du (Royaume du) Maroc sur le territoire du Sahara occidental vis[ait] à modifier les structures sociales et [à] pervertir l'idée même du référendum".

...*omissis*...

164. Selon la jurisprudence, les institutions de l'Union jouissent, dans le domaine des relations économiques extérieures dont relève l'accord visé par la décision attaquée, d'un large pouvoir d'appréciation (voir, en ce sens, arrêt du 6 juillet 1995, *Odigitria/Conseil et Commission*, T-572/93, Rec, EU:T:1995:131, point 38).

165. Par conséquent, il ne saurait être admis qu'il ressort des "valeurs fondant l'Union" ou des dispositions invoquées par le Front Polisario dans le cadre du présent moyen que la conclusion par le Conseil d'un accord avec un État tiers susceptible d'être appliqué sur un territoire disputé est, en toute hypothèse, interdite.

166. Du reste, la question de l'exercice par le Conseil du large pouvoir d'appréciation que lui reconnaît la jurisprudence citée au point 164 ci-dessus, ainsi que des éléments pertinents dont il doit tenir compte dans ce contexte, sera examinée ci-après (voir points 223 et suivants ci-après).

167. Sous réserve de cet examen, il convient de rejeter le cinquième moyen.

– Sur le sixième moyen

168. Dans le cadre du sixième moyen, le requérant fait valoir que la décision attaquée est contraire à l'objectif du développement durable "dès lors qu'elle permet à la puissance occupante d'amplifier l'exploitation des ressources naturelle d'un peuple autonome". Il se réfère à cet égard à l'article 11 TFUE, aux termes duquel "[l]es exigences de la protection de l'environnement doivent être intégrées dans la définition et la mise en œuvre des politiques et actions de l'Union, en particulier afin de promouvoir le développement durable". Il invoque également plusieurs textes de l'ONU et de l'Organisation des Nations unies pour l'alimentation et l'agriculture (FAO).

169. Le requérant ajoute que le Royaume du Maroc "conduit une politique d'annexion, gérant les affaires du Sahara occidental via son ministère de l'Intérieur et refusant [...] de rendre compte de son administration auprès de l'ONU". Le Front Polisario en déduit que la décision attaquée "non seulement [...] prive le peuple sahraoui du droit à son développement, mais elle encourage une politique de spoliation économique qui a pour but principal de détruire la société sahraouie".

170. Dans la réplique, le Front Polisario ajoute que "de grandes sociétés, contrôlées par le Maroc, procèdent à une exploitation des ressources [du Sahara occidental] dont le but explicite est de piller le peuple sahraoui, pour renforcer l'économie du Maroc et conforter dans les faits l'annexion marocaine".

171. À ce stade, il suffit de relever qu'il ne résulte pas davantage des allégations susvisées du Front Polisario ni des dispositions qu'il invoque une interdiction absolue pour le Conseil de conclure un accord avec un État tiers susceptible d'être appliqué sur un territoire disputé.

172. Partant, pour autant que ce moyen doive être compris comme faisant valoir la violation d'une telle interdiction, il doit être rejeté. Du reste, l'argumentation du Front Polisario doit être examinée dans le cadre de l'analyse de la question de l'exercice par le Conseil de son pouvoir d'appréciation (voir points 223 et suivants ci-après).

– Sur le septième moyen

173. Le septième moyen est, selon l'intitulé retenu par le requérant, tiré de la "contrariété de la décision [attaquée] aux principes et objectifs de l'action extérieure de l'Union dans le domaine de la coopération au développement". Le requérant se réfère à l'article 208, paragraphe 2, TFUE, aux termes duquel "[l]'Union et les États membres respectent les engagements et tiennent compte des objectifs qu'ils ont agréés dans le cadre [de l'ONU] et des autres organisations internationales compétentes". Il invoque également l'article 220 TFUE (voir point 129 ci-dessus).

174. Concrètement, le Front Polisario relève que "[l]a formulation de [l'] article [208, paragraphe 2, TFUE], qui emploie le terme "agrees", permet de fonder l'opposabilité à l'Union [...] des engagements et objectifs qui figurent dans les résolutions de l'[ONU], dont la Déclaration du millénaire et les résolutions à l'élaboration desquelles l'[Union] a participé".

175. Force est de constater que l'argumentation du requérant telle qu'exposée au point 174 ci-dessus ne permet nullement de comprendre ce qu'il reproche au Conseil et pour quel motif la décision attaquée serait contraire "aux principes et objectifs de l'action extérieure de l'Union" ou aux textes de l'ONU, dont la Déclaration du millénaire. Partant, le présent moyen doit être rejeté comme irrecevable.

...omissis...

– Conclusion sur l'existence ou non d'une interdiction absolue de conclusion d'accords internationaux applicables sur un territoire disputé

215. Il ressort de l'ensemble des considérations qui précèdent que rien dans les moyens et arguments du requérant ne permet de conclure qu'il est absolument interdit, par le droit de l'Union ou par le droit international, de conclure avec un État tiers un accord qui serait susceptible d'être appliqué sur un territoire disputé.

216. La jurisprudence du Tribunal confirme également cette conclusion.

217. Le Tribunal a eu à connaître de la question de la licéité d'un accord international, conclu entre l'Union et un autre État tiers et susceptible de trouver également application sur un territoire disputé, dans son

affaire ayant donné lieu à l'arrêt *Odigitria/Conseil et Commission*, point 164 *supra* (EU:T:1995:131).

218. Cet arrêt concernait un recours indemnitaire introduit par une société propriétaire d'un bateau de pêche battant pavillon grec, lequel avait été arraisonné par les autorités de la Guinée-Bissau, au motif qu'il pêchait sans licence dans la zone maritime de ce dernier État. Il s'était avéré que le bateau en question disposait d'une licence de pêche délivrée par les autorités sénégalaises, mais qu'il pêchait dans des eaux revendiquées comme faisant partie de leurs zones maritimes respectives tant par la République du Sénégal que par la République de Guinée-Bissau. La Communauté économique européenne, telle qu'elle était à l'époque, avait conclu des accords de pêche tant avec l'un qu'avec l'autre de ces États tiers portant, dans les deux cas, sur l'ensemble de leurs zones maritimes. La requérante dans cette affaire poursuivait la réparation, par la Communauté, du préjudice qu'elle prétendait avoir subi en raison de l'arraisonnement de son bateau et, dans ce contexte, invoquait la prétendue illégalité de l'omission d'exclure du champ d'application des accords de pêche conclus entre la Communauté et chacun des deux États tiers en question la zone qui faisait l'objet du différend entre eux (arrêt *Odigitria/Conseil et Commission*, point 164 *supra*, EU:T:1995:131, points 1 à 13 et 25).

219. Le Tribunal a considéré que cette omission n'était constitutive d'aucune illégalité. En substance, il a conclu que, dans l'exercice du large pouvoir d'appréciation dont jouissaient les institutions de l'Union dans le domaine des relations économiques extérieures ainsi que dans celui de la politique agricole commune (dont relève également la pêche), elles auraient pu, sans commettre d'erreur manifeste d'appréciation, décider qu'il ne convenait pas d'exclure la zone en question des accords de pêche conclus avec les deux États susmentionnés, malgré le différend existant entre eux s'agissant des eaux revendiquées comme faisant partie de leurs zones maritimes (voir, en ce sens, arrêt *Odigitria/Conseil et Commission*, point 164 *supra*, EU:T:1995:131, point 38).

220. Il ressort ainsi a contrario de l'arrêt en question que la conclusion, entre l'Union et un État tiers, d'un accord susceptible de trouver application sur un territoire disputé n'est pas, en toute hypothèse, contraire au droit de l'Union ou au droit international, que l'Union doit respecter.

...omissis...

222. Il convient également de rappeler qu'une interdiction absolue de conclure un accord portant sur un territoire disputé ne ressort pas davantage des considérations figurant dans la lettre du conseiller juridique de l'ONU, mentionnée aux points 207 à 210 ci-dessus. En effet, le conseiller juridique de l'ONU a en substance relevé que, seulement dans

le cas où l'exploitation des ressources naturelles du Sahara occidental était entreprise "au mépris des intérêts et de la volonté du peuple" de ce territoire, elle "contreviendrai[t] aux principes de droit international".

Sur le pouvoir d'appréciation des institutions de l'Union et sur les éléments dont elles doivent tenir compte

223. Au regard de l'ensemble des considérations qui précèdent et ainsi qu'il ressort de la jurisprudence rappelée au point 164 ci-dessus, il doit être conclu que les institutions de l'Union disposent d'un large pouvoir d'appréciation, s'agissant de la question de savoir s'il y a lieu ou non de conclure avec un État tiers un accord qui s'appliquera sur un territoire disputé.

224. Leur reconnaître un tel pouvoir se révèle d'autant plus justifié que, ainsi qu'il ressort au demeurant de la lettre du conseiller juridique de l'ONU mentionnée ci-dessus, les règles et principes du droit international applicables en la matière sont complexes et imprécis. Il s'ensuit que le contrôle judiciaire doit nécessairement se limiter à la question de savoir si l'institution compétente de l'Union, en l'occurrence le Conseil, en approuvant la conclusion d'un accord tel que celui approuvé par la décision attaquée, a commis des erreurs d'appréciation manifestes (voir, en ce sens, arrêt du 16 juin 1998, *Racke*, C-162/96, Rec, EU:C:1998:293, point 52).

225. Cela étant, en particulier dans les cas où une institution de l'Union dispose d'un large pouvoir d'appréciation afin de vérifier si elle a commis une erreur manifeste d'appréciation, le juge de l'Union doit contrôler si elle a examiné, avec soin et impartialité, tous les éléments pertinents du cas d'espèce, éléments qui appuient les conclusions qui en sont tirées (arrêts du 21 novembre 1991, *Technische Universität München*, C-269/90, Rec, EU:C:1991:438, point 14, et du 22 décembre 2010, *Gowan Comércio Internacional e Serviços*, C-77/09, Rec, EU:C:2010:803, point 57).

226. Or, ainsi que cela a été relevé au point 125 ci-dessus, le Front Polisario reproche en substance au Conseil, précisément, de ne pas avoir examiné, préalablement à l'adoption de la décision attaquée, les éléments pertinents du cas d'espèce, s'agissant tout particulièrement de l'éventuelle application de l'accord dont la conclusion a été approuvée par la décision attaquée au Sahara occidental et aux produits exportés à partir de ce territoire.

227. À cet égard, s'il est certes exact que, comme cela a été relevé au point 146 ci-dessus, il ne ressort pas de la charte des droits fondamentaux, invoquée par le requérant dans le cadre de son troisième moyen, une interdiction absolue pour l'Union de conclure un accord susceptible de trouver application sur un territoire disputé, il n'en est pas moins exact que la protection des droits fondamentaux de la population d'un tel territoire

revêt une importance particulière et constitue, par conséquent, une question que le Conseil doit examiner avant l'approbation d'un tel accord.

228. En particulier, s'agissant d'un accord tendant à faciliter, notamment, l'exportation vers l'Union de divers produits en provenance du territoire en question, le Conseil doit examiner, avec soin et impartialité, tous les éléments pertinents afin de s'assurer que les activités de production des produits destinés à l'exportation ne sont pas menées au détriment de la population du territoire en question ni n'impliquent de violations de ses droits fondamentaux dont, notamment, les droits à la dignité humaine, à la vie et à l'intégrité de la personne (articles 1er à 3 de la charte des droits fondamentaux), l'interdiction de l'esclavage et du travail forcé (article 5 de la charte des droits fondamentaux), la liberté professionnelle (article 15 de la charte des droits fondamentaux), la liberté d'entreprise (article 16 de la charte des droits fondamentaux), le droit de propriété (article 17 de la charte des droits fondamentaux), le droit à des conditions de travail justes et équitables, l'interdiction du travail des enfants et la protection des jeunes au travail (articles 31 et 32 de la charte des droits fondamentaux).

229. Les considérations du conseiller juridique de l'ONU quant aux obligations découlant du droit international, telles qu'elles ont été résumées aux points 208 et 209 ci-dessus, conduisent à la même conclusion.

230. À cet égard, le Conseil fait valoir que, "[d]u fait d'avoir conclu un accord avec un pays tiers[,] l'Union ne devient pas et ne peut pas devenir responsable pour des éventuelles actions commises par ce pays, qu'elles correspondent ou pas à des violations des droits fondamentaux".

231. Cette thèse est correcte, mais elle ignore le fait que, si l'Union permet l'exportation vers ses États membres de produits en provenance de cet autre pays qui ont été fabriqués ou obtenus dans des conditions qui ne respectent pas les droits fondamentaux de la population du territoire dont ils proviennent, elle risque d'encourager indirectement de telles violations ou d'en profiter.

232. Cette considération est d'autant plus importante dans le cas d'un territoire, comme le Sahara occidental, qui est administré, dans les faits, par un État tiers, en l'occurrence le Royaume du Maroc, tout en n'étant pas inclus dans les frontières internationalement reconnues de cet État tiers.

233. Il convient également de tenir compte du fait que le Royaume du Maroc ne dispose d'aucun mandat, décerné par l'ONU ou par une autre instance internationale, pour l'administration de ce territoire et qu'il est constant qu'il ne transmet pas à l'ONU de renseignements relatifs à ce territoire, tels que ceux prévus par l'article 73, sous e), de la charte des Nations unies.

...omissis...

235. L'absence de communication des renseignements prévus par l'article 73, sous e), de la charte des Nations unies par le Royaume du Maroc à l'égard du Sahara occidental est à tout le moins susceptible de faire surgir un doute quant à la question de savoir si le Royaume du Maroc reconnaît le principe de primauté des intérêts des habitants de ce territoire et l'obligation de favoriser dans toute la mesure du possible leur prospérité, ainsi que cela est prévu par cette disposition. De plus, il ressort du dossier et, notamment, du texte produit par le requérant, en l'occurrence un discours tenu par le roi du Maroc le 6 novembre 2004, que le Royaume du Maroc considère que le Sahara occidental fait partie de son territoire.

236. Le Conseil a fait valoir qu'aucune des dispositions de la décision attaquée ou de l'accord approuvé par elle "n'[amenait] à conclure que l'exploitation des ressources du Sahara occidental se ferait au détriment des habitants dudit territoire, ni n'empêche[rait] le [Royaume du] Maroc de garantir que l'exploitation des ressources naturelles est menée au profit des habitants du Sahara occidental et dans leur intérêt".

237. Il est exact que le Front Polisario n'a pas reproché au Conseil d'avoir inclus dans la décision attaquée des termes de nature à conduire à une exploitation des ressources du Sahara occidental au détriment de ses habitants.

238. Toutefois, ainsi que cela a été relevé au point 231 ci-dessus, l'exportation vers l'Union de produits en provenance, notamment, du Sahara occidental est facilitée par l'accord en question. En effet, cela fait partie des objectifs dudit accord. Par conséquent, s'il devait s'avérer que le Royaume du Maroc exploitait les ressources du Sahara occidental au détriment de ses habitants, cette exploitation pourrait être indirectement encouragée par la conclusion de l'accord approuvé par la décision attaquée.

239. S'agissant de l'argument selon lequel le Royaume du Maroc ne serait pas empêché par les termes de l'accord de garantir que l'exploitation des ressources naturelles du Sahara occidental est menée au profit de ses habitants, il suffit de relever que l'accord ne garantit pas davantage une exploitation des ressources naturelles du Sahara occidental profitable à ses habitants. Il est à cet égard entièrement neutre, se limitant notamment à faciliter l'exportation vers l'Union des produits du Sahara occidental, qu'ils proviennent ou non d'une exploitation profitable à ses habitants.

240. En réalité, cet argument du Conseil démontre que, pour lui, il incombe au seul Royaume du Maroc de s'assurer du caractère profitable, pour les habitants de la partie du Sahara occidental qu'il contrôle, de l'exploitation de ses ressources naturelles.

241. Or, compte tenu notamment du fait que la souveraineté du Royaume du Maroc sur le Sahara occidental n'est reconnue ni par l'Union et ses États membres ni, plus généralement, par l'ONU, ainsi que de l'absence de tout mandat international susceptible de justifier la présence marocaine sur ce territoire, le Conseil, dans le cadre de l'examen de tous les éléments pertinents du cas d'espèce en vue de l'exercice de son large pouvoir d'appréciation concernant la conclusion, ou non, d'un accord avec le Royaume du Maroc susceptible de s'appliquer également au Sahara occidental, devait s'assurer lui-même qu'il n'existait pas d'indices d'une exploitation des ressources naturelles du territoire du Sahara occidental sous contrôle marocain susceptible de se faire au détriment de ses habitants et de porter atteinte à leurs droits fondamentaux. Il ne saurait se limiter à considérer qu'il incombe au Royaume du Maroc d'assurer qu'aucune exploitation de cette nature n'a lieu.

242. À cet égard, il y a lieu de relever que le Front Polisario qualifie l'exploitation des ressources naturelles du Sahara occidental sous contrôle marocain de "spoliation économique dont le but est la modification de la structure de la société sahraouie". Il ajoute qu'il a fait connaître à l'ONU ses protestations sur le projet d'accord approuvé par la décision attaquée. Ses arguments présentés dans le cadre des cinquième et sixième moyens (voir points 159, 169 et 170 ci-dessus) vont également dans le même sens.

243. Le Front Polisario a également versé au dossier un rapport détaillé de son conseil qui contient notamment des allégations selon lesquelles, en substance, les exploitations agricoles dans le Sahara occidental seraient contrôlées par des personnes et des entreprises étrangères non indigènes, seraient exclusivement orientées vers l'exportation et reposeraient sur l'extraction d'eau issue de bassins non renouvelables situés en profondeur. Il est renvoyé dans ce rapport à un rapport publié par une organisation non gouvernementale qui confirmerait ces allégations.

244. Il ne ressort ni des arguments du Conseil ni des éléments que ce dernier a versés au dossier qu'il a effectué un examen tel que celui mentionné au point 241 ci-dessus. S'agissant des allégations du Front Polisario mentionnées aux points 242 et 243 ci-dessus, le Conseil n'a présenté aucun commentaire particulier et ne les a pas démenties, ce qui donne à penser qu'il ne s'est pas penché sur la question de savoir si l'exploitation des ressources naturelles du Sahara occidental sous contrôle marocain se faisait ou non au profit de la population de ce territoire.

245. Toutefois, il apparaît des éléments invoqués par le Front Polisario que ces allégations ont connu une certaine diffusion et ont notamment été portées par lui à l'attention de l'ONU. Elles ne pouvaient dès lors être ignorées du Conseil et méritaient d'être examinées quant à leur vraisemblance par celui-ci.

246. Les arguments du Conseil, résumés aux points 230 et 236 ci-dessus, montrent au contraire qu'il considère que la question de savoir si l'exploitation des ressources du Sahara occidental se fait ou non au détriment de la population locale ne concerne que les autorités marocaines. Or, pour les motifs exposés aux points 227 à 233 ci-dessus, cette thèse ne saurait être admise.

247. Il en résulte que le Conseil a manqué à son obligation d'examiner, avant l'adoption de la décision attaquée, tous les éléments du cas d'espèce. Par conséquent, il convient de faire droit au recours et d'annuler la décision attaquée en ce qu'elle approuve l'application de l'accord visé par elle au Sahara occidental.

248. Au vu de cette conclusion, il n'est pas nécessaire de se prononcer sur la recevabilité des pièces mentionnées au point 27 ci-dessus, dont la prise en considération ne se révèle pas nécessaire en l'espèce.

...omissis...

Par ces motifs,

LE TRIBUNAL (huitième chambre)

déclare et arrête :

1) **La décision 2012/497/UE du Conseil, du 8 mars 2012, concernant la conclusion de l'accord sous forme d'échange de lettres entre l'Union européenne et le Royaume du Maroc relatif aux mesures de libéralisation réciproques en matière de produits agricoles, de produits agricoles transformés, de poissons et de produits de la pêche, au remplacement des protocoles nos 1, 2 et 3 et de leurs annexes et aux modifications de l'accord euro-méditerranéen établissant une association entre les Communautés européennes et leurs États membres, d'une part, et le Royaume du Maroc, d'autre part, est annulée en ce qu'elle approuve l'application dudit accord au Sahara occidental.**
2) **Le Conseil de l'Union européenne et la Commission européenne supporteront chacun leurs propres dépens ainsi que ceux exposés par le Front populaire pour la libération de la saguia-el-hamra et du rio de oro (Front Polisario).**

...omissis...

13. Court of Justice of the EU, General Court (Eighth Chamber), Case T-180/14, Front populaire pour la libération de la saguia-el-hamra et du rio de oro (Front Polisario) v. Council of the European Union, pending.

Action brought on 14 March 2014 – Front Polisario v Council

(Case T-180/14)

2014/C 184/55

Language of the case: French

Parties

Applicant: Front populaire pour la liberation de la saguia-el-hamra et du rio de oro (Front Polisario) (Laâyoune) (represented by: G. Devers, lawyer)

Defendant: Council of the European Union

Form of order sought

The applicant claims that the Court should:

- declare its action for annulment to be admissible;
- annul the decision of the Council;
- order the Council to pay the costs.

Pleas in law and main arguments

The applicant relies on 12 pleas in law in support of its action against Council Decision 2013/785/EU of 16 December 2013 on the conclusion, on behalf of the European Union, of the Protocol between the European Union and the Kingdom of Morocco setting out the fishing opportunities and financial contribution provided for in the Fisheries Partnership Agreement between the European Union and the Kingdom of Morocco ([1]).

The applicant considers that, as representative of the Sahrawi people, it is directly and individually affected by that act.

1. First plea in law, alleging breach of the obligation to state reasons, the contested decision not permitting an understanding of how the Council integrated into its decision-making process the fact that the Western Sahara is a non-self-governing territory occupied by the Kingdom of Morocco.

([1]) OJ 2013 L 349, p. 1.

2. Second plea in law, alleging breach of the principle of consultation, the Council having taken the contested decision without consulting the applicant, whereas international law requires that the exploitation of natural resources of a people of a non-self-governing territory be conducted in consultation with its representatives. The applicant argues that it is the sole representative of the Sahrawi people.

3. Third plea in law, alleging breach of the principle of consistency, in so far as the contested decision allows the entry into force of an international agreement which applies in the territory of the Western Sahara even though no Member State has recognised the sovereignty of the Kingdom of Morocco over the Western Sahara. The contested decision strengthens the Kingdom of Morocco's control over the Sahrawi territory, which is contrary to the aid provided by the Commission to Sahrawi refugees. In addition, the contested decision is inconsistent with the usual reaction of the European Union to breaches of obligations under peremptory norms of international law and is contrary to the objectives of the Common Fisheries Policy.

4. Fourth plea in law, alleging failure to achieve the goal of sustainable development.

5. Fifth plea in law, alleging breach of the principle of legitimate expectations, in so far as the contested decision runs counter to the expectation the applicant garnered from the repeated statements by the European Union institutions on the conformity of the agreements concluded with the Kingdom of Morocco with international law.

6. Sixth plea in law, alleging breach of the Association Agreement concluded between the European Union and the Kingdom of Morocco, the contested decision being contrary to Article 2 of that agreement in so far as it infringes the right to self-determination.

7. Seventh plea in law, alleging breach of the United Nations Convention on the Law of the Sea, in so far as the contested decision allows the entry into force of a protocol by which the European Union and the Kingdom of Morocco set fishing quotas for waters not under their sovereignty and authorised European Union vessels to exploit fisheries resources under the sole sovereignty of the Sahrawi people.

8. Eighth plea in law, alleging infringement of the right to self-determination, the contested decision bolstering the Kingdom of Morocco's control over the Western Sahara.

9. Ninth plea in law, alleging breach of the principle of permanent sovereignty over natural resources and of Article 73 of the Charter of the United Nations, the applicant not having been consulted even though the contested decision permits the exploitation of natural resources under the sole sovereignty of the Sahrawi people.

10. Tenth plea in law, alleging breach of the principle of the relative effect of treaties, the contested decision giving rise to international obligations in respect of the applicant without its consent.

11. Eleventh plea in law, alleging infringement of international humanitarian law, in so far as the contested decision provides financial support to the Kingdom of Morocco's policy of colonising the Western Sahara.

12. Twelfth plea in law, based on the law of international responsibility, the contested decision engaging the international responsibility of the European Union.

United Kingdom

14. High Court of Justice, Queen's Bench Division, Administrative Court, R (Western Sahara Campaign UK) v. The Commissioners for HMRC and the Secretary of State for the Environment, Food and Rural Affairs, [2015] EWHC 2898 (Admin).

Judgment Approved by the court for handing down. Western Sahara v HMRC & SSEFRA

Neutral Citation Number: [2015] EWHC 2898 (Admin)

Case No: CO/1032/2015
CO/1034/2015

IN THE HIGH COURT OF JUSTICE
QUEEN'S BENCH DIVISION
ADMINISTRATIVE COURT

Royal Courts of Justice
Strand, London, WC2A 2LL

Date: 19/10/2015

Before:
THE HON MR JUSTICE BLAKE

Between:

THE QUEEN on the application of WESTERN SAHARA CAMPAIGN UK	**Claimant**
– and –	
THE COMMISSIONERS FOR HER MAJESTY'S REVENUE AND CUSTOMS	**Defendants**
– and –	
THE SECRETARY OF STATE FOR THE ENVIRONMENT FOOD AND RURAL AFFAIRS	

...omissis...

Approved Judgment

The Honourable Mr Justice Blake:

Introduction

1. The claimant is an independent voluntary organisation founded in 1984 with the aim of supporting the recognition of the right of the Saharawi people of Western Sahara to self-determination and independence and to raise awareness of the unlawful occupation of the Western Sahara. It brings two related claims against each defendant pursuant to permission granted by Walker J on 23 April 2015.

2. Both claims contend that each defendant is acting unlawfully by applying provisions of EU law to matters within their jurisdiction. The Commissioners for Her Majesty's Revenue and Customs (HMRC) are the defendants in the first application where what is challenged is the preferential tariff given on import to the United Kingdom of goods that are classified as being of Moroccan origin but in fact originate from the territory of Western Sahara. The second challenge is brought against the Secretary of State for the Environment and Rural Affairs (DEFRA) in respect of the intended application of the EU-Morocco Fisheries Partnership Agreement to policy formation relating to fishing in the territorial waters of Western Sahara.

3. Both decisions challenge acts of the European Union in making agreements with Morocco with respect to customs tariffs and fisheries that do not distinguish between goods and activities arising in the sovereign territory of Morocco and the territory of Western Sahara over which Morocco has exercised jurisdiction, in whole or in part, since November 1975. The claimant contends that Morocco has annexed the territory of Western Sahara and claims it as part of its sovereign territory despite decisions of the United Nations and the International Court of Justice (ICJ) that the people of Western Sahara have the right to self-determination. Accordingly it is said that Morocco's occupation is in breach of the principles of international law and the Charter of the United Nations.

4. It is common ground that only the Court of Justice of the European Union (CJEU) has competence to determine the legality of the disputed EU measures. The claimant therefore seeks a reference for a preliminary ruling pursuant to Article 267 of the Treaty on the Functioning of the European Union (TFEU). The defendants oppose such a reference primarily because they submit that the issues raised by the claimant are matters of public international law that the CJEU will decline to adjudicate on in the present circumstances and the claims should accordingly be dismissed.

...omissis...

6. The defendants' detailed grounds also raised the question of delay as a reason to refuse relief. Delay was only faintly argued by Mr Kennelly

for the defendants in opposition to the claim. In my judgment, it affords no bar to making a reference, if that is otherwise considered to be the appropriate course, for a number of reasons. Permission has been granted without the question of whether the claims were made out of time being reserved, applying the principle in R v CICB ex p A [1990] 2 AC 330 as explained by the Court of Appeal in R (on the application of Lichfield Securities Ltd) v Lichfield DC [2001] EWCA Civ 304 delay should normally only remain an issue if there are good grounds for the refusal of relief pursuant to s.31 (6) of the Senior Courts Act. It is not contended that making a reference would cause substantial hardship, or prejudice to the rights of anyone or be detrimental to good administration. No licence has yet been granted has yet been granted to anybody in the UK to fish in the waters of Western Sahara, and the second defendant suggests that in some respects the challenge is premature and it would be appropriate to see how revised measures more recently adopted bilaterally between the EU and Morocco work out before any court should endeavour to adjudicate on the issues. In respect of the importation of goods, this is an allegation of a continuing breach of international and EU law and not a challenge to a historic specific import. The outcome of the proceedings if successful would not prevent goods being imported from Western Sahara but would merely for the future prevent those goods receiving preferential tariffs on the basis that they are Moroccan goods. In any event, if the issue of the timeliness of these applications were still live today, I would grant an extension of time given the significance of the issues, the factors mentioned above and the history of the issue to which further consideration will be given elsewhere in this judgment.

7. The defendants' principal objection, that for short hand I will label 'justiciability', is altogether more substantial. There is little doubt that if the present challenge was solely based on common law rules, a domestic court might dismiss a claim that depends on an assessment of the legality of actions of a foreign sovereign: see Buttes Gas v Hammer (No 3) [1982] AC 888 per Lord Wilberforce at 931-2; Shergill v Khaira [2015] AC 359 at [42]. The developing exceptions to this rule, where the fundamental human rights of an individual are in issue, would have no application in the present case: see Lloyd-Jones LJ in Belhaj v Straw [2014] EWCA Civ 1394 at 114-121.

8. Mr Beal QC for the claimants contends, however, that the common law rules have no application to challenges to EU acts taken before the CJEU. He points out that Article 3 (5) of the consolidated Treaty of the European Union (TEU) states that in its relations with the wider world the Union shall uphold and promote its values and shall contribute to the strict observance and the development of international law including respect for the principles of the United Nations Charter. The CJEU has

stated that the EU must respect international law including customary international law. Thus in Case C-366/10 Air Transport Association of America and others v Secretary of State for Energy and Climate Change [2012] 2 CMLR 4 the CJEU noted:

> 101. Under Article 3(5) TEU, the European Union is to contribute to the strict observance and the development of international law. Consequently, when it adopts an act, it is bound to observe international law in its entirety, including customary international law, which is binding upon the institutions of the European Union (see, to this effect, Case C-286/90 *Poulsen and Diva Navigation* [1992] ECR I-6019, paragraphs 9 and 10, and Case C-162/96 *Racke* [1998] ECR I-3655, paragraphs 45 and 46).
>
> 102. Thus, it should be examined first whether the principles to which the referring court makes reference are recognised as forming part of customary international law. If they are, it should, secondly, then be determined whether and to what extent they may be relied upon by individuals to call into question the validity of an act of the European Union, such as Directive 2008/101, in a situation such as that in the main proceedings.

9. A little later the Court observed:

> 107. The principles of customary international law mentioned in paragraph 103 of the present judgment may be relied upon by an individual for the purpose of the Court's examination of the validity of an act of the European Union in so far as, first, those principles are capable of calling into question the competence of the European Union to adopt that act (see Joined Cases 89/85, 104/85, 114/85, 116/85, 117/85 and 125/85 to 129/85 *Ahlström Osakeyhtiö and Others v Commission* [1988] ECR 5193, paragraphs 14 to 18, and Case C-405/92 *Mondiet* [1993] ECR I-6133, paragraphs 11 to 16) and, second, the act in question is liable to affect rights which the individual derives from European Union law or to create obligations under European Union law in his regard.
>
> …
>
> 110. However, since a principle of customary international law does not have the same degree of precision as a provision of an international agreement, judicial review must necessarily be limited to the question whether, in adopting the act in question, the institutions of the European Union made manifest errors of assessment concerning the conditions for applying those principles (see, to this effect, *Racke*, paragraph 52).

10. The defendants contend that this statement of the law does not assist the claimant:

i. It has no rights under EU law that it is asserting.
ii. There is a respectable legal opinion from counsel to the Secretary General of the United Nations that exporting goods from and exploiting the

natural resources of an occupied territory is not inherently unlawful if the occupying power complies with the legal obligations on such a power to promote the welfare of the population of the territory.

iii. The EU has never recognised that the Western Sahara is part of Morocco but is not required to specify what the limits of Moroccan territory are in entering agreements with it.

iv. The EU and its institutions have had proper regard to the principles of international law in its dealing with Morocco and it cannot be said to have arguably made any manifest error in its examination of the issue.

11. With this brief introduction to the issues in dispute, this judgment will now examine:

i. the status of the Western Sahara;

ii. the terms of the EU agreements in question;

iii. the respective arguments as to why it is contended that the agreements do or do not breach international law.

...omissis...

The EU Agreements

23. In March 2000 the Member States of the European Union and the European Community entered into an Association Agreement with the Kingdom of Morocco (OJ 1/70/2 18 March 2000). Article 9 of that Agreement deals with industrial products and states 'products originating in Morocco shall be imported into the Community free of customs duties and charges having equivalent effect'. Article 17 of the Agreement relates to agricultural and fishery products and refers to more detailed schemes of tariff free entry into what is now the European Union set out in the protocols. Article 29 of the Agreement is common to all products and states that concept of originating products is set out in Protocol 4.

24. Article 94 of the Agreement states that it shall apply to 'the territory of the Kingdom of Morocco'. Article 6 (4) of Protocol 4 to the Agreement states that 'the terms Morocco and the Community shall also cover the territorial waters which surround Morocco and the Member States of the Community'.

25. On the basis of these provisions, it is, in my judgment, arguable that this agreement refers to products that originate in Morocco and Morocco means the internationally recognised sovereign territory of Morocco and its associated territorial waters on the one hand and the similar territories of the Member States on the other.

26. Case C-386/08 Firma Brita GmbH v Hauptzolamt Hamburg-Hafen [2010] ECR 1-1289 concerned whether goods originating from

areas occupied by Israel but outside its internationally recognised borders could benefit from the EU Israel-Association Agreement. Advocate General Bot in his opinion at [113] records that the Council took the view that a reference to the territory of the State of Israel and its territorial waters meant its internationally recognised territory in accordance with UN Security Council resolutions. As we shall see below (at [36]) the Court reached its decision in this case on a different basis.

27. In 2006 the European Community and the Kingdom of Morocco reached a Fisheries Partnership Agreement (OJ L 141/4 29 May 2006) enabling fishing vessels of the EU Member States to fish in the Moroccan fishing zone in exchange for a significant financial payment by the Community. Article 2 of the Agreement states that 'Moroccan fishing zone means the waters falling within the sovereignty or jurisdiction of the Kingdom of Morocco'. Article 11 of the Agreement states that its area of application is 'the territory of Morocco and to the waters under Moroccan jurisdiction.' Detailed regulations assign fishing quotas to the Member States and applications for a licence within the allocated quota are determined by the national authority (in the instant case the Marine Management Organisation or relevant devolved fisheries administration, but pursuant to policy made by the second defendant). The United Kingdom has been assigned a quota but has not yet issued any licences.

28. Whatever the terms 'territory of Morocco' and 'waters under Moroccan jurisdiction' mean, there is undisputed evidence that agricultural products originating from the territory of Western Sahara have been imported into the United Kingdom tariff-free on the basis of a declaration that they originate from Morocco. Despite being made aware of this state of affairs, HMRC, as the responsible national authority has never exercised its powers to investigate and query the stated place of origin of these products. It contends that EU and international law permits exporters to make the declarations concerned.

29. Equally, it is undisputed that where Member States have issued licences to vessels within its jurisdiction to fish in the Moroccan fishing zone, such fishing has taken place within the territorial waters of the Western Sahara and catches have been landed and port fees paid to the Moroccan authorities in ports located within the territory of Western Sahara.

30. There has been debate between the European Parliament, or some members thereof, and the European Commission as to whether an agreement that permits vessels from EU Member States to take fish from the waters of Western Sahara is in accordance with international law. The material before this court includes exchanges between Parliament, the Legal Service and the Commission and on this issue since at least February 2006.

31. The response of the Commission to the various queries raised by members of the European Parliament is reflected in a joint written answer given by the High Representative, Baroness Ashton, on behalf of the European Commission in June 2011. It states:

> "According to the United Nations position on the subject, which the EU adheres to, Western Sahara is considered a 'non-self-governing territory' and Morocco its de facto administering power. To the extent that exports of products from Western Sahara are 'de facto' benefitting from the trade preferences, international law regards activities related to natural resources undertaken by an administering power in a non-self-governing territory as lawful as long as they are not undertaken in disregard of the needs, interest and benefits of the people of that territory. The 'de facto' administration of Morocco in Western Sahara is under a legal obligation to comply with these principles of international law. The same applies to the envisaged Agreement on the liberalisation of trade on agricultural and fisheries products, which would modify the trade chapter of the Association Agreement. The Association Agreement establishes formal bodies which aim to ensure follow-up on the implementation of the Agreement and give each contracting party the opportunity to raise issues and facilitate discussions of policies implemented by the parties."

32. This statement and the legal opinions on which it is based, in substance refer back to the opinion of Hans Corell[1], although without any reference to the concomitant duty of the administering authority to promote self-determination, or the need to consult the representatives of the people of the territory. It may be debatable whether the need to demonstrate that actual exploitation is used for the benefit of the Saharawi people is sufficiently reflected in the observation made in the words quoted that the needs of the people of the territory should not be disregarded.

33. In 2013 a further Protocol was agreed between the Commission and Morocco to establish a Joint Committee to monitor how revenues generated by the agreements were to be spent and the minutes of the early meetings of that Committee have been placed before the court.

The claimant's contentions on conflict with international law

34. In the course of his written and oral submissions, Mr Beal contends that the EU and the Commission, in entering into these agreements with Morocco, have acted on a mistaken and erroneous understanding of international law. A vague expression of intent by Morocco to benefit the local population by these agreements is insufficient to make them lawful

1 See also reply of European Commission 23 June 2010 cited in Dawidowicz at p. 270 footnote 110.

agreements by an administering power pending the expression of self-determination by the people of the territory concerned. In particular:

i. Morocco has never acknowledged that it is an administering power or has an obligation to promote the self-determination of Western Sahara. On the contrary, it claims the territory as its own sovereign territory because of historic links, despite the opinion of the ICJ to the contrary. It has thus not merely failed to report to the UN on the progress being made to self-determination but has refused to accept peace proposals based on a referendum, of the original population of Western Sahara in 1975 and their descendants and at the most has accepted the possibility of limited self-government within the auspices of Moroccan sovereignty.

ii. Neither the Saharawi people nor their legitimate representatives have been consulted as to how natural resources should be exploited and they have not consented to such exploitation. The Frente Polisario itself is opposed to these agreements as it perceives them as a means where Morocco legitimises its occupation of the country and can use the resources generated by them for the general purposes of benefitting the Moroccan people as a whole and not (or not just) the people of Western Sahara in particular. Further by moving its own nationals into the territory and assigning land and commercial licences to such nationals, Morocco has ignored the principle that the indigenous inhabitants of the territory should determine the fate of its natural resources. For a state to rely on the approval of people transferred to the occupied territory after the unauthorised assertion of jurisdiction is inevitably to legitimise such occupation that was, at inception, and remains, illegal in international law.

iii. Whilst the 2013 Protocol and its Committee may be a good faith endeavour to ensure that fish caught in Western Saharan waters are landed at Western Saharan ports and landing fees paid there, that is no guarantee that the benefit of the agreements goes exclusively to the people of Western Sahara. There is nothing in the Agreements or the Protocol or the terms of references of the Committee to require Morocco to do so and its own statements about the projects developed with the EU are that this is part of a general economic expansion of Morocco.

iv. Morocco has in fact exercised administrative control of the territory as a result on the location of its armed forces there, in violation of the principles of the UN Charter and respect for the right to determination. Despite the cease-fire, Morocco has not proceeded to legitimise its exercise of authority by arranging for a free expression by the people of Western Sahara as to the arrangements for their future governance.

v. In such circumstances it is wrong for Member States, let alone an international body such as the EU, that abides by the principles of international law and the UN Charter, to aid and abet what is in effect an illegitimate occupation of the Western Sahara. Such assistance is in breach of emerging principles of state responsibility for unlawful acts that violate the principle of self-determination.

Discussion

35. In addition to the Air Transport case (cited at [8] above) the advocates placed particular reliance at the oral hearing on three further authorities.

36. Mr Beal submitted that Brita was precisely a case where certification of goods from the West Bank as Israeli was declared unlawful applying principles of international law. The ratio of the Court's decision at [44] to [52] was the principle that in entering a bi-lateral treaty a state cannot impose obligations on a third state and a fortiori where the third state (the Palestinian authority) has entered its own Association Agreement with the Commission. The Court therefore concluded at [52]:

> "Accordingly, to interpret Article 83 of the EC-Israel Association Agreement as meaning that the Israeli customs authorities enjoy competence in respect of products originating in the West Bank would be tantamount to imposing on the Palestinian customs authorities an obligation to refrain from exercising the competence conferred upon them by virtue of the abovementioned provisions of the EC-PLO Protocol. Such an interpretation, the effect of which would be to create an obligation for a third party without its consent, would thus be contrary to the principle of general international law, "*pacta tertiis nec nocent nec prosunt*", as consolidated in Article 34 of the Vienna Convention".

37. I am not persuaded by Mr Beal's submission that the situation is analogous here. Western Sahara is not recognised by the European Union and its Member States as an independent territory. No self-governing body exercises jurisdiction over the agricultural land and fishing area of Western Sahara. There has been no agreement entered into between the Community and the Frente Polisario in respect of these matters. Applying the Morocco Agreement to all areas where the state of Morocco exercises authority would thus not conflict with the rights of a third state or state-like entity.

38. Mr Kennelly relied on case T-572/93 Odigitria AAE v Council of the European Union and Commission of the European Communities. The Community had entered agreements with the states of Guinea-Bissau and Senegal for licensed operators to fish in their territorial waters. The precise boundary between the two states was disputed. The Association Agreement did not define what the boundary was or exclude the disputed area from the agreement. A Greek vessel that had a national quota and authority from Senegal was fishing in the disputed zone when it was boarded by the authorities of Guinea Bissau, its cargo confiscated and the master fined for fishing without a licence. The vessel brought an action for damages against

the Council and the Commission for negligent discharge of their duties in making Agreements that provided a hidden peril for those who relied on them. The claim was dismissed and the General Court explained (at [38]):

> "As regards the content of that agreement, it must be observed that the Community institutions enjoy a wide discretion in the field of the Community's external economic relations, as in the corresponding internal field of the common agricultural policy. In concluding the agreements and protocols with the two States in question, the Council and the Commission did not go beyond the limits of the discretion which they have in this matter and did not in any case adopt a measure manifestly inappropriate in relation to the objective which they were pursuing. The Council and the Commission could not have asked for the zone in dispute to be excluded from those agreements without taking a position on matters forming part of the internal affairs of non-member States. If the Community opposed the claims of the States concerning the zones over which they claim to have jurisdiction or opposed the exercise of that jurisdiction when a dispute exists, those non-member countries would very probably refuse to conclude such agreements with the Community. Moreover, if the Community asked for zones to which other States lay claim to be excluded, that move would certainly be interpreted as interference by the Community in those disputes. The exclusion of such zones at the Community's request would also have the effect of weakening the claim of the non-member State in question to have the right to exercise such jurisdiction. The fact that such disputes are submitted to arbitration or are the subject of legal proceedings strengthens that argument, since, where proceedings are pending before the ICJ, it is not appropriate for the Community to take a position on disputes between non-member States."

The judgment was upheld on appeal by the CJEU but the discussion there focused on different issues.

39. I accept that if there is an unresolved territorial dispute between two states, the Commission is not obliged to endeavour to resolve it before entering Association Agreements with either state. It does not follow that the Commission is always entitled to be indifferent to where the sovereign borders of a state end, particularly where there is an unlawful occupation of territory of another. Such a submission would be contrary to the principles of the UN Charter and the principles that bind the European Union, however wide the discretion may be with respect to foreign affairs. Further it would be contrary to the decision in Brita, for the Union to accept one state's *de facto* assertion of jurisdiction with respect to the origin of goods, where it would conflict with another state's rights. The dispute between Senegal and Guinea-Bissau was not about whether one state could claim jurisdiction outside its sovereign territory but where the limits of its sovereign territory in fact lay.

40. The present position is different. Morocco may claim Western Sahara to be part of its sovereign territory but the international community generally and the European Union, in particular, does not recognise that claim. Indeed, the Western Sahara is one of the few pieces of disputed territory where a claim by a neighbouring state to sovereignty has been examined by the International Court of Justice. In my judgment, Morocco's claim to the territory must be based on:

i. the pre-existing links before 1975 that it relied on its submissions to the International Court; or
ii. the November 1975 agreement with the former colonial power; or
iii. its military occupation in December 1975; or
iv. a free act of self-determination by the people of Western Sahara.

However, the first basis of claim was considered and rejected by the Court in its Advisory Opinion of 16 October 1975 (Western Sahara Advisory Opinion ICJ Reports 1975 p. 12 at [162]). The second and third bases would unambiguously conflict with the principles of the UN Charter. A colonial power cannot gift an occupied territory to a neighbouring state for some reason of diplomatic advantage, particularly where it has been directed by the UN to supervise the process whereby the 72,000 odd people of the Western Sahara should express their right to self-determination. Equally, unauthorised military occupation cannot found the basis for legitimate territorial claims. The fourth potential basis of sovereignty has not come to pass; despite long engagement by the UN no free expression of the will of the Saharawi people has yet been undertaken. In these circumstances, I am of the view that this is not a dispute as to where the sovereign territory of Morocco extended; this was at all times clear. Rather the issue is whether it is legitimate for a body respecting the principles of the UN Charter to make an agreement with an administering power in respect of territory outside its recognised boundaries. The principle in Odigitria is accordingly directed to a different issue and does not resolve the present problem.

...omissis...

43. In the end, the best prospects of Mr Kennelly dealing a knockout blow to making a reference lay in the combination of the Hans Corell opinion and the application of the test of manifest error identified in the Air Transport case (at [9]) above. I accept that in the light of the state of the learning and the submissions made to me, it would not be a manifest error for the Commission to conclude that the fact of Morocco's continued occupation of the territory of the Western Sahara did not preclude, as a matter of international law, the making of any agreements for the exploitation of the natural resources of the territory in question. If so,

I also recognise that it is but a short step to say that what agreements can be reached and whether the benefit of the agreements is being given to the people of the region is a matter of judgment for the Commission rather than adjudication for the CJEU. I recognise that there is a real possibility that this is an approach that will find favour.

Conclusions

44. In the end, I am not persuaded that I can with complete confidence decline to make a reference on the basis that the claimant's arguments are bound to fail (see R v International Stock Exchange ex parte Else [1993] QB 534 at 551D per Sir Thomas Bingham). My reasons on this part of the argument are as follows.

45. First, whilst I recognise the eminence and expertise of the author, the Hans Corell, the opinion is an opinion of a legal adviser on a difficult topic and not a judgment of the ICJ.

46. Second, there are issues that arise in these proceedings that were not considered in Mr Corell's opinion, in particular, who it is who must benefit from the exploitation of Western Sahara's natural resources: the whole population of the territory, assessed in 2000 to be some 250,000 or so, or the 86,000 original inhabitants and their descendants then assessed to be eligible to vote. This seems to be rather central to the principle of self-determination reflected in the Charter and emphasised in Mr Corell's opinion. No learning on the topic has been directed to me, but I can see why Mr Beal's submissions, that I have summarised at [34] above, may well find favour.

47. Third, the answer to who represents the people for the purpose of self-determination may prove decisive to the question of the relevance and sufficiency of the Commission's efforts to ensure that the financial benefits of the Agreements are felt in territory of the Western Sahara. It may be that the benefits need to be directed specifically to the indigenous population. If this cannot be achieved as a matter of political practicality then no agreement should be entered with an administering power that:

i. does not recognise that this is its status and
ii. does not act in accordance with all the obligations imposed by Article 73 of the Charter,
iii. and in particular does not acknowledge the obligation to promote the self-determination of the people of Western Sahara.

48. Fourth, Mr Corell's opinion was cautious in tone and addressed the making of a contract, in principle, between Morocco and a commercial enterprise not itself bound by public international principles (contrast the

Member States and the Commission itself). Some of the legal opinions and statements made on behalf of the Commission, seem wide-ranging and unqualified in scope; they may suggest that it is appropriate to contract with an occupying administering power as long as *some* benefit is created for the region generally. It seems to me that that there are good reasons why the CJEU may take a narrower view.

49. Fifth, the non-state nature of the commercial companies who made exploration agreements with Morocco meant no consideration was given to the status of the International Law Commission's 2001 Document on the Responsibility of States for Internationally Wrongful Acts (see Chapter III Articles 40 to 41 and the duty on states to cooperate to end serious breaches of a peremptory norm of international law). If such an obligation is now part of customary international law, it is possible that a failure by an administering power to promote self-determination will be considered such a serious breach. Equally, the fact that trade agreements are made that benefit the population of the occupied territory generally without regard to the fact that some of the population are said to be present in the territory as a result of the original unlawful act may be evidence of a serious breach of international law. Further, no consideration was given in the Corell opinion to the UN Convention on the Law of the Sea.

50. Sixth, it is clear that the status of these agreements have been controversial, not merely within the European Parliament but also in respect of declarations made by Member States to the 2013 Protocol (see for example the declarations of Denmark and Sweden opposing the Protocol, the United Kingdom in abstaining and the expressions of concern by the Netherlands and Finland). There would appear to be a strong public interest in ascertaining what the CJEU has to say on the question, thereby clarifying the limits of the Commission's broad powers in the sensitive arena of international relations.

51. Seventh, it is pertinent to note that amongst public expressions of concern about the legality of these agreements are writings by scholars. Reference has already been made (at [18] above) to the essay by Martin Dawidowicz 'Trading fish or human rights in Western Sahara?' that is critical of the agreements made by the Commission. His is not a lone voice. Of particular interest to the present proceedings is that Hans Corell himself authorised publication of a paper he delivered as a private individual at a conference in Western Sahara at the University of Pretoria in December 2008. In the paper he makes a number of points about the limited nature of the issues on which he had been asked to advise and the caution he expressed in reaching them. He further noted that as Morocco did not have the status of an administering power, the application of

Article 73 by analogy had to be examined with the utmost sensitivity. He continues:

> "If the principle is that the interest of the peoples of Non-Self-Governing Territories are paramount, and their well-being and development are the sacred trust of their respective administering powers, this principle had to be applied with an extra margin in the present case. To what extent had the people of Western Sahara been involved in the process of granting the contracts? I believe that the fact the situation obtaining in the territory for so many years and the fact that the question was raised in the Security Council, are a clear indication that there might be a problem here."

52. Noting the final paragraph of his opinion (summarised at [22] (vi) above) he added:

> "From this sentence it follows that Morocco would have to engage in proper consultations with persons authorised to represent the people of Western Sahara before such activities would be allowed as was done by the United Nations in East Timor."

53. Of particular relevance are his comments on the Fisheries Agreement.

> "I must confess that I was quite taken aback when I learnt about this agreement. Without doubt, good relations between Europe and Morocco are of the greatest importance. And there is also a mutual interest in the fisheries off the coast of western Africa being effectively managed and supervised. But I am sure that it would have been possible to find a formulation that would have satisfied both parties while at the same time respecting the legal regime applicable in the waters off Western Sahara. Any jurisdiction over those waters is subject to the limitations that flow from the rules on self-determination. It has been suggested that the legal opinion I delivered in 2002 has been invoked by the European Commission in support of the Fisheries Partnership Agreement. I do not know if this is true. But if it is I find it incomprehensible that the Commission could find any such support in the legal opinion, unless, of course, it had established that the people of Western Sahara had been consulted, and accepted the agreement, and the manner in which the profits from the activity were to benefit them".

Having then examined the text of the agreement and noting the absence of delimiting factors he reaches the conclusion:

> "Under all circumstances, I would have thought that it was obvious that an agreement of this kind that does not make a distinction between the waters adjacent to Western Sahara and the waters adjacent to the territory of Morocco would violate international law."

54. Mr Kennelly invites me to disregard this expression of opinion altogether. I recognise that caution should be exercised when considering the weight to be attached to remarks made informally in a private capacity at a conference in Africa, where the position of the OAU is markedly different from that of other states. However, although no longer holding a position as Legal Counsel to the Secretary General, Mr Corell remains a distinguished expert in this field of law. In January 2015 he was appointed Co-Chair of the International Bar Association's Human Rights Institute, and the biographical details then provided demonstrate that after his 10 years of service with the UN he has been active in this field as a judge, legal adviser and scholar. His 2008 remarks precisely address some of the concerns I have had with the Commission's reliance on the UN Charter to justify its actions. They are reflected in Mr Beal's submissions about the absence of any evidence of consultation and consent to these agreements by the Saharawi people or their recognised representatives.

55. I conclude that there is an arguable case of a manifest error by the Commission in understanding and applying international law relevant to these agreements.

56. I recognise that the claimant is not an exporter of goods or applicant for a fishing licence whose commercial rights have been infringed by the decision in question. The claimant has standing in English law to bring this challenge and relies on the principles of international law as applied in the EU to do so. I consider that the challenge is real and genuine. I cannot conclude that the CJEU would decline to answer these questions simply because an individual Saharawi or anyone else with commercial interests affected by the Agreements have not been joined as co-claimant.

57. I accordingly conclude that I should make a reference to the CJEU as the relevant criteria to do so have been established. I will give the parties an opportunity to agree the questions pursuant to a timetable to be agreed at the handing down of this judgment. At present, I consider that there may be a difference between the issues with respect to the Fisheries Partnership Agreement 2006 where the text refers to waters 'falling within the sovereignty or jurisdiction of the Kingdom of Morocco' and the customs tariff point under the Association Agreement of 2000 where the reference is simply to the territory of Morocco. It may be as a matter of simple interpretation that this excludes produce from territories outside of Morocco's recognised border. Otherwise, the core issues seem to me to be whether the Commission was able to make the agreements it has done and remain in conformity with international law and the UN Charter without the consultation and consent of the Saharawi people and their recognised representatives first having been obtained.

Biographical notes

Marco Balboni is Professor at the School of Political Science, University of Bologna – Forlì. His main research interests include: the role of the EU in promoting the principles of the rule of law in the international arena; international refugee law and EU immigration law; international and EU non-discrimination law; the role of the domestic courts in the implementation of EU law. Among others, he is a member of the scientific board of the legal academic review *Diritto, Immigrazione e Cittadinanza* and of the PhD Commission on EU Law – University of Bologna. Finally, he has been responsible for the University of Bologna of the Italian National Focal Point of the EU Agency on Fundamental Rights (Wien).

Hans Corell was Under-Secretary-General for Legal Affairs and the Legal Counsel of the United Nations between March 1994 and March 2004. He was head of the Office of Legal Affairs in the United Nations Secretariat. Before joining the United Nations in 1994, Corell was an Ambassador and Under-Secretary for Legal and Consular Affairs in the Swedish Ministry for Foreign Affairs. Hans Corell graduated with a Master of Laws at Uppsala University. He was Chairman of the Board of Trustees of the Raoul Wallenberg Institute of Human Rights and Humanitarian Law at Lund University from 2006-2012.

Francesco Correale, historian and Ingénieur de recherche on the analysis of the sources at the CNRS – UMR 7324 CITERES (CNRS / A. F. Rabelais, Tours – http://citeres.univ-tours.fr/spip.php?article410), he analyzed the history of the French colonization of the Western Maghreb using the sources of the most important French and Spanish archives. He is coordinator of a research program for the digitization of the sources for the history of Western Sahara (BIBLIMOS Program: http://citeres.univ-tours.fr/spip.php?article1195). He is currently doing research on the colonial history of the Sahara in a research group of the UAM Madrid.

Erik Hagen is chair of Western Sahara Resource Watch (Norway) and director of the Norwegian Support Committee for Western Sahara. He has followed the issue of plundering of Western Sahara's resources since 2002, both as an investigative journalist and civil society activist.

Giuliana Laschi is professor of Contemporary History and History of European Integration (Jean Monnet Chair *ad personam*) at the University of Bologna, Forlì Campus. President of the Scientific Committee of Punto

Europa Forlì (Europe Direct Centre of European Commission since 2007 and Jean Monnet centre of Excellence since 2014), she cooperates with many institutions in the organization of awareness events on EU. Her books include *L'Italia e il processo di integrazione agricola europea, 1947-1962* (Peter Lang, 1999), *Europa, potenza civile o entità in declino?* (with Mario Telò, Il Mulino, 2007), *L'Europa nel sistema internazionale* (with Mario Telò, Il Mulino, 2009), *The European Community and the World* (PIE Peter Lang, 2014). Her last work is the monography *L'Europa e gli altri. Le relazioni esterne della Comunità dalle origini al dialogo Nord-Sud* (Il Mulino, 2015).

Enrico Milano is Associate Professor of International Law at the University of Verona (since 1 January 2011). He is Member of the Board of the Department since March 2013. Courses taught: Public International Law, Law of International Organizations, Advanced International Law. Guest lecturer at the University of Milan, University of Parma, University of Catania, University of Trento, University of Palermo, University of Bologna, Second University of Naples. Responsible for the area "International Law" in the School for Legal Professions of the University of Verona and the University of Trento. He taught a Module on cooperation policy of EU in the framework of the Master "Diritti umani e intervento internazionale" during 2011/2012 and 2012/2013.

Ricardo Passos worked at European Commission on Human Rights (1978-1986); European Court of Justice (referendaire) (1986-1988); European Parliament (1988-Present) as Head Secretariat of the Legal Affairs Committee. During 2002-2003 he was member of the Secretariat of the European Convention which drafted the substance of the Treaty of Lisbon; he also represented the European Parliament at the European Court of Justice.

Carlos Ruiz Miguel is Professor of Constitutional Law at the University of Santiago De Compostela. He is the author of 11 individual books, editor of two, contributor to 35 collective books, author of 70 articles in scientific journals. His work has been published in Spanish, English, French and Italian.

EUROCLIO – Published Books

N° 97 – *Europe between Imperial Decline and Quest for Integration. Pro-European Groups and the French, Belgian and British Empires (1947-1957)*. Laura Kottos, 2016.

N° 96 – *Réinventer la diplomatie. Sociabilités, réseaux et pratiques diplomatiques en Europe depuis 1919 / Reshaping Diplomacy. Networks, Practices and Dynamics of Socialization in European Diplomacy since 1919*. Vincent Genin, Matthieu Osmont and Thomas Raineau (eds.), 2016.

N° 95 – *Sometimes Speaking with a Single Voice. The European Community as an International Actor, 1969-1979*. Lorenzo Ferrari, 2016.

N° 94 – *Competition Law Challenges in the Next Decade*. Sofia Oliveira Pais (ed.), 2016.

N° 93 – *The Borders of Schengen*. Alice Cunha, Marta Silva, Rui Frederico (eds.), 2015.

N° 92 – *Que dire à l'Espagne ? De l'isolement franquiste à la démocratie européiste, la France au défi, 1957-1979*. Pablo Martin-Pañeda, 2015.

N° 91 – *Francis Delaisi, du dreyfusisme à « l'Europe nouvelle »*. Éric Bussière, Olivier Dard, Geneviève Duchenne (dir.), 2015.

N° 90 – *European Parties and the European Integration Process, 1945-1992*. Lucia Bonfreschi, Giovanni Orsina, Antonio Varsori (eds.), 2015

N° 89 – *Européanisation et démocratisation des États baltes dans la période de préadhésion à l'UE. Le rôle de la conditionnalité politique des organisations européennes*. Anne-Sylvie Pigeonnier, 2015.

N° 88 – *Le Continent basket. L'Europe et le basket-ball au XX*e *siècle*. Fabien Archambault, Loïc Artiaga, Gérard Bosc (dir.), 2015.

N° 87 – *The Convention on the Future of Europe. How States Behave in a New Institutional Context of Negotiation*. Francesco Marchi, 2015.

N° 86 – *Christian Democrat Internationalism. Its Action in Europe and Worldwide from post World War II until the 1990s. Volume III. The European People's Party Continental and Social Cooperation*. Jean-Dominique Durand (ed.), 2014.

N° 85 – *Pela Paz! For Peace! Pour la paix ! (1849-1939)*. Maria Manuela Tavares Ribeiro, Maria Fernanda Rollo, Isabel Maria Freitas Valente, Alice Cunha (eds.), 2014.

N° 84 – *Economic Crisis and New Nationalisms. German Political Economy as Perceived by European Partners*. Antonio VARSORI, Monika POETTINGER (eds.), 2014.

N° 83 – *European Constitutionalism. Historical and Contemporary Perspectives*. Alexandre DUPEYRIX, Gérard RAULET (eds.), 2014.

N° 82 – *Cross-Border Cooperation Structures in Europe. Learning from the Past, Looking to the Future*. Luis DOMÍNGUEZ, Iva PIRES (eds.), 2014.

N° 81 – *The European Community and the World. A Historical Perspective*. Giuliana LASCHI (ed.), 2014.

N° 80 – *Christian Democrat Internationalism. Its Action in Europe and Worldwide from Post World War II until the 1990s. Volume II: The Development (1945-1979). The Role of Parties, Movements, People*. Jean-Dominique DURAND (ed.), 2013.

N° 79 – *Christian Democrat Internationalism. Its Action in Europe and Worldwide from Post World War II until the 1990s. Volume I: The Origins*. Jean-Dominique DURAND (ed.), 2013.

N° 78 – *Investment Banking History. National and Comparative Issues (19th-21st centuries)*. Hubert BONIN & Carlo BRAMBILLA (eds.), 2013.

N° 77 – *Citizenship and Solidarity in the European Union. From the Charter of Fundamental Rights to the Crisis, the State of the Art*. Mariana CANOTILHO, Pedro MADEIRA FROUFE & Alessandra SILVEIRA (eds.), 2013.

N° 76– *The OSCE: Soft Security for a Hard World. Competing Theories for Understanding the OSCE*. Roberto DOMINGUEZ (ed.), 2013.

N° 75 – *Euroscepticism, Europhobia and Eurocriticism. The Radical Parties of the Right and Left* vis-à-vis *the European Union*. Cesáreo RODRÍGUEZ-AGUILERA DE PRAT, 2013.

N° 74 – *Fermer les mines en construisant l'Europe. Une histoire sociale de l'intégration européenne*. Nicolas VERSCHUEREN, 2012.

N° 73 – *Reflets de la construction européenne. Réflexions, références et refus du débat sur l'Europe*. Bertrand VAYSSIÈRE (dir.), 2012.

N° 72 – *The International Relations of Local Authorities. From Institutional Twinning to the Committee of the Regions: Fifty Years of European Integration History*. Fabio ZUCCA, 2012.

N° 71 – *Histoire du Conseil de l'Europe (1949-2009)*. Birte WASSENBERG, 2012.

N° 70 – *The EU, Security and Transatlantic Relations*. Finn LAURSEN (ed.), 2012.

N° 69 – *Européanisation au XXe siècle. Un regard historique / Europeanisation in the 20th Century. The Historical Lens*. Matthieu OSMONT, Émilia ROBIN-HIVERT, Katja SEIDEL, Mark SPOERER & Christian WENKEL (dir./eds.), 2012.

N° 68 – *Consensus and European Integration. An Historical Perspective / Consensus et intégration européenne. Une perspective historique*. Daniela PREDA & Daniele PASQUINUCCI (eds./dir.), 2012.

N° 67 – *Générations de fédéralistes européens depuis le XIXe siècle. Individus, groupes, espaces et réseaux*. Geneviève DUCHENNE et Michel DUMOULIN (dir.), 2012.

N° 66 – *Raymond Aron, penseur de l'Europe et de la nation*. Giulio DE LIGIO (dir.), 2012.

N° 65 – *Europe Twenty Years after the End of the Cold War. The New Europe, New Europes? / L'Europe vingt ans après la fin de la guerre froide. Nouvelle Europe, nouvelles Europes?* Bruno ARCIDIACONO, Katrin MILZOW, Axel MARION & Pierre-Étienne BOURNEUF (eds./dir.), 2012.

Euroclio European Network

together with the SEGEI Network

Coordination : Chaire Jean Monnet d'histoire de l'Europe contemporaine (Cehec)
Collège Erasme, 1, place Blaise-Pascal, B-1348 Louvain-la-Neuve

Germany

Jürgen Elvert
Wilfried Loth

Belgium

Julie Cailleau
Jocelyne Collonval
Yves Conrad
Gaëlle Courtois
Pascal Deloge
Geneviève Duchenne
Vincent Dujardin
Michel Dumoulin
Roch Hannecart
Pierre-Yves Plasman
Béatrice Roeh
Corine Schröder
Caroline Suzor
Pierre Tilly
Arthe Van Laer
Jérôme Wilson
Natacha Wittorski

Spain

Enrique Moradiellos
Mercedes Samaniego Boneu

France

Françoise Berger
Marie-Thérèse Bitsch
Gérard Bossuat
Éric Bussière
Jean-François Eck
Catherine Horel
Philippe Mioche
Marine Moguen-Toursel
Sylvain Schirmann
Matthieu Trouvé
Laurent Warlouzet
Emilie Willaert

Hungary

Gergely Fejérdy

Italy

David Burigana
Elena Calandri
Eleonora Guasconi
Luciano Segreto
Antonio Varsori

Luxemburg

Charles Barthel
Etienne Deschamps
Jean-Marie Kreins
René Leboutte
Robert Philippart
Corine Schröder
Gilbert Trausch

The Netherlands

Anjo Harryvan
Jan W. Brouwer
Jan van der Herst

Poland

Józef Laptos
Zdzisiaw Mach

Switzerland

Antoine Fleury
Lubor Jilek

Discover the general website
of the Peter Lang publishing group
www.peterlang.com

For the avoidance of doubt, input of the whole or any part of this publication into any generative artificial intelligence model, chatbot, program, software or technology is expressly prohibited without the prior written consent of the publisher.